Discovering the Scottish Revolution

Also available by Neil Davidson: *The Origins of Scottish Nationhood*

'Neil Davidson's book on *The Origins of Scottish Nationhood* is extremely timely. ... Shock, horror! (Or Jings! Crivvens!) This man says we owe our "nationhood" to our fusion in one state with the Auld Enemy!! Yet once one has dispensed with the ludicrous notion that Scotland was "colonised" by England...Davidson's case seems unassailably strong. ... Neil Davidson's account of the role of Scots in the conquest and exploitation of the British Empire...is as good a summary as I've seen of the suture which fixed Scottish "nationhood" proudly together with "Britishness".'
Angus Calder

'Because [Davidson] writes as a Marxist, our nationalists may manage to disregard his argument for the late, post-Union emergence of Scottish nationhood. They will find it harder to ignore the evidence he offers for the way in which the idea of Britain and the sense of Britishness evolved from the interaction of Scots and English, an argument which renders untenable the proposition that Scotland was in any sense an oppressed or colonised nation. ... The great merit of *The Origins of Scottish Nationhood* is that it encourages clear thinking about the national condition. ...clear thinking has been in short supply in Scotland, driven out by "correct thinking". A book which demonstrates that much of this "correct thinking" is baloney is therefore to be welcomed.'
Alan Massie, *Times Literary Supplement*

'This is not a book for the faint-hearted. ...an important book because it raises pertinent questions about about attitudes and beliefs in Scotland today. ...controversial and provocative.'
Bill Howatson, *Aberdeen Press and Journal*

'The development of capital and class are central to the Scottish historical experience and Davidson is absolutely right to place them centre stage. His bold endeavour to offer a conceptual framework is something that Scottish historians should engage with and not ignore, although Scottish history is a subject which is not exactly renowned for its love of theoretically informed discussion. ...Davidson is to be congratulated for taking to task a number of historians who have been too cavalier in their assertions concerning Scottish national identity. As a taskmaster demanding the most rigorous intellectual standards, Davidson is one of the best critics the Scottish historical profession has.'
Richard Finlay, *Scottish Affairs*

'Davidson's important study provides a very different account of Scots history...[his] demolition of nationalist myths is very convincing. ... Davidson is very informative on Scots economic and political participation in the British Empire.'
John Sullivan, *Revolutionary History*

'*The Origins of Scottish Nationhood* is a remarkable piece of work that dares to seriously challenge the basis for the nationalist myths accepted by many historians and a number of socialists. It does so in a fraternal, sophisticated and rigorous way...'
Angela McCormick, *Socialist Review*

'Davidson's book...is in many respects more penetrating and convincing than several recent attempts by established scholars to explain the phenomenon of Scottish nationhood.'
Colin Kidd, *English Historical Review*

'Davidson has written a well-argued and stimulating book. *The Origins of Scottish Nationhood* follows in the footsteps of the ground-breaking work of the Communist Party's historians group... Davidson's book provides both a theory and abundant historical evidence...'
Jack Conrad, *Weekly Worker*

Neil Davidson

Discovering the Scottish Revolution 1692–1746

Pluto Press
LONDON • STERLING, VIRGINIA

First published 2003 by Pluto Press
345 Archway Road, London N6 5AA
and 22883 Quicksilver Drive,
Sterling, VA 20166–2012, USA

British Library Cataloguing in Publication Data
A catalogue record for this book is available from
the British Library

ISBN 0 7453 2054 6 hbk ⱦ
ISBN 0 7453 2053 8 pbk

Library of Congress Cataloging in Publication Data applied for

10   9   8   7   6   5   4   3   2   1

Designed and produced for Pluto Press by
Chase Publishing Services, Fortescue, Sidmouth, EX10 9QG, England
Typeset from disk by Stanford DTP Services, Towcester, England
Printed in the European Union by
Antony Rowe Ltd, Chippenham and Eastbourne, England

To Robyn

Contents

A Note on the Cover Illustrations

The cover illustrations for the paperback edition feature representations of real and symbolic participants in the Scottish Revolution taken from the work of the English artist, William Hogarth (1697–1764). Hogarth directly dealt with the climax of the Revolution, the suppression of the '45, in two works. One was his portrait of *Simon, Lord Lovat*, awaiting trial for treason (1746). The other, *The March To Finchley* (1749), depicts soldiers preparing to march up Tottenham Court Road to Finchley Common to defend London from the advancing Jacobite army.[1] The two images reproduced here, however, relate more obliquely to the outcome.

The front cover reproduces *The Mackinen Children* (1745). The children represented, Elizabeth and William Mackinen, were the grandchildren of Daniel Mackinnon of Skye (1658–1720), one of the Scottish 'new merchants' who built their fortunes through the sugar trade with the West Indies, where he was a landowner and member of the legislative council of Antigua (see Chapter 1 below). His son William (1697–1767), the children's father and 32nd chief of Clan Mackinnon, changed the conventional spelling of his family name to what he took to be the Anglicised version. The sunflower which stands between Elizabeth and William, dominating the painting, is a symbol of the House of Hanover, the dynasty whose succession was secured by the final defeat of the House of Stuart in 1746.[2] The Mackinen family are among the victors.

The back cover reproduces a detail from the bottom right-hand corner of *The Gate of Calais* (1749). The anonymous figure represented here is a defeated Jacobite. His tartan trousers and jacket indicate that he has served as a junior officer in a clan regiment during the '45. He is now an exile in the territory of the main foreign state to have backed the rising: Catholic, absolutist France. The price of his opposition to the new order in Britain is signalled by his hunger. The implication is that, had he been loyal to the Hanoverian state, he would not now be sitting in the gutter with an apple – sharing the pitiable condition of the French – but at home enjoying fare similar to the sirloin of English beef at the centre of the painting.[3] He is among the vanquished.

Acknowledgements

Early in 1993 I submitted a handwritten publication proposal for a 40,000 word book on the Anglo-Scottish Union to the now defunct Northern Marxist Historians Group. It was intended as a contribution to a series entitled *A Socialist History of Britain*, to be published by Pluto Press. That proposal underwent considerable development over the subsequent decade, not least in terms of length, until it became the present work. The themes discussed in *Discovering the Scottish Revolution* were presented in embryonic form at a number of forums: the Association of Scottish Historical Studies annual conference, *Scotland and War*, in March 1995; the History Workshop Journal/Ruskin College conference, *Scottish Dimensions*, in March 1995; the Socialist Workers Party events, *Marxism '96*, in July 1996 and *Socialism in Scotland*, in November 1998; the Northern Marxist Historians Group meeting in March 1997; the London Socialist Historians Group conferences, *Writing History*, in May 1997 and *Political Change*, in May 1998; and the Social Movements Research Group conference, *Making Social Movements: the British Marxist Historians and the Making of Social Movements*, in June 2002. I also had the opportunity to present my arguments at some length at more informal seminars within the Departments of Sociology at the Universities of Abertay and Liverpool during 1996. Every year between 1994 and 1998 I was able to present the developing argument to students and tutors attending the Supplementary Studies Programme of the Open University Summer School for what was then the Social Science Foundation Course, *Society and Social Science*, held at Stirling University. I am grateful to everyone who participated in these discussions for helping me clarify my own position. A rather lengthy summary of my argument (as it stood at the time) was published in a collection of papers from the *Socialism in Scotland* conference of 1998.[1] Earlier drafts of this book included a section, which at one point was the final chapter, on the formation of national consciousness in Scotland. The importance of this subject for post-Devolution Scotland ultimately led me to detach that chapter and expand it into a book in its own right, prior to the completion of the present work, although some brief passages appear in both.[2]

A number of people helped ensure that this book was eventually completed. Chris Bambery, Colin Barker, Angus Calder, Donny Gluckstein, John Robertson and Ian Wall all read various draft versions of the book and provided me with helpful comments. As the stock phrases have it, 'I have not always followed their advice' and 'Any remaining errors are entirely my responsibility'. Nevertheless, I am deeply grateful to them for engaging with what I wrote in such a serious way, especially where – in the cases of Messrs Calder and (especially) Robertson – my theoretical approach was different from their own. I have also more personal thanks to offer for the friendship and encouragement shown to me since I began writing. It is possible that the people involved were not aware of the extent to which they kept me going at different times during the process. My thanks are particularly due to the following individuals; John Bissett, Michelle 'Fifer' Campbell, Douglas and Margaret Davidson, Liz Ford, Alex Law, Tricia McCafferty, Raymond Morell, Janine Stenhouse and Cathy Watkins, whose name appears last, not simply for alphabetic reasons, but because I owe more to her than anyone else.

Neil Davidson
Leith
Edinburgh
8 September 2002

Preface

This book is about a revolution, the only successful revolution Scotland has ever experienced, but one whose very existence is rarely recognised. Several American historians have attempted to define their Civil War of 1861–65 as a Second American Revolution (the first being the War of Independence).[1] They are fortunate, not only in having two revolutions rather than none, but because both have beginnings and endings whose dates are universally agreed. The period which I describe as that of the Scottish Revolution (1692–1746) has not previously been discussed in these terms. Indeed, it has rarely been treated as a distinct period for any purpose, at least in modern historiography.[2] And this is not my only difficulty. There could scarcely be a less propitious moment in which to add a hitherto undiscovered revolution to the existing roster. The revisionist wisdom of the closing decades of the twentieth century was that revolutions, even – or especially – great revolutions like the English, French or Russian, were not historic turning points, but irruptions of popular violence by irrational mobs, calculated struggles for supremacy between rival elites or, at most, the former in the service of the latter. Nevertheless, the cumulative effect of events in Scotland between 1692 and 1746 was not only to transfer social and economic power from one class to another, but also to transform a relatively backward feudal economy into one of the centres of emergent capitalism.

The transition from feudalism to capitalism seems a small enough difference when typed on the page. Yet concealed beneath the substitution of one word for another lies the beginning of a global transformation which Scotland was among the first nations to experience, which the Scots were pre-eminent in carrying abroad, and whose impact we have yet to transcend. Whatever we think of the Scottish contributions to the Enlightenment, the Industrial Revolution, and the British Empire, they had a global, as much as a local significance. Britain was not the first capitalist state – that honour, if honour it be, falls to the United Provinces – but it was the first capitalist state to form the basis of an international system. Events in Scotland were integral to the survival and consolidation of British capitalism, and consequently to the phase of world history which its expansion and imitation initiated. If the word 'revolution' retains any meaning, then this process is surely one to which it can be applied.

Contrasts and Comparisons

The international context is also relevant in another respect. To understand the nature and extent of change in Scotland during this period we must be able, not only to measure the process of internal development over time, but to compare the experience of Scotland with that of other states. Throughout this book I have therefore drawn parallels with areas of Europe and North America at analogous moments in their history, the majority of which fell in the 1860s. Nevertheless, the two nations that appear most frequently in these pages are geographically nearest: Ireland and England. Not only because they share the territorial framework of the British Isles with Scotland, but because by 1692 they had begun their respective journeys toward opposite ends of Western European development, journeys whose progress the Glorious Revolution of 1688, and the Wars of the British and Irish Succession which followed, did much to complete.

Comparisons with Ireland are acceptable to most historians of Scotland, comparisons with England are not. For some this is because both Scotland and Ireland were subject to English imperatives which left them as strategic bulwarks against foreign invasion, captive markets for English goods, and with home industries bound by regulations designed to protect English exports from competition. According to Daniel Szechi and David Hayton: 'In terms of government and politics, England's relationship with Scotland and Ireland in the late seventeenth and early eighteenth century was classically imperial.' It is then claimed that what was first tested on the Irish and the Scots was then exported – by the English alone, note – to the rest of the world: 'The internal mechanics and rhetoric behind the later global empire owed not a little to the attitudes and institutions generated by the earlier *Imperium Anglorium*.'[3] Contrary to these claims, Scotland was in no sense an imperial dependency of England. Indeed, some Scots were at the forefront of imposing British imperialism across the globe, not least in Ireland itself, where Ulster has some claim to have been a Scottish colony during the seventeenth century.

But even those historians who balk at describing Scotland as a colony tend to reject comparisons with England. Rosalind Mitchison, for example, writes: 'It is more fruitful to look at [Scotland] in the company of the less developed parts of northern and western Europe than to draw comparisons between her and England.'[4] Nor is this merely a defensive reaction on the part of Scottish historians; Fernand Braudel, the late doyen of French historiography, was even more emphatic: 'Seventeenth-century Scotland was a poor country which it would be ridiculous to compare for a moment with England.'[5] Even those historians prepared to countenance some level of comparison are careful to restrict the areas in which this is permissible. As the English social historian, Keith Wrightson, has written: 'Where distinctions can and should be made between the Scottish and the English experience they surely must lie not in the stark juxtaposition of backwardness and precocity, stasis and momentum, but in the subtler exploration of differences in the contexts, the pace, the precise chronology and the degree of change.'[6]

Yet despite this distinguished body of opinion, the comparison with England is unavoidable.[7] Not because England represents an Ideal Type or normative model – English development was exceptional before 1688 and unrepeatable after[8] – but because after 1707 Scotland fused with England into one state. The source of the conflicts which were to plunge that state into civil war twice in 40 years was precisely the unevenness in development between its two component parts. To emphasise these differences is therefore highly instructive – indeed, failure to do so obscures the meaning of the events we wish to discuss. A comparison between Scotland and, for example, Sweden, might well be interesting in its own terms, and certainly more favourable to Scotland than one with England, but it would contribute little to understanding the actual course of Scottish history. To discuss the socio-economic backwardness, not only of Scotland compared with England, but of Ireland compared with Scotland, and of the Highlands compared with the Lowlands, is not to make a moral judgement condemning the Irish, the Highlanders or the Scots. Nor, conversely, is it to extol the English. Contrary to nationalist myth, nations and peoples cannot be spoken about in the singular, for all of them were, and still are, internally divided, most importantly in terms of class. To use these terms is therefore simply to register the fact that in the early modern period there was no more equality between nations than there was within them. And in these respects at least, the situation is no different 300 years later.

Structure, Narrative and Critique

How then have I approached the history of this pivotal, if largely unknown revolution? Georg Lukacs once wrote that 'the facts' in any historical case were only comprehensible through their 'integration into the totality'.[9] And what is true for the individual facts is also true for the sub-disciplines of history. Without 'integration into the totality' they can only be of limited value in understanding the historical process. This book is therefore not a political history, an economic history, a social history, a cultural history, an ecclesiastical history, a military history, a history of ideas, a history from above, a history from below, nor all of these in turn, but a history which aspires to represent the totality of the revolutionary epoch in Scottish history. The political, economic, social, cultural, religious, military and intellectual aspects of that epoch, the roles of patricians and plebeians, all assume greater or lesser importance at different moments, but in each case only as aspects of the whole. This approach does not involve attempting to convey every aspect of life during the period under consideration, a project as pointless in conception as it would be impossible of execution. Our subject is revolution, and my focus is therefore on what Antonio Gramsci called the 'moments of force':

> ... the moments in which the conflicting forces are formed, are assembled and take up their positions; the moment in which one ethical–political system dissolves and another is formed by fire and steel; the moment in which one system of social relations disintegrates and falls and another arises and asserts itself.[10]

We pan across relatively static decades in long shot, registering only the broadest impressions. We zoom in to register the 'moments of force' in close-up, omitting no detail.

If the decisiveness of the moment determines the extent of the treatment, it also suggests the approach I have taken to discuss it. In general, historical writing can take one of two modes; either a structural analysis of institutions, activities and beliefs, or a narrative of events. The former tends to be concerned with continuity, the latter with change, although the difference between the two is often simply a matter of duration.[11] An exclusive reliance on either approach is in any case impossible, since institutions, activities and beliefs are themselves subject to transformation and events take place within the context of structural constraints. The recent historiography of Scotland includes excellent examples of both approaches, but structural analysis is currently dominant, for two reasons. First, because the most influential figures on the current scene are social and economic historians like Thomas Devine and Christopher Whatley for whom it is the most appropriate mode. Second, because the claims of narrative are tainted by association with a tradition of popular history whose woeful products can still be found in the 'Scottish Interest' section of any bookshop north of the Tweed, generally between volumes recounting the story of Greyfriars Bobby and those proving the existence of alien life in the skies over Bonnyrigg.

As a result of these unhappy associations, it is perhaps worth stating why the sections of this book which deal with 'moments of force', such as popular opposition to the Treaty of Union in 1706 or the suppression of the last Jacobite rising in 1746, have a narrative framework. It is for similar reasons to those set out by James McPherson in his outstanding history of another great revolution, to which I have already referred, the American Civil War:

> This choice proceeds ... from my own convictions about how best to write the history of these years of successive crises, rapid changes, dramatic events and dynamic transformations. A topical or thematic approach could not do justice to these dynamics, this complex relationship of cause and effect, this intensity of experience ... A topical or thematic approach that treated military events, diplomacy, slavery and emancipation, anti-war dissent and civil liberties, and northern politics in separate chapters, instead of weaving them together as I have attempted to here, would leave the reader uninformed about how and why the battle of Antietam was so crucial to the outcome of all these other developments.[12]

If 'Culloden' is substituted for 'Antietam' then the relevance of these remarks to Scottish history should be obvious. The difficulty of a pre-dominantly non-narrative approach, certainly in periods of rapid transformation, is not only that events become disconnected from each other, as McPherson suggests, but that their outcomes appear inevitable. The ratification of the Treaty of Union by the Scottish Parliament, for example, is often presented in precisely this way. Another benefit of the narrative mode of presentation is therefore that it can help us identify the alternative courses of action which were available to the historical actors at any given moment in time.

The text which follows therefore switches from analysis to narrative depending on the precise period and subject under discussion. At several points I have, however, also employed another mode of presentation which, for want of a better term, can be called critique. All scholars have occasion to take issue with the methods or conclusions of their colleagues, but these disputes are usually confined to reviews or articles in specialist journals, and are less frequently integrated into their books.[13] I have not followed this convention, which seems to me appropriate only in the case of 'micro-histories' which seek to reconstruct particular life-worlds in minute detail. In works of this kind, disputes over historical interpretation have the effect of constantly recalling the reader from the recreated world, and should therefore be excluded from the main text.[14] Given the breadth of the subject matter dealt with in this work, however, it has of necessity been written at a 'macro'-level where these restraints need not apply. In the case of many of the themes discussed below I am in radical disagreement with both the hitherto dominant interpretations and those which are coming to replace them. Current claims that Jacobitism represented a pan-Scottish movement for national liberation, for example, do not seem to me to be any more credible than earlier claims that it was the political expression of Highland clan society. Since these views are associated with particular writers, it is entirely legitimate to engage with what they have written in the course of setting out my own positions.

Sources and Conventions

In spite of these differences of interpretation, I am happy to acknowledge my personal debt to the now substantial body of work produced by contemporary historians of Scotland, much of it in areas of research whose materials are inaccessible to the non-specialist. Reliance on the findings of other historians is to be avoided as far as possible, of course, but given my own lack of familiarity with the primary sources in certain areas, I have sometimes found it necessary. I trust that I have not mis-represented their work by incorporating it into my own. The richness of much contemporary Scottish historiography does not mean, however, that I have not entirely ignored the work of earlier scholars. Some of it, including some very venerable works indeed by William Law Mathieson and George Pratt Insh, has proved of lasting value and is often more concerned with giving a total picture of the social dynamic than is that of their successors.[15]

Nevertheless, my main sources have been the records left by the historical actors themselves – the legislation, memoirs, correspondence, proclamations, eyewitness accounts and contemporary theoretical works which are the basic components of any history of this period. When quoting from seventeenth and eighteenth century texts I have referred where possible to editions which are in print and consequently most easily accessible to the reader. Alas, as every historian of early modern Scotland becomes aware (usually after hours peering over fading print with a pencil and a shorthand notebook), such consideration is not always possible. With a handful of important exceptions – notably Ferguson, Fletcher, Hume and Smith – the leading authors of the period are out of print and, in some cases, have been so for over two centuries. With the current revival of interest in Scottish history and culture one hopes that some enterprising publishers will detect the possibility of profit in making the works of Dalrymple, Kames, Millar, Robertson, Shields and others available to new generations.[16]

In addition to problems of accessibility, one also has to balance between authenticity and intelligibility. In order to give a sense of how texts from this period appeared to their readers, I have retained the random capitalisation typical of the time. As an aid to understanding, however, I have modernised spelling throughout, except when citing the titles of pamphlets or books. In the case of particularly incomprehensible passages (notably by Gilbert Burnet and the anonymous author of *The*

Smoaking Flax Unquenchable), I have added punctuation. Scottish words are given, where necessary, with the English equivalent in parenthesis. In quoting from *The Complaynt of Scotland* and other works of similar vintage, I have rendered the relevant passages from sixteenth century Middle Scots in modern English. Throughout, interpolations by me are always within square brackets. Many quotations report, directly or indirectly, the utterances of the Scottish feudal lords. Individual members of this class are introduced in one of two ways. Members of the peerage are introduced by their name and title (e.g. Archibald Campbell, ninth Earl of Argyll) and thereafter referred to by their title (Argyll). As the reader will soon discover, there have been a great many Argylls. Mere landowners, on the other hand, are introduced by their full name and the location of their estate (e.g. John Clerk of Penicuik) and thereafter by their name (Clerk). It seems appropriate that, in a society as conscious of rank as was early modern Scotland, social distinctions should mark men down to their very names.

Marxist Theory and Scottish History

No matter how deeply one immerses oneself in the primary sources, however, unless the material found there is used in a way informed by some theory of history, the resulting work is likely to remain a compendium of more or less interesting facts about the past. According to Alex Callinicos, a theory of history contains at least three elements. First, a theory of structure which explains the differences between types of society. Second, a theory of transformation which explains how these societies change and, in particular, are transformed into other types of society. Third, a theory of directionality (progressive, regressive or circular) which identifies the overall pattern of human history suggested by the sum of these social transformations. This book is written within the classical Marxist theory of history, which has its own distinctive perspective on these constitutive elements. The Marxist theory of structure claims that types of society are based on particular modes of production, which combine the means of production (nature, the capacity to labour, skills, tools, techniques and the labour process through which these are integrated) and the relations of production (which determine how the exploitation of one class by another takes place, and consequently whether these antagonistic classes are slaves and slaveowners, peasants and feudal lords, or wage labourers and capitalists). The Marxist theory of transformation claims that one type of society changes into another because of a series of inherent structural contradictions. The forces of production develop to the point where they are prevented from further expansion by the relations of production, leading to economic crisis. This in turn intensifies the conflict between the exploiting and the exploited classes which can either lead to social collapse or, if the latter has the capacity, to the reconstruction of society on a new basis. The Marxist theory of directionality claims that social development is progressive, since the tendency, referred to above, is for the forces of production to grow, at least over the longer historical term.[17]

The classical Marxist tradition in which these theories have been deployed is represented here by Marx, Engels, Lenin, Trotsky, Lukacs, Gramsci, and Benjamin – although these names do not exhaust it. How relevant can the work of these Germans, Russians, Hungarians and Italians be to the understanding of Scottish history?[18] In fact, all but two (Gramsci and Benjamin) discussed Scottish history and politics at some time in their lives, although not always very accurately.[19] The point, however, is not the extent to which Scotland features in their work, but whether the Marxist tradition – and their specific contributions to it – can explain the pattern of Scottish history. There is also a more direct connection between Scotland and historical materialism. The Scottish Enlightenment, or least the aspect concerned with the process of social development, was one of the major influences on Marx and Engels, and one which extended to their successors. One of the central themes of Gramsci's work, for example, was the nature of civil society, a concept first developed in the work of Adam Ferguson and other contributors to this decisive moment in European history. In a sense, therefore, to make a Marxist analysis of Scottish history is to apply, in a more complete form, the historical concepts first developed in Scotland during the period under discussion. It will be up to the reader to decide whether or not that analysis is convincing.

Introduction

On the morning of Wednesday, 12 May 1999, in the Assembly Hall of the Church of Scotland, the recently elected Members of the Scottish Parliament signalled the opening of the new body by swearing an oath of loyalty to 'Her Majesty, Queen Elizabeth, Her Heirs and Successors, according to Law', a third of them doing so under protest. Around 9.30, after the last oath had been sworn, Winifred Ewing of the Scottish National Party rose to her feet and said: 'I want to start with the words I have always wanted to say, or hear somebody else say – the Scottish Parliament, adjourned on the 25th day of March 1707, is hereby reconvened.'[1] The immediate cause of the 'adjournment' to which Dr Ewing referred in her speech was, of course, the Treaty of Union with England, which the original Scottish Parliament ratified by a majority of 110 votes to 69 on 16 January 1707.[2] The Treaty united the two kingdoms in the new state of Great Britain, which formally came into being on 1 May with the opening of the first British Parliament. After the Scottish Parliament adjourned on 25 March it was quietly dissolved by royal proclamation on 28 April. It never met again.[3] What meanings have been ascribed to these events?

Three Interpretations of the Anglo-Scottish Union

There are three main political interpretations of the Treaty of Union and, implicitly, of the British state which it brought into being. I will refer to these as the British Unionist, Scottish nationalist and constitutional reformist interpretations.

The oldest of the three, the British Unionist interpretation, was first formulated by Scottish Enlightenment intellectuals after 1746. The period during which it exercised the greatest influence was, however, between the defeat of Chartism in 1848 and the outbreak of the First World War in 1914, when the British bourgeoisie enjoyed relative social peace at home, and near absolute military and economic dominance abroad.[4] The main theme of this interpretation is that England had evolved, at a suitably gradual pace, a constitution so finely balanced between the different powers and interests that it could incorporate new social forces (such as the industrial bourgeoisie and working class) without disrupting the state. Other nations reached this level, if at all, only after enduring centuries of absolutist rule and recurrent revolutionary crises. Those aspects of English history which appeared to deviate from the evolutionary path (such as the occasional civil war), were the result, not of irreconcilable social differences, but of the folly of individual monarchs and their advisers, and were in any case ended by the Revolution of 1688. Scotland, despite its geographical proximity to England, is decidedly one of these other nations. Scottish history before 1707 is accordingly viewed as one of economic backwardness, political division and religious fundamentalism which historians should decently pass over in silence. Consequently, for England – and in this account British history after the Union is very much a continuation of English history before it – 1707 is scarcely a significant date at all, and certainly not one to compare with 1832, 1945, or even 1979.[5] For Scotland, however, it was the moment of redemption. In the words of Hugh Trevor-Roper:

> The impact of the Union on England was superficial ... But to Scotland it was a far more fundamental change ... it was in fact the beginning of a radical and permanent change: the opening up of a closed society, a social transformation, a revolution.[6]

According to British Unionism, everything worthwhile in Scottish society is a result of the Union with England. Needless to say, this doctrine is unacceptable to those who wish to see the re-establishment of a Scottish state. After the Second World War, accelerating economic decline and the accompanying social tensions made it clear that Britain could neither sustain its previous role in the world state system nor pretend it had no significant internal conflicts. 'Official' British historiography still survived, of course, as nostalgia or wish fulfilment, but with the passing of the conditions under which it originally flourished it could no longer command the field. One of the internal conflicts that helped undermine it was the appearance, during the 1960s, of a Scottish nationalist politics that had for the first time a degree of permanent electoral support, the first sign of which was the election of Winifred Ewing in the Hamilton by-election of November 1967. For this movement the nature of the British state is less important than the fact that the Scottish state was sacrificed to bring it into being. Even if it could be demonstrated that, after 1707, Britain had the most democratic polity and advanced economy possible at the time, and that, before 1707,

Scotland had been less developed in both respects, consistent nationalists would still be unsatisfied, since these benefits only became available to the Scots through the loss of their sovereignty. The illegitimacy of the Union is therefore held to lie in the fact that it was opposed by the majority of the Scottish people and was, according to the Scottish nationalist writer Paul Scott, 'not a bargain of any kind, but an imposition which the Scottish Parliament was brought to accept by the carrot of bribery and the threat of the big stick of military force'.[7] All nationalisms require positive historical myths, however, and in practice Scottish nationalists usually deny the extent of Scottish backwardness before 1707, stressing instead the positive aspects of Scottish history, like the extent of popular literacy, or more elusive qualities such as 'the democratic intellect'.

The British Unionist and Scottish nationalist positions can be summarised as follows. The former celebrates the Union as a gift which Scottish leaders wisely accepted on behalf of a nation that has never subsequently wished to reject it. The latter denounces the Union as a trap into which an unrepresentative oligarchy led a Scottish people who have never subsequently found the will to escape.

There is, however, an intermediate position that takes a less than exalted view of British developments without necessarily seeing the pre-existing Scottish state as a historically viable alternative. Constitutional reformism was predominantly a response to the succession of Conservative governments between 1979 and 1997 which, although supported by only a minority of the electorate, were able to launch a radical onslaught on the social-democratic settlement of 1945. In this interpretation, 1688 appears not as the climactic assertion of constitutional principle against royalist pretension, but as a narrow compromise that preserved most of the attributes of absolutism. Later generations were therefore bequeathed a non-existent Constitution and uncontrolled executive through which prime ministers can – in theory at least – do as they please with both the individual citizens (or rather, subjects) and the constituent nations of the Great British state. But although constitutional reformism presents a mirror image of British Unionism in matters of interpretation, it does not contest the facts themselves. It accepts that Scotland was incorporated into a Greater England after 1707, for example, although this is presented, not as a timely deliverance from backwardness, but as a permanent incarceration in a state of pre-modernity. Such a position is theoretically quite compatible with the dismissive British Unionist view of pre-Union Scotland. In practice, however, constitutional reformers, like Scottish nationalists, have tended to emphasise what they see as the positive aspects of Scottish society, particularly in the elements of popular sovereignty supposedly embodied in the Scottish Parliament. As Neal Ascherson writes of contemporary British society: 'There is no doctrine of popular sovereignty – the half-formed Scottish version of that doctrine vanished with the Union of Parliaments.'[8] The implication is that, even if popular sovereignty was at least half-formed in Scotland before 1707, this was in advance of the situation in England, and subsequently of that in Britain.

Contextualising the Treaty of Union

These then are the interpretative frameworks within which the Union is usually discussed. All contain the same underlying flaw. It may be the case that Scotland did derive greater benefit from the Union with England than it would have done had it retained sovereignty, but does this necessarily mean that these benefits continue to flow in equal measure today? It may be the case that the majority of contemporary Scots do regard the Union as frustrating their national aspirations, but did – could – their ancestors have felt this way in 1707? It may be the case that the British state is an archaic formation compared to its closest rivals, but does the same verdict apply to that state in the period between 1707 and 1789? All three interpretations are in effect applications of the Whig Interpretation of History, which, as Michael Fry has written, involves 'judging the past by the standards of the present ... distorting the past by interpreting it in terms of the present ... searching the past for the origins and evolution of ideas and institutions to be recommended for the present'.[9]

Contemporary political preoccupations influence the assessment of historical events everywhere, and in Scotland the particular reason for this is easy to discern. The Treaty of Union is not simply an object of historical study, but is still the constitutional basis of Scotland's relationship with England. That relationship was increasingly called into question as the twentieth century progressed and, as the century ended, was altered by the establishment of the new Scottish Parliament which Dr Ewing was so anxious to claim as a restoration of the old. Any discussion of the origins of the Union is therefore heavily influenced – and sometimes completely determined – by whether the participants think it should be preserved from further change, modified still further, or completely abolished. Yet most contributions to the debate made on this basis are not only anachronistic in form but also empty of content. The themes of Progress, Sovereignty and the Constitution that they take as central each omit a crucial question. Whose Progress? Whose Sovereignty? Whose Constitution? In other words, they lack a class dimension, both in relation to Scotland and to the other nations – England, France and Ireland – whose internal development was affected by the events of 1707. There is, however, an alternative approach that integrates the issue of social class into the debate over the Union. This involves situating the Union, not merely as a moment – albeit the most important moment – in Anglo-Scottish relations, but as part of the Revolution which Scotland underwent during the seventeenth and eighteenth centuries. At this point it is, however, necessary to introduce a distinction between different types of revolution, which can be respectively characterised as political and social in nature. What do these terms signify?[10]

Political revolutions are struggles within society for control of the existing state, but which leave the social and economic structure intact. These revolutions have been relatively frequent in history, from the Roman Civil Wars, which led to the abandonment of Republican rule for the Principate in AD 27, to the Eastern European revolutions of 1989–91, which swept away the Stalinist regimes and began the transformation of Eastern state capitalism into an approximation of the Western trans-state model. They may involve more or less popular participation, may result in more or less improvement in the condition of the majority, but ultimately the class which was in control of the means of production at the beginning will remain so at the end (although individuals and political organisations may have been replaced on the way), and the class which was exploited within the productive process at the beginning will also remain so at the end (although concessions may have been made to secure its acquiescence).

Social revolutions, however, are not merely struggles within existing society, but result in the transformation of one type of society into another. Such revolutions are extremely rare, taking place only when the existing organisation of production has become an obstacle to further development, not only in the sphere of economics but also, by extension, in those of society and politics. The bourgeois revolutions which formed the climax of the transition from feudalism to capitalism belong in this category.

Marxism and the Scottish Revolution

Even after decades of relative decline, Scotland today still occupies a position near the summit of the capitalist system. Yet the question of whether it owes that position to a prior bourgeois revolution has proved difficult to answer for Marxist writers and historians. It will be useful to begin this discussion with a review of the few who do accept the existence of a Scottish Revolution. Generally speaking, they have adopted one of two interpretations, neither of which is satisfactory.

The first claims that the Revolution took place in the form of a struggle between two geographically distinct societies, the capitalist Lowlands on the one hand and the pre-feudal Highlands on the other. Eric Hobsbawm writes, for example, that:

... Scotland was a dual society and economy, in which the tribal Highlands coexisted with the entirely different and far more advanced Lowlands. The struggle for the equivalent of a bourgeois revolution in Scotland was also the struggle between two societies. Its major victories, reflected in revolutionary legislation in 1695 and 1748, were the consequence of military victories of the Whig Lowlands (allied with, and later deliberately merged with, England) against the tribal levies of the Highlands.[11]

This is certainly plausible, but several problems remain. It assumes that the Jacobite rebellions between 1688 and 1746 were political manifestations of Highland clan society. Although a popular view (reproduced, for example, in the section of the National Museum of Scotland devoted to Jacobitism), it is wrong: Jacobitism was as much a Lowland movement as a Highland one. Moreover, if the transformation of the Highlands after the '45 is the key episode in the Scottish Revolution, then the central process must be the Highland Clearances. But the majority of these – certainly the majority of forcible clearances – took place between 1815 and 1860, long after Lowland Scotland had established itself at the summit of world capitalist development. The timing is simply too late. Finally, for Lowland society to effect this change in the Highlands, it must also have experienced a bourgeois revolution beforehand. But when? Concentrating on the opposition between Highland and Lowland leaves the central question unanswered.

The second interpretation appears to answer it. There are two variants. In one, the Scottish bourgeois revolution takes place in the Lowlands at the same time as in England, between 1638–60 and 1688–89. An editorial in *International Socialism* from the early 1970s, for example, while attempting to explain the emergence of Scottish nationalism to its readers, noted that: 'The struggles of the Scottish bourgeoisie against the remnants of feudalism took place more or less simultaneously with similar struggles in England, in the 1640s and 1688, with the movements in one country being intimately bound up with movements in the other.'[12] In the other variant, the Treaty of Union of 1707 becomes the missing Scottish bourgeois revolution, by allowing the 'structural assimilation' of Lowland Scotland to England. John McGrath, for example, wrote that: 'Scotland, to put it crudely, did not have its own bourgeois revolution, it inherited the fruits of the English one by the Act of Union.'[13] The same point is made, although less crudely, by Tom Nairn, for who, 'the Scottish bourgeoisie had been able to exploit (by alliance) some of the consequences of the English bourgeois revolution'.[14] This is a position close to that held by right-wing British Unionists such as Hugh Trevor-Roper, although they would, of course, reject the actual term. Both variants of the second interpretation revert to the first regarding the fate of the Highlands after their respective closing dates for the revolution in the Lowlands. The problem here is that Scotland – including Lowland Scotland – was not dominated by the capitalist mode of production either after 1688 or immediately after 1707. All the economic indicators show that the transformation of Lowland Scotland along capitalist lines took place in the second half of the eighteenth century – over 50 years after the Treaty of Union was signed. Furthermore, between 1707 and 1746 Scotland was the base for four counter-revolutionary Jacobite risings against the British state, all but one of which were combined with actual or potential foreign invasions. And these risings were by no means confined to the Highlands – indeed, the '15 was almost entirely a Lowland affair. Two of these risings, in 1708 and 1719, were of little consequence, but the other two, in 1715 and 1745, led to civil wars which, in different ways, had the potential to undo, not merely the Union, but the English settlement of 1688 whose transference to Scotland the Union was supposed to have achieved.[15]

Perhaps conscious of these difficulties, the majority of Marxists have been either doubtful or dismissive of the existence of Scottish bourgeois revolution. In a pioneering article first published in 1973, for example, John Foster opined that: 'If we want to assess the nature of the English union (to discover at what point and on what terms the independent development of the Scottish nation came to an end), it is essential to determine to what extent Scotland had previously experienced a bourgeois revolution of its own.' After reviewing some evidence indicating the growth of capitalist relations of production in the sixteenth and seventeenth centuries, however, Foster could only conclude: 'How far a bourgeois revolution actually occurred is far less certain.' The level of uncertainty experienced by Foster is suggested by a subsequent passage which begins: 'Whether or not there was a decisive capture of state power ...'.[16] Whether or not? Whatever attributes can otherwise be expected from Marxist historians, the ability to recognise decisive captures of state power is surely one of them. James Young is at least definitive in his assessment:

> A distinctive feature of the overall Scottish experience was the absence of a bourgeois revolution through which the middle ranks and philosophes might have expressed their *own* authentic confidence, mission and path-breaking role comparable to what the English were already doing. In contrast to the English and the French the Scots still had not experienced a bourgeois revolution in the nineteenth century ...[17]

Both Foster and Young work with an underlying model of bourgeois revolution in which the bourgeoisie themselves must accomplish a 'decisive capture of state power'. Barrington Moore has characterised this position, with only a hint of caricature, as involving:

> ... a steady increase in the economic power of the commercial and manufacturing classes in the towns up to the point where economic power comes into conflict with political power still in the hands of an old ruling class based mainly on the land. At this point there supposedly occurs a revolutionary explosion in which the commercial and manufacturing classes seize the reigns of political power and introduce the main features of parliamentary democracy.[18]

Since nothing of this sort took place in Scotland, even during the national and civil wars between 1637 and 1651, Foster and Young are left without an event to designate as 'the revolution'. At this point it is tempting simply to declare that the concept of the bourgeois revolution has little to offer in understanding the historical process, at least with respect to Scotland. And the concept has indeed been subjected to numerous criticisms since the 1950s, most damagingly, perhaps, by writers who in other respects claim adherence to some form of non-Stalinist Marxism.[19] The standard method is to identify the bourgeois revolution with one or two specific instances (usually the English Revolution of 1640 or the French Revolution of 1789) and then to demonstrate that the bourgeoisie was neither 'rising' in the pre-Revolutionary period, nor in the vanguard of the struggle against absolutism during the revolution, nor yet in power after the revolution was complete. And if there are doubts over the claims made for these supposedly 'classic' examples of bourgeois revolution, what remains to be said about the lesser affairs experienced by the vast majority of other nation-states? In fact, these arguments are not so much wrong as irrelevant, for there is an alternative theory of bourgeois revolution which does not rely on the existence of a self-conscious bourgeois class subject responsible for taking political power on its own behalf. According to this version a bourgeois revolution is a sequence of social and political conflicts which remove institutional barriers to local capitalist development and allow the establishment of an independent centre of competitive accumulation within the framework of the nation-state. The cumulative effect of the individual bourgeois revolutions was the establishment, by the late nineteenth century, of a world system economically dominated by the capitalist mode of production and politically divided into actual or aspirant capitalist nation-states. This definition does not require bourgeois revolutions to take a particular form, nor does it even require them to be carried out by the bourgeoisie. Nevertheless, some generalisations are possible regarding the patterns of process and agency involved.

Patterns of Bourgeois Revolution

Marxists from Engels onwards have tended to see the decisive moments in the individual bourgeois revolutions as belonging to one of two cycles of development. The first extended over several centuries and consisted of the Dutch Revolt against the Spanish Habsburgs between 1565 and 1609, the English Civil Wars and Interregnum between 1640 and 1660 together with their coda in the Glorious Revolution of 1688, the American War of Independence from Britain between 1776 and 1784, and the French Revolution of 1789 together with its coda in the Revolution of 1830.[20] The end of this first cycle came only with the abortive European revolutions of 1848–49. The second was compressed into the years between 1859 and 1871, and consisted of the Italian Risorgimento, the American Civil War, the Meiji Restoration in Japan, Confederation in Canada and the Unification of Germany. All of these revolutions took place within their own particular epoch. What does this term mean?[21]

Each individual epoch of bourgeois revolution began only when three objective conditions were fulfilled. First, the organic crisis of the feudal system had become fully declared. Such a crisis was general in late medieval Europe, but feudalism nevertheless re-emerged at the end of the fifteenth century, transformed but still dominant. A second condition is therefore required: a capitalist solution to the crisis. This does not simply mean the existence of capitalist production. The epoch of the Italian Revolution, for example, did not begin with the city-states of the twelfth century, when feudalism itself had been consolidated as a system for little over 100 years, but at the end of the eighteenth century, by which time capitalism, and the classes associated with it, had developed sufficiently to dominate the national economy and society. The second condition suggests, in turn, a third: the existence of some class agency capable of rising from a position of economic and social influence to one of political power. Each individual epoch of bourgeois revolution ended only when capitalist property relations were irreversibly installed and could only be threatened by a class still more advanced than the bourgeoisie, which is to say, the proletariat. The conjunction of crisis, solution and agency can, of course, exist for a period of time without the situation being resolved. The epoch of the German Revolution, for example, was not restricted to the years between 1862 and 1871 when Unification actually took place, but can be dated, like the Italian case, from the late eighteenth century. Pre-Bismarkian attempts at revolution, notably that of 1848, failed not because the objective conditions were unripe, but because of a subjective failure on the part of the bourgeoisie themselves.

'The bourgeois revolution was not therefore a single event,' writes Goran Therborn, 'but a historical process of economic, political, juridical, and ideological ruptures between old social institutions and new bourgeois forms.'[22] Those who reject the notion that revolution – any revolution – can be a process may find this argument difficult to accept. The very word 'revolution', according to Perry Anderson, means the destruction of the existing state and the construction of a new one, and this can scarcely occur gradually in the way that the words 'epoch' and 'process' imply.[23] This objection assumes, however, that bourgeois revolutions have to take the same form as proletarian revolutions – that is, a frontal assault on the state apparatus. As we have already noted, however, this is not the case. With the exceptions of the English and French absolutist regimes which fell during the first cycle, the feudal states against which the bourgeois revolutions were directed differed in several ways from their capitalist successors, most significantly in that they were not all unitary machines against which such an operation could be mounted. Some revolutions, such as the Dutch, took the form of extended wars against foreign dynasties, gradually liberating territories where the capitalist mode of production was already dominant. Others, such as the German, took the form of unification movements incorporating different regions at varying levels of development within the most advanced. In neither case is there any reason why the establishment of a state committed to capital accumulation should not be the result of a prolonged period, involving more than one moment of 'convulsive transformation', and the process still be classifiable as a revolution.

In the same way as the bourgeois revolutions can belong to more than one type, so too can the agents responsible for their accomplishment, who were by no means always members of the bourgeoisie. What then was the role of this class? Since the very term 'bourgeoisie' is frequently subjected to ridicule, it is perhaps first worth explaining what I mean by it. In the original Old French *burgeis* meant a town-dweller, as did similar terms in other European languages, like *burgher* in German. By the time Marx and Engels used the term in the 1840s, it stood, in relation to town-dwellers, for something both shallower than previously (because it excluded the new class of urban industrial labourers) but also wider (because it included rural capitalists). In short, it meant capitalists, both urban and rural, in the literal sense of the those who owned or controlled capital, but also encompassed a larger social group over which this class was hegemonic. Hal Draper describes the bourgeoisie in this sense as 'a social penumbra around the hard core of capitalists proper, shading out into the diverse social elements who function as servitors or hangers-on of capital without themselves owning capital'.[24] As Edward Thompson once pointed out, the capitalist 'hard core' of the bourgeoisie 'are not historically notorious for their desperate propensity to rush, bandoliers on their shoulders, to the barricades. More generally they arrive on the scene when the climatic battles of the bourgeois revolution have already been fought.'[25] If not capitalists themselves, then who did fight these battles? It is in this context that Draper's 'outer penumbra' is significant.

The bourgeoisie in this broader sense were certainly present in the leadership of the first cycle of revolutions – think particularly of the role of pastors in the Dutch Revolt or of lawyers in the French Revolution – but the forces which they mobilised tended to be from the petty bourgeoisie – small commodity producers in the towns, yeoman farmers in the countryside, shopkeepers and tavern owners in both – whose aims by no means coincided with those of the capitalist class as such. Indeed, in some cases, they would be either individually undermined or collectively expropriated by the triumph of the latter. It is important to note that, although these revolutions of the first cycle generally involved an alliance 'from below' of against the absolutist state or its colonial extensions, even this contained elements of revolution 'from above' and 'from outside', most notably in the activities of the New Model Army during the Protectorate, and of the French armies during the Republican and Napoleonic periods. Even during the episodes of maximum mass involvement, bourgeois revolutions are minority affairs, whose ultimate achievement is to establish a new ruling class, albeit one with a broader base than feudal absolutism.

During the second cycle the role of existing state power became more marked. Engels wrote of Germany that: 'The gravediggers of the Revolution of 1848 had become the executors of its will.'[26] The point, however, is of general application. In all these cases a fraction of the existing ruling class, under pressure from nation-states that had already undergone their bourgeois revolutions, simultaneously restructured the existing state from within and expanded its territorial boundaries through conventional military conquest. Antonio Gramsci wrote of 'a period of small waves of reform rather than by revolutionary explosions like the original French one' which combined 'social struggles, interventions from above of the enlightened monarchy type, and national wars – with the two latter phenomena predominating':

> The period of 'Restoration' is the richest in developments of this kind: restoration becomes the first policy whereby social struggles find sufficiently elastic frameworks to allow the bourgeoisie to gain power without dramatic upheavals, without the French machinery of terror. The old feudal classes are demoted from their dominant position to a 'governing' one, but are not eliminated, nor is there any attempt to liquidate them as an organic whole; instead of a class they become a 'caste' with specific cultural and psychological characteristics, but no longer with predominant economic functions.[27]

Popular involvement in the revolutions of the second cycle, although present in Italy and, to a lesser extent, America, only appears as a subordinate element in a process otherwise directed from above.

The shift in agency after 1849 can be explained as the result of two related factors, both products of the growth and dynamism of the capitalist system. The first factor was the creation of the working class itself. During the French Revolution even the most class-conscious members of the bourgeoisie drew back from the actions necessary to achieve victory over the old regime, paralysed as they were by a fear of the urban plebeians who might – and in the event, did – push beyond the limits that the former considered acceptable. It was therefore inevitable that once the potentially even more dangerous working class appeared as a social force, as it did during the revolutions of 1848–49, the bourgeoisie would seek accommodation with the existing regimes rather than risk igniting a conflagration that might engulf them too. The second factor was the availability of agencies that could provide capitalist leadership in the place of this increasingly cautious bourgeoisie. The states which had undergone revolutions during the earlier cycle – pre-eminently Britain and France – were now not merely the competitors of those which had not, but potential models for them to follow. Once the system of which these nation-states were the pre-eminent members had achieved a certain momentum, its very success became the most decisive argument in persuading sections of the non-capitalist ruling classes that they must effect internal self-transformation or be overtaken by their more developed rivals.[28]

The ideological banners under which the two cycles of revolution advanced were therefore very different from each other. During the first, revolutionaries presented their actions as having universal significance – although whether this was for Protestantism or the Rights of Man depended on whether the revolution in question lay nearer to the Reformation or the Enlightenment. Their successors, precisely because they were consciously striving for the establishment of a capitalist nation-state, had none of this universalising impulse towards religious or political freedom. 'Instead of the banners of Liberty, Equality and Fraternity,' writes Perry Anderson, 'the new elites drove conscript masses under the signs of Nationality and Industry.'[29]

We should not therefore be surprised that the bourgeoisie were not always actively involved in the bourgeois revolutions, nor that, where they were involved, they did not always play a leading role in overthrowing the old regime. As Alex Callinicos has argued: 'Bourgeois revolutions must be identified, not as revolutions consciously made by capitalists, but as revolutions which promote capitalism.'[30] Once it is understood that the bourgeoisie have largely been the beneficiaries rather than the instigators of the revolutions that bear their name, the argument that dismisses the concept of bourgeois revolution because a self-conscious revolutionary bourgeoisie cannot be identified loses much of its force.

The diversity both of the means by which the bourgeois revolutions were accomplished and of the social forces which accomplished them had implications for the nature of the post-revolutionary states. As Georg Lukacs observed shortly after the First World War:

> The bourgeoisie had far less of an immediate control of the actual springs of power than had ruling classes in the past (such as the citizens of the Greek city-states or the nobility at the apogee of feudalism). On the one hand, the bourgeoisie had to rely much more strongly on its ability to make peace or achieve a compromise with the opposing classes that held power before it so as to use the power-apparatus they controlled for its own ends. On the other hand, it found itself compelled to place the actual exercise of force (the army, petty bureaucracy, etc.) in the hands of petty bourgeois, peasants, the members of subject nations, etc.[31]

The political forms taken by post-revolutionary states therefore showed considerable variation and some writers have argued that without the attainment of representative ('bourgeois') democracy bourgeois revolutions must be considered incomplete. Paul Ginsborg, for example, writes that:

> The epoch of bourgeois revolution can perhaps be best characterised in terms of a twofold process, both economic and political. In economic terms, the period witnesses the definitive triumph of capitalism as the dominant mode of production. In the political sphere, the absolutist state comes to be replaced by one founded on the principles of bourgeois democracy.[32]

The question was raised in Scotland itself. The Scottish peer, Basil William Douglas, second Lord Daer, witnessed the early stages of the French Revolution and was radicalised by the experience. In 1792, after his return to Scotland, he became a leading figure on the constitutional wing of the Society of the Friends of the People.[33] In a letter of 1793 to Charles Grey he complained about the effects of the Treaty of Union:

> You say that we have gained emancipation from feudal tyranny. I believe most deliberately that had no Union ever taken place we should in that respect have been more emancipated than we are. Left to ourselves we should probably have had a progression towards Liberty and not less than yours. Our grievances prior to the accession of the Stewarts to your throne were of a kind that had that event not taken place, must before this time have been annihilated. Any share of

human evil that might have awaited us we are ignorant of, whereas we feel what we have undergone.[34]

In one sense Daer was right: 'emancipation from feudal tyranny' in the socio-economic sense did not involve the attainment of democracy in Scotland, any more than German unification introduced it in Germany. There are, however, three reasons why an insistence on a democratic criterion is both unnecessary and misleading.

First, representative democracy is a completely arbitrary measure of bourgeois revolutionary success. States characterised by both a capitalist economy and bourgeois democracy have, alas, been known to regress to a condition without the latter, and even to one of oppressive dictatorship. Such has been the fate of most Latin American states at one time or another. And not only them. Tom Nairn (writing in 1988) sets the period by which capitalist democracy became dominant in the 1960s and 1970s, 'to allow for France's last fling with the quasi-Monarchy of General de Gaulle, and the end of military dictatorship in Spain, Portugal and Greece'.[35] But is it seriously being suggested that nations regress to a point before the bourgeois revolution every time civilian rule is replaced by that of the military? The effect is to trivialise the concept of bourgeois revolution by reducing it from a systemic shift of historic proportions to a momentary change in the form of the capitalist state.

Second, if we take bourgeois democracy to involve, at a minimum, a representative government elected by the adult population, where votes have equal weight and can be exercised without intimidation by the state, then, as Goran Therborn writes, 'the fact [is] that none of the great bourgeois revolutions established bourgeois democracy'.[36] Of course, the first cycle involved previously unknown levels of participatory democracy, notably in England and France, although such popular involvement was nowhere sustained in the post-revolutionary period. Two alternative positions are therefore made possible by invoking the establishment of representative democracy as a criterion of successful bourgeois revolution; either (as I have argued) bourgeois democracy is not an essential component in their completion, or the revolutions listed above were not completed by the conventional dates. The logic of the latter position is to extend the chronological boundaries of 'the great bourgeois revolutions' until they include all the political episodes up to the point at which bourgeois democracy was established. Perry Anderson has argued that 'between the initial bourgeois revolution that breached the old order and the final completion of bourgeois democracy as the contemporary form of the capitalist state, there typically lay violent intervening convulsions that extended the work of the original upheaval and transformed the political framework of the nation'.[37] He draws the line for (West) Germany, Italy and Japan at the end of the Second World War. The implications of this position are that the American state which was largely responsible for democratising the Axis Powers had not completed the bourgeois revolution itself, since the Afro-American population of the Southern states were effectively denied the right to vote until the victory of the Civil Rights movement signalled by the passing of the Voting Rights Act in 1965. More generally, it is vulnerable to any definition of bourgeois democracy which is set at a high enough level of perfection. Indeed, it could quite plausibly be argued that the bourgeois revolution has nowhere been completed to this day. Think, for example, of the restrictions on rights of citizenship which are currently placed on migrant labourers in the USA and the EU, or the generally precarious nature of democracy in the post-Stalinist states.

Third, as the example of the American Civil Rights movement suggests, the achievement of representative democracy was generally the result of demands for representation by the working class and oppressed groups. Yet these groups were either brought into being or subjected to oppression in the first place by the capitalist industrialisation which the bourgeois revolutions (in the sense that I use the term) made possible. Other than as the result of defeat in war, national bourgeoisies have only agreed to such demands as a series of necessary concessions to forestall what were, for them, still more dangerous outcomes.

Alex Callinicos once wrote, against attempts to draw up lists of specific tasks which the bourgeois revolution is supposed to accomplish, including the establishment of representative democracy: 'Surely it is more sensible, rather than to invoke the metaphysical concept of a "complete and genuine solution", to judge a bourgeois revolution by the degree to which it succeeds in establishing an autonomous centre of capital accumulation, even if it fails to democratise the political order, or to eliminate feudal social relations.'[38] This does indeed seem a more sensible approach, the relevance of which to Scottish history will shortly become apparent.

The Bourgeois Revolution in Scottish History

The parameters of the bourgeois revolutionary epoch in Scottish history must lie within the cycle of revolutions 'from below' which concluded in 1849, since Scotland had become one of the most dynamic components of the international capitalist order long before that date. Let us now try to set the opening parameter more precisely, remembering that our focus is on the period beginning when Scottish feudalism could potentially have been overthrown, and ending at the moment when that overthrow actually took place. The period between 1637 and 1692 is full of dramatic and 'revolutionary' events, but clearly does not meet these criteria. The survival of Scottish feudalism throughout these years was not the result of subjective factors, but of objective conditions which could not be overcome, no matter how heroic the participants or how passionately they held their beliefs. Less heroic, less passionate, but infinitely more decisive for the triumph of capitalism was the period which followed 1692.

I wrote above that for each individual nation the epoch of bourgeois revolution began with the conjunction of three objective conditions: a crisis of feudalism, a capitalist solution to the crisis, and an agency capable of imposing the solution. For Scotland, this suggests the decade of the 1690s. On the one hand the twin catastrophes of famine at home and colonial misadventure abroad constituted the crisis, while on the other the growing wealth and power of the English bourgeoisie in the same decade demonstrated, for the first time in history, the possibility of a capitalist solution. It is the identity of the third condition, an effective agency, which at first seems elusive. Revolutions are not made by acts of will, but according to the availability of social forces capable of carrying them out, and these forces are themselves the products of prior economic development. Even by the late seventeenth century, when both the feudal impasse and capitalist alternative to it were clearly visible, the Scottish bourgeoisie were still incapable of breaking through the first to reach the second – or rather they were incapable of doing so on their own. The Scottish revolutionary epoch therefore opened with the completion of the process in the neighbouring kingdom of England, after which the English bourgeoisie and their state became, potentially at least, allies for the weaker bourgeois forces north of the Border, although it would take several decades for that potential to be realised. It is time, therefore, to meet the contending forces – the social classes, professional or occupational groups and ethnic communities – which comprised the Scottish people as they, unknowingly at first, entered their own age of revolution.

1

Scotland in the Late Seventeenth Century

By the late seventeenth century the majority of Scots lived either in the central belt between the Clyde and Forth estuaries, or on that part of the Lowlands plain which follows the east coast from the Firth of Forth up to Aberdeen. The precise number of these inhabitants is impossible to determine, since there are no completely reliable statistics, but one interpretation of the hearth tax returns for 1691 calculates it to be 1,234,575 (of whom only 245,699 lived in the Highlands and Islands), compared with nearly 2 million in Ireland, 6 million in England and 20 million in France.[1] Who were they? How and where did they live?

Lords, Peasants and Industrial Serfs

Between 80 and 90 per cent of Scots lived in the countryside, in hamlets which were called fermtouns in the Lowlands (kirktouns if they included a church) and clachans in the Highlands. The majority of them also drew their livelihood from the land, but at most only 10,000 of them owned any of it, and these landowners themselves varied enormously in the wealth they possessed and the power they exercised over others.

Lords

At the summit sat the upper reaches of the peerage, the Lowland nobles and Highland chiefs who held tenure directly from the Crown (although it is important to note that one person could, and in many cases did, simultaneously occupy both roles). The Scottish peerage had a large and growing membership, proportionate to the population, throughout the seventeenth century. At the Union of Parliaments in 1603 Scotland and England both had between 50 and 60 peers; but the former had a population of around 1 million, the latter a population of around 5 million. The number of peers grew equally in both countries while the population ratio remained constant. Consequently, at the Union of Parliaments in 1707 there were 154 peers in Scotland and 168 peers in England.[2] The former consisted of, in descending order by title, 10 dukes (including Argyll in the western Highlands, Gordon in the north-eastern Lowlands and Hamilton in the central Lowlands), three marquises (Atholl, Douglas and Montrose), 75 earls (including Seaforth and Haddington), 17 viscounts (including Dupplin and Kenmure) and lastly, 49 lords.[3] Let the greatest of all, the House of Argyll, stand for the rest.

Between 1607, when Archibald Campbell, the seventh Earl of Argyll, destroyed the power of Clan Donald on the Scottish mainland, and 1701, when Archibald Campbell, the tenth Earl, was created a Duke, the territory from which family drew their feudal rents grew fourfold in size to over 500 square miles. By the latter date Argyll himself held at least four major social roles. As representative of his family he was both Chief of Clan Campbell and feudal superior over the majority of the other chiefs and landowners in Argyll and areas of western Inverness-shire – an area of nearly 3,000 square miles. As representative of the central state in Argyll he embodied the law (as hereditary sheriff) and military power (as hereditary lord lieutenant).[4] Only a handful of other nobles or chiefs – Atholl, Hamilton, Queensberry – could aspire to such authority as this, but the example shows in the most extreme form the different roles and powers which could be combined in one person.

Below the peers were the lairds, of whom there were perhaps 1,500. Since the lairds are sometimes taken to be the progressive element in rural Scottish society it is important to note that, like the English gentry, they were not a class but an estate, whose representatives sat as such in the Scottish Parliament. Their members fell into two main subcategories. The first, the barons, held tenure directly from the crown in the same way as members of the peerage. The second, the non-baronial lairds, were sub-vassals of the nobility, although they could be, and often were, wealthier than the barons who stood above them in the social hierarchy.

The ruling class in the countryside, to which I will henceforth refer as the lords, therefore consisted of the entire nobility, from the dukes down to the barons, plus those non-baronial lairds who themselves exercised jurisdiction over a feudal superiority. Their defining characteristic was that their wealth came in the form of feudal rent from those beneath them who, whatever the specific nature of their tenure, carried out their own labour on the land or paid others to help them do so. The majority of the lords were uninterested in orientating themselves towards market relations, since this would have meant undertaking long-term investment to which few could afford to commit themselves, particularly when the results would have been slow in making themselves felt. They were more concerned with maintaining a stable level of income and the social power that came from their traditional form of proprietorship. A conspicuous display of social position, not an ascetic commitment to capital accumulation, was the mark of a great man in seventeenth century Scotland. In 1699 John Hamilton, second Lord Belhaven, dedicated a precocious contribution to the literature of Improvement to his fellow lords, but felt it necessary to do so in these terms: 'Up then brave Youths, leave off Courts and Politics, especially at so great a Distance from you, and in another Kingdom: follow Husbandry and Trade, two necessary Twins, who like Man and Wife, ought not to be separated.'[5] Belhaven, whatever else one may wish to say about him, knew where the actual interests of his audience lay, and why they would have to change; but he was virtually alone, at least among the lords, in making these arguments at the time.[6]

The lords maintained their authority over their tenants through the exercise of the heritable jurisdictions, which both helped define the feudal mode of production and represented one of the main sources of counter-vailing power to the Crown. These jurisdictions took two main forms, baronies and regalities, which differed in terms of size and the powers which they conferred, but in both cases were private, hereditary and unalienable. As the title suggests, a barony corresponded to the domain of the local baron and accompanied the granting of land from the Crown. A baron court could try all criminal offences except treason and the 'four pleas of the crown' – arson, murder, rape and robbery. A regality was a larger unit, often comprising several baronies, and usually in the possession of a lord with greater status than a mere baron. As an index of his superior position, the lord of a regality could try all criminal offences except treason, which remained the preserve of the Crown. Where fines were imposed on offenders the revenues went directly to the feudal superior – the implications of which, given the parlous state of many noble finances, it should not be necessary to labour. Neither type of court was, however, concerned solely or even mainly with crime, but with the management of the estate and enforcing the duties of tenants. Neither the Crown nor its appointed sheriffs had any right to interfere with the lord within his own jurisdiction. Indeed, many sheriffdoms had themselves become hereditary and the property of men who were already lords of regality. Because the state had not been successfully reorganised on an absolutist basis, the economic functions of the territorial jurisdictions retained their former importance. The Stuarts attempted to curb or assume control over various type of jurisdiction on at least six occasions between 1455 and 1637, to little avail: 'Such grants, however, continued to be made; sometimes they were confirmed by Parliament; often they were not, but they were exercised all the same. They were revoked again and again, and still continued to be granted.'[7] Had the Stuarts succeeded it would have massively increased the authority of the central state, and their failure is in itself eloquent testimony to the real balance of power between the lords and the Crown. Instead of creating a centralised authority to control the lords, the Crown strategy became one of supporting particular territorial lordships, such as those of Gordon in the north-east and of Argyll in the central west, in order to maintain local stability and act as counterweights to each other. The effect was, however, to help create the alternatives to royal power which it was intended to avoid. In this respect the territorial expansion of the Earls of Argyll, both as feudal superiors and as Chiefs of Clan Campbell, is only the most extreme example of a general process. The Cromwellian regime that ruled Scotland between 1651 and 1660 had temporarily suppressed the heritable jurisdictions, but they were reintroduced at the Restoration in 1660: Charles II needed the lords as much as they needed him, if the state was to function in Scotland.

The records of one, unexceptional baron court session held in Castle Forbes on 3 March 1662, show the operation of these jurisdictions. On this day, William, Master (i.e. eldest son) of Forbes, handed down instructions concerning when the tenants should pay their rent ('The said day, all tenants who pay victual duty are ordained to pay their whole rent in meal before the last day of March and their rent in malt before the 20th of May, under pain of paying ten pounds for the meal and twelve pounds for the malt'), the attitude they should take towards baronial officials ('The said day, it is enacted and ordained that all tenants within the lordship of Forbes give obedience to their ground officers in all matters concerning the law, under the penalty of twenty pounds for those who are able to pay it and of sitting for four days in the stocks for those who are not') and the punishments reserved for those who had the temerity not to turn up ('The said day, John Couper of Westhills is incited and ordained to pay forty shillings for his absence from the court').[8]

The penalties that the jurisdictions made available to the lords extended, at least theoretically, to the death penalty. 'Every laird (of note) hath a gibbet near his house,' noted Thomas Kirke, an English visitor in 1679, 'and has power to condemn and hang any of his vassals; so they dare not oppose him in any thing, but must submit to his commands, let them be never so unjust and tyrannical.'[9] Kirke was prone to exaggeration, but not to outright invention. An account of the same year, taken from the baron court of the Right Worshipful Sir Robert Gordon of Gordonstoun, reveals the continued exercise of the death penalty, although not by the gibbet. At the session of 25 August, the case of a woman called Janet Grant, who had been accused of theft by a local weaver, was heard:

> The assizers [i.e. jurors] ... being enclosed by themselves, did give their verdict sealed, by the hand of John James their chancellor [i.e. spokesperson] by which they found the said Janet guilty of the crimes for which she was accused. Whereupon the judge gave sentence that she shall be conveyed back from thence to prison, and to remain till the morrow, being the 26th instant, and thence to be carried, betwixt

2 and 6 o'clock in the afternoon, to the Loch of Spynie and there to be drowned under water till she be dead.

On the next day the sentence was carried out 'and the said Janet went down evacuating curses on her persecutors'.[10] The point here is not the nature of the sentence passed on Janet Grant, for even in a non-hereditary sheriff court the death sentence would likely have been imposed. Nor is it the means by which the sentence was executed. In the same source we learn that, during 1700, the magistrates in Elgin paid the marshal £20 for the equally barbarous if non-fatal work of whipping two people, cutting the ears off two more and branding a further two with a hot iron. The point is rather that the death penalty was in the power of a lordly jurisdiction outwith the authority of the central state. These powers were not removed by the Revolution of 1688. In the regality of Grant during September 1697, three men who confessed to the theft of cattle were first imprisoned at Grant Castle, then hanged at Gallowhill in Belintomb. In the barony of Breadalbane during May 1701, a man found guilty of the theft of three wedders and a horse was condemned to be hanged at Killin by John, Earl of Breadalbane.[11]

Nor were the jurisdictions all archaic survivals. Shortly after the fall of the Stuarts in 1688 the Grants of Speyside were given a regality as a reward for supporting William of Orange.[12] Shortly before the Treaty of Union in 1707 Lovat was granted to William Mackenzie of Prestonhall.[13] By the first quarter of the eighteenth century, Lanarkshire alone was the site of one heritable sheriffdom belonging to the House of Hamilton, eight regalities, two baronies, four commissary courts and the magistracy of Lanark and Hamilton.[14] By the time the jurisdictions were finally abolished in 1747, there were in Scotland a total of 16 hereditary sheriffdoms, 200 regalities and 1,000 baronies.[15]

After the Jacobite rising in 1745 made the issue unavoidable, one anonymous English commentator noted the authority which these jurisdictions conferred on the lords, writing that 'the Barons ... have power not only in Life and Limb but in an absolute sense too ... So that in fact these Lords of Regality are Sovereigns, not subjects.'[16] This had been recognised far earlier by the Scots themselves. In 1700, William Seton of Pittmeden proposed that the Scottish Parliament should pass an Act appointing 'some judicious Gentlemen of every County, to be chosen annually by Land-Proprietors of 40 pounds Sterling a year, and above, who should have power to decide all controversies arising between Master and Tenant, (for it is not just, that the Master should be both Judge and Party, as it often happens in Baron courts)'.[17] Where Parliament was composed of the very people who benefited from the existing arrangements, however, such reforms were unlikely to be forthcoming.

The heritable jurisdictions were not the only form of power which the lords exercised. The form of tenure known in Scotland as wardholding was the most fundamental to military feudalism. Sir Thomas Craig was legal adviser to James VI and I before his accession to the English throne, and the author of an important work on the feudal law, dedicated to James, which remained unpublished for nearly 50 years after his death in 1608. His book, *Jus Feudale*, as several authorities have noted, is not so much an analysis of Scots law during the feudal period, as a codification of the feudal law in general with special reference to Scotland. It is a codification that was only possible in retrospect, as the classic age of military feudalism gave way to that of absolutism. Yet precisely because Scotland had not made that transition, much of what Craig wrote about military feudalism was not a matter of historical retrospect but of contemporary description, as events would confirm on several occasions over the next 150 years. Craig attempts to play down the relevance of military tenures: 'In Scotland, where military holdings are now old fashioned and feudal grants have become matters of commerce and profit, the feudal oath is entirely forgotten; but notwithstanding, we continue to hold our vassals bound by the obligations of fealty.' Yet he undermines his own argument in two respects. First, fealty requires the vassal to protect the 'life or person ... honour and reputation' of his lord. If the lord requires vassals to participate in an 'armed endeavour', then no special form of requisition is required: 'For military service differs from all other kinds of feudal service in that it is (as every vassal knows) the radical condition of his tenure.' Second, even where lands were feued out 'it is important to remember that a feu is presumed to be proper unless it is shown by the terms of its investiture to be that its proper or genuine character has been modified.' 'Proper', in this context, means 'military'.[18] As late as 1681, Sir James Dalrymple, first Viscount Stair, in a further codification of the existing feudal law much influenced by Craig, could write of wardholding that: 'It is the most proper feudal right we have; and therefore wherever the holding appeareth not, or is unclear, there wardholding is understood [i.e. assumed to be the prevailing form of tenure].'[19] What this meant in practice, outside these works of legal theory, was expressed with admirable clarity by Macdonell of Keppoch, who, when questioned as to the size of his rent roll, simply replied: 'I can call out and command 500 men.'[20]

Peasants

Who were the people over whom jurisdiction was exercised, or who were expected, albeit less frequently, to fight as a condition of their tenancy? The rural population below the ruling class can be usefully, if inadequately, described as the Scottish peasantry.

The most independent were a group, without jurisdictions or separate legal status, who have come to be known, after Sir Walter Scott, as the bonnet lairds. They farmed the land themselves with their servants and families, and were often little better off than the tenant farmers who stood directly below them in the social structure. What distinguished the bonnet lairds was that they held their land, either directly or indirectly from the Crown, under a distinct form of tenure known as *feuferme*. They were descended from the beneficiaries of the great sub-infeudation movement of the fifteenth and sixteenth centuries, in which feudal superiors granted a charter (the 'feu') effectively conferring perpetual heritable possession in return for a large initial downpayment and a fixed annual sum payable in perpetuity. A further payment on the death of the feuar transferred possession to his kin. Even when land had been feued out, however, the rights of jurisdiction remained with the feudal superior, so that even those farmers who were no longer tenants could not completely escape his authority. Bonnet lairds were therefore in a contradictory position. Like the lords above them, they had effective possession of their land; unlike the lords, they did not live off the rent of tenants. Like the tenants below them, they worked their own land; unlike the tenants, they did not pay rent to a lord. They were resentful of the social power of the lords and yet had enough economic independence not to be completely cowed by it. With as many as 8,000 in their ranks, they were the most numerous of the non-tenant farmers. If the lairds are comparable to the English gentry, then the bonnet lairds are comparable to the English yeoman. Yet the total proportion of land occupied by them was low. No region of Scotland can be taken as typical, since all had their own peculiarities, but Aberdeenshire provides some indication of the general pattern of landownership and was close to the national average for bonnet laird occupancy of 5.5 per cent. By 1667, 25 family groups, who had between them controlled landownership in the county since the fourteenth century, accounted for nearly 33 per cent of the landowners and were in receipt of 66 per cent of the valued rent. Of the 621 landowning families in Aberdeenshire, 51 families (8.1 per cent) owned 50 per cent of land; 503 families (81 per cent) held only 35.3 per cent. Of the lesser landowners, those identified as lairds owned 41.6 per cent and the bonnet lairds, only 5 per cent.[21] There were so few bonnet lairds across Scotland as a whole that, with the exception of the south-west they nowhere attained the numerical mass necessary to act as a social or political vanguard.

Below the bonnet lairds stood the tenant farmers who, theoretically at least, had no security over the land they occupied. Their condition varied greatly. A minority worked holdings which were actually larger and more prosperous than those of the bonnet lairds. William Nisbet, for example, was the sole tenant in the small kirktoun of Crimond in Aberdeenshire, and the main employer in that community, providing work for, amongst others, six farm servants and six artisans, in addition to acting as landlord for two subtenants. Nisbet was typical of farmers who broadcast their status by classifying themselves as 'gentleman' in the poll-tax returns, even though this increased the amount they would be required to pay.[22] Farmers with more than 8 oxen and 50 Scots acres might 'be expected to have some commitment to commercial production and some opportunity to accumulate capital'. Farmers with less than this 'would not have been able to furnish their own ploughteam without co-operating with their neighbours. One would expect them to have little market orientation and to have been closer to the margin of subsistence.'[23] As Thomas Devine writes: 'It is not difficult to see men like ... Nisbet of the upper rank of the tenantry as part of an embryonic farming bourgeoisie whose unusually large consolidated holdings were increasingly committed to servicing the market for grain and stock.'[24] Nevertheless, the majority of the tenants correctly felt themselves to be so insecure that they were unable even to guarantee that their tenancy would pass to their children. Christina Larner described their situation as 'an excellent structural recipe for docility and deference'.[25] The tenants were therefore ill-suited for the role of leading the rural masses against their landlords.

Any attempt to identify a class of potential capitalists in the Scottish countryside must therefore combine the precise, if extra-legal, category of the bonnet lairds with the much less definite category of large tenant farmers. Both had an incentive to produce for the market that was denied to either the lordly proprietors above them or the smaller tenant farmers below them. But few tenants farmers approached the degree of local importance attained by Nisbet. Take Aberdeenshire as an example once more; only 2 per cent of tenants held more than 100 acres, but 45 per cent held less than 20 acres.[26]

Whatever the problems of the tenantry, however, they were fewer than those endured by the classes below them in the social structure. In descending order of poverty and dependence, these were the crofters, cottars, farm servants and last of all, of course, their wives and children. If the tenant farmer generally had just enough land to sustain himself and his family, the crofters and cottars tended to have much smaller holdings, typically sub-let from the tenant himself, from whom they also had to seek employment. And their occupancy was even more precarious. The voice of these peasants went largely unrecorded, and most of the attempts to articulate or explain their condition come rather from sympathetic individuals among their social superiors. In one of the early classics of Scottish vernacular literature, *The Complaynt of Scotland*, published anonymously in 1549, 'the labourer' expresses his anger at the misery of his life:

> I labour night and day with my hands to feed lazy and useless men, and they repay me with hunger and the sword. I sustain their life with the toil and sweat of my body, and they persecute my body with

hardship, until I am become a beggar. They live through me and I die through them.[27]

It might be objected that this is a literary invention, and one written 140 years before the opening of our period at that. A reference from the close, however, in a letter of 1759 from Sir Robert Pollock to the Duke of Douglas, indicates that, in relative terms at least, their conditions had not improved significantly: 'These cottars uphold their own houses and work all the work, for I have rarely observed a Tenant work here; the Cottar's slavery is incredible and what is worse they are liable to be turned out at the Master's pleasure.'[28]

By the late seventeenth century some commentators had begun to analyse the dilemmas of the tenants and those below them. Two writers in particular, Andrew Fletcher of Saltoun and Sir William Seton of Pitmedden, despite taking very different positions over the Union of 1707, came to virtually identical conclusions on this question. Fletcher was himself a baronial laird and consequently a lesser member of the ruling class. Nevertheless, in 1698 his analysis of the problems faced by the majority of the tenants placed responsibility mainly with his fellow landowners, assigning:

... the principal and original source of our poverty ... in the letting of our lands at so excessive a rate as makes the tenant poorer even than his servant whose wages he cannot pay; and involves in the same misery day-labourers, tradesmen and the lesser merchants who live in the country villages and towns; and thereby influences no less the great towns and wholesale merchants, makes the master have a troublesome and ill-paid rent, his lands not improved by enclosure or otherwise, but for want of horses and oxen fit for labour, everywhere run out and abused.[29]

From a similar class position, Seton wrote in 1700 of:

... the Husband-men, which [sic] in my Opinion are the most miserable of all our Commons; and I believe, we have learned that Method of oppressing our Peasants, from the French, amongst many of their good customs. The reason for this Oppression proceeds from small Farms and High valued Duties. For the Poverty of the Nation and the smallness of Trade does occasion, That Land-Estates are frequently shifted from hand to hand, so long as they keep Possession of them: and are sure to rack every Tenant in his Duty, when they are disposed to sell them, for drawing the greater price from the Buyers.[30]

The dominance that the lords had over their tenants, of which both writers complained, was expressed, in the first instance, through the lease itself, both in terms of its duration and the conditions which the tenant was expected to fulfil. Tenants were said to 'sit at will' – the will of the lord, of course, not their own – and leases were usually for one, or perhaps two years; the implication being that if the lord was unsatisfied with the tenant's behaviour – or that of the subtenants for whom the tenant was also held responsible – it would not be renewed. Short-term leases gave tenants little incentive to improve their yields, since the likely result of so doing would either be a rent increase, or eviction and replacement by another tenant who was prepared to pay the difference. By 1688 the written lease had begun to replace the purely verbal agreement which had previously characterised the landlord–tenant relationship, particularly in arable areas. The importance of this should not, however, be exaggerated. Where the length of tenure was for such short periods a tenant were unlikely to be evicted before even a verbal lease expired. When it did, the lords still rarely evicted tenants, not through benevolence, but because the threat itself was sufficient to instil obedience and the acceptance of increased rents. There are even recorded examples of lords forcing up rents by making potential tenants bid for holdings, a tactic with which Fletcher concluded his list of grievances: 'To all this may be added the letting of farms in most part of those grazing countries every year by roup or auction.'[31] It is sometimes suggested that written leases, by providing greater security for the tenant, contributed to early experiments in Improvement.[32] It seems more likely that the majority of written leases were a means, in an age where the law was playing a more significant role in defining contractual relationships, of establishing beyond question the nature of the labour services which the tenant was expected to provide for the landlord.

The majority of rents were still mainly paid in kind; but if tenants failed to deliver their full quota, the lords were not above calculating the outstanding amounts in cash terms. If tenants of the Earl of Panmure in Forfarshire failed to deliver the required amount of grain in any year, they were charged with what would have been the market price of the grain. As a result, when a bad harvest led to high prices, the tenants fell deeply in debt from which they had to extract themselves by selling the surplus of a good harvest – by which time, of course, the price had fallen. This was not exceptional. Two authors who generally take an optimistic view of social relations in the countryside at this time conclude that: 'While the survival of such rent structures into the eighteenth century may be attributed in part to inertia and a lack of economic growth, the system may also have been a method of social control which prevented tenants from accumulating enough capital to enter the land market.'[33]

In addition to these constraints, tenants were also required to perform the labour services referred to above. These generally involved such duties as ploughing, harrowing or harvesting on the mains or home farm; moving grain supplies for the lord ('carriage'); cutting, drying and bringing in the peat supply; quartering the lord's livestock; and helping maintain the estate mill, to which they would also have to take their grain for grinding ('thirlage'), before paying the lord in kind for the privilege of doing so ('multure'). All of this took up time and effort that the tenants could have spent more productively on their own land. Occasionally, they complained. In 1669 Colonel David Barclay 'was informed [that] some of his tenants did calumniate him as an oppressor and exactor'. Barclay said that that he was willing for their case to be heard in his court – by his baillie, Alexander Keith of Cowton: 'Whereupon the tenants being called and present to give in their complaints, they refused to do it in regard they confessed they had no reason to do so.' Barclay then 'freely offered' that his tenants should have the option of either carrying out these services or paying him ten merks a year in compensation. They agreed to continue doing service, on the understanding that they would be penalised in the sum of 28 shillings and 8 pence for every day of service which they failed to perform.[34]

As this example suggests, some tenants refused to submit without at least offering token resistance, although this usually took the form of refusing to perform labour service, paying rent in kind with spoiled or poor quality produce, and poaching from or cutting peat on the lord's estate. The barony of Urie felt it necessary to repeatedly ordain that tenants – sometimes the subtenants of specific villages – were forbidden to cut and carry off peat, on pain of being fined. These ordinances are so frequent that we can only assume the laird experienced a continuing problem.[35] This is one aspect of a 'hidden' class struggle which hardly ever escalated into an 'open' challenge to the ruling class. Why not?

The pattern of human settlement militated against collective responses. Scotland had a relatively small population which was for the most part widely scattered into isolated rural communities. There was little contact between these communities and little co-operation or sense of collectivity within them.[36] Consequently, an integrated national economy did not exist. Instead there was a multitude of small regional economies that were to a great extent self-contained. Thus, although there might be scarcity and the resulting dearness of essential foods in one region, there was no guarantee that the same situation would exist in the next.[37] The basis for a generalised response was usually absent and noble feuding or civil war tended not to provoke one, but rather to force individual communities to seek the protection of the local lord – a situation which, as we shall see later in this chapter, was formally embodied in the clan system, particularly in the western Highlands where these activities were most disruptive. One Scottish commentator, John Barclay, compared English and Scottish plebeian attitudes in 1614. He noted of the former that 'the pride of the common people is not more bitter and distasteful towards strangers, than towards their own gentry, who account themselves equal almost to the best and most ancient of them', but of the latter that:

> ... the people courageous also against themselves, are divided by many fierce enmities, and cruel to each other, beyond all laws of humanity or hatred. For being divided by Families and Names, they hold these as Princes of their factions, which possess the most ancient inheritance of the Family ... to them when they are wronged, they fly for succour ...[38]

Yet there was one region in which the peasantry did regularly engage in open confrontation, not directly with the landlords, but with the state itself: the south-west. It was here, in 1648, that the Battle of Mauchline Moor was fought by local lairds and tenant farmers resisting conscription into what they regarded as the ungodly army of the Scottish state. It was here, again in 1648, that the 'Whiggamore Raid' was launched to overthrow the Royalist regime in Edinburgh and established the radical Kirk Party in power. It was here, yet again in 1648, that the paramilitary Western Association was founded and began a succession of campaigns against Royalists, the official army of the Scottish state and eventually the New Model Army. It was after the Restoration of 1660, however, that the region became the centre of militant opposition to the Episcopalian religious settlement. There was not a continuous regional revolt between 1660 and 1688, but rather two insurrections separated by 13 years (1666 and 1679), both of which were initially responses to state provocation. These events involved relatively large numbers of people; around 1,000 in the first and around 4,000 in the second. Subsequently, between 1682 and 1685, an intermittent *guerrilla* was waged by a tiny minority of activists who could not have numbered more than a few hundred at most. Finally, between 1688 and 1690 a mass uprising played a major role in both evicting the ecclesiastic appointees of the Stuart regime and militarily defending the new monarchy of William and Mary from Jacobite counter-revolution. A unique combination of four circumstances provided the peasants of the south-west with conditions for action unavailable elsewhere in Scotland.

First, as we noted above, there was a higher level of bonnet laird occupancy. The national average was only 5.5 per cent, but it was highest in the south-western shires of Ayr and – in particular – Dumfries and Galloway, where it rose to 17 per cent.[39] Here, the bonnet lairds were numerous and concentrated enough to lead collective action in defence of their religious principles or material conditions. The religious distaste which they felt towards the Commonwealth regime of 1651–60 prevented them from acknowledging the extent to which it had freed them from their feudal superiors. When these were reimposed at the

Restoration, the constraints on their liberty were felt all the more strongly, after nearly a decade of relative freedom.

Second, the tenant farmers immediately below the bonnet lairds were experiencing a regional crisis. Large parts of the area were pastoral, and because of the impossibility of self-sufficiency in these areas, rents were typically paid in cash raised from the sale of cattle and sheep in the markets of the east. On the Hamilton estates in Clydesdale the price of essential items of food had increased between 9 and 10 times in the 100 years preceding the Battle of Mauchline Moor in 1648. In the arable east, where rents tended to be paid in kind, they rose as prices rose, relatively steadily through the great inflation of the sixteenth and early seventeenth centuries. In the south-west, rents did not rise semi-automatically in the same way. It required a conscious decision by the landlord which they often postponed, not only because of the threat of disorder, but because of the social obligations which their position in feudal society placed on them, not least by the kirk. Many of the tenants, on the lands of both the church and the lords were secure, having granted the feu directly or through the process of sub-infeudation from the laird. Yet between 1625 and 1670, on the Hamilton estates at least, rents began to rise, sporadically and inconsistently, but nevertheless remorselessly upwards. And rent became ever more exclusively paid in cash. In some cases rents would be 'augmented', sometimes by as much as two-and-a-half times the money rent. In others, the tenant would be offered the chance to pay a downpayment or entry fine ('grassum') which would postpone the increase until his death, so that his son would inherit the new rent along with the tenancy. Whatever the respective weight which should be given to these various mechanisms for increasing proprietorial income (and that is by no means clear), the effect was dramatically to increase the burden on the tenantry.[40] The tenants had, however, an ideological basis for resistance to these additional burdens in the doctrines of a church which treated their imposition as something approaching a sin.

Third, the area described by Walter Makey as running from 'the northern edge of the Southern Uplands from the city of Edinburgh to the Solway Firth' was open to traffic in intellectual movements from two directions: 'At the one end it absorbed radical influences from London and the Continent; at the other, it received presbyterian zealots returning from exile in Ulster.'[41] The second of these – proximity to the Presbyterian colonies in Ulster where, in Antrim and Down, Scots were in the majority – is likely to have been the more significant. The shortage of ministers in Ulster before 1637 meant that radicals from the south-west like John Livingstone and Robert Blair were able both to obtain parishes there denied them for political reasons in Scotland and to use the province as a launching pad for conventicling expeditions back to their home terrain. But their exile impacted on them in other, less material ways. Like all colonial outposts, the settlers in Ulster developed intense ideological positions both to justify their imperial mission and to distinguish themselves from the natives. These positions communicated themselves to the temporary migrants from Scotland: 'The nearness of Ulster, where [Alexander] Peden could find sanctuary at need in a Scottish settlement planted with the sword, with a Presbyterian fervour kept in constant heat by confrontation with popery, must have reinforced the intransigence of the south-west.'[42] The connection with Ulster is confirmed by an Act of 7 October 1663 intended to restrict the arrival in Scotland of 'many seditious and turbulent persons, ministers and others, in the kingdom of Ireland, who by reason of their fanatic principles could not comply with the administration of his majesty's authority and government so happily established in that kingdom', and who were crossing the Irish Sea to agitate in Scotland.[43] These concerns were sustained throughout the period. In 1678 Sir Joseph Williamson, the Secretary of State, was writing to the Duke of Ormonde, the Lord Lieutenant of Ireland, requesting a 'strict guard to be kept in all the passages between the north of Ireland and Scotland for apprehending any suspected persons' who attempted to use Ulster as a refuge from persecution in Scotland or base from which to plan readmission.[44] But although the ideas carried by travellers to and from Ulster gave ideological sustenance to believers in the south-west, they would not have made this impact had their audience not already been predisposed to find them attractive.

Fourth, and finally, the area was geographically inaccessible. Fife and the Lothians, where large numbers of ministers had also been excluded, were too near to the centres of state power in Edinburgh, with all the military resources it had to hand: 'Ayrshire, Dumfriesshire, and the neighbouring Borders were rich in trackless moors, bogs, hills, where unlawful meetings could avoid detection or baffle pursuit, as smugglers and cattle-reivers had done in times still not quite gone by.'[45] This terrain allowed open displays of religious dissent lacking in Edinburgh, where the ousted ministers tended to preach to the faithful in small indoor gatherings where the emphasis was on bearing witness rather than expressing defiance.

The struggle in the south-west provided the Stuarts with part of their rationale for constructing the absolutist state in Scotland, particularly after 1685, and reminded the lords of their previous experience sufficiently for them to acquiesce in its construction. Nevertheless, it presented more of a local irritation than a mortal threat to the existence of the regime. Indeed, it is difficult to see how an almost entirely localised rebellion could present such a threat when the rest of the country lay supine, or at best engaged in passive resistance. Nevertheless, the fact that there was resistance at all is significant, given the lack of such a historical tradition. The failure of their rebellion to generate a supportive response elsewhere only confirms how exceptional it was in the annals of the Scottish peasantry.

Industrial Serfs

A small but economically significant section of the rural population laboured, not in the fields, but in the coal and lead mines (and the subsidiary salt industry). For the most part these labourers and their families lived in communities little bigger than the fermtouns and clachans occupied by the peasants. In some ways, however, their conditions were even worse. Unlike the peasants, miners and panners were juridically defined as serfs, bound to their place of employment – and in the case of the colliers to the very coal which they dug – in the same way as rural serfs had been tied to the land over 300 years earlier. We tend to think of the coal industry as fuelling the initial process of industrialisation in Britain. We are equally used to regarding British miners, not least their Scottish contingent, as exemplars of proletarian solidarity, attested to time and time again in innumerable local battles and in their four great twentieth-century confrontations with their employers and the British state. It might seem strange, therefore, to refer to workers so closely identified with the class struggle under capitalism as serfs. 'Serfdom' is, however, more than a figure of speech. A man digging coal is no more a proletarian by virtue of his activity than a man ploughing a field is necessarily a peasant by virtue of his.[46] Their class position derives instead from the social relationships within which these activities take place.

In Scotland, coal mining, lead mining and salt panning were activities dominated by the lords, who supplemented their income from feudal rent by exporting the mineral wealth of their lands. To ensure the continual supply of this supplementary income, however, they used means that had been abandoned in agriculture several centuries before. The process by which the workforce in these industries was enserfed is therefore worth recounting in some detail, precisely because it was not made possible by legal remnants of the medieval period, unaccountably retained long after similar restrictions had effectively ceased to function elsewhere. The first of these laws was in fact only 100 years old in 1707, and its successors continued to be ratified and added to until the last quarter of the eighteenth century, by which time the social relations they originally embodied had fundamentally changed.[47]

Small-scale mining had taken place on monastic estates since the twelfth century, but the real period of expansion in the industry took place after 1580, when an increased demand for both domestic and industrial fuel made it worthwhile expanding production. Both the old monastic coal deposits and new seams as yet unmined were now in the possession of various lords, from the dukes (including, needless to say,

Argyll) at the top end of the ruling class pyramid to lairds such as the Clerks of Penicuik at the bottom. Their difficulty lay in persuading anyone to undertake the type of work required in extracting the coal. Few peasants would voluntarily commit themselves to the dangerous and unaccustomed work involved in mining or panning, but since many of the greater lords were commissioners to the Parliament, or even members of the Privy Council which effectively controlled the legislative process, they had the opportunity to enact laws which could resolve their dilemma by compulsion.

There were useful precedents in a succession of Acts – some of which were constituent of the Scottish Poor Laws – beginning with the Act Permitting Assessment of the Poor in 1574, which attempted to bring the perceived problem of vagrancy under control. The effect of these enactments was to allow vagrants to offer themselves up for enserfment to an employer and, more significantly, to allow employers the right to seize vagrants against their will for this purpose. Basing themselves on these models, some of which had already been used to obtain labourers for the mines, an Act of 1606 forbade the employment of colliers, coal bearers or salters by anyone unless they possessed a testimonial from their previous employer or magistrate confirming they had been lawfully released from service. Given the shortage of labour that had impelled this legislation in the first place, such testimonials were unlikely to be forthcoming. Any miner leaving employment without one – that is to say, escaping – could be prosecuted as a thief if recaptured within a year and a day. The logic behind this charge was that they had removed part of the owner's property, their own person, which belonged to the master as surely as did the chains and buckets with which the coal was brought to the surface. Any person who wrongfully employed a runaway or failed to return one within 24 hours was subject to a fine of £100 Scots. A further Act of 1641 extended serfdom from the colliers and panners themselves to the surface workers and lengthened the working week for everyone in these industries to six days. Once the workforce had been established the problem of reproducing it was partly accomplished by making the condition of servitude hereditary. On the christening of a male child the master would present the collier and his wife with a gift (the 'arle') in return for their promise that the child would enter the mine on coming of age. But of course, the children did not have to wait that long before experiencing the rigours of the mining life; along with their mothers and sisters they were obliged to work, for nothing, in carrying the coal hewed by their fathers to the pithead. The conditions of the panners was no better. In 1656, Thomas Tucker, the registrar to the English commissioners for appeals charged with regulating the Scottish excise, wrote of the condition to which they had been reduced: 'And to require an account or any thing else of the workmen (who, besides their infinite poverty and miserableness, are (were it not a breach of charity) to be esteemed brutes rather than rationals).'[48]

In addition to the main legislation, several other Acts refined the terms of industrial servitude. The Act for Establishing Correction Houses for Idle Beggars and Vagabonds of 1672 states:

> It is always hereby Provided, that it shall be lawful for coalmasters, Salt-Masters and others who have Manufactories in this Kingdom, to seize upon any Vagabonds or beggars, wherever they can find them and put them to work in their Coal-heughs or other Manufactories, who are to have the same power of Correcting them, and the benefit of their work, as the Masters of the Correction-houses.

The 'powers of correcting' to which the Act refers included, 'in case of their disobedience, to use all manner of severity and correction, by whipping or otherwise (excepting torture)'.[49] No doubt the subtlety of the distinction between whipping and torture was one which the colliers and panners appreciated as the skin was being lashed from their backs. Discipline did not of course simply rely on enforcing the Acts of the Scottish Parliament. The mine owners who were also lords had at their disposal the authority conferred by the heritable jurisdictions. Clerk of Penicuik was one who used his baronial status to impose order on his workforce: 'Any labourer who questioned his orders, or those of his overseers, was to be removed from the mine and brought before the court for punishment.'[50] Nor was the desire for control restricted to the labour process; Clerk also sought to regulate to the personal lives of the labourers through the same means. The serfdom imposed on Scottish colliers and salters is therefore comparable, albeit on a much smaller scale, to the 'second serfdom' imposed on East European peasants during the same period. And, as Christopher Whatley has written, the motivation was similarly 'to retain scarce labour'.[51]

Finally, before leaving the extractive industries, it is worth considering how members of the Scottish ruling class regarded the workers involved not directly involved in their exploitation. A number of writers have reacted to what they consider an unnecessarily bleak view of late seventeenth century Scotland by emphasising the cultural achievements of the time. Central to such accounts is the monumental codification of the Scots Law by Sir James Dalrymple, first Viscount Stair, published in 1681.[52] *The Institutions of the Law of Scotland* is indeed a major landmark in the development of Scots Law. In it he writes of juridical serfdom that:

> ... there remain some vestiges in colliers and salters, who are astricted to those services by law, though there be no paction or engagement, which is introduced upon the common interest, these services being so necessary for the kingdom, where the fuel of coal is in most parts

necessary at home and very profitable abroad; and seeing we have no salt of our own, but that which is made by the boiling of salt water, salters are also so astricted: so that colliers and salters, while they live, must continue in these services.[53]

There is not a hint of criticism in this learned account of how these 'necessary and profitable' activities are organised. Dalrymple reminds us, by his very acceptance of the cruelties of his age, that the subject of his great work was not 'the law' in some abstract sense, but the feudal law by whose provisions the colliers and salters had been enserfed.

Burgesses and Indwellers

If neither agriculture nor rural industry offered an immediate challenge to the prevailing feudal order, what of the towns? By the 1690s Scotland ranked only tenth out of 16 areas in Western Europe in the league of 'urbanised societies'.[54] There were a relatively large number of towns, but they were mainly small and, with the exception of Inverness, all of them were in the Lowlands. Only 15.4 per cent of the population lived in towns of more than 1,000 people and only 7.2 per cent in towns of more than 10,000, of which there were only two – Edinburgh and its environs with 40,000, and Glasgow with 13,000.[55] Although the capital Edinburgh was the largest town, it did not yet play the same central role in Scottish economic and political life that other capital cities like Paris, London or even Dublin did in their respective nations. Scotland was characterised instead by a series of regional capitals, notably the so-called 'four great towns' of the late medieval and early modern period (Aberdeen, Dundee, Edinburgh and Perth), but also Inverness, Stirling and, of increasing importance throughout the seventeenth century, Glasgow.

Most towns were classified as burghs – urban communities which had been given the right to trade by the crown, to elect magistrates with the authority to enact and enforce local laws, and to establish merchant and craftsman guilds. As with everything else in Scottish society, they were ranked in hierarchical order. In the first rank were the 70 royal burghs, which (until 1672) had the sole rights to conduct foreign trade, to meet in their own collective forum (the Convention of Royal Burghs), and to be represented as an Estate along with the Nobility and the Church in the Scottish Parliament. Below the royal burghs lay the burghs of barony, which had considerably smaller areas of control and were restricted to conducting internal trade. As many as 270 burghs of barony were created between 1500 and 1707, but in many cases their populations were below the 500 mark usually taken to mark the demarcation between rural cluster and urban community. Paisley, the largest burgh of barony in the late seventeenth century, had only 2,200 inhabitants in 1695.[56] Many of the smaller burghs of barony were erected by the feudal superior of the land on which they stood for the specific purpose of collecting tolls from travellers and traders, and generating rents from the inhabitants. As we have already seen, others were more specifically built to service local mineral extraction; Saltcoats and Leadhills reveal the reason for their existence in their very names. These burghs required little outlay from the lord beyond the initial costs of construction, creating the burgesses and establishing their governing institutions. In return he received the benefit of all the revenues which accrued. These closely controlled creations were not to be the site of a developing bourgeois class to challenge the rule of the lords. Indeed, the Act of 1672 which secured the privilege of foreign trade for the burghs of barony should be seen as a temporary victory for the lords (it was partially reversed in 1690) in breaking into the hitherto merchant monopoly of the royal burghs, rather than a furthering of any distinct capitalist interest. It was not only the burghs as corporate bodies that were assigned different ranks, of course, but their inhabitants. If there was one primary social division, it was between the third of the urban population who were merchant and craftsmen burgesses on the one hand and the two-thirds who were mere 'indwellers' of the burghs on the other.

Burgesses

By 1688 no more than 7 per cent of the inhabitants of Edinburgh were classed as burgesses.[57] The former were permitted to trade, vote, and stand for election; the latter could do none of these things – although they were still considered to be part of the burgh 'community', a characterisation which at any rate entitled them to receive poor relief. The unfree were not encouraged to get above themselves. The burgh records of Edinburgh for 9 December 1668 contain a warning to the burgesses to be on the lookout for unfreemen pretending to have burgess status and, above all, to refuse to assist them in their schemes to surmount the burghal restrictions on trade:

> And whereas the Council is informed that several freemen of this burgh do colour unfreemen's goods under colour of their own, expressly contrary to their oath in their burgess ticket and highly derogatory to the interest of this burgh, by connecting the privilege and benefit of a free burgess to them that has no right thereto and hereby rendering the said privilege useless and contemptible.[58]

Patrick Lindsay, once the Lord Provost of Edinburgh, complained of these practices, not in the sixteenth century, but in 1733, when their effectiveness had already greatly diminished:

> How unlike it is to Freedom and Liberty that a Trader in a Royal Burgh cannot employ a Tradesman in the Country, who by his superior Industry and Diligence can work cheaper; and that the County Manufacturers cannot bring in his Goods for Sale, but on a certain Day, and at a certain Hour, as if Commodities for Exportation ought to be subjected to the same Rules of Sale with Market-provisions? How much is the Trade within Burghs discouraged by the Practice? And who are the Gainers by this great loss to the Country?[59]

Even the burgesses held unequal stations. At the pinnacle were the merchants. Like the term 'laird', however, 'merchant' conceals a number of class positions. The top layer were a narrow elite of the wealthiest who constituted the urban ruling class and occupied most major political positions, including those of the magistrates, who were empowered to fix the rates for prices and wages. These not only had the financial capacity to engage in foreign trade but were also members of the guild, which conferred upon them the right to do so. In Aberdeen during the 1690s, for example, this stratum consisted of 27 out of 239 merchant burgesses, all with stock valued at 10,000 merks or over, although on average the elite could encompass as many as 20–25 per cent of the merchants in any burgh.[60] Below these were the majority of merchant burgesses, who were allowed to trade within Scotland but not abroad, either because they were not members of the guild or simply because they could not afford the initial outlays which entering foreign trade involved.

How easy was it to join the merchant class? An aspirant could buy his way in, or serve an apprenticeship, or marry the daughter of an existing guild brother. The easiest route, however, was to choose your father with some care. Between 1623 and 1626, the merchant guild in Aberdeen admitted 148 new guild brothers and in this, as in everything else, the city proved to be one of the most conservative areas of Scotland; 70 (64.5 per cent) were sons of existing merchant burgesses, six (5.5 per cent) were recommended by 'prominent' men, three (4.5 per cent) were sons of craftsmen burgesses, eight (7 per cent) were married to the daughter of a merchant burgess and 20 (18.5 per cent) were not categorised.[61] The last group would have included apprentices and those who had simply bought their way in – and for those with no familial connections the cost of doing so would have been steep indeed.

How much did the merchants contribute to the development of capitalism in Scotland? Throughout early modern Europe mercantile capitalism played an ambiguous role in the development of the system. They drew their profits, not from realising the value added to commodities in the process of production, but from the discrepancy in price between their initial outlay and the ultimate selling price at the end of long-distance trade routes. Alex Callinicos has described their activities as a 'necessary but not sufficient' condition for the dominance of capitalist relations of production: 'As long as capitalism did not conquer production it was forced (and indeed largely content) to co-exist with feudalism.'[62] Marx noted that by taking control of production, the merchant 'cannot bring about the overthrow of the old mode of production itself, but rather preserves and retains it as its own precondition'. More specifically, where 'the merchant makes the small masters into his middlemen, or even buys directly from the independent producer[,] he leaves him nominally independent and leaves his mode of production unchanged'.[63] This is borne out by the behaviour of the Scottish merchants. One aspect of capitalism is production for an unknown competitive market, but this was resisted by the merchant guilds, who were still imposing sanctions on their members for the crime of buying goods before they had been displayed in an authorised market ('forestalling') at the end of the seventeenth century.[64] As late as 1690 the guild in the Royal Burgh of Lanark can be found invoking an Act passed 130 years earlier against forestallers buying or selling hide skin or bone before the carcasses can be brought to market:

> Therefore they do hereby strictly prohibit and discharge all guild brethren within this burgh at any time hereafter to buy either hide or skin before the same be presented to the market, and that under the pains and penalties contained in the Acts of Parliament made against forestallers and regrators.[65]

Yet the block which the merchants presented to the development of competitive markets went further than this type of petty feudal restriction and into the process of production itself. Raw wool, for example, was exported by merchants to the Scottish staple (i.e. officially recognised trading port) at Campveere in the Netherlands where it was worked up by local weavers before being re-exported back to Scotland by the same merchants. The fact that the wool had to be processed outside of Scotland was partly the result of a shortage of skilled labour, which the merchants saw no need to spend time and money overcoming while an acceptable alternative was available. The result was not simply that such skills were never developed – leading such manufacturers as did exist to employ more expensive English workers – but that the chance to link production to trade was lost, for the merchants had no control over the weavers to whom the work was subcontracted.

Where did the profits acquired in trade go? Seton wrote in 1700:

So soon as a Merchant has scraped together a piece of money ... instead of employing it for promoting Trade or by projecting any new thing that may be serviceable to his country ... nothing will satisfy him but laying it out upon a land Estate, for having the Honour to make his son a Laird, that is, an idle person.'[66]

In fact, Seton is less than accurate here. Unlike their contemporaries elsewhere in Europe, the Scottish merchants showed little inclination to buy their way into the landowning classes. Indeed, before 1660 their external investments had largely gone into loans to the existing lords. The losses they suffered as a result of the financial collapse of the nobility during the Civil Wars and English occupation persuaded them to find a safer alternative for their money: manufacturing.[67] As many as 78 enterprises may have been founded between 1660 and 1707, producing such commodities as glass, sugar, paper, soap and wool.[68] Of those established between 1660 and 1710, 52 were situated in the towns. It was once believed that the same proprietors who sank the coal and lead mines on their land mainly established these manufactories. More recent research has shown that merchants were the sole source of capital in 35 cases out of the 49 whose investment history can be traced, and were responsible for contributing capital along with landowners and professional groups in other cases. It is possible to interpret this as the origins of the much greater wave of industrial investment that can be traced in the second half of the eighteenth century. Yet against this three qualifications must be made. First, this influx of merchant capital came exclusively from Edinburgh (19 establishments) or Glasgow (16 establishments). It was not generalised across the country. Second, the very fact that these investments were made in order to secure a safe return does not suggest an excess of thrusting entrepreneurial zeal. Third, without exception, these enterprises had failed by the first decade after the Union of 1707. There is, in other words, a discontinuity between these initial forays into industrial investment and their later reappearance as a normal feature of merchant activity.[69]

Why did the merchant capitalist class not move into production in any consistent way? The internal market was too small to sustain a manufacturing sector for goods beyond those staple products required for everyday consumption, and the luxury market for the rich could not compensate. Their focus therefore came to be on export markets, particularly in northern Europe where raw materials and semi-processed goods had traditionally been sold. In the period after 1660 the state encouraged the establishment of manufactories, but also attempted to protect them from foreign competition until they were capable of entering the world market on a competitive basis. Such protectionism inevitably brought retaliation in the form of increased duties or outright prohibitions on certain goods. Since their main impulse was to treat manufacturing as an insurance policy rather than an expansionist strategy, the inability of the resulting products to capture markets meant it became a decreasingly attractive option. On an individual basis this was perfectly rational. Gordon Marshall has argued at great length that the 'spirit of capitalism', identified by Max Weber as being generated by Calvinism, was present in seventeenth century Scotland. Whatever one thinks of this judgement, Marshall is surely correct to add that the mere existence of such attitudes was not enough to induce capitalist development in material circumstances that were otherwise unconducive:

> The spirit of modern capitalism may well be consistent with the *non*-appearance of the modern capitalist form of enterprise. The capitalist, when the conditions of action (economic, social, political, legal, and other circumstances) are inappropriate, does not invest in the modern capitalist form of enterprise. If capitalists maximise returns by investing in less developed forms of enterprise they are nevertheless acting in accordance with the dictates of modern capitalist rationality – despite the fact that the more 'developed' capitalist form of enterprise has not yet appeared.[70]

Why Marshall considers this to be a specifically 'capitalist' form of rationality is not clear, but he nevertheless accurately describes the logic underpinning the mercantile withdrawal from production.

The clearest contrast with Scottish merchant activity can be found in England. Here too were guilds under conditions of state-protected monopoly, exporting semi-processed woollen goods (albeit of much higher quality) to the same north European markets, but also trading in luxury food and textile commodities from the Levant and the East Indies. As Robert Brenner has shown, however, the most significant development in the English merchant community, particularly in the City of London, was the appearance of the 'new', 'interloping' merchants, often of plebeian origin ('shopkeepers, small producers and ship captains') who were excluded from the existing monopolies and who therefore specialised in colonial products like sugar and tobacco. These had not been incorporated into the restricted trade circuits protected by the Stuart state precisely because the crops required long term investment which the 'old' merchants were unwilling to make, and because many of them originated in territories which were already controlled by Spain. The new merchants, by contrast, were prepared to co-operate with the planters in determining the quantity and nature of their output, in some cases even to take over ownership themselves and to sell directly to their customers without recourse to middlemen.[71] The fact that this stratum did not rely on the Crown for their privileges led them to regard the policies and, ultimately, the existence of the Stuart state as an impediment to their further expansion – a fact which saw them take the lead in the parliamentary opposition to Charles I. The difference between Scotland and England is, however, best illustrated by comparing how the two most important merchants in their respective nations – Sir William Dick and Maurice Thompson – acquired their wealth and what they did with it.

Sir William Dick (?1580–1655), was the richest Scotsman of the period. His father was a landowner in Orkney and a merchant trader with Denmark – a classic example of the combination of feudal lordship and traditional mercantile interests. Dick inherited these, but also increased his wealth through tax farming (customs and excise) and negotiating bills of exchange. He was elected Lord Provost of Edinburgh during the Covenanting agitation of 1638 by which time his fortune stood at £200,000. Dick lent 100,000 merks to Charles I to enable him to visit Scotland in 1641 and was duly knighted the following year before the Civil War broke out in England. Once the Covenanters entered the war on the Parliamentary side, however, Dick used his resources to supply their army, but this proved a drain even to him. By 1644 he was petitioning the Scottish Estates for repayment of 840,000 merks he was owed; in return he was paid £40,000 and given control over the Customs and Excise in Orkney and the tobacco industry throughout Scotland.[72]

Now contrast this trajectory with that of his English equivalent. 'Maurice Thompson,' writes Brenner, 'was certainly the greatest colonial merchant of his day.'[73] Born in 1600 to a family of little property, he had emigrated to Virginia by 1617. By 1623 he had accumulated sufficient wealth as a ship's captain involved in provisioning and transporting passengers to the colony, that he was able to buy an estate himself. By 1626 he had returned to London (while retaining links with a partner in Virginia) where he attempted to break into the tobacco export trade in the Caribbean – so successfully that by 1634 he was responsible for shipping out 25 per cent of tobacco exports from Virginia. His second intended area of expansion was to be in the Guinean slave trade, but this was blocked by the holders of the royal monopoly, the Guinea Company. It was only after the Company had its privileges withdrawn by the Long Parliament that the way was open for Thompson and other 'new merchants' to intervene. He was at the forefront of dismantling the semi-absolutist government of the West Indies and establishing in its place a system where colonial settlers held their land in freehold tenancies and were able to elect their own government. He was similarly involved in overthrowing the royalist government of Maryland, which threatened the expansionist commercial policies that Thompson and the other 'new merchants' favoured, and active as a privateer intercepting ships sailing from the Netherlands to royalist ports. Finally, he was among those who successfully petitioned Parliament in April 1645 for permission to trade with the West Indies, thus breaking the monopoly enjoyed by the East India Company, as a prelude to forcing themselves into its leadership.[74]

The differences between the two men are stark. Dick was born into traditional forms of mercantile wealth; Thompson had to acquire his own through intervening in new patterns of trade. Dick was awarded many of his sources of income by the existing state; Thompson had to obtain his through a struggle against that state and its current beneficiaries. The Civil Wars, for Dick, were merely a drain on resources, to be made good by further subventions from the state in competition with other claimants. The Civil Wars, for Thompson, were an opportunity to refashion the state for the purposes of the interloping merchant fraction to which he belonged. The differences between them extend to their ultimate destiny. The last years of Dick give some indication of how low many of the merchant section of the ruling class had fallen by the end of the Civil Wars. Dick adopted the position taken by the majority of his class, so that after the Scottish Estates moved to support Charles II in 1649, he joined the committee for organising resistance to Cromwell and still had the financial wherewithal to lend his new king £20,000. Classified as a 'malignant' by the Protectorate regime, he was fined £64,934 that, on top of the £160,854 owed to him by successive Covenanting regimes, ended his career and his fortune. Despite various petitions he was only ever repaid £1,000 of his many debts and, when he died at his lodgings in Westminster on 19 December 1655, he left insufficient money to provide the funeral his status required.[75] Thompson, on the other hand, was at the time of Dick's downfall simultaneously a member of the commission of militants assigned to sequester the property of royalists like Sir William, a member of the High Court of Justice established to investigate and proceed against counter-revolutionaries and a member of the 16-man commission for regulating the navy and customs.[76] Rarely can the opposite political fates consequent on different economic orientations have been so starkly illustrated as by these two men.

Yet for a small minority of the Scottish merchant class, their experience is not so much qualitatively as quantitatively different from that of England. The Scottish equivalents of the 'new' merchants appeared not before but after the Civil Wars and occupied a much less strategically important position within their society. By the latter half of the seventeenth century, Perth had slipped from its position among the 'four great towns' to be replaced by Glasgow, even though, at the beginning of this phase of expansion, Glasgow bore no relation to the 'second city of Empire' it would one day become, resembling more a large village than a town, despite its population of nearly 14,000.[77] Why was it in this location that the majority of the Scottish new merchants were to be found? An answer is suggested by comparing it with the royal burgh that was most closely wedded to the established trading patterns and methods of guild recruitment: Aberdeen.

Some of the differences were circumstantial. Aberdeen was devastated on several occasions between 1637 and 1651 by different armies, notably by the Royalists in 1644. Glasgow was largely spared from involvement at this level and had less from which to recover after the latter date. Aberdeen was perfectly situated for participation in trade with northern Europe through the staple at Campveere and had orientated itself accordingly; Glasgow was situated in a position which made such an orientation difficult, but which did allow it to take advantage of the Atlantic trade with the American colonies and the West Indies. There were, however, also deeper social reasons for the disparity between the two cities. Aberdeen was an established royal burgh from the classic period of military feudalism and was governed by a constitution that reflected these origins. We have seen the difficulties which this posed for entrants to the merchant guild who were not of the male line of existing members. The Glaswegian constitution, on the other hand, had been drawn up as recently as 1605 and took account of the fact that the city was entering its period of expansion with a small number of trading merchants; it therefore allowed greater upward mobility in order to regularly renew the guild membership. Christopher Smout has calculated that, based on a sample taken from four periods between 1610–15 and 1700–05, only 30 per cent of new entrants were sons of existing merchants, 30 per cent had married the daughters of existing merchants, 15 per cent were the sons of craftsmen burgesses and 25 per cent married the daughters of craftsmen burgesses. This more fluid social structure was echoed in the change to the relative position of both cities in the burghal hierarchy: Glaswegian burghal taxation, based on the level of trading activity, increased fivefold by the end of the seventeenth century; that of Aberdeen had halved.[78] Much of this trade was with the areas of North America and the Caribbean that had made the fortunes of the English new merchants in the first half of the century. The precariousness of this trade may also have contributed to the openness of the Glaswegian merchant elite, since that class was subject to a far higher proportion of failures and consequently, bankruptcies, than were their less intrepid brethren on the east coast. They welcomed to their ranks, for example, the clan chief Daniel Mackinnon of Skye, whose grandchildren are represented on the front cover of this book (see 'A Note on the Cover Illustrations', above). The English merchants, and the state that they had helped to fashion, were not now willing to share the source of their wealth with a new set of interlopers, particularly when they belonged to a different nation. Despite the Navigation Laws and the risks involved in breaking them, however, at least 70 ships arrived from America between 1672 and 1707 bearing tobacco, sugar, rum, wood and spices.[79]

The ruling elites in the towns consisted not only of members of the merchant guilds, but also of their counterparts among the craftsmen. The conflict between the craft and merchant guilds carried on throughout the period of war, revolution, occupation and restoration; although the participants attempted to use the shifts in power to their own advantage. The craftsmen were almost always the losers. But however ferocious their disputes became, particularly in the sixteenth century, they were ultimately inter-class disputes between different factions of the ruling elite, often about the extent of their representation on the town council. Take Elgin, for example, a small but prosperous town which, by 1660, had a population of upwards of 2,500. Over half the workforce whose details are preserved in the town records between 1540 and 1660 were craftsmen; they were under-represented both on the burgh council and in the civic office, usually in inverse proportion to the presence of the merchants. They seem to have enjoyed a brief period of self-government in the mid-sixteenth century before being declared illegal by 1570. A further, even briefer, attempt at incorporation during the 1650s was ended after a craft revolt in April 1660 (itself a response to threats to their status) after which they were suppressed, losing the right to regulate entry to the trade and assess quality of work.[80]

It is as common to treat the craft guilds as proto-trade unions as it is to treat the merchants as proto-industrialists, and even more mistaken.[81] There are two excellent reasons for refusing to treat the former as some early manifestation of the working class presence. First, the dividing line between merchant and craftsman was never absolute, with some occupations being classified differently from burgh to burgh: 'A maltman, for instance, was a craftsman in Dundee and Perth but a merchant in Edinburgh and Glasgow.'[82] In at least one burgh (Elgin), three members of the skinners craft guild appear to have also been admitted to the merchant guild on its foundation in 1640, but they seem to have renounced their craft membership in order to be elected to the burgh council in 1643. An agreement establishing the precise demarcation between crafts and merchants on the one hand, and between the individual crafts on the other, was only reached in February 1658.[83] Second, the craft guilds were perhaps even more insistent than the merchants that their exclusiveness be preserved, an attitude that was determined by the greater precariousness of their economic position. It is simply a category mistake to confuse restrictions on entry imposed by small employers with the type of controls later forced on employers by trade unions. In Scotland, as everywhere else, the emergence of a working class depended at least in part on the destruction of the restrictions that they imposed and the consequent 'freeing' of labour.

Indwellers

Who were the unfree two-thirds of the population who stood below the guildsmen in the urban hierarchy? Some were wage labourers. In the majority of enterprises the workforce would never have achieved three figures, a master craftsman typically working with a handful of journeymen. At the other extreme were the textile manufactories where numbers could be as high as 1,500, but this was exceptional. We do not know how many wage labourers there were, since the lists of pollable persons compiled at this time do not, alas, use Marxist categories, but the classifications 'manufacturers' and 'labourers', in which they cannot be distinguished. Many of them were almost as distant from the urban centres as the colliers and panners, since the majority of manufactories were situated in the suburbs or rural hinterlands of the burghs. Indeed, as Michael Lynch has suggested: 'The century after 1650 saw the consolidation of a rural proletariat rather than the creation of an urban one.'[84] We also know that where the manufactories were founded by the same landowners that established the coal and lead mines, and salt refineries, the same methods of obtaining a workforce were enforced. 'In yet another attempt to deal with the problem of reluctant labour,' writes Hamish Fraser, 'the Earl of Eglinton in 1662 was given the monopoly of any vagrants in Galloway, Ayr and Renfrew to work in his new, and short-lived, woollen factory in Ayr.' This privilege was subsequently extended to all manufacturers the following year.[85] Despite this use of feudal enactments, particularly in the early stages of the manufactory movement, the workforce were nearer to being full-blown wage labourers than their counterparts down the mines. Yet some care must be exercised when classifying them 'proletarians'. As Jairus Banaji writes: 'The slaves and hired labourers who intervened in [the feudal] economy were as much part of specifically *feudal relations of production* as the serf population itself.'[86] And this applied, not only to the miners and panners, but to the vast majority of wage labourers who were both unaffected by any sort of juridical serfdom and involved in manufacturing essential commodities for stable local markets, as they had been for centuries. Workers in the manufactories were a slightly different case, but the process by which they might have become part of an emergent proletariat was short-circuited by the fact that the vast majority of the enterprises in which they worked followed that of the Earl of Eglinton into failure, with few surviving into the first decade after the Union of 1707. When the proletariat did emerge it was not from this source. Greater numbers were involved in what would now be called the 'service' sector. Male domestic servants comprised 24.1 per cent of the pollable population of Edinburgh in the 1690s, and also featured strongly in the lesser burghs of Saint Andrews, Selkirk, Turrif, Huntly and Eyemouth.[87] Others had classic petty-bourgeois occupations as shop or tavern keepers. Others still were small traders like peddlers, ale-sellers or stablers who were neither burgesses nor guildsmen and whose activities were often on the fringes of legality. Yet the very fact that they traded for a living placed them in the category of 'merchant' alongside the great merchants who traded in the Baltic ports or the Caribbean.

The urban crowd could be volatile – Edinburgh was particularly notorious in this respect – but can rarely be seen engaged in activities that were exclusively in the interests of the indwellers. As Rab Houston writes, 'until the late eighteenth century, riot did not apparently present a threat to the social fabric. Protest was usually structured and orderly: at least partly an attempt to remind the authorities of their responsibilities.'[88] The riots in Perth which initiated the Reformation in 1559 and in Edinburgh which opened the Covenanting rebellion in 1637 were, at least partially, exercises in channelling popular discontent behind factions of the ruling class. The riots which accompanied the Revolution of 1688 were by no means solely the work of the plebeian masses, but were led and partly executed by the burgesses themselves. This is less surprising than it first appears. The very immaturity of urban social classes meant that the divisions between them were often less significant than the formal division into free and unfree would suggest. A craftsman of the cordiner or cooper guild would work alongside his apprentices and hired labourers in a small workshop and, leaving aside the pressures which he could bring to bear on them, would share many of their views and experiences. Certainly the perceived differences would have been far less than those between the laird and the cottar or the coalmaster and the collier.

Officers, Lawyers and Ministers

The structural capacity of the exploited and oppressed classes to challenge the existing order was therefore severely limited in both the countryside and the towns. Some sections of the population were increasingly antagonistic to the existing social order but they were not, in the majority of cases, directly involved in the productive process. Let Edinburgh serve as an example. By the late seventeenth century the capital was the largest Scottish town, with a population of 40,000, perhaps 47,000 at the absolute outside. Only 349 of these inhabitants belonged to the 'middling sort', and of them, only 47 or 13 per cent were manufacturers; 209 or 60 per cent belonged to the professions.[89] It was among the latter that alternative views of society – albeit partial and fragmented – tended to emerge most strongly, although for different reasons in each case. These groups did not yet constitute the 'social penumbra' of the bourgeoisie discussed in the Introduction, if only because the capitalist class did not yet have sufficient social weight to act as a nucleus around which an outer layer of dependent groups could form. Non-capitalist professional groups could only assimilate to the bourgeoisie, let alone act as its political vanguard, if capitalist production and the social attendant classes already existed. They could not express the interests or demands of a capitalist class which was either absent or subordinate, as it was in Scotland throughout most of the seventeenth century. They could, for reasons of their own, weaken the structure of feudal society from within, leaving it more vulnerable to attack from bourgeois class interests when they did finally emerge. Three groups in particular had grievances against feudal society, but as yet had no class alternative to which they could identify. These were, in ascending order of importance, the Scottish officer caste of the British army, the legal profession and the ministers of the Church of Scotland.

Officers

Just as the British Empire came into existence with the colony of Ulster, over 100 years before the British nation-state, so too did a British army, at least in embryo.[90] The Scottish army consisted of around 2,000 men at the beginning of the Restoration in 1660, and had only risen to around 3,000 by the Revolution of 1688. Following the Cromwellian experience, no standing armies were to be tolerated by either the English or Scottish Parliaments. The function of internal repression therefore fell in Scotland to a militia of 20,000 foot and 2,000 horse which was approved by the Parliament in 1663, to be raised as and when it proved necessary, first of all in repressing the Pentland Rising of 1666. A military career was therefore more easily sought outside Scotland, either as a mercenary on the European mainland or as part of the larger English and Irish establishments. Many among the nobility, particularly the younger sons, had to follow the profession of arms, either in the absence of other viable alternatives, or because it provided the type of honour and stimulation which the alternatives did not: 'Military service at home or abroad was ... one means by which an over-bloated and financially precarious nobility might avoid slipping into a kind of petty, debased nobility.'[91]

But it was not only the otherwise superfluous sons of the Scottish nobility who were led to enter military service outside Scotland. All sections of the ruling class had traditionally used the armed forces as a depository for male children which their estates or enterprises were unable to absorb. Their search for a role was complimented by the strategy of a British monarchy which increasingly desired the integration of the different national officer corps. As opposition to his rule took shape during the 1670s, particularly in relation to the succession, Charles II began to regard officers from throughout the British Isles as interchangeable components of a supra-national army which would do his bidding: 'All three kingdoms, together with overseas outposts, were increasingly organised as a singe military unit through and between which men freely moved.'[92] This project never reached fruition under Charles or James VII and II – it had to wait until the reign of their nemesis, William III – but it is nevertheless here that a British army can be seen in the process of formation.

For at least some of the Scottish officers in this proto-British army their new military careers offered a tangible alternative in miniature to the society over which their fathers ruled. The British army involved a command structure different from that of either the military feudalism which still prevailed in parts of Scotland or the newly professionalised apparatuses which were emerging from the 'military revolution' on the continent. The former relied on the ability of feudal superiors to raise their tenants to fight; the latter on the aristocracy to command armies of foreign mercenaries and conscripts. The British army was a product of the same changes in military tactics and technology adopted by the absolutist states, but it differed from them in that command was increasingly less the prerogative of social rank as such, and more the prerogative of money acquired either from the profits of agrarian and merchant capital, or from political influence bestowed for supporting one of the competing factions at Westminster. For young men from the ruling class whose origins lay beneath the nobility these were new routes to promotion and position that did not depend on the possession of a title. In that sense the British army embodied the difference which now existed between English society and the rest of Europe, including Scotland – one might almost say, especially Scotland. And, although it would be wrong to make too much of this, it also offered more limited possibilities for talented plebeians to progress up the ranks. Levels of advancement that would have been denied these officers in Scotland, if only because of the absence of comparable opportunities, came to be associated with what we might call proto-Britishness, a new form of national consciousness which had, as yet, no other institutional embodiment outside of the colony in Ulster – a place where the nobility were conspicuous by their absence. The significance of this shift in – or perhaps it would be more accurate to say, this extension of – existing loyalties would not be fully apparent for another two decades, when the Treaty of Union was in the process of being ratified in the Scottish Parliament.

Lawyers

One of the professions to which the younger sons of the nobility were increasingly denied access, forcing them to turn to military careers, was the law. Lawyers originally emerged from the clerical Estate. Before the Reformation professional lawyers were almost unknown outside of church courts, where they appeared on behalf of litigants, but every churchman was educated in civil law as part of his education and during the reigns of James I and, in particular, James IV, attempts were made to make up the deficiency of lawyers trained in civil law by extending such training to the clergy. It was only after the Reformation, when the kirk effectively prevented ministers from accepting civil appointments, that a genuine class of non-clerical lawyers began to emerge.[93]

The legal profession grew dramatically during the seventeenth century – particularly in Edinburgh, which was home to both the Court of Session and the professional bodies, the Faculty of Advocates and the Society of Writers to the Signet: 'By the 1690s the professions in the capital rivalled the merchants in numbers – there were some 600 and 580 respectively – but the wealth of the 320 lawyers was greater than that of the merchants and craftsmen combined.'[94] Such growth had two main causes. On the one hand, both the Commonwealth and Restoration regimes had in their different ways imposed a degree of order in the countryside, and the consequent decline of inter-magnate feuding led landed proprietors to seek redress in their territorial disputes at law rather than at the head of their feudal host. On the other hand was the increased use of the legal process of sequestration as the predilection of landowners for conspicuous consumption, together with their unwillingness to increase their incomes through commercialisation of their property, led inevitably to a greater number of bankruptcies. It was not unknown for the two causes to be combined. Archibald Campbell, ninth Earl of Argyll, had expanded his empire in the western Highlands in part by bringing bankruptcy proceedings against vassals whose lands he wished to let out at more 'economic' rents.

The social class whose activities provided much of the increased demand for legal services also began to enter the profession themselves. Before 1670 the Faculty of Advocates had been a corporation dominated by the sons of the lesser lords. This had changed by the end of the century: 'Between 1690 and 1730 sons of peers and baronets constituted between 27 and 35 per cent. of all intrants and between 1691 and 1702, 21 per cent. had fathers who were Members of Parliament.'[95] As disputes began to be conducted in the courtroom rather than on the field of battle, the progeny of the greater nobility were sent to colonise juridical institutions, secure in the knowledge that the social position of their fathers would contribute as much towards victory as their knowledge of the law. Yet despite their wealth the social position of the lawyers was still ambiguous. A man practising as a surgeon, an occupation long recognised as a feudal craft, was eligible to become a burgess and, in the majority of cases, would be accepted as such. A man practising as an advocate, an occupation of more recent provenance, was not. The advocate might be – indeed was almost certain to be – wealthier and might enjoy higher status within burghal society, but was excluded from standing for political office in the burgh, not only by surgeons – who were at least of comparable social status – but by such plebeian types as skinners and bonnet-makers. Lawyers therefore had excellent political reasons for wishing to overthrow feudal obstacles to their advancement in burghal government, but status group closure was not their only reason for complaint. The universalisation of legal norms was blocked by a barrier that ran across almost every part of Scottish society: the existence of the heritable jurisdictions. The functions of the courts of barony and regality overlapped and competed with those of the sheriff courts, and had far greater significance than the jurisdiction of the Justices of the Peace.[96] Not only were the lords still entitled to apply 'law' within their own domains, they were themselves in some respects outwith its reach. As late as the 1740s the Earl of Cromarty was avoiding bankruptcy by the simple fact that no one could sue him in his own baron court.[97] The expansion of their profession across all areas of civil society was therefore dependent on removing alternative sources of legal authority.

Ministers

Ministers of the Church of Scotland also held a contradictory position within Scottish society. Like lawyers, ministers were exempt from burghal taxation and excluded from burghal office. Like lawyers, ministers had become a self-perpetuating caste by the end of the seventeenth century. To a far greater extent than the legal profession, however, their fate was intertwined with the political events between 1637 and 1688. Indeed, some historians have insisted that the clergy provided the leadership of the Scottish bourgeoisie during this period. S. R. Gardiner wrote in his classic account of the English Civil War, first published in 1894: 'In Scotland it was by the Presbyterian clergy that the middle classes were organised and the organisation thus given enabled them to throw off the yoke of the feudal nobles and ultimately assert their own dominance.'[98] The same theme recurs, nearly a century later, in the chapter by Willie Thompson in *Scottish Capitalism*, only here it is claimed that, although the bourgeoisie themselves did not achieve state power, they did achieve in the kirk 'an institutional expression of their interests and demands, whose structures, theology and discipline expressed a regime of frugality, toil, sobriety and conspicuous non-consumption'. As a consequence: 'The consolidation of this implicitly anti-feudal and bourgeois institution as a state Church decisively marked off the Scottish class from its English counterparts, enhancing their separate identity and consciousness.'[99] These claims are deeply implausible. In order for a social group not directly related to production to embody bourgeois values one must first have a bourgeoisie with a degree of social weight, which Scotland signally lacked. Sections of the Scottish clergy became increasingly opposed to the organisation of their society as the seventeenth century progressed and, of all the professional groups discussed here, their opposition had the greatest impact, but it was not one directly informed by a desire to see the extension of capitalist relations of production.

During the first quarter of the seventeenth century the clergy may have experienced the biggest improvement in conditions of any of the professional groups. By the accession of Charles I in 1625 the annual stipend of a minister was at least £30 sterling, while some English vicars subsisted on £5. Twenty years later, in the midst of a civil war, some ministers in Edinburgh were earning as much as £100 a year:

> The result of this new-found prosperity, which gives a novel twist to the Weber thesis, was that the average rural minister, earning something like ten times the average income of his congregation, had money to spare in a society usually short of cash; so he lent it, at interest, to his flock.[100]

Yet the point here, as Rosalind Mitchison remarks, is that: 'In a world where there was no large bourgeois class the clergy's income marked them out from others.'[101] In addition to having some of the qualities of a 'hereditary caste', through intermarriage between clerical families, their professional solidarity was consolidated by the self-enclosed world of the seminaries and the experience of the presbyteries. Yet prior to 1637 the ministers were not necessarily the most radical elements within the kirk. How could they be when their appointment was typically dependent on the Crown, the prelacy or the nobility? In the last 15 years of James VI's reign only 21 ministers were actually punished by the Court of the High Commission. The session, on the other hand, was more likely to reflect the views of the congregations, or at least the 'middling sort' among them. But the session members were excluded from participation in the higher courts of the kirk; it would only be if these were opened to them that these opinions would be able influence national life.[102]

Radicalisation only came with a change in the social composition of the clergy. If the class basis of the legal profession rose during the latter half of the seventeenth century, then that of the clergy fell in equal measure. Walter Makey has estimated that over 90 per cent of the elders (lay officials elected by the parish congregation) present at the General Assemblies of 1638 and 1639 were either lords of varying status or Members of Parliament.[103] One result of the wars and political revolutions between 1637 and 1651 was that these social layers were replaced by those from lower down the social scale among 'the middling sort'. In most cases elders were neither subtenants nor landowners, but tenants or feuars. Similarly with the clergy. 'Only a few of the ministers of the middle seventeenth century were drawn from the feudal classes,' writes Makey, who goes on to summarise the class origins of 'a typical minister of the 1640s': 'He was born at about the turn of the century, the son of another minister, the proprietor of a small estate, a tenant farmer or a lesser burgess.'[104] What was the significance of this shift in class composition?

The attitudes of the new ministers tended to be hostile to the landowning classes and consequently, as Makey argues, they were unlikely to preach acceptance of the existing order to their congregations: 'It might as easily, and as convincingly, be argued that they represented those – the feuar and, in a different way, the younger son – who had most reason to resent [the values of feudal Scotland].'[105] Ministers were highly educated men, not only compared to their parishioners – many of whom were illiterate – but to the landowners who had the power of patronage over clerical appointments. The necessity to make oneself acceptable to intellectual inferiors, to whom one might already feel a strong class antipathy, bred resentment among the parish clergy – particularly among those most committed to pastoral care, who did not see their role as announcing rent increases from the pulpit on behalf of the local laird. But even after the question of patronage was temporarily resolved during the Glorious Revolution, three areas of tension remained between the clergy and the society in which they carried out their ministry.

First, without in any way minimising the repressiveness and intolerance of which the kirk was only too capable, it was the only institution in civil society which allowed democratic participation by those outside the ruling class; it mattered who was elected as an elder to the kirk session. Although a numerical minority of the elders, the major landowning members of the session undoubtedly exercised a greater influence over the proceedings than the lesser lairds and burgesses who formed the majority; but this did not mean that they were totally dominant. In the class antagonisms which lay beneath the surface of the kirk session, the ministers tended to align themselves with the majority, the backgrounds of whose members more closely resembled their own.

Second, both the kirk session and the baron court were concerned, in different ways, with exercising social control. They complemented each other in some respects, but in others functioned as alternatives. The kirk session had no economic role and, crucially, involved degrees of participation and consent which were alien to the exercise of the heritable jurisdictions. The degree of territorial overlap between the two forms of jurisdiction can be seen from the example of Stirlingshire. The shire covered an area of 50 miles from north to south and 25 miles from east to west. The population (according to the first census of 1755) numbered 37,014. Yet this relatively small and sparsely populated shire held, on the one hand, two regalian courts and nine baron courts and, on the other, five presbyteries and 24 kirk sessions. And the jurisdiction of the presbyteries extended beyond the boundaries of the shire into those of other heritable jurisdictions.[106]

Third, in a situation analogous to that of the lawyers prevented from practising in areas where the heritable jurisdictions held sway, the ministers were excluded from preaching across whole areas of the Highlands by the physical remoteness and the inability of the Scottish state to exert full control over the region. The attitude of most Lowland ministers to the unconquered terrain in the north and west was no doubt formed by as mixed a set of motives as the attitude of most lawyers to the heritable jurisdictions. On the one hand they desired to see the word of God spread to those whom they regarded (quite wrongly, in most cases) as benighted papists or semi-heathens. On the other, in a situation where an oversupply of ministerial graduates meant close competition for every post, this vast territory offered unparalleled opportunities for clerical appointments. Yet the ambitions of the kirk in the Highlands embody more than a mere frustrated sectional interest, but an issue of more general concern which is the subject of the next chapter: the mutual hostility between the inhabitants of the two main regions of Scotland which has passed into history under the name of the Highland–Lowland divide.

Highland and Lowland

Even in England, the early modern state which contained the most advanced areas of capitalist development, the economic and cultural divisions between the north and the south of the country prevailed at least until the mid-seventeenth century.[107] By 1688, however, the spread of capitalist relations of production extended so far that none of the regional distinctions within England were strong enough to prevent the formation of a unified national consciousness across the territory of the state. The situation in Scotland was different. It contained – or at least appeared to contain – not merely regional differences within a single society, but two different societies, situated on either side of the Highland line. From this perspective, the question of whether Lowland society was predominantly feudal or capitalist is of less importance than the claim that the clan system of the Highlands was different from either and opposed to both. How accurate is this claim? Were the Highlands and the Lowlands component parts of the same socio-economic system, or did they represent antagonistic modes of production which happened to coexist within the same territorial framework?

By the late seventeenth century it was widely believed that two different societies lay within the boundaries of the Scottish kingdom. Duncan Forbes of Culloden, for example, noted in a memorandum written during the early 1690s that: 'The strength of the kingdom of Scotland did stand anciently in the power of superiors over their Vassals, and of Chiefs over their Clans.'[108] Most modern commentators accept this distinction between feudal and clannic modes of production. Audrey Cunningham, for example, held that clan society in the Highlands and feudal society in the Lowlands were based on incompatible forms of land tenure. The former on a 'natural' right to land established by (clan) chiefs through conquest, the latter on an 'artificial' system whereby (feudal) lords were granted parcels of land in return for service to the king.[109]

Marxist historians have also maintained the distinction. Eric Hobsbawm, for example, refers to the 'feudal Lowlands and the tribal Highlands'.[110] In a more nuanced version of this position, Christopher Smout encapsulated the difference as being that 'Highland society was based on kinship modified by feudalism, Lowland society on feudalism tempered by kinship'.[111] This at least acknowledges that the two regions were not completely alien to each other. However, since Smout identifies feudalism with what I have more specifically referred to as military feudalism, his comments do not amount to much more than saying that vassalage was less widespread in the Highlands than the Lowlands. For our purposes, the central question is the same as that which we have asked for Scotland as a whole. Which mode of production prevailed north of the Highland line?

The key issue here is the nature of clan society. During the seventeenth century Scotland was widely considered to be one of the few remaining areas in Europe where groups descended from a common ancestor, distinguished by a common name, and united within a common territory under the patriarchal authority of the chief could still be found. The English republican James Harrington, for example, wrote in 1659 that: 'The patriarchs in Israel ... were such as, till of late years in Scotland, were they that could lead the whole name or kindred, and be followed by them.'[112] Once established, each clan sought historical legitimisation through the construction of elaborate pedigrees and lineages dating back to the first syllable of recorded time. The literary productions of the bards and poets are, however, no more accurate a guide to the history of clan society than those of contemporary nationalists necessarily are to the histories of their nations. It is only if we accept the ideology of the clans themselves, and the mirror image thrown back at them from the Lowlands, that they appear to have existed from time immemorial. Clans are also said to have enjoyed relative social equality, despite the scarcity that characterised their material conditions. Three supposedly distinct aspects of clan life in particular are cited to support the view that they represented a permanent bonding of 'kin' whose loyalties and activities lay outwith the structure of feudal society.

The first was the practice of collective agriculture. The form of tenure known as runrig is often thought to have involved communal farming, with the strips of land being reallocated by lot on an annual, or at least regular basis, so that the best land was never permanently in the possession of any one tenant family. In fact, runrig was practised in parts of Scotland other than the Highlands and involved a type of shareholding tenancy. Tenancy granted on these terms gave each shareholder a separate title to a specific quantity of land, but not to a specific location, which might vary at different times in the history of the lease. The allocation of the actual land would happen either at the start of a lease or upon its renewal, which – given the short-term nature of most leases

– would often be on an annual basis, but this would be a condition of the individual lease, not a collective decision by the tenants.[113] In short, far from representing what Max Weber called a 'diluted village communism', it is hard to see runrig as anything other than a form of private property in land.[114]

The second supposedly distinctive aspect of clan life was less the material situation of the Highland peasants than the beliefs they held about their place in society. The peasants who took the name of Fraser, or MacDonald, or Campbell were aware that this was a symbolic act. As Robert Dodgson has written: 'For those who adopted a clan name, this was not an act of self-deception but acceptance of the socio-political order that sprang from clanship and the need to have a place in that order.'[115] In another respect, however, they did practise self-deception, or perhaps were genuinely mistaken. Lowland peasants knew how dependent their continued occupancy of the land was on the will of the lord; but Highland clan members believed that they had rights as kinsmen of the chief – artificial or not – to heritable possession of the land. The chiefs were prepared to encourage this belief as long as they needed the presence of fighting men on their territory, but, as was to become all too apparent after 1746, a right which subsists on the sufferance of the powerful is no right at all.

The third and final distinctive aspect of clan society was the fact that clan territories tended to cut across those of the heritable jurisdictions. If peasants had all been tenants of the chief whose name they adopted, then clanship would appear little more than an elaboration of existing feudal relationships; but their conditions of life drove many to seek the protection of the nearest lord capable of delivering it, even though he was not their own feudal superior, and indeed, might even be in dispute with their feudal superior, as the Camerons of Locheil and MacLeans of Duart were with the House of Argyll. At one level, therefore, clanship appears to be both different from, and perhaps opposed to feudalism. At a deeper level, however, the differences and oppositions assume a lesser significance. A feudal superior might indeed act as chief to a clan whose members only partially corresponded to his own tenants, but if some clan members were not his tenants they would certainly be those of some other lord. None of the peasantry were free from the necessity of handing over the product of their labour to one lord or another, and it was this labour which provided the wealth enjoyed by the Highland nobles, whether they were considered lords, or chiefs, or both. Indeed, those who entered a clan led by a man who was not their feudal superior might also have to pay a tribute to him in addition to paying feudal rent to their lord. If a member of the Highland elite ceased to be a clan chief, he would still be a feudal lord in his own right. As Walter Scott wrote of the Border clans, where 'the patriarchal power of the chieftains was broken, those who were landed proprietors retained their feudal power over the vassals and their tenants'.[116] Clan organisation was therefore not only compatible with but also dependent upon the feudal exploitation of the peasantry. The point has been put best, ironically enough, by a member of the family who were in turn the greatest clan chiefs, feudal superiors and capitalist landlords in Scottish history:

> The ruinous customs and usages which we have seen established among the Celts were feudal in their root, in their origin and in their essence. But they represented Feudalism in its most barbarous form – unrestrained by any sense of justice or of law. Cognate ideas – analogous rights and duties – were embodied in the Anglo-Norman Feudal System; but they were moulded and governed by more civilised conceptions of an orderly and settled jurisprudence.

This argument, from the pen of George Campbell, eighth Duke of Argyll, is scarcely disinterested, since the Campbells were usually and rightly credited with being the individual family most responsible for destroying Highland society, and therefore had an interest in presenting it in the worst possible light. Yet it is hard to disagree with his final verdict: 'The dream of any simple patriarchal system in the Highlands within living memory, bound together in peaceful village Communities like those of the mild Hindu, is a dream indeed.'[117]

The clan system must therefore be understood as part of the political superstructure of Scottish feudalism. It corresponded to no other mode of production. If anything, the clans, far from being opposed to feudalism, were representative of its most extreme form. There is a certain irony in the fact that, contrary to the myths of Highland exceptionalism, by 1688 the majority of the clans had organised themselves on the classic military feudal system of vassalage supposedly so alien to their nature.[118] Indeed, along with Poland, Scotland was the last area in Europe where such organisation still flourished at the end of the seventeenth century.[119] The differences between Highland and Lowland society were therefore matters of degree rather than of kind. In most respects the class structure in the Highlands was simpler than, but otherwise comparable to that of the rural Lowlands. As one traveller, James Walker, noted in 1750, shortly before the old order was completely swept away:

> The possessors of land over the Highlands in general, are of three different kinds; tacksmen, tenants and sub-tenants. The tacksmen hold their land of the proprietor, by lease; the tenants hold their farms, without any lease, at the will of the landlord; the sub-tenants have small possessions of land, let out to them from year to year, by the tacksmen and tenants.[120]

The tacksmen were as unique to the Highlands as the bonnet lairds were to the Lowlands. They acted as middlemen between the chiefs and their tenants, not only collecting rents, from which they drew their own income, but also raising the tenantry to fight. They acted, in other words, as a local bureaucracy, if that expression does not carry too many inappropriate connotations of modernity. The tacksmen only appeared during the seventeenth century, but were to be of crucial importance in exercising the class power of the lords over the peasants. They tended to hold their land because of this military function, rather than because of their farming abilities, for in Highland society land was primarily a source of social power rather than of rental income. An English commentator whom I have already quoted wrote of this power, while it was being demonstrated during the '45, that 'he who can command his Clans, on Pain of Death, to take up Arms against the Sovereign and Legislature is simply himself a Sovereign to all Intents and Purposes, independent of that Sovereignty under which he is specifically protected'.[121] There was one respect, however, in which the tacksmen could even be seen to follow a parallel route to the bonnet lairds. During the Restoration period in particular, clan chiefs and those directly below them among the Highland elite were forced, because of restrictions on lending by the Lowland merchants, to borrow from their tacksmen to meet their debts and continue their consumption levels. These debts were secured on mortgages (wadsets) which conferred hereditary title to part of the estate on the lender. As elite indebtedness grew, they tended to sell off the mortgaged lands giving hereditary title to their creditors, although retaining the feudal superiority.[122] The tacksmen who become hereditary proprietors by this route differed from the bonnet lairds in one crucial respect: they do not seem to have resisted the continuing power of the feudal superior, a fact which is at least partly explicable by their adherence to clan ideology.

In Argyllshire, 42 per cent of land transfers between 1660 and 1688 were acquisitions by wadset and sale. But the territory of the House of Argyll was already the one area in the Highlands where some attempt was being made to commercialise estate management. It was here that the role of the tacksman was subject to the greatest modification. Unlike many of the other great families the House of Argyll consciously awarded wadsets to younger sons of the lesser lairds to undertake the role of tacksman in territories which had been colonised or acquired through forfeiture. They were forbidden to incur debts over a certain amount, usually £2,000. The tacks which they oversaw were consolidated and tacksmen expected to move from one supervisory role to another within the Argyll territories in order to retain their positions. The tenants themselves were given much shorter leases – 5–19 years – than those in force elsewhere in the Highlands, with the clear understanding that failure to abide by the terms of the lease would lead to eviction, regardless of whether or not they belonged to Clan Campbell.[123]

Failure to take account of the underlying similarity between the Highlands and the Lowlands has contributed to more than one form of mystification. A danger with the 'pre-feudal' view of clan society is that it can provoke an equally mistaken reaction. Bruce Lenman, for example, has described Donald Cameron of Locheil as 'a brisk and enterprising businessman very much involved in the most advanced and far-flung developments of his day', and it is true that Locheil was involved in several commercial ventures, notably growing wood on his estate for sale of both timber and such by-products as ash.[124] By emphasising these activities Lenman hopes to dispel the illusion that Locheil or similar Highland chiefs were 'uncommercialised Gaels' living a bucolic existence untainted by contemporary civilisation. This is a project with which I am in complete sympathy, but it is almost as misleading to go to the opposite extreme and present Locheil as an enterprising capitalist who simply liked to surround himself with an armed retinue of 700 men for the sake of appearances. Individual clan chiefs were as capable as other feudal lords were of introducing elements of capitalist production to their domains without this in the slightest altering the basis of their social power. What enabled Locheil to raise a military force to support Charles Stuart in 1745 or his father to mount a similar operation in support of James Stuart in 1689? It was not, I suspect, their role as small-scale timber merchants.

Apart from timber, the other major commodity Highlanders were involved in trading was cattle, mainly at the market towns on the Lowland side of the Highland–Lowland border. Given the arable economy of the Highlands the trade was essential in raising money with which to buy grain and meal.[125] Commerce, in a situation of general backwardness, does not necessarily indicate a move towards capitalism, but may simply be a prerequisite for the survival of communities which are not relatively self-sufficient in goods. In any case, the profits raised from the grain trade did not tend to be used by the elites for accumulation, but 'to pay off pressing creditors, redeem outstanding debts and justify rent increases ... as clansmen were acutely aware, such regular income was used principally to underwrite absenteeism and conspicuous expenditure'.[126]

If there was a Highland–Lowland divide, the reason for its existence was not that the two regions contained societies based on different modes of production. As Gordon Donaldson has argued, the geographical basis for the sociological divisions within early modern Scotland lay elsewhere:

The 'north and the 'south' which are contrasted are not to be identified with 'highlands' and 'lowlands'. Contrary to what is often assumed, the division between highlands and lowlands is not a division between north and south, but much more truly between east and west, to the extent that almost the entire east coat is lowland and almost the entire west coast is highland. The 'highland line' which divides the two should be thought of as a line which meanders roughly from west to east or even from south-west to north-east. The highlands proper barely come into the subject under discussion, for they played hardly any part in the main stream of Scottish affairs in the sixteenth century and intervened only occasionally in the seventeenth. It can, however, be said that to some extent the pattern of a conservative north and a radical south existed within the highlands as well as within the lowlands, because the southerly part of the highlands, namely Argyll, tended to follow the pattern of the southern lowlands: Argyll was the most protestant, the most presbyterian, the most Hanoverian, part of the highlands. It would seem, therefore that racial and linguistic differences cut across, rather than coincided with, the division of opinion on political and ecclesiastical matters, or, at least, that if racial distinctions explain the pattern of opinion they must be racial distinctions other than those between Celt and Saxon.[127]

Donaldson is right to identify a dividing line within Scotland between the 'radical' south and the 'conservative' north, a division which was based in turn on the extent to which capitalist relations of production had become rooted in these regions.[128] This does not mean that southern Scotland had experienced significant capitalist development, only more capitalist development than the north. To suggest otherwise would merely be to replace the existing 'clan Highland versus feudal Lowland' division with an equally erroneous 'feudal north versus capitalist south' alternative.

Does this mean then that Highland–Lowland divide is simply a myth? This would be going too far. In fact, the Highlands (including the 'radical' south-west) and the Lowlands (including the 'conservative' north-east) had, over several centuries, developed antithetical cultures which led each to regard the other with deep suspicion. Captain Edmund Burt, an English soldier stationed in Scotland during the 1720s, registered these differences on entering the Highlands after passing through (for him) more familiar Lowland territory:

The Highlanders differ from the People of the Low-Country in almost every Circumstance of Life. Their Language, Customs, Manners, Dress, etc., are unlike, and neither would be content to be taken for the other, inasmuch that in speaking for an unknown Person of this Country (I mean Scotland) as a Scotchman only, it is as indefinite as barely to call a Frenchman a European, so little would his national character be known by it.[129]

This would have been less significant if it had not also led their respective inhabitants – especially those of the Lowlands – to feelings of hostility or even hatred. The basis for these feelings lay not in the existence or otherwise of clans (which scarcely feature in discussions of the Highlands before 1688), but in different attitudes to the rule of law, different languages and different religions .[130]

Law and Order

Highland disregard for law and order was often put down to the environment. Samuel Johnston, touring the Highlands in 1773, shortly after order had finally been imposed, noted:

> Mountaineers are warlike, because by their feuds and competitions they consider themselves as surrounded with enemies, and are always prepared to repel incursions, or to make them. ... Mountaineers are thievish, because they are poor, and having neither manufactures or commerce, can grow richer only by robbery. ... Mountainous regions are so remote from the seat of government, and so difficult to access, that they are very little under the influence of the sovereign, or within the reach of national justice.[131]

Fletcher of Saltoun had already provided the answer to Johnsonian environmental determinism in 1698, noting that the nature of Highland society cannot be the result of geography alone, since the Alps provided an example of a country which, although in many ways even less naturally endowed, was the very model of civilised industriousness:

> ... but they had no lords to hinder them from being civilised, to discourage industry, encourage thieving, and to keep them beggars that they might be more dependent; or when they had any that oppressed them, as in that part of the mountains that belongs to the Swiss, they knocked them on the head.[132]

These comments point towards an explanation of Highland criminality that rests on their social relationships rather than their surroundings. The poverty to which Fletcher refers provided an incentive for some of the warriors to engage in large-scale plundering, particularly of cattle, from the more settled Lowland communities. These onslaughts resembled more the lordly marauding typical of the feudal system in its formative years than the normal condition of the late medieval or early modern period. Nevertheless, two qualifications need to be made to this assessment.

One is that these raids were not directed solely at the Lowlands, but also at other Highland communities. For they would have been committed not by lordly dependants (i.e. the tacksmen), who maintained their standard of living through collection of rent from the tenantry, but mainly by bands of 'broken men' who were outside the structure of Highland society. The Lowland Perthshire peasant, watching his herd being driven off by armed clansmen was, however, unlikely to give this fact consideration. On 15 June 1650 the burghers of Lanark informed their fellow inhabitants of the following:

> It is stated and ordered that no highlander, young or old, remain within this burgh, but remove out thereof betwixt and Tuesday next, and orders any who have set them houses to remove them furth thereof betwixt and the said day, and discharge all persons whatsoever to reset or harbour or give them any entertainment thereafter, under the pain of ten pounds each person.[133]

The other qualification is that the level of Highland disorder had reduced by the second half of the seventeenth century in keeping with the greater stability of the country as a whole. Between 1661 and 1674, Highlanders were involved in less than 30 per cent of crimes of aggression against persons and crimes against property brought before the Lords Commissioners of Justiciary. Indeed, the greatest source of disorder came not from the Highlands at all but from the political and religious revolt of the south-western peasantry, 1,000 of whom fought in the Pentland Rising of 1666, 4,000 of whom fought at Bothwell Bridge in 1679 and between 3,000 and 14,000 of whom were involved in illegal armed religious assemblies during the 1670s.[134] If the twentieth century has shown us anything, however, it is that groups can be scapegoated as the cause of social ills on the most spurious of grounds. Although less sophisticated than modern ruling classes in the manipulation of such techniques, the Scottish ruling class certainly applied them to the Highlanders. A semi-official history of the Revolution of 1688, published in 1690, says:

> The Highlanders of Scotland are a sort of wretches that have no other consideration of honour, friendship, obedience, or government, than as, by any alteration of affairs or revolution in the Government, they can improve to themselves an opportunity of Robbing and plundering their bordering Neighbours.[135]

The identification of the Highlanders as a pariah group was made easier by a second factor: the distinctiveness of their language.

Language

Gaelic was originally the language of the majority of the population within the territory of present-day Scotland. The Scots, one of the tribes who went on to form the Scottish people, originally came from present-day Ireland, and had by the sixth century established their own kingdom called Dalriada in what is now Argyll. By the late fourteenth century, however, Fordun was noting that the inhabitants of Scotland spoke two languages, 'the Scottish [i.e. Gaelic] and the Teutonic [i.e. English]: the latter of which is the language of those who occupy the seaboard and plains, while the race of Scottish speech inhabits the highlands and outlying islands'.[136] Mair notes the same distinction between his 'wild' and 'householding' Scots: 'The Irish tongue is in use among the former, the English among the latter.'[137] What these comments reveal is the extent to which Gaelic, once the dominant language within the territory of the Scottish kingdom, had given ground since the eleventh century to its main rival, the Scots vernacular, which was at any rate comprehensible to those who spoke the English language of trade and administration. The first reference to the language spoken in the Lowlands as being *Scottis* or Scots is from 1494.[138] It is possible that this may indicate the point at which the Gaelic had definitely ceased to be the language of the majority, or simply that the regnal solidarity of the ruling class required that they had their own language, separate from the English. Either way, from around this time a further layer of separation was formally interposed between the Highlanders and the other inhabitants of Scotland. At a meeting of the Synod of Moray in 1624 the problems of a local minister were noted: 'Donald McQueen, minister at Pettie, regrets that Mr Patrick Dunbar his travels are unfruitful in the place wherein he serves and that only through want of the language.'[139] Thomas Tucker noted in 1656 that: 'The Inhabitants beyond Morayland (except in the Orkneys) speak generally Gaelic, or Highlands, and the mixture of both [i.e. both Gaelic and English] in the town of Inverness is such that one half of the people understand not one another.'[140]

The extent of the Gaidhealtachd at the end of the seventeenth century cannot be exactly defined, not least because of the way in which it shaded into areas on its south and eastern border where both Gaelic and Scots were spoken, often by the same people. Nevertheless, from the early eighteenth century onwards a number of attempts were made to map the boundary. From a study of these sources, Charles Withers has concluded that a working borderline can be established which, starting around the Clyde estuary in the south-west, follows 'a curving line from Dumbarton through central Perthshire and upland Aberdeenshire and Banffshire along the edge of the Grampians to a point at or near Nairn and thence along to the Easter Ross and Cromarty Lowlands'.[141] What is clear from this is that the Gaidhealtachd was increasingly synonymous with the geographical Highlands of Scotland. As James Walker noted in 1750: 'The Highlands is a very general name for a large tract of the kingdom, which appears to be the boundary of the Gaelic language.'[142]

Gaelic was held to be a contributory factor to the supposed degradation of those on the Highland side of this line.

How important were linguistic distinctions to the Highlanders? The difficulty for the historian is that the voices of the Highland peasants are even less audible than those of their Lowland counterparts. Only in the period after 1746, when Highland society was collapsing round about them, can the songs, memoirs and protests of the peasants be distinguished from those of their lords, or, more precisely, from those of the clan poets and mythologists who served the lords. It is true that the Highlanders made an absolute distinction between English (Sasannach) and Scottish (Albannach), the latter term encompassing both Highland and Lowland.[143] It is also true that they made a similarly absolute distinction between Highlands (Gaidhealtachd) and Lowlands (Galltachd). The distinctions are different in kind, but both pre-national in nature. The former is racial, where race is equated with a particular kingdom; the latter is linguistic, where language (and, by implication, other elements of culture) divide the subjects of the kingdom. The division was not seen in neutral terms either; the contemptuous contrast between the warriors of the Gaidhealtachd and the peasants of the Galltachd is one which runs through the poetry of the Highland elites. Aonghus mac Alasdair Ruaidh of Glencoe wrote after the Battle of Killiecrankie (1689) of how the Jacobite clansmen were: 'Being felled with lead – which even the cowherds can throw'. The key to the definition of Alba is kingship.[144] The point is not that Highland clans were particularly noted for the respect they showed for any particular king, but rather the way in which the idea of kingship is significant in the ideological self-conception of the clan elites.[145] A late example, from the work of the Highland Jacobite poet Alexander MacDonald, asserts that the Gaelic speakers were the true representatives of the Scottish 'race', as opposed to the Lowlanders who had abandoned their original linguistic traditions. He writes of the Gaelic:

> She still survives
> and her glory will not be lost
> in spite of the deceit
> and great ill-will of the Lowlander
> She is the speech of Scotland
> and of the Lowlanders themselves
> of our nobles, princes
> and dukes without exception.[146]

In the Lowlands, the two distinguishing features of the Highlanders continued to be reiterated down to and beyond the opening of our period: on the one hand, their disregard for the laws passed by the central state; on the other, their inability to communicate in the language spoken by most Scots by the late seventeenth century. The supposed criminality of Highland social behaviour and the actual incomprehensibility of Highland language led the Lowlanders to compare their neighbours, not to themselves, but to the native Irish and the settlers who had over the centuries been assimilated to that culture. For although the Scots version of Gaelic is distinct from the Irish, it contains enough similarities for the former to be described as 'Erse' or simply 'Irish' by non-Gaelic speakers in Scotland. Around 1746 Duncan Forbes of Culloden, himself a Highlander, wrote: 'What is properly called the *Highlands of Scotland*, is that large tract of mountainous ground to the Northward of the Forth and the Tay, where the natives speak the Irish Language.'[147] The comparison between Highlanders and the Irish was not itself new. Fordun himself refers to 'The Scottish nation [i.e. the Highlanders] ... is that which was once in Ireland, and resembles the Irish in all things – in language, manners and character.'[148] Yet without a third and final factor, which had not yet been introduced into Scottish society when Fordun or even Mair wrote their accounts, it is unlikely that the hostility between Lowland and Highland would have reached the extent that it did or that the identification of Highlander and Irish would have been so close. This final factor was religion.

Religion

What forms of religious life dominated the area in the absence of the kirk? The history of the Revolution quoted above comments: 'If there be any smack of religion amongst them, 'tis generally of the Roman Catholic persuasion.'[149] Although still widely believed today, such observations were inaccurate; by the late seventeenth century the majority of Highlanders were Protestants, and had been for the preceding century.[150] In 1681 the Vatican agent Alexander Leslie reported to the Congregation of Propaganda that there were around 14,000 Catholic communicants in Scotland, of whom 12,000 lived in the Highlands and Islands.[151] The reliability of these figures is supported by the respective totals of 16,490 and 10,022 calculated in 1755 by Alexander Webster in the first census of the Scottish population.[152] The other main concentrations of Catholic belief were to be found in Aberdeen, its rural hinterland, and Banffshire to the north.

In the early years of the Scottish Reformation the Church of Scotland was successful in converting the majority of Highlanders, particularly where the local lords had already converted and used their authority to impose their personal beliefs: in 1562 Archibald Campbell, fifth Earl of Argyll, swept through the Campbell lands of the south-west physically destroying Catholic iconography in the churches and expelling priests.[153] The Episcopalian form of church government imposed after the Restoration of 1660 nevertheless remained dominant across most of the central and eastern Highlands, and in the north-east, after the kirk was permanently established on a Presbyterian basis in 1689. Episcopalian communicants were therefore greater in number than Catholics (although until 1746 they were less strictly penalised by the state), but the combined effect of these religious alternatives meant that the Church of Scotland was hardly recognised across the entire area north of the Tay.

Nor were Catholicism and Episcopalianism the only barriers to the forward march of the Church of Scotland. In many areas, often not in the Highlands but simply in the remote north, peasant superstitions prevailed under a veneer of religious observance. Martin Martin, an unusually sympathetic English traveller in Scotland during the 1690s, noted with irritation their persistence in Orkney:

> Ladykirk, in South Ronaldsha [i.e. Ronaldsay], though ruinous and without a roof, is so much revered by the natives, that they choose rather to repair this old one, than to build a new church in a more convenient place, and at a cheaper rate: such is the power of education, that these men cannot be cured of these superfluous fancies transmitted to them by their ignorant ancestors.

Martin himself was not entirely free of irrational beliefs, devoting as he does pages to defending the existence of second sight in Skye and elsewhere.[154]

Lowland kirk ministers constantly complained of the failure of the Reformation to make permanent inroads beyond the Highland line. One of their key preoccupations was that the perpetuation of the Gaelic language was preventing the Highlanders from being converted to the Calvinist version of Christianity practised by the Church of Scotland. We are dealing here with the effect of perceptions, not their relationship to reality. Hugh Mackay, son of General Mackay (himself a Highlander), wrote more generally of the religious condition while describing his father's campaigns in the Highlands during the same period that:

> ... in all the progresses and marches of the General benorth Tay, he testified to have remarked no true sense of the deliverance which God had sent them, except in a very few, and that the people in general were disposed to submit to and embrace the party which they judged most like to carry it, their zeal for the preservation of their goods going by them, far beyond the consideration religion and liberty, which he attributed to the gross ignorance occasioned by the negligence of their ministers, as well as the large extent of their parishes, which made most of them come seldom to church.[155]

One aspect of this negligence was an unseemly empathy on the part of local ministers for the Highland culture of their flock. In 1624 an

Inverness minister whom we have already encountered, Mr Patrick Dunbar, was upbraided by visitors to the presbytery for holding infrequent meetings and indulging in 'uncomely habits such as [wearing] bonnets and plaid', in the same way as his parishioners. Dunbar was instructed to hold more frequent meetings and adopt a manner of dress more becoming his station.[156] Another sign of negligence was the failure to suppress peasant superstitions. The second sight, as Martin Martin noted, was an established aspect of Highland culture, which Gaelic-speaking ministers saw no reason to challenge. As Jane Dawson notes: 'The Gaelic clergy took a similar relaxed attitude towards the fairy culture of Gaeldom.' This attitude was sustainable because of the separation that existed between the world of 'elves, fawns and fairies' and the Catholic world of saints, angels and devils: 'The clergy could therefore accept the fairies and yet attack all those practices associated with Catholic worship and reverence for the saints.'[157] The Lowland ministers were not so much concerned with substituting reason in the place of superstition, as with imposing the particular superstitions sanctioned by the King James Bible ('Thou shalt not suffer a witch to live') in place of those which were part of the peasant tradition. Anyone claiming to have the gift of second sight or admitting to a belief in fairies in the Lowlands was likely to find himself or herself accused of witchcraft. Toleration of such abominations in the sight of the Lord introduced a further degree of separation between Highland and Lowland. The four great witch-hunts that blighted early modern Scotland (1590–97, 1629–30, 1649 and 1661–62) were almost exclusively Lowland affairs. 'In the Highlands,' writes Christina Larner, 'especially those parts outside the Kirk sessions system and within the dominion of the clans there was no witch hunting, or none that reached the records.'[158]

The Mid-Seventeenth Century Watershed

We can summarise the argument concerning the Highland–Lowland divide as follows. Scotland by the late seventeenth century was dominated by the feudal mode of production, but one part of the country ('the south') was more developed than the other ('the north') in both feudal terms and as the site of what little capitalist production existed. Superimposed over this economic division lay another, more cultural and ideological in nature, between the Highlands and the Lowlands, which led the inhabitants of these regions to regard each other as members of two separate societies. Indeed, many Lowlanders treated as the 'other' to their own society not the Highlands alone, but the Highlands and Catholic Ireland together. As we have seen, from the fourteenth century onwards the behaviour, language and, in a minority of cases, religion of the Highlanders led to them being described as 'Irish'. In particular, all the negative characteristics which the Lowland mind identified with the Highlands appeared to be confirmed by the close links which existed between Ulster and the western Highlands (which James VI had identified as lacking in all 'civility'). The seventeenth century, from the Scottish entry into the War of the Three Kingdoms, was the watershed during which attitudes on the Lowland side of the Highland line hardened into a hostility whose full and terrible consequence would only become apparent at the climax of the Revolution in 1746. Two events in particular were crucial in consolidating this hostility.

The first took place during the Civil Wars. The British colonists in Ulster who came under attack in the Irish rising of 1641 largely consisted of Protestant Scots from the Lowlands. In Scotland itself some of the clans, led by the royalist commander James Graham, Marquis of Montrose, leagued with the Irish Confederacy, led by Alasdair MacColla, in support of Charles I: the Scottish MacDonalds fighting alongside the Irish MacDonnells. In fear for relatives in Ireland and in reaction to the violence of royalist supporters in Scotland it became easy to ascribe such behaviour to all Highlanders, and to explain it as arising from their nature. The massacre of the local population after the battle of Aberdeen on 13 September 1644 is perhaps the most notorious example of such violence. As one participant recalled how:

> Montrose entered the town, where his army made great havoc and spoil, plundered them of their goods and killed the inhabitants, without distinguishing of age or of sex, to the number of eight score, which was done chiefly by the Irish and Scots Highlanders.[159]

No individual event did more than the massacre at Aberdeen to fuse the Highlander and the Catholic Irish in the Lowland mind not simply as alien, but as murderously alien, even though the Irish were far more heavily involved than the Highlanders. The extent of civilian losses was not great by the contemporary European standards of the Thirty Years' War – perhaps a hundred non-combatants were killed. Indeed, far greater numbers had been slain in Argyllshire by the troops of MacColla and Montrose before the sack of Aberdeen, and still more were to fall between 1644 and 1647. These victims were themselves Highlanders, however, notwithstanding the adherence of Argyll and Clan Campbell to the Covenant. Aberdeen saw the first major Lowland civilian losses of the war in Scotland, in a burgh which had a record of support for the King, and moreover these losses were perpetrated by troops who were already supposed to have committed atrocities upon Protestants in Ulster – largely imaginary events which nevertheless appeared to receive confirmation with this new and verifiable atrocity. 'The double standard that allowed and even encouraged atrocities in Ireland [i.e. against Catholics] but expressed revulsion at atrocities in Great Britain might be hypocritical,' writes David Stevenson, 'but it was a double standard that was generally accepted.'[160]

The second event took place during the Restoration, as part of the repression directed against the Presbyterian opposition to the religious policy of the regime. During late January and February 1678, troops were quartered among the inhabitants of the south-west in an effort to impose 'order' and, in particular, to prevent open air conventicles from being held. The practice of quartering was not itself new; it was the nature of the troops doing so which was to prove significant.

Out of a total force of 750 horse and 7224 infantry, 590 and 6124 respectively were from the Highlands.[161] The conventicling minister Alexander Shields wrote of the so-called 'Highland Host' that:

> they [i.e. the Privy Council] brought down from the wild Highlands a host of Savages upon the Western shires, more terrible than Turk or Tartar, men who feared not God nor regarded man; and being also poor pitiful Skybalds, they thought they had come to a brave world, to waste and destroy a plentiful country, which they resolved to make as bare as their own.[162]

Another minister, James Kirkton, agreed with Shields about those whom the latter called this 'hellish crew', these 'barbarous savages', stressing their otherness from the Lowlanders: 'After they past Stirling they carried as if they had been in an enemy's country, living upon free quarter where ever they came.' But, apart from living off the western peasants, what did the Highland Host actually do to earn such approbation?

Kirkton writes that 'the oppressions, exactions, injuries and cruelties committed by the Highlanders among the poor people of the west country' are 'above my reach to describe', but that a 'thinking man may apprehend what a company of barbarous Highlanders would do, when they were sent upon design to turn the innocent people of the west country mad by oppressions, in which office you may believe they were very faithful'.[163] This is all remarkably vague. In fact, the experience of Lanark seems to have been typical of that of the south-west:

> A great host of highland forces were sent into the west, whereof the most part of the Earl of Strathmore's regiment was quartered in Lanark the space of 21 days, where by oppression they extracted of the inhabitants, of free and dry quarters, the sum of 3544 pounds, whereof there is a particular account yet extant, and this besides the demolishing of the tolbooth and other houses in the town and what they robbed.[164]

Confirmation can be found in a letter dated 17 February, evidently written by a Lowland officer commanding the regular forces who made up a minority of the 'Highland Host', from one of the south-western towns. ('We are all quartered in and about this town, the Highlanders only in free quarters.') The author, who, it must be recalled, was engaged in the same activity as the Highlanders, describes them as:

> ... this unhallowed, and many of them unchristian, rabble, besides the free quarters, wherein they kill and destroy bestial at their pleasure, without regard to the commands of their discreeter officers, rob all that comes to hand, whether in houses or in the highways; so that no man may pass safely from house to house; and their insolency in the houses where they are quartered fills poor women and children with terror, and both men and women with great vexation.

Indeed, the writer favourably compares the regular troops with the Highlanders, noting that 'when these men, lately this people's only persecutors, are now commended by them for sobriety, and in effect are looked on by many of them as their guardians and protectors, you may easily judge what is the others' deportment'.[165]

Kirkton describes the departure of the Highland army in the same terms as its arrival: 'But when this goodly army retreated homeward, you would have thought by their baggage they had been at the sack of a besieged city; and therefore, when they passed Stirling Bridge, every man drew his sword to show the world they had returned conquerors from their enemy's land.' Yet even he is compelled to admit that there was only one fatality during the entire episode: 'Yet under all this oppression the poor people bore all; only in Campsie there was one of the plunderers killed by a country man, yet escaped punishment.'[166] In other words, the only person to die was himself a Highlander. Kirkton puts this down to the heroic self-restraint of the inhabitants under provocation, yet the episode reveals something other than this. On 22 March 1678 John Campbell, then Earl of Caithness, complained to the Committee of the West of the Privy Council that 'there was one of his men killed at Campsie and several of them wounded in their goings home by a multitude of people convocated in arms'. Nor was Campsie the only parish to display 'great insolence'. 'Several disorders' were reported 'in the parishes of Strathblane, Killin, Balfron, Fintry and Gargunnock in Stirlingshire'. Three days later it was reported to the Council that a man named Brash had been committed to the tolbooth in Edinburgh for the 'slaughter' of Alexander McGregor.[167]

What does this demonstrate? Essentially that the Highlanders were not regarded as belonging to the same nation as, not only the radical south-west, but the southern Lowlands more generally, and even the 'conservative' north-east. Perhaps as a result of the earlier experience of

Highland participation in the sack of Aberdeen in 1644, Alexander Brodie, scion of a long-established north-eastern family with lands in Elgin and Nairn, wrote in his diary of 'what desolation was done in the west country', which was not an area whose inhabitants would normally have attracted his sympathy.[168] The Lowland officer quoted above noted the difference in historical time which the Highlanders seemed to embody:

> As for their armies and other military accoutrements, it is not possible for me to describe them in writing; here you may see head pieces and steel bonnets raised like pyramids, and such as a man would affirm, they had only found in chamber boxes; targets [targes?] and shields of the most odd and antique form, and powder horns hung in strings, garnished with beaten nails of burnished brass. And I truly doubt not but a man, curious in our antiquities, might in this host find explications of the stranger pieces of armour found in our old laws ... above what any occasion in the lowlands would have afforded for several hundred years.[169]

In his discussion of this episode, John Prebble, the great radical historian of the Highlands, writes: 'It was as if several thousand Afghan hillmen were to be billeted in Sussex.'[170] The effect of such exaggerated comparison is, however, quite unintentionally to lend retrospective support to the arguments of those who, in 1746, were to justify their violence against the Highlanders precisely on the grounds that they were barbarians – although their favoured comparison was with 'Red' Indians rather than with Afghan hillmen. In fact, as Hamish Henderson has pointed out: 'The level of material culture and comfort was not markedly higher in the Galloway of 1678 than in the lands of the Earls of Strathmore and Airlie, whence many of the levies came.'[171] But this fact had no impact on the way in which the Highlands were regarded.

Highlanders seem to have returned the same levels of hostility. In 1724, shortly after taking up his position as Commander-in-Chief of the British army in Scotland, George Wade – himself an Irishman – attempted to explain Highland attitudes in a report to George I:

> They have still more extensive adherence one to another as Highlanders in opposition to the people who Inhabit the Low Countries whom they hold in the utmost Contempt, imagining them inferior to themselves in Courage, Resolution, and the use of Arms, and accuse them of being Proud, Avaricious, and Breakers of their Word. They have also a tradition that the Lowlands were in Ancient Times, the Inheritance of their Ancestors, and therefore believe that they have a right to commit Depredations, wherever it is in their power to put them in Execution.[172]

But if Highlanders felt no affinity with the Lowlanders, neither did they look across the Irish Sea for an alternative. Scottish clan poets of the seventeenth century occasionally invoked pan-Celtic solidarity between the native Irish and the Highlanders. Ian Lom MacDonald, celebrating the royalist massacre of Clan Campbell at the Battle of Inverlochy in 1645, gives high praise to the Irish leader Alasdair MacColla:

> Alasdair, son of handsome Colla,
> skilled hand at cleaving castles,
> you put to flight the Lowland pale-face:
> what kale they had taken came out again.[173]

As Allan MacInnes has pointed out: 'The poet felt an immediate hostility towards the Campbells who, as the main upholders of the Covenanting Movement among the clans, were promoting cultural assimilation with the racially inferior Lowlander, the *Gall*.'[174] But no general movement of solidarity among the two Gaelic peoples was present in the Scottish Highlands, at any rate beyond the MacDonald strongholds on the western seaboard. Indeed, even the links which did exist between the western clans and those in Antrim should not be taken to mean that the former regarded themselves as more 'Irish' than 'Scottish' – that would simply be to adopt the ideological framework through which the Lowlanders viewed them. Neither the Scottish nor the Irish clans – or more precisely their respective nobilities – would have recognised the concept of the nation as having any significance to their way of life. As late as 1617 the 'Irish' MacDonnells came out best in a dispute with the 'Scottish' Campbells over which had the superior claim over Rathlin Island off the coast of Antrim.[175] Such a dispute could be resolved without bloodshed – as happened in this case – only where the debatable land was not felt to belong to a national territory which must be defended at all costs.

The Balance of Social Forces

What then was the overall balance of social forces within Scotland by the late seventeenth century? There was as yet no conscious struggle for power between opposing classes, or alliances of classes. Nevertheless, we can, in retrospect, discern three broadly aligned congeries of groups within society.

The first consisted of the majority of the established ruling class, the Lowland magnates and Highland chiefs – a class in economic decline, but whose members still possessed greater individual social power than those of any other in Western Europe. They were supported by other social groups whose horizons were limited to maintaining the traditional order, but making it function more effectively and profitably; the vast majority of baronial lairds, clan tacksmen, and traditional east coast merchants. Elements from each of these might have been persuaded to consider new ways of organising economic and social life – the ways that were so obviously coming to dominate in England – if it could be demonstrated that the potential benefits were worth the risks. But this demonstration would require some form of alternative leadership, which was exactly what Scotland lacked.

The second congeries consisted of those groups which had been part of the existing order but which had either been displaced or threatened by the political revolution of 1688. Two in particular stand out. On the one hand, the dispossessed Episcopalian clergy. On the other – and more significant in material terms, those Highland clans alienated from the new regime. Both groups were excluded from the Revolution settlement and prepared to act respectively as the ideologues and foot soldiers of Jacobitism when it eventually emerged as a serious movement. For it to do so would require a more substantial social base than either of these groups could provide. That would come in due course, but this embryonic movement was already infinitely more coherent in ideological terms than the directionless elites at the apex of late feudal Scotland. It was also more coherent than the fragmented forces groping their separate ways towards a new form of society:

The third congeries consisted of those actual or potential sources of opposition to the existing order – or rather, to specific aspects of it. Bonnet lairds in Fife or the south-west found that their economic independence was compromised by the social control which the heritable jurisdictions conferred on the lords within whose superiorities they held their land. Edinburgh lawyers found that the same heritable jurisdictions both rivalled and restricted the functioning of the central legal system whose agents they were. Glasgow merchants found that their ambitions were frustrated both by the privileges afforded by the Scottish state to their traditional east coast rivals and by the limitations imposed by the English state on their trade with the Americas. The Church of Scotland found that it was prevented from exercising dominion over the northern territories where Episcopalianism and even Catholicism still held sway. The House of Argyll found its territorial expansion into the west on the basis of new, commercial forms of tenure slowed down by the resistance of clans hostile to Clan Campbell. But all these groups had different aims and, even where these did not contradict each other, no faction or ideology existed to unite them, let alone to form a pole of attraction for those whose interests were currently served by maintaining the status quo. No group like the Independents, still less the Jacobins, was waiting in the wings to meld these disparate groups of the dissatisfied into a coherent opposition.

If Scotland had been isolated from the rest of the world, and the future of Scottish society made entirely dependent on these three groups, then the most likely outcome would have been an epoch of stagnation similar to that which affected the north-western states of mainland Europe, which in most respects Scotland closely resembled. But Scotland was neither isolated nor, consequently, entirely dependent on its own resources. For several of the main players lay outside the borders of Scotland, although they sought to influence, or even determine what happened within them. These players were the states – Spain, France, England – locked in competition for hegemony over Europe and, increasingly, its colonial extensions. What was the nature of this competition, which would affect the future of Scotland, Europe and, ultimately, the world?

Three Dimensions of Socio-economic Crisis (the 1690s)

Capitalism and the social classes associated with it were still undeveloped in Scotland by the late seventeenth century, but the country was by no means unique in this respect. 'By 1650,' claims Immanuel Wallerstein, 'the basic structures of historical capitalism as a viable social system had been established and consolidated.'[1] Such a judgement mistakes the existence of pre-existing components of the capitalist system – money, wage labour, commodities – for the system itself, where these are combined in the cycle of competitive accumulation. Capitalist relations of production, although still largely subordinate to feudalism, were indeed present in Western Europe and colonial America, but only in a handful of territories had they separated and become dominant in their turn, and none of the states founded on these relations was secure.

Two areas had earlier been balanced precariously at the leading edge of development, only to be pushed backwards before their position could be consolidated. In the earliest, the republican city-states of Northern and Central Italy, the source of this reversal was the failure of attempts to form a unified state under Frederick II and the resultant submission of the communes, over several centuries, to the feudal barons of the surrounding countryside; a defeat compounded by conquest at the hands of the Spanish Habsburgs at the end of the fifteenth century. In the case of Bohemia, less developed than the Italian communes, but a coherent territorial state with a population ideologically bound together by the Hussite proto-reformation of the fifteenth century, defeat came more suddenly at the hands of the armed Counter-Reformation when, during the early stages of the Thirty Years' War, the Austrian Habsburgs reimposed both the Catholic religion and feudal economic relations on the defeated Estates.

If two other states, Switzerland and the United Provinces, survived in spite of the best efforts of the Habsburg empire, this was not simply due to their internal strength, but also because they did not fundamentally challenge the economic and political structures of absolutist Europe. The Swiss Confederation was formed at the end of the fourteenth century after 100 years of struggle against the Austrian monarchy, but progress towards capitalism was slow. The first cantons to join the Confederation in 1291 had thrown off a foreign feudalism before capitalism had a chance to develop, leaving a population of small commodity producers in possession of their land. By the time Calvin set up his dictatorship in Geneva during the sixteenth century Switzerland had some claim to being the first bourgeois republic, but this land of free peasants and urban oligarchs was the very opposite of a centralised nation-state. Divided by language, a fragmented canton structure and, after the Reformation, opposed religious affiliations, it made much of its wealth by hiring out the population as mercenaries to the very absolutist regimes that were stifling bourgeois development elsewhere in Europe. The formation of the United Provinces, on the other hand, was the first breakthrough to have taken place after the Reformation and under the banner of Calvinism. The climax of the 80-year struggle by the Dutch against the Spaniards coincided with the end of the Thirty Years' War in 1648 and the proclamation of the Republic in England in the following year. Yet, contrary to what Wallerstein has written, this was far from being the consolidation of bourgeois rule in Western Europe. The wealth of the United Provinces also depended ultimately on servicing the existing feudal regimes, not through the supply of military manpower, but through its vast trading and financial networks. Adapted to this feudal environment, the very moment of political triumph saw the United Provinces falter under the combined impact of economic crisis among its more backward feudal clients and competition from its more advanced capitalist rival, England. The United Provinces were to remain a bulwark against French expansionism, but that role was also played by such notably non-bourgeois regimes as Austria. It was not to be at the centre of a new world system.

As a result of this series of reversals and accommodations, England was by 1688 the only surviving source of a systemic alternative to feudal absolutism. From Marx himself onwards, the majority of Marxist historians have claimed that the events of 1688–89 in England ended the revolutionary process begun in 1640 by confirming a new capitalist ruling class in power and establishing a state geared to the accumulation of capital. In these accounts it is accepted that the state had still to undergo several subsequent transformations, largely to accommodate the process of industrialisation and the classes that it produced, but on the essential point – that there was no longer any question of a retreat to feudal economic relations or absolutist political rule in England – the decisive nature of the Glorious Revolution has never seriously been in doubt.[2] Yet there is a difficulty associated with this verdict. According to Eric Hobsbawm, the seizure and maintenance of state power is not enough to bring a revolution to an end: 'Revolutions cannot be said to "conclude" until they have either been overthrown or are sufficiently safe from overthrow.'[3] This observation is accurate with regard to political revolutions, but profoundly misleading in relation to social revolutions. Any revolution that introduces a new type of society is liable to be overturned by a mixture of external pressure and internal subversion as long as it remains isolated in a world where a different and hostile system prevails. Only when the cumulative impact of several revolutions has established a new social system can safety be assured. The English Revolution had not yet been overthrown, but was it safe from overthrow? In fact, as Roy Porter writes, '1688 could in nowise be a final solution'.[4] The finality usually ascribed to that year is only possible if events in England are treated in complete isolation. As Fred Halliday has noted:

> There is an extensive literature on the origins of the English revolution and indeed the character of this, the second – after the Dutch – 'bourgeois' revolution. The overwhelming majority of this literature focuses on changes in the social and economic structure of Britain prior to the 1640s and on variant interpretations of the social character of the parliamentary cause. One can, indeed, say that virtually the whole of this literature is written as if England [sic] was not just an island, but was a closed entity, separate from the political, economic and intellectual world of the rest of Europe.[5]

More specifically, it is not possible to separate developments in England from either the wider struggle with France for European and colonial hegemony, or the impact of that struggle on the other nations of the British Isles, as the English ruling class themselves were only too well aware at the time.

Justin Rosenberg has argued that the wars between England and France were essentially pre-capitalist in character: 'We see here neither nation-states nor capitalism; we see dynastic and oligarchic state-organisation, in collaboration with mercantile groups, deploying territorial strategies to secure monopoly control over resources (mostly the trade in luxury goods) to supplant the income from their agricultural estates.'[6] The work from which this assessment is taken scores many telling points against the Realist theory of International Relations, but here Rosenberg misses his target. Relations between states have varied in history according to the modes of production upon which they are based. We cannot assume, therefore, that the wars between actual or aspirant absolutisms in the seventeenth century are comparable to the international wars between competing capitalist powers in the nineteenth and twentieth centuries. There was, however, a transitional period from the absolutist to the capitalist state system in the same way as there was a transitional period from the feudal to the capitalist modes of production. Of course in the War of the Spanish Succession bourgeois

England was ranged alongside, not only the bourgeois United Provinces, but also the absolutist Austria. The latter alliance was, however, the result of military necessity, not of any deeper affinity between the two regimes. French politicians were themselves aware of the difference between their state and that of England. De Cominges, French ambassador to the court of Charles II, wrote to Louis XIV about the British state early in the Restoration: 'It has a monarchical appearance, as there is a king, but at bottom it is very far from being a Monarchy.'[7] English politicians were also aware of this fact, whatever rhetoric they sometimes employed. As Frederick North, second Earl of Guilford, said to Charles Fox while in opposition during the 1780s: 'The King ought to be treated with all sort of respect and attention, but the appearance of power is all that a king of this country can have.'[8] The French Revolution of 1789 would go further than the English Revolution of 1688 by removing the person of the king, in addition to his power, but for the hundred years between them, the position of the monarch in England was uniquely restricted in Europe. As Adam Smith noted: 'The absolute power of the sovereign has continued ever since its establishment in France, Spain, etc. In England alone a different government has been established from the natural course of things.'[9]

The essential difference between England and France is however perhaps best illustrated by focusing on a subject which in different ways was dear to the hearts of both ruling classes: money. As Colin Mooers has stressed, the nature of taxation and office holding in England were unique in Europe at the time. The principle form of taxation was the Land Tax which was self-imposed on the landowners by the Parliament which they controlled, then assessed and collected by the lower levels of that class and their tenants. This preference for a Land Tax over Customs and Excise was conditioned by the connections there had always been under the Stuarts between Custom and Excise, the financial independence of the Crown, and its attempts to impose absolutist rule. There was however another aspect of the Land Tax which marked it as bourgeois in nature. English landowners were taxed on capitalist ground rents paid to them by tenants whose incomes derived from the employment of wage labour.[10] These arrangements strongly contrast with those current in France, where the nobility was exempt from taxation, but was responsible for collecting it from a peasantry already oppressed by demands for feudal rent. Frank McLynn is therefore correct to write that 'Britain and France were for the entire Jacobite period engaged in a titanic economic and commercial struggle, waged world wide'. At the heart of this struggle lay the fundamental difference between the two states, 'the divine right of kings versus the divine right of property'.[11] But until 1707 it was not 'Britain' but England which was engaged in this inter-systemic conflict, and it is here that the differences between England and Scotland were of the greatest importance.

Counter-revolution can have both external and internal sources. The external danger to England after 1688 mainly lay in France. The internal threat in the British Isles lay not in England, nor in Ireland, which had been quiescent since the Treaty of Limerick in 1691, but in Scotland. The Scottish and English states were still harnessed together in a multiple kingdom, even though they remained at different stages of socio-economic development. The absolutist project of the Stuarts had, at one level, attempted to even up the situation by extending the power of the feudal state in Scotland as it retarded the development of capitalist economy in England. The new, constitutional monarchy had no comparable ambitions of its own for Britain as a whole and the English ruling class regarded Scotland as a disruptive element to be contained, rather than a potential ally to be transformed. But as long as Scotland remained untransformed, there was always the possibility that the classes which had found it convenient to remove James VII and II might, through a further change in circumstances, wish to bring him back, and with him his French supporter – the global rival of the English state. Neither the English Revolution nor the new world system which it promised (or threatened) to bring into being would be secure while this possibility remained. The oft-stated desire of the Stuarts to reclaim all of their previous kingdoms, combined with the French need to remove their opponents from the international stage, meant that the English ruling class was faced, not only with impoverishment, but also with a threat to its continued survival on a capitalist basis.

Within Scotland, the three main congeries of social groups identified in Chapter 1 did not align themselves between France and England according to any clear-cut division into progressive or reactionary, feudal or capitalist. The first, comprising the majority of the established ruling class, hoped to avoid the choice if possible, while retaining their freedom of movement within the composite monarchy of the British Isles. The second, comprising those who were excluded (the Episcopalian clergy) or endangered (the Jacobite clans) by the Revolution Settlement, were willing to contemplate an alliance with France to secure their goal of a second Stuart Restoration. The third, comprising the forces who wished to transform Scottish society in various different ways, did not counterbalance the second by displaying an equal level of support for an alliance with England. On the contrary, they were hostile to English influence, either because they hoped to protect from it their own sectional interests (the Church of Scotland, Scots law) or because they were in direct competition with English rivals (the Glasgow tobacco merchants). An attempt by the latter to raise these competitive stakes contributed to an economic crisis of such proportions that it effectively marks the opening of the epoch of the Scottish Revolution. This is not unique in history, as Perry Anderson explains:

... among the most fundamental of all mechanisms of social change, according to historical materialism, are the systematic contradictions between *forces and relations of production*, not just social conflicts generated by antagonistic relations of production alone. The former *overlap* with the latter, because one of the major forces of production is always labour, which simultaneously figures as a class specified by the relations of production. But they do not coincide. Crises within modes of production are not identical with confrontation within classes. The two may or may not fuse, according to the historical occasion. The *onset* of major economic crises, whether under feudalism or capitalism, has typically taken all social classes unawares, deriving from structural depths below those of direct conflict between them. The resolution of such crises, on the other hand, has no less typically been the outcome of prolonged war between classes. In general, *revolutionary* transformations – from one mode of production to another – are indeed the privileged terrain of class struggle.[12]

Scotland had enjoyed modest economic growth during the Restoration, perhaps sufficient to bring output up to the level attained before the Civil Wars of the 1640s, but this was largely the result of conjunctural accident, rather than structural transformation. Social relations remained essentially feudal and, consequently, the economy remained trapped within the twin-track of subsistence agriculture and raw material exports. The danger was that once favourable circumstances passed, as they did even before the Revolution Settlement had been accomplished, gains of such a purely quantitative nature could be wiped out, leaving Scottish society no further forward, or even further back, than it had been in 1660. In the 1690s a threefold crisis, of appalling social cost, brutally revealed the limits of Scottish development. First, the involuntary surrender of long-established trade links at the behest of the British monarchy showed the political constraints acting on the ruling class. Second, the failure of the agricultural sector to cope with a massive subsistence crisis revealed the socio-economic constraints on production. Third, and finally, an attempt to transcend these boundaries by opening up new colonial markets was to expose the underlying weaknesses of the state itself.[13] The result was to make some alteration in Anglo-Scottish relations – although not necessarily an incorporating Union – inevitable.

Trade Wars and Shooting Wars

By the late seventeenth century economic competition between states had taken the form of the zero-sum game that we know as mercantilism. Put crudely, each state sought to restrict imports to the raw materials needed for industry while excluding, through protectionist legislation, those manufactured goods whose production was simultaneously being encouraged internally. The ultimate effect of the universal adoption of this doctrine would have been to reduce the level of trade across all the participant states, had it not been for the fact that the major international players were all in possession of colonies where trade, or simple plunder, could be carried out without the risk of encouraging the industrial development of rival states. Scotland, however, had no serious colonies. The tariff barriers that her exports faced were not restricted to the manufactured goods that formed the lesser part of national output, but extended to the raw materials which formed the greater. After 1660, the English state treated Scotland as a foreign country for economic purposes by imposing tariffs on Scottish coal and salt, and barring Scotland from imperial trade unless Scottish goods were carried in English ships (which were subject to high levels of duty), or in the ships of their country of origin (which were subject to even higher levels of duty). The Scottish Parliament retaliated with similar legislation, which, needless to say, failed to bring the English economy to its knees. The later Stuarts had, however, provided one service for the Scottish ruling class. Their admiration for and, more to the point, financial dependence on the French monarchy prevented the inevitable systemic conflict between England and France for as long as they sat on the throne. Thus, although Scottish trade with the United Provinces was disrupted by enforced participation in the various Dutch Wars of the Restoration period, the dependent nature of aspirant Stuart absolutism meant that Scotland was not involved in a far more disruptive war with its major trading partner. With the accession of William, and the immediate outbreak of the long-delayed hostilities against France, even this advantage was lost. The Wars of the British and Irish Succession lasted from 1688 to 1697 and would in any event have had a generally disruptive effect on trade, but the outbreak of hostilities led to the cessation of all commercial relations with France. The impact of war was also felt in two other areas. Scottish shipping was now exposed to attack from French privateers and had little chance of protection from an English fleet who were instructed to treat the task as very low down on its list of priorities. Nor were there any Scottish frigates that could provide self-protection until 1697, the last year of the war, and the Scots had to buy even these from England. Similarly, conscription removed Scottish men, particularly skilled mariners, from economic activity and exposed them – already in proportionally higher numbers than those of England – to the threat of death or mutilation.

The Scottish Parliament used the freedom gained at the Revolution of 1688, and royal embarrassment over the Massacre of Glencoe (1692), to try and legislate a way out of this economic impasse. On 14 June 1693, two Acts were passed, one for encouraging foreign trade and the other allowing the formation of joint stock companies with the power to undertake both colonial and trading activities.[14] More importantly, on 9 May 1695, the fifth session of the Scottish Parliament met to be told by the Marquis of Tweedale that, amongst other things, a Commission of Inquiry into Glencoe would be set up. He also said that the King was willing, in very general terms, to contemplate the establishment of a Scottish plantation in Africa, India or elsewhere that would be granted the same rights and privileges as those afforded his other subjects. The two matters were connected. The initial Acts had been given royal assent in order to pacify injured national feelings in the immediate aftermath of Glencoe. Their successor was now hurried through Parliament in the shadow of the attempt to allocate blame for that atrocity. William had returned to the European mainland to resume the military struggle with Louis, hoping to divert attention from the events in the Highlands by endorsing a scheme from which he probably believed nothing would ever come. In fact, the Scots moved with remarkable speed to put it into effect. John Hay, second Marquis of Tweedale and Lord Commissioner, formally gave royal assent to the Act on 26 June. He almost certainly exceeded his authority by doing so, for as we shall see, it is certain that William would not have extended his general approval to this specific proposal.[15]

The Act for a Company Trading to Africa and the Indies allowed a monopoly of trade in the named continents 'forever' and, in the case of America, for the somewhat shorter period of 31 years. All goods could be traded free of duty for 21 years, except sugar and tobacco, the most profitable. Colonies could be established anywhere in the three continents, except where another European power had already established sovereignty. Anyone who became a member or employee of the Company, or who settled in any colonies which it might establish, would become a subject of the Kingdom of Scotland, with all the rights and privileges which accompanied that condition. Among the clauses designed to attract likely investors and allay the suspicions of European powers with interests in the area was, however, one that hinted at problems to come. The property and personnel of the Company were to be secure from confiscation, damage or other interference – presumably by privateers or other states. And what was supposed to guarantee this happy state of affairs? The knowledge that the Company would be protected by the King in the first instance, and, should anyone be foolish enough still to proceed against the Company, they would be pursued by him for reparations.[16] This clause would return to haunt the men who drafted it.

The Acts establishing the Company was not the only legislation passed during 1695 and 1696 which sought to transform Scotland's economic condition. The fifth session had also passed Acts for erecting two incorporated bodies, a linen manufactory at the Citadel in Leith and a woollen manufactory at Newmills. The Act Anent Lands Lying in Runrig allowed application to be made, to whoever held local jurisdiction, for such lands to be divided and consolidated, even if this was against the wishes of some of the parties. If only by implication, it also allowed for the consolidated land to be enclosed.[17] The Act for the Division of Commonties allowed such lands to be divided in proportion to the size of the estates held by landowners that could prove their rights. Again, this could be forced through by the application of one person rather than by agreement as in the earlier 1647 Act.[18] The Act for Settling Schools ordered that a school be established in every parish where this had not already been done, with the local heritors providing funding for both the schoolhouse and the schoolmaster's salary.[19] These Acts demonstrate a desire on the part of the Scottish ruling class to force the pace of national development, but it is only by establishing thoroughly artificial links to economic expansion after 1746 that they can be said to have helped accomplish that goal. The agrarian legislation was permissive, but it was to take over 50 years before the cumulative effect of piecemeal applications was to have any impact on agriculture. The educational legislation was compulsory, but merely reaffirmed an aspiration first voiced during the Reformation 150 years before, and which would still remain unaccomplished 100 years after this restatement.

The difference between the sluggish implementation of these enactments and the frenzy that was to surround the Company will soon become apparent. A still greater contrast is provided by the one piece of legislation passed by the Scottish Parliament whose effects are still visible on any Scottish high street. The Act for the Establishment of the Bank of Scotland was passed on 17 July 1695, three weeks after the passage of the Act establishing the Company.[20] Much has been made of the foundation of the Bank as an indication of the extent to which capitalism – or at any rate the capitalist 'spirit' – was already present in Scotland at this time. Gordon Marshall, for example, writes that:

Reduced to its fundamentals, the Bank of Scotland at this time represented nothing more than an extremely large and sophisticated organisation for money-lending. ... Can one imagine a more 'pure' instance of the spirit of modern capitalism at work – of capital being used to generate money, of money begetting money?[21]

The spirit may have been willing, but as so often in seventeenth century Scottish history, the flesh was all too weak. The initial capital stock of the Bank was £800,000 (although this was later increased), to be raised by 172 subscribers – 136 of them based in Scotland, 36 in London. Nearly half the stock was subscribed by 24 nobles and 30 lairds, a further £300,000 by 25 merchants and the residue mainly by members of the legal profession.[22] Without the support of the nobility and the landowners it is unlikely that the Bank would ever have been launched. Two comparisons are instructive here.

The first is with the Bank of England, which had been established the previous year. The difference between these institutions was not limited to the respective capital stock fixed by their founding Acts – that of the Bank of England was £1,200,000, that of the Bank of Scotland £120,000 – although the proportionality is telling. Rather it extends to their origin, function, and relationship to the state and the nature of their subscribers:

> The [Bank of England] was primarily a creation of the City of London, with management controlled by a group of powerful financiers and merchants who worked closely with the Treasury. The strengths of this financial interest were such that they had little need of government office-holders, members of the House of Lords or judges. ... While the initial subscribers numbered 1,272 and were widely spread throughout the mercantile classes and the professions, few of the nobility subscribed.[23]

The Bank of England was chartered as a machine for lending to the state and indeed for ensuring its supply of credit. The Bank of Scotland was founded as a purely private affair, independent of the state and unconnected with managing the public debt. Indeed, it was forbidden to lend to the Crown without explicit parliamentary approval.

The second comparison is with the Company itself. William Paterson, the Scottish merchant most associated with its activities, was one of the founders of the Bank of England, yet he was not similarly involved in establishing the Bank of Scotland. On the contrary, he regarded that institution as a rival to the Company. Indeed, he tried to prevent the Bank charter being granted by the Scottish Parliament. Even after failing to abort the Bank the directors of the Company did not rest in their attempts to strangle it at birth. The Bank was not allowed to trade, but the Company was allowed to act as a bank. The latter institution proceeded to crowd out its rival by issuing loans and to pay for its activities by issuing banknotes, although both activities proved unprofitable and were quickly abandoned.[24]

What does this episode demonstrate? The failure of the absolutist project meant that the state lacked a semi-autonomous officialdom capable of overriding the individual concerns of noble factions on behalf of their collective class interest. The politicians who occupied the leading positions in the Scottish state were too preoccupied with their own internal struggles to see the possibilities for national development in either a financial body like the Bank or a trading venture like the Company. Both projects were therefore left in the hands of private individuals. Looking back from 1733, Patrick Lindsay noted the failure of the independent Scottish state to encourage manufactures: 'Strange! that when we had the Power in our own hands, to tax ourselves for the Improvement of our Manufactures, we did it not as the Irish have done.' As with agriculture, the problem was not that laws were not passed, but that they were ignored: 'These Laws could have no effect, as they were attended by no certain Execution, but left at large to the Discretion of every Sheriff, Steward, Lord, or Baillie of Regality.'[25]

It is therefore a measure of the frustration, perhaps even the desperation, of the bourgeoisie that they were prepared to take the enormous gamble involved in the Company to break through the developmental barriers at one bound. The Dutch and English states had prospered. Was this not due to the trade which flowed through their colonial possessions? As A. M. Carstairs writes, 'for a country plunged in poverty and urgently seeking the means for greater prosperity, commercial policy then, as always, seemed to be the easy solution, the line of least resistance – much easier than attempting to raise productivity per head on the land and in a multitude of economic activities'.[26] Why did this 'easy solution' take the form of the Company Trading to Africa and the Indies?

George Pratt Insh finds 'three distinct forces' involved: 'the Scottish desire to find, in a Scottish colony, a new market overseas; the project of the London Merchants to break through the monopoly of the East India Company by establishing in Scotland a base for English trade; the persistent efforts of the Edinburgh merchants to establish an African trade'.[27] In fact, there were but two 'distinct forces' in operation, since the Edinburgh focus on African trade was merely a specific example of the general drive to establish new markets. Pratt Insh is correct to say that the venture was Anglo-Scottish in origin, but the backers in England were different from those in Scotland.

In England a group of London merchant capitalists (including a large number, like Paterson himself, of Scottish origin) who were excluded from lucrative trading areas by the monopoly positions of the English African Company – and, more importantly, the East India Company – saw as many possibilities in the Scottish legislation of 1693 as did the Scots themselves. The East India Company in particular had forfeited its charters in November of that year after failing to pay tax on the value of its stock. Although the charters were reconfirmed by William in December, Parliament denied them once again the following month. By March 1695, the House of Commons had appointed a committee to investigate possible irregularities in the accounts. The East India Company looked to be on the verge of collapse. For the new men – the 'interlopers' as they were known to the East India Company – the Scottish Company would either be the vehicle for their back-door entry into the African and Indian markets, or it would act as a stopgap until the – surely inevitable – fall of the existing East India Company opened up the way for a new company to replace it. In fact, they may well have anticipated becoming the dominant interest in the Scottish Company. Such was their confidence in the project that they pressurised the Scottish directors into raising the original capital target from £360,000 to £600,000.

In Scotland the principal backers were also merchants, but with a very different relationship to their national economy. Far from trying to compete with an already established monopoly interest, they were themselves seeking to erect such an interest. This in itself speaks volumes about the relative level of economic development attained by their respective societies. These men tended to be active both as elders in the Church of Scotland and as commissioners to the Scottish Parliament. 'William Arbuckle,' writes John Prebble, 'a merchant of Glasgow and one of the first to dip into his purse for the company, was able to subscribe more stock than peers whose estates spread across three shires.'[28] In particular, two Edinburgh merchants at the heart of the Company, Robert Blackwood and James Balfour, had been involved in the earlier 'manufactory' movement during the Restoration. Nor were they alone. As Gordon Marshall has demonstrated, of the 48 original sponsors of what eventually became the Act for Encouraging Foreign Trade in 1693, twelve were partners in the Newmills Cloth Manufactory. More striking still, seven of the ten directors based in England were also partners in Newmills.[29] Their presence indicates the extent to which the relative failure of the manufactories movement (of which Newmills is the best documented example) had driven the bourgeoisie to turn from a project of increasing productive efficiency in order to become more competitive with England, to one of capturing monopoly markets through which to guarantee demand for Scottish products, no matter how uncompetitive these were compared with those of England.

The English subscription book opened in London on 13 November 1695 and closed nine days later after pledges for the full £300,000 were received. An investigation into the company by the House of Lords began on the very same day, during which various interested parties – most notably the East India Company – produced evidence designed to demonstrate the harmful effects of the Company – the Scotch East India Company, as it was invariably, if misleadingly, described – on English trade. The most damaging clause of the Act, it was argued, was that which exempted commerce and capital from taxation for 21 years; the result of which, it was claimed, would be the transfer of English capital to Scotland and the smuggling of East Indian goods from there into England. The English Parliament responded to these arguments for reasons other than simply the protection of trade. If Scotland did succeed in raising its material level to one nearer that of England, it might act as a source of revenue for the King which would allow him independence from Parliamentary control. Consequently, neither the East India Company nor the English Parliament found it acceptable that William had chosen to support the foundation of Scottish trading monopoly. The accumulated 'evidence' was presented to William on 17 December, when the implications of what Tweedale had done by permitting the Act to pass finally became apparent. 'I have been ill-served in Scotland', William famously pronounced, and in truth he had little choice but to side with the East India Company: '[It] invested time, money and effort into courting the Lords and Commons because it believed that they and not the King now held the reigns of power.'[30] The East India Company was right.

The immediate effect of events in England was not the crippling of the Scottish enterprise but, under the threat of royal displeasure and, more importantly, impeachment by the House of Commons, the effective withdrawal of English subscriptions. From this point on, the Company was to be a purely Scottish affair. Its activities ceased to be regarded as the most promising means of improving the nation's economic situation and became regarded instead as the only source of national salvation. The level of capital to be raised locally was necessarily increased from £300,000 to £400,000, with a minimum subscription of £100. Given the poverty endemic in Scotland at this time it is astonishing to record that £50,400 was raised on the day on which the book opened on 26 February 1696, and that the target figure was in fact oversubscribed by the time it closed on 1 August. By that date 1,300 subscribers, both as individuals and, at the lower end of the social scale, in syndicates, had pledged their often hard-earned funds for a project that seemed to offer the chance of national renewal. As might have been expected, given their previous attempts to break out of established Scottish trade routes to north-western Europe, the Glasgow merchants were to the fore with contributions. The burgh went so far as to draw up its own separate subscription list which opened on 5 March 1695 and was fully subscribed by 22 April. In short, despite noble involvement, in so far as any episode in Scottish history can be said to embody bourgeois leadership at the head of popular aspirations and in a purely secular venture, then this is it. The Scottish nation they sought to lead was almost exclusively concentrated in the Lowlands, however, and in the urban Lowlands at that. In the Highlands, apart from the internal border town of Inverness, support came solely from Clan Campbell and those otherwise associated with the House of Argyll – the only one of the great Highland magnates to support both the Revolution Settlement and the expansion of 'commerce'. Few subscribers were identified from the central Highlands and the Western Isles.[31]

The excitement and sense of possibility generated by the venture found their way into the popular songs of the period: 'The mood of the country before the *debacle* is expressed in the somewhat McGonagalesque *Trade's Release: or Courage to the Scotch-Indian-Company. Being an Excellent New Ballad; To the Tune of, the Turks are all*

Confounded'. The theme of this offering, according to Thomas Crawford, was that, 'Scotland, under the leadership of her economic genius, Paterson (the founder of the Bank of England), will spread the bourgeois revolution to every corner of the globe':

> To Scotland's just and never-dying Fame,
> We'll in ASIA, AFRICA and AMERICA proclaim
> *Liberty! Liberty!* nay, to the shame
> of all that went before us;
> Wherever we plant, TRADE shall be free,
> In three years time, I plainly foresee,
> GOD BLESS THE SCOTTISH-COMPANY
> *Shall be the Indian-Chorus.*[32]

There was, however, a note of hysteria in these tunes of glory, which signalled how easily optimism could turn into its opposite. Shortly after the commissioners for the Scottish East India Company arrived in Hamburg to raise money during February 1697, Sir Paul Rycaut, the English Resident in Hamburg and the man responsible for their failure, reported a conversation between himself and William Paterson which captures the injured national feeling that English blocking manoeuvres had produced:

> In the first place Mr Paterson told me that he was always well affected to the English nation and looked on them as one people with theirs under one denomination of Britons, so that his great and chief desires were to unite the Scotch and English East India Companies, engaging to bring in £500,000 Stock to be employed joint with ours; but this proposition was rejected and whereas their people were so provoked by this contempt and scorn that they could stand upon their own legs and raise such a fund as was sufficient to carry on this great design, to which their people had freely and unanimously contributed.[33]

Yet the tone of desperation captured here was not simply due to frustration at English manoeuvring, but at the internal crisis which had erupted in Scotland while the plans for the Company were still being laid.

'Death in the Face of the Poor'

The capitalist system has always been characterised by the cycle of boom and slump; recurrent patterns quite separate from the broader waves of expansion and contraction within which they occur. Feudalism too had its own regular tendencies to short-term depression, but the chief characteristics of these were not merely overproduction, unemployment and unused capacity, but a more directly catastrophic one for the direct producers: a subsistence crisis.

A downturn in global weather conditions had significantly increased the incidence of harvest failure throughout the early 1690s, and by 1694 this had already led to famine in France and Sweden. In August 1695, the Scottish harvest failed for the first time since 1674 and, by December, it was obvious that the country was on the verge of a famine. It lasted, with peaks in 1696 and 1699, until normal harvests resumed in 1700. So great was the extent of the disaster that the government was sufficiently shaken from its mercantilist dogma to allow duty-free food imports to enter the country on two occasions (June 1696 and January 1697). Indeed, during the first two years grain was actually shipped from the Highlands to the Lowlands, although the Western Isles were not spared indefinitely. While visiting Lewis in the second half of the 1690s, Martin Martin noted of the inhabitants of Melbost, in the parish of Ey, that 'the late years of scarcity brought them very low, and many of the poor people have died by famine'.[34] If the worst effects of the famine in the Highlands were mitigated by the greater assistance shown by chiefs to clan members, feuding and raiding continued and indeed saw a 'massive' increase as the clans looked to robbery as a way of maintaining revenues unobtainable from tenants who were unable to pay their rent.[35]

It was nevertheless the Lowland upland areas like the Borders and the inland north-east that suffered the most complete crop failure. The north-east was the area hardest hit. It is also the one about which we have the most information. On the west coast there was, at best, access to imported food from Ireland or, at worst, the possibility of fleeing temporarily to the Ulster plantation for relief. In the north-east these options did not exist. Worse, the pre-existing crisis of Scottish exports exacerbated the problem. The majority of landless labourers and subtenants in the rural areas relied on the small-scale manufacture of plaid and stockings to supplement their meagre income from the land; between 1695 and 1700 the level of cloth exported had fallen by perhaps 50 per cent. Tradesmen were therefore doubly squeezed: the collapse of exports meant that their incomes fell, the harvest failure meant that they had to spend more of what remained on imports. Between 1691 and 1695 the average number of foreign grain and salt shipments to Aberdeen was less than two a year. By 1698–99 they had risen to 31. By 1700 the population may have fallen from 124,000 to 98,000, or by nearly 21 per cent, a loss which had not been made up even by 1755.[36]

We may never know the full extent of population loss across the country as a whole, since not every area had comparably accurate statistics. The overall figure cannot, however, have been less than 5 per cent and may have been as high as 15 per cent; that is to say between 50,000 and 150,000 people. These are staggering losses, but the bare recitation of statistics cannot convey what a disaster of these proportions meant to the people suffering it. There are, however, a number of all too graphic contemporary accounts which do precisely this. Looking back from the relative security of the 1720s, Patrick Walker, biographer to the Cameronian ministers, testified to conditions in the south-west:

> I have seen, when Meal was all sold in the Markets, Women clapping their Hands, and tearing the Clothes off their Heads, crying, 'How shall we go home and see our children die in Hunger? They have got no Meat these two Days and we have nothing to give them.[37]

The comments of Sir Robert Sibbald, written while the famine was still raging in 1699, present an even bleaker picture:

> Everyone may see Death in the Face of the Poor that abound everywhere; the Thinness of their Visage, their Ghostly Looks, their Feebleness; their Agues and their Fluxes threaten them with sudden Death, if Care be not taken of them. And it is not only common Wandering Beggars that are this Case, but many House-Keepers, who lived well by their Labour and their Industry are now by Want, forced to abandon their dwellings, and they and their little Ones must Beg ...[38]

These observers drew different lessons from the catastrophe. Walker condemned those farmers whose lack of Christian charity allowed them to profit from the shortages by raising their prices – 'Persons who dwelt in low-lying fertile Places, who laid themselves out to raise Markets when at such a Height, and had little sympathy with the Poor' – and recounts with glee turning one such Philistine away from his door after his crops also failed.[39] Sibbald was more concerned that the attitude held by Walker did not manifest itself in collective action, for, 'where there are many Poor, the Rich cannot be secure in the Possession of what they have'.[40] The rich were, however, to remain in possession of what they had for some time yet. It is a regrettable fact, as often observed in famines during our own time as in seventeenth century Scotland, that prolonged undernourishment leads more often to apathy and resignation than to the will to seize the means of survival from those to whom the market price is more important than human life.

The normal source of institutional relief in such situations, the kirk, had still not fully recovered from the internal divisions attendant on the Revolution of 1688. Such help as it could provide depended first on whether any parish organisation existed, given that one effect of the purges was to leave many parishes vacant. Even if the kirk session was organised for distribution of relief, the funds to do so would have to come from the contributions of parishioners who might themselves be in need of help. Finally, the attitude of the elders had to be taken into account, and this was by no means always inclined to act. It would be wrong, however, not to mention the one recommendation which the General Assembly made repeatedly during the famine. In order to placate their God (whose judgement upon them this clearly was) the Scottish people should undertake a traditional method of penance, which had apparently proved its efficacy in ages past: a fast.[41]

In addition to death from hunger and disease went the displacement of a population in search of food. By 1698 Andrew Fletcher could write:

> There are at this day in Scotland (besides a great many poor families very poorly provided for by the church-boxes, with others, who by living upon bad food fall into various diseases) two hundred thousand people begging from door to door.

These figures are almost certainly wrong (and were subsequently cited too uncritically by Marx in *Capital*), since there was no reliable way of gathering statistics at the time, and Fletcher was using them to make a particular case, as we shall shortly see. Nevertheless, the fact that he considered them even remotely plausible gives some idea of how desperate matters appeared to an intelligent observer.[42] Yet despite the extent of the crisis, two arguments are often put to minimise the significance of the famine. These are summarised by the English historian, Keith Wrightson, as part of his case against pessimistic readings of early modern Scottish history: 'The famine of the 1690s was both an exceptional misfortune and the last such national disaster in Scottish history.'[43]

The first argument, for 'exceptional misfortune', rests on the assertion that the famine resulted from climatic changes whose effects could not have been anticipated beforehand or countered once they had begun, as demonstrated by the comparable – and in some cases considerably greater – levels of mortality elsewhere in Europe. At one level this is correct, but only in the same way that 'natural causes' can be invoked to explain more recent famines in sub-Saharan Africa. It would be truer to say that these natural events, rather than causing their respective crises, triggered them by exposing the underlying weakness of existing socio-economic relationships.[44] In the case of Scotland these relationships were the still dominant forms of feudal tenure which had prevented the com-mercialisation and increased productivity of agriculture that might have prevented the actual level of devastation. In some areas the collection of rent from tenants who had barely enough on which to survive went on throughout the famine. This was not a new experience. In Orkney, for example, the unremitting demand for compliance with the terms of the lease, even in conditions of subsistence crisis, had heightened the impact of harvest failure throughout the century. In 1631, during a famine comparable with that of the 1690s, the tacksmen extracted 'a hundred lasts of malt and two hundred and fifty lasts of bere' from the tenants for export as part of their rent. In 1696, when the harvest is reported to have fallen to less than 5 per cent of the normal crop, two of the most rapacious tacksmen, Sir Robert Elphinstone and Sir Alexander Brand, continued to insist that the tenants deliver up what little produce they had. Indeed, so ferocious were the exactions demanded by the latter that the famine years were called not – as they were elsewhere in Scotland – 'King William's Ill Years', but 'Brand's Years'.[45] It is worth considering that while some countries did indeed suffer even greater loss of life than Scotland (Finland lost perhaps as many as a third of its population), two others suffered a sharp increase in food costs, but no actual starvation. It is perhaps unnecessary to add at this stage in the argument that they were the two that had broken through to commercial agriculture: England and the United Provinces.[46]

The second argument is fast becoming the orthodox viewpoint on the subject. 'No one doubts that there was a desperate famine in the 1690s', writes Eric Richards, 'but now its significance rests on the fact that it was the last such famine in Scottish history.'[47] Scotland certainly suffered no further famines, but this in itself proves nothing, and certainly not what is implied, namely that agriculture had already begun to be transformed at this point and that the catastrophe of the 1690s was a regrettable but unrepeatable throwback to an earlier time. Theoretical discussion about the urgent need for improvement was stimulated by the famine – in the works of Lord Belhaven, Sir Robert Sibbald, Andrew Fletcher, and James Donaldson. The assumption with which all of these writers began, however, was precisely that Scottish agriculture was constricted by current forms of tenure and agricultural practice, which hardly suggests that these problems were nearing an end. In a postscript to his Improving work, *Husbandry Anatomized* (1697) Donaldson observed that 'I am not fully understood by any, nor the Project received with that Applause I humbly conceive it deserveth'. As he himself recognised, however, this was not due to a lack of intelligence on the part of his readership, but to the social relationships which held them in thrall:

> I know that Landlords are generally too severe upon their Tenants, and if they see them in a thriving Condition, they either heighten their Rent or oblige them to remove, so that Farmers are altogether discouraged to make any Improvements whatever.[48]

The writings of these reformers had little impact at the time since the famine had removed for most tenants the material possibility of doing anything to improve their condition, at least in the short term. Their views would only become a material force in a changed social context which none of these writers would live to see. And the one proposal that any of these writers offered as an immediate solution to the crisis was profoundly contradictory in its social implications. This was a proposal by Fletcher to extend the scope of legal servitude from the colliers and salters to all members of the non-property-owning classes. Attempts had already been made in the previous decade to extend servitude to fishermen in the north-east, but these had been rejected by the lords of the Privy Council 'as tending to introduce slavery; contrary to the principles of the Christian religion and the mildness of our government'. It is difficult not to be cynical when discussing the motives of the Scottish nobility in any context, but in this case, their sensibilities may have been awakened by the fact that it is considerably more difficult to police men whose means of production allow them to escape to sea on a regular basis than it is those who are confined to a mining village. At any rate the Principles of the Christian Religion did not extend to relieving those already enserfed. Fletcher, however, wanted to go much further.

His starting point was the same legislation from the Scottish reign of James VI that formed the basis of the Acts of 1606 and 1641: in this case the Acts of 1579 and 1597, which allowed landowners to seize the children of beggars and press them into service for life – theoretically at least. According to Fletcher these Acts ('either from some mistake about Christian or civil liberty') did not go far enough, foolishly failing to make provision for the continuing servitude of the next generation, for example. In the circumstances of the 1690s, when the numbers of beggars had risen so dramatically, a radical and systemic extension of the legal framework was required:

> Now what I would propose upon the whole matter is, that for some present remedy of so great a mischief, every man of a certain estate in this nation should be obliged to take a proportional number of these vagabonds, and either employ them in hedging and ditching his grounds, or any other sort of work in town or country; or if they happen to be children and young, that he should educate them in the knowledge of some mechanical art, so that every man of estate might have a little manufacture at home which might maintain those servants, and bring great profit to the master.[49]

One difficulty he foresaw was that hordes of vagabonds, failing to appreciate the rationality of his suggestion that they be sent to serve as Venetian galley slaves, might flee to the Highlands. Fletcher was nothing if not a systematic thinker. If his plan was to have any chance of success, the Highlands must be prevented from playing this role. It is significant that in his Modest Proposal for dealing with the economic crisis of the 1690s Fletcher also argued that the Highland problem would have to be tackled at some stage: 'And it were to be wished that the government would think it fit to transplant that handful of people and their masters (who have always disturbed our peace) into the low-country, and people the Highlands from hence, rather than they should continue to be a perpetual mischief to us.'[50]

These passages from the *Second Discourse* have tended to cause some embarrassment among their author's present-day acolytes. Paul Scott, for example, oscillates between seeing these proposals as anticipating the health and education provisions of the modern welfare state and as an exercise in Swiftian satire.[51] An earlier commentator wrote rather more realistically of 'the sworn friend of liberty': 'That Fletcher wrote this pamphlet need cause no surprise, for both colliers and salters wrought his estate in East Lothian. The astounding thing is that the enlightened portion of the nation did not condemn so retrograde a proposal.'[52] But this is both too cynical with regard to Fletcher and too naive with regard to 'the enlightened portion of the nation'. The reason that his proposal fell on deaf ears was not revulsion at the extremity of his solution, but because it did not stop at enserfment. Linked to these measures against the poorest were others designed to break the tyranny of the landlord that he elsewhere so ably condemned. The two most important of these were a ban on the charging of interest on money loans and the enforced sale of all land beyond that which a landowner could farm with his own servants (i.e. without sub-letting).[53] There was more, but these proposals alone were probably enough to persuade his contemporaries that Fletcher was principled, but mad.

His aim seems to have been a society that combined the independent peasant proprietors of the Swiss cantons with the aristocratic republicanism of the Venetian city-state – or at least idealised versions of these models. His difficulty was that he had no social forces with which to accomplish it. Landlords greater than himself would scarcely abandon the income they accrued from interest and rent in pursuit of an abstract model of civic virtue, and the classes below him were unlikely to be won to a banner – even supposing he had been prepared to raise it – which promised them permanent servitude as a penalty for slipping further down the social order. In short, Fletcher, the most brilliant representative of the lairds who formed the lowest rung of the ruling class, was propounding a classic petty-bourgeois utopia. John Pocock has written of Fletcher that:

It would be wrong to suppose that Fletcher naively desired to restore an agrarian world of self-sufficient farming warriors; he wrote at length about the undeniably urgent problems of introducing some degree of commercial prosperity in the desperate society of Scotland; but his history of liberty, his 'discourse of government in its relation to militias', reveals to us a condition of thought about 1700 in which a bourgeois ideology, a civic morality for market man, was ardently desired but apparently not to be found.[54]

Hence his attempt to offer military training as a means of inculcating civil virtue in the absence of economic mechanisms. By the time his work appeared in print, however, the crisis which had provoked it was nearly over, but the same contradictions were to resurface again in a situation – the debate over the Union – where his contribution was to be of considerably more importance to the course of events.[55]

To conclude our discussion of this episode, we can note that the main economic effect of the famine was to further retard development by forcing tenants to devote whatever surplus they produced towards paying off rent arrears accumulated during the 1690s. We referred earlier to the situation in Orkney during the famine. In 1707, 220 rigs of earldom land in Sheatown, Deerness, were still uncultivated after the departure of their tenants ten years before. As late as 1713, half the bishopric land in Walls was still untenanted:

> Even a hundred years later 'miserable skeletons' of rigs abandoned at this time were still visible. The University of Aberdeen which held the tack of the bishopric from 1699 to 1704 had to resort to the use of troops to extract payment from James Moodie of Melsetter, and he was one of the sixty leading landowners 'put to the horn' for debts still owing on expiry of the university's tack.[56]

Nor were such occurrences limited to far-off Orkney. On the estates of the Earl of Panmure, between Dundee and Arbroath:

> Arrears began to build up rapidly after the first sharp rise in prices following the harvest of 1696, but although prices fell after 1701, arrears remained at far higher levels than during most of the second half of the seventeenth century until the data for most baronies terminate in 1714. ... As late as 1717 the barony account list appears specifically for 'crop 1699 and before' and sums of money described as old rests were listed separately through the 1720s and 1730s, gradually diminishing, in all probability, as tenants died off rather than as debts were repaid.[57]

As Thomas Devine has noted: 'A disaster of that magnitude must have drained tenant capital and reinforced conservative instincts.' Later harvest failures, in the quite different circumstances of the 1780s and 1790s, still had the effect of retarding rural investment: 'One can only speculate on the more destructive consequences of the catastrophe of the 1690s on a much poorer farming class.'[58]

As early as 1693 one Presbyterian minister had warned of the dangers of 'Seven Ill Years' befalling Scotland, on the model of those visited by God on Egypt, as a punishment for its failings. The Jacobites later took this up, after their emergence from hibernation, as a description of the years between 1693 and 1700. In fact, as we have seen, the famine only lasted for four years, but taken in conjunction with concurrent events the case had a certain plausibility, for famine was not the only crisis facing the Scottish economy. The Anglo-French struggle had temporarily come to an end with the Treaty of Ryswick in 1697, but this had no benefit for Scotland. Apart from the immediate problem caused by now unemployed officers and men returning to a country which could not feed its existing population, the expected upturn in trade did not transpire. Many of the alternative trading patterns which had been set up as a result of the War survived it. Between 1697 and 1702 France banned the import of Scottish wool and fish, and imposed heavy duties on coal, as did the Spanish Netherlands. Most seriously of all, however, was the decline in trade with England, which had become increasingly significant during the seventeenth century and, unlike trade with the European mainland, was not liable to disruption by the French. Yet between 1698 and 1706, the value of Scottish exports fell by 50 per cent, from an average yearly figure of £114,000 sterling in 1698–1700 to £54,000 in 1704–06.[59] In these circumstances it is little wonder that 'God save the Scottish Company' became 'the Indian Chorus'.

The Debacle of Scottish Colonialism

Largely under Paterson's influence, the nature of the enterprise had meantime shifted from being a trading endeavour to something quite different: the launching of a colony at Darien on the Panamanian Isthmus. The precedents in Scottish history for such a project were not propitious. Prior to 1695, Scottish colonies outwith the British Isles had all been situated in North America. But from the first colony in Newfoundland during 1617 to the Covenanting attempt at Stuart's Town in South Carolina 1684–86, all were intermittently maintained, poorly resourced and small-scale compared to the English ventures in the same continent. Paterson's ambitions outran these previous efforts. As he famously expressed it, in his retrospective justification of the Darien expedition:

> The time and expense of navigation to China, Japan, the Spice Islands, and the far greatest part of the East Indies will be lessened more than half, and the consumption of European commodities will soon be more than doubled. Trade will increase trade, and money will beget money, and the trading world shall need no more to want work for their hands but will rather want hands for their work. Thus, this door of the seas and key of the universe, with anything of a sort of reasonable management, will of course enable the proprietors to give laws to both oceans and to become arbitrators of the commercial world, without

being liable to the fatigues, expenses and dangers, or contracting the guilt and blood of Alexander and Caesar.[60]

The story of the three successive attempts to establish a colony at Darien belongs more properly to an account of what Angus Calder calls the 'English-speaking Empire' (which would become the British Empire after 1707).[61] Our concern is more with the impact of their failure in Scotland itself. Nevertheless a brief account of their fate is relevant here.

High hopes accompanied the five ships and 1,200 people who left the Port of Leith on 18 July 1698. Those who survived the journey landed at Darien on 31 October and began to construct a fort called Saint Andrew, and, a short swamp away from it, a fermtoun called New Edinburgh. They faced three sets of obstacles.

The first was their own lack of preparation. They laboured to construct their communities in totally unaccustomed heat, prey to diseases, including malaria, to which they had no immunity, and at the mercy of torrential rains which on at least one occasion destroyed what they had built. Supplies failed to appear from famine-ridden Scotland, and they had insufficient money to buy more provisions. In any case, from whom would they have bought them? The Company had failed to appoint factors in New York or the Caribbean who could have arranged for provisions to be sent.

The second obstacle was the hostility of the Spanish state. By the late seventeenth century the Spanish Empire was in decline. It only held a weak grip on some of its territories and was often reduced to claiming sovereignty without being able to enforce it. Darien was one of the areas that had been claimed, but not settled, not least because of resistance from the native inhabitants. 'A dozen leagues from the new settlement slaves under Spanish masters were digging for gold, and on the island within five miles a small Spanish garrison had been massacred by the Indians only two months before the Scots arrived.'[62] The Spanish had given way to intruders into their territory only where they could do little to stop it – the English, French, Dutch and Portuguese had settled respectively in Mexico, San Domingo, Guiana and Brazil. Nor was their authority threatened only by other states. Spanish forces had also been beaten in the same area by Henry Morgan's buccaneers who sacked Panama with 1,200 men, took Portobello with 300 and defeated the Spaniards with canoes against men-of-war at Santa Maria. Darien was different. The fact that the Spanish had experienced difficulty in subduing the natives did not mean they would allow any other power to occupy the region in their stead. Decline should not be mistaken for outright collapse – an error frequently made by telescoping the 15 years between the launch of the Darien expedition in 1698 and 1713, when the Habsburg dynasty fell and 'the Spains' lost all their European territories outwith the Iberian Peninsula. A successful Scottish colony at Darien would have threatened the Spanish Empire in three ways. First, by undermining the already fragile prestige of the monarchy. Second, by intruding into Spanish strategic interests in the Pacific, potentially giving strategic access north to Mexico, south to Peru, east to Cuba and perhaps even to the Philippines. Third, by carrying the virus of Protestantism into nominally Catholic territory – a major issue given that it was only 50 years since Spain had finally been forced to abandon all claims to the United Provinces after the revolt of another people united by Calvinist ideology.[63] The Spanish were also acutely aware that their own empire had begun with the landing of Cortes and a small expeditionary force – one smaller than that of the Scots. They did not want the experience to be repeated with the Scots playing the role of the Spanish and the Spanish that of the Aztecs:

> A territory so important from its position, and so closely adjacent to the chief seat of their power, was not to be abandoned without a struggle; and they could not stand in such awe of a nation whose naval force was represented by four foreign-built ships, whose ordinary revenue was some £110,000 a year, and the disavowal of whose enterprise by the English Government exposed its colonists to be treated as little better than buccaneers.[64]

The political difficulties facing the colonists were not, however, only the result of intruding into territory claimed, however ineffectively, by Spain.

The third obstacle was the malign neglect and, ultimately, conscious obstruction by the English state. Despite the failure of their own Company to give them proper support, they might at least have expected to receive support and protection from the existing English colonies in the Caribbean. According to the very Act that founded the Company, England would have to protect the Scottish fleet from foreign interference. Even in their negotiations with the Spanish after armed struggle had broken out, the colonists continued to play on the supposed fact of Royal support:

> We do therefore, by these, signify to you that we are the subjects of the King of Great Britain, by virtue of whose power and authority granted to us, with advice and consent of his Parliament of Scotland, we have settled here, for the encouraging, advancing and carrying on of trade and commerce.[65]

There was only one problem in this respect: England was allied to Spain. The Scots had blundered into the complex web of international alliances which characterised Europe as it awaited the death of Charles II of Spain and the impending struggle over the Spanish succession between France, Bavaria and Austria. William was not prepared to allow their ambitions to upset the power balance against Louis and, in particular, to jeopardise his manoeuvring over the Spanish succession, which he was anxious to prevent Louis obtaining at any cost – thus, no help was forthcoming from English colonies elsewhere in the Americas. An instruction, drawn up in 1695, but significantly only issued on 2 January 1699, after the first expedition had landed, told the Governors of nearby English Plantations not to assist the Scottish Company under any circumstances. Discovery of this Proclamation was the final blow to the first colony. By 22 June it had been abandoned except for six remaining settlers who were two ill to make the return voyage. Less than a year had elapsed from setting sail to collapse, with a quarter dead and only one ship – appropriately enough, the *Caledonia* – able to make the return journey. Meanwhile a second expedition, consisting of 300 colonists and two ships, set sail on 12 May 1699. A third expedition, of 1,300 colonists and four ships, followed on 24 September, only days after confirmation arrived that the first colony had collapsed. The second expedition arrived at Caledonia Bay at the end of November, to find the settlement of New Edinburgh and Fort Saint Andrew reclaimed by the jungle.

Previously, reports received second-hand from continental Europe were not believed. During the summer of 1699 Robert Wodrow wrote to a friend in the United Provinces whom he believed to be in receipt of 'bad information' about the colony, claiming that:

> ... we have an abundance of accounts that they [i.e. the colonists] are well supplied in provisions from the English plantations, who have encouragement to it by the good returns they get from their efforts from Caledonia, and this sways more with them than prohibitions on the other hand, so that, your fears of their want of provisions are not well grounded. As to the Spaniards, truly here we are not so much afraid of them, if Monsieur has not his hand in the plot.[66]

The assumption that the main threat to the colony would come from the French ('Monsieur'), rather than the Spanish was not universally shared. By the launch of the second expedition some supporters of the venture had recognised the centrality of the Spanish question to the survival of the colony and addressed themselves to it. One anonymous pamphleteer, who may have been Fletcher, argued:

> Then as to the hazard of a Rupture with Spain, we reply, that the Spaniards are in no condition to break with England, when they are not able to maintain themselves against the Insults of the French by Sea and Land: and the only way to secure them in the British interest is to have a powerful Colony on Darien which lying in the very centre of their American Dominions, and within reach of their Silver and Gold

Mines, will be an effective Curb upon them, and not only prevent their own Hostilities, but their joining at any time with our Enemies; or if they do, being Masters of the Money, we shall speedily cut the sinews of their war.[67]

The argument that, on the one hand the Spanish were in no position to break with England, but on the other a colony was required to keep them in line, was never likely to prove very convincing, nor did it prove to be. What these machinations revealed was the ultimate inadequacy of the Regal Union, and the weakness of the personal monarchy. William was supposed to give equal weight to the needs of each kingdom, but in a situation where these interests were in conflict, what determined his attitude?

As the extent of the disaster was becoming apparent, Melville wrote to Carstares of the way in which the opposition in the Scottish Parliament were using William's evasive reasons for refusing to support the Darien scheme – that they 'do not concern Scotland' – to make propaganda against the Court:

> If they do not concern Scotland, then, say they, this gives ground for an unanswerable argument, that the crowns of England and Scotland are incompatible, seeing it is not to be supposed that, where the interests of England and Scotland do irreconcilably interfere, the king must act in the favours of England.[68]

Although their own reasons for making these arguments were less than public spirited, the opposition was right. For William, the maintenance of the anti-French alliance took first place, the wishes of the more powerful of his English subjects second and those of his Scottish subjects – however powerful – a very poor third.

Final abandonment of the project came with submission to the Spanish on 30 March 1700. The balance sheet reveals the loss of 2,000 people – although this was a drop in the ocean compared to the thousands dying of starvation at home – and something between a fifth and a half of the national capital – money that was now unavailable for any more achievable end. A letter by Wodrow, written after all illusions had finally been dispelled, conveys the public mood:

> ... we are all in a fearful ferment, which I pray God may not cast us in a confusion and a field of blood. Our colony is broke and that (as it seems) for ever; our money, and which is worse, our credit and reputation lost, and after all we know [not] where or how to help ourselves. All the blame is laid upon the King ...[69]

Which of the obstacles discussed above contributed most to this disaster? The Spanish could be expected to oppose any intrusion by another power, but they were by no means destined to be successful – their forces were beaten at Tubuganti by the second expedition and native American allies as late as 15 February 1700. Spanish hostility was therefore unwelcome, but not necessarily decisive. Neither, however, was the 'disavowal of the enterprise by the English Government' – although the fact that it was believed to be by the Scots was, of course, to be highly significant in the years ahead. The action of the British monarchy which was most offensive to the Scots was not enforcing the withdrawal of English subscriptions – since that might be seen as inadvertently freeing the project from the domination of London based economic interests – but the obstacles which were subsequently put in the way of obtaining finance elsewhere before the colony was launched, and of material assistance afterwards. Leaving aside the inherent absurdity of complaining that a project which was supposed to establish Scotland as a trading nation independent of England failed from the lack of English help, such a perspective ignores the fact that English hostility had not stopped the Glaswegian merchant class from earlier establishing trading links elsewhere in America, when they were faced with not only lack of support but illegality.

In fact, the principal reason for the failure of the colony was neither military intervention by the Spanish Empire nor diplomatic opposition by the British Crown. These certainly compounded the difficulties experienced by the colonists, but both could have been coped with, had either the Scottish state or civil society been resilient enough to sustain the venture. They were not. Recall that one of Paterson's conditions for success was 'anything of a sort of reasonable management'. Fletcher (who himself subscribed £1,000) commented in similar terms on 'that affair that presses most, and on which the nation is so universally concerned', noting that:

> ... if it be considered, that provisions, or the smallest things necessary, falling short but by a few days, have often been the ruin of the greatest undertakings, and chiefly of those of this kind; there cannot be any more urgent affair than that of providing incessantly a supply for the necessities of so many men as are on board those ships, who may be brought under extraordinary sufferings by a delay.[70]

Yet consideration of some of their cargo indicates that planning and provisioning had not been as complete as Fletcher had urged. Among the cargo were 4,000 periwigs (to trade with the native Americans) and 1,500 copies of the King James Bible. After setting sail it was discovered that only six months stock of provisions had been laid in instead of the expected nine, and as the bread was mouldy it would not in fact be enough to keep the colonists for three months. We have already seen the inadequacies of the provisions sent with the first expedition. Matters did not improve significantly in subsequent voyages. As late as the third expedition, the minister Alexander Shields could write:

> Our chest of medicines ignorantly or knavishly filled and ignorantly dispensed by our surgeons, our water in wooden bound casks very unsavoury and unclean, our beef, much of it rotten. ... Many things sent out were useless, and many things needful wanting. It is a wonder of mercy so many of us escaped.[71]

Contrast this debacle with the one successful colonisation in Scottish history, that of Ireland. 'Ulster was almost a Scottish colony in the seventeenth century,' writes Tom Gallagher.[72] Yet the colony, as Michael Maxwell notes, 'was not begun as a result of private enterprise, but was a project of the state'. It was in fact initiated by the composite monarchy that emerged from the Union of the Crowns in 1603 for two purposes. The first was to remove disruptive elements from Scottish territory, committed Presbyterians who refused to accept compromise with Episcopalianism and displaced Border reivers squeezed out by the combined pressure of the Anglo-Scottish repression. The second was to use the colonists as agents of regal power over the native inhabitants. In that sense we can speak of a 'British' Empire taking shape in Ireland over a hundred years before 'Britain' itself came into existence. The main difference, as Maxwell makes clear, was that: 'When Scottish settlement began in Ulster it was supported by English power.'[73] The Scottish settlement in Darien was not.[74]

As Christopher Storrs points out:

> It was almost inconceivable that the Scots colony could survive without the support framework (diplomatic, financial, military and naval) – one experienced in supplying the sinews of war both locally, in the Americas, and over vast distances, across the Atlantic – that their Spanish opponents clearly did enjoy.[75]

This had of course been recognised in the original Act, with its clauses allowing the Company the right to militarily defend itself and invoking Crown protection in the last resort. Given that the Crown had no intention of protecting the Company, this actually meant that the state had thrown the sole responsibility for organising, financing and defending this crucial project onto a civil society that was equally incapable of accomplishing the task. Shortly before surrendering to the Spanish, the besieged colonists attempted to negotiate. Hidden among the ensuing bluster is a passage which, in its quiet way, is one of the most tragic in Scottish history:

We have sent herewith the Act of Parliament, letters patent under the great seal of the Kingdom of Scotland, one in English, and another in Latin, whereby you may have a clear and full view of the just ground of our settlement, and great powers and privileges granted to us.[76]

There is something desperately moving in the picture of these bedraggled colonists, disease-ridden, dying, exhausted, outnumbered and abandoned, waving aloft these pathetic bits of paper giving notice of their 'great powers and privileges', as if the words of the Scottish Parliament could substitute for the power that the Scottish state so evidently lacked. Was there any alternative to the eventual outcome? Bruce Lenman has suggested that a scaling down of ambitions might have resulted in modest, but real achievements: 'The only worthwhile objective for [Scotland] in the colonial field was other nations' colonists. Trade with these was feasible and could be so lucrative as to cover the marginal risk of its technical illegality.'[77] This was certainly feasible, but a parasitic existence dependent on other empires would not have allowed Scotland to break out of the circuit of backwardness in which it was situated. 'Especially since the nation has so great a concern in this enterprise,' wrote Fletcher of the first colonists, 'that I may well say all our hopes of ever being more than a poor and inconsiderable people are embarked with them.'[78] Paterson, Fletcher, Wodrow and everyone else who shared these hopes had asked, essentially, whether Scotland could become what we would today call an independent centre of capital accumulation. With the return of the colonists lucky enough to survive, their question was now answered.

The Balance Sheet of the 1690s

It is difficult to view the cumulative disasters surveyed in this chapter merely as minor obstacles on the road to the ultimate success story enjoyed by the Scottish bourgeoisie. Difficult, but not impossible. Michael Lynch writes:

> In reality, the barrage of economic and social disasters of the 'seven ill years' of the 1690's were no more than a blip in an economy which was in a slow, piecemeal but notably steady state of transition towards more coherent organisation and greater productivity.[79]

Willie Thompson makes the same point in Marxist terminology:

> The firm social entrenchment of the lowland bourgeoisie is made clear in the relative ease with which it survived the economic and political disasters of the following decade: a devastating famine and the massive commercial losses sustained in the abortive Darien colonisation scheme and the bankruptcy of the Bank of Scotland.

And the reward for enduring these trials? 'Finally [Scotland] negotiated an advantageous parliamentary and commercial Union with England in 1707 and progressed to the attainment in due course of a fully fledged capitalist economy and social order.'[80] Was the loss of between 50,000 and 150,000 people, and between a fifth and a half of the available national capital a 'blip'? The point made earlier in relation to agriculture is also applicable to the Scottish economy as a whole: the fact that Scotland did experience 'take-off' into self-sustaining growth relatively soon after these disasters is no evidence that such a development was inevitable, nor that similar disasters could not have struck again. In fact, the 1690s serve as a demonstration, not of the strength of the Scottish bourgeoisie, but of their weakness. The twin crises were not an accidental diversion from an otherwise unbroken upward progression, but the inevitable result of failing to break the existing mould of society.

Indeed, the overall effect was to reinforce conservatism at all levels, not least that of the state. Take, for example, the execution of Alexander Aitkenhead for blasphemy on 8 January 1697. This episode has often been taken as one of the last examples of Calvinist bigotry being put to noxious practical effect. In fact, it is more likely to have been a determined effort by the Privy Council to make an example of those rejecting conventional beliefs. Aitkenhead was summoned to appear before the Council on November 1696 and charged with blasphemy. Four witnesses were produced who swore that, among other things, he had referred to the New Testament as the History of the Impostor Christ, whom he compared unfavourably to Moses; Aitkenhead apparently regarded the latter as a better magician, actor and politician. The indictment also claimed that Aitkenhead expressed a preference for Mohammed over Christ and that he expected a majority to have accepted his views within a few centuries, leading to the 'extirpation' of Christianity. The savagery of the death sentence passed on Aitkenhead was a reflection of the laws under which he was condemned – not those of the Covenanting regimes, which had all been repealed at the Restoration, but the blasphemy law passed in 1661 under Charles II and re-enacted by the Revolution Parliament in 1695. The fear of social breakdown which, in different ways, had possessed the politicians of both Covenanting and Restoration regimes (unsurprising given the identity of their class locations), was once again manifest in the 1690s. The issue in 1696 was not, however, fear of revolutionary overthrow so much as social disintegration under the pressure of economic collapse. Aitkenhead was the second person to be tried for blasphemy towards the end of 1696, but the first, Archibald Pitcairne, was merely imprisoned and made to wear sackcloth, as the law prescribed for a first offence, before being released in February 1697. Although Pitcairne recanted and Aitkenhead did not, the implication is that the Privy Council wished to make an example.[81] It is suggestive that the Council was also responsible for launching the last major Scottish witch-hunt in Renfrewshire in the same year as Aitkenhead's death, against a steady rise in acquittals, or minor sentences on conviction, since the great witch-hunt of 1661–62. In this case, the penultimate outbreak in Scotland, seven out of twenty accused were executed.[82]

The effect of this decade of disaster was ultimately paradoxical. On the one hand it raised popular hostility to the supposed English source of national humiliation, and to those among the Scottish elite who appeared insufficiently supportive of the endeavour:

> Upon Thursday night last there fell out a very insolent and violent rabble in this city [i.e. Edinburgh]. The occasion was, some news come of the advantage the Scots got against the Spaniards in Darien, which did put the people in a very frolic humour. ... The rabble rose and made themselves masters of the Netherbow Port, fell a-breaking the windows where there were no illuminations, beat off and commanded the guard within the town who came to resist them. They broke down in great madness many windows, especially those of the houses of the President of the Council, the Lord Seafield, the Lord Carmichael, the Lord Treasurer Depute, the Lord Provost, and some others of the Magistrates; and in short all in the Fore street who did not please them by putting up illuminations.[83]

On the other hand, the ruling classes were made aware that, whatever solution was adopted, the existing situation could not continue. Patrick Hume, first Earl of Marchmont, and a supporter of the Court in the Scottish Parliament, wrote to Seafield in the dying months of the century: 'You may remember, Your Lordship was speaking a little to me about an Union of the two kingdoms; I have thought much upon it, and am of the opinion that the generations to come of Scotsmen will bless them and their prosperity who can have a good hand in it; and I could wish that you and I both, who (thanks to God) have hitherto been acceptable both to our King and country, may have some good hand in an affair that may be of so great advantage and honour to our King and to our country.'[84] Some months later, in a letter to an English correspondent, he wrote that he had taken sounding of 'the more intelligent and significant men' and was confident that 'if such a thing came to be treated in any way tolerable, it would find a ready concurrence of the far greater part of people of all ranks of this nation'.[85] What 'significant men' would find 'in any way tolerable' was shortly to be put to the test. 'Increasingly the ruling classes of Scotland were ready for drastic, nay revolutionary change', writes Bruce Lenman.[86] Was a union with England to be the source of that change?

From Hanoverian Succession to Incorporating Union (1700–1707)

Scotland entered the eighteenth century in a constitutional relationship to England that was no longer tenable, as the fate of the Darien expeditions had conclusively demonstrated. Yet there was no agreement within the Scottish ruling class over what should replace it. In the debate that followed, the key issue was initially not that of a union with England, but of who would succeed to the three Crowns of the British Isles and whether the same person should succeed to all three. The context was a series of deaths among the monarchies of Europe.

First, the Duke of Gloucester, last surviving son of William's sister-in-law Anne, died in July 1700. As Anne was designated to succeed William in the short term, but not expected to successfully conceive a further heir, the English Parliament passed an Act of Settlement on 10 June 1701, settling the further succession on her nearest Protestant relative, Princess Sophia, Dowager Empress of Hanover. Second, Charles II of Spain died on 1 November 1700, leaving as his successor Phillip, the second grandson of Louis XIV of France. As had been expected, neither Austria nor England recognised Phillip, thus making the long-awaited War of the Spanish Succession inevitable. Third, James VII and II died at Saint Germains on 16 September 1701 and Louis immediately proclaimed his 13-year-old son James King of England, Scotland, Ireland and (rather generously under the circumstances) France. Anne began to refer to young James as 'the Pretender' (i.e. pretender to the thrones of the British Isles), a designation which both he and his son Charles would bear to their graves. The continuation of support for Jacobitism by France ensured that the War of the Spanish Succession was also a resumption of the earlier War of the British and Irish Succession. Fourth, and finally,

William himself died on 8 March 1702 and was succeeded as planned by Anne.

This survey of royal mortality may seem beside the point, but in fact it takes us right to the heart of the problem faced by the Scottish ruling class. Following an Act of 1696, the Scottish Estates should have been summoned within 20 days of William's death, but they were not recalled until 9 June – 70 days late and quite obviously in order that the Lord Commissioner could declare war on France, as he did on 4 May, without the possibility of opposition. The proclamation by the Privy Council on 30 May 1702 was not the first time that the Scottish Parliament had been forced into a war against its will. Under the Commonwealth, Scotland had been compelled to participate in an English war against the United Provinces between 1652 and 1654. Under the Restoration, Scotland had been embroiled in two more wars against the Dutch, in 1665–57 and 1672–74 respectively. In all three cases enforced intervention had damaging effects on the Scottish economy, since the Dutch were Scotland's leading trading partners in northern Europe. The Revolution Parliament had endorsed Scottish involvement in the War of the British and Irish Succession in order to defend itself against French attempts to restore James; but as Darien had demonstrated, there was no guarantee that the views of the Scottish Parliament would always coincide with those of the Crown. William had refused to assist the expedition as part of his diplomatic offensive to prevent Phillip succeeding to the Spanish throne. Since Phillip had now done so in spite of these manoeuvres, the Scots could be forgiven for wondering to what purpose their ambitions had been sacrificed. The English state that had apparently done so much to injure Scottish economic interests had now engineered Scottish participation in yet another war whose impact on Scotland would be further disruption of established trading patterns. As a final indignity, the Parliament would now be asked to approve a succession which would leave the country permanently helpless in the face of such impositions in the future. Why were English politicians so anxious to see the Hanoverian Succession accepted in Scotland?

The War of the Spanish Succession, together with the War of the British and Irish Succession which it continued, was the latest instalment in the inter-systemic conflict between England, centre of the still insecure capitalist order (with some support from the declining United Provinces) and France, the dominant feudal absolutist power. As Anthony Ashley Cooper, Lord Shaftesbury, wrote to Jean Le Clerc in 1707:

> There is a mighty light which spreads itself over the world, especially in those two free nations of England and Holland, on which the affairs of Europe now turn and, if Heaven sends soon a peace suitable to the great successes we have had, it is impossible but that letters and knowledge must advance in greater proportion than ever before.[1]

If Louis XIV succeeded in pressing his claim to the Spanish Crown then, whatever the formal terms of the ensuing settlement, the territories of the Spanish monarchy would simply be absorbed by the French, with decisive consequences for future European development: 'Never, it seemed, had the nemesis of Universal Monarchy come so close to realisation.'[2] The English ruling class faced the prospect of its greatest rival presiding over a world empire which stretched from the manufactories of Flanders to the gold mines of the Americas, and which was positioned to seize the English colonies and so cut off one of their main sources of English ruling-class wealth. John Churchill, first Duke of Marlborough and Captain General of what were in effect the British armed forces, wrote to the Pensionary of Holland in December 1701, on the eve of the English general election, that 'we have here no talk but of elections; I hope to God they will be such as do their utmost power against France'.[3] Marlborough famously hated William of Orange, referring to him as 'Mr Caliban', but on one point the two were agreed: successful prosecution of war against France, temporarily suspended in 1697 at the close of the War of the British and Irish Succession, and shortly to be resumed in 1702 with the opening of the War of the Spanish Succession, was absolutely necessary for the security of the English state. This was the context in which the entire debate over Anglo-Scottish relations took place.

It was therefore a strategic necessity for the English ruling class to prevent a Stuart restoration in Scotland which would almost certainly see that country align itself with France. The solution, they believed, was to impose the Hanoverian Succession in Scotland. Early in 1702 Robert Pringle, Under-Secretary of State in the English Ministry, wrote to Marchmont, then acting as Scottish Chancellor, about the debate over Scotland in the House of Commons, noting that:

> ... the Earl of Nottingham made a discourse, as I am informed, to this purpose, that they could not reckon themselves secure in the settlement of the succession, so long as the same was not done in Scotland, for that were to leave a large gap for the Prince of Wales [i.e. James] to enter at.[4]

Sidney Godolphin, the Lord Treasurer, made the international implications of the succession issue explicit in a letter to John Ogilvie, first Earl of Seafield:

> At another time, what should be done of this kind [i.e. about the Succession] would perhaps concern Scotland alone. But we are now at so critical a conjuncture with respect to other nations, that all Europe must in some measure be affected by the good or ill ending of the Parliament of Scotland.[5]

The reasoning of the English ministers was perfectly comprehensible to at least some members of the Scottish ruling class. 'It is nothing strange,' wrote Marchmont to an English peer late in 1704,

> ... that the Parliament of England is earnestly desirous to have the successor to the crown of England named successor to the crown of Scotland, and to have the pretensions of the popish pretender extinguished here, as it is there, both for the security of her Majesty's life and person, and of our religion and liberties.

In the same letter he goes on to suggest that, however reasonable this concern might be, unless the English Parliament ceased interfering in Scottish affairs the succession was likely to be hindered.[6] Marchmont had good reason to complain, for it was this interference which triggered off the crisis between the two states.

The Lord Commissioner, James Douglas, second Duke of Queensberry, eventually summoned the Scottish Parliament on 9 June 1702. Almost immediately, his great rival and fellow magnate James Douglas, fourth Duke of Hamilton, led 57 of his followers out of the opening session, declaring that the assembly was illegal as a result of the delay in Parliament being called. Thus relieved of opposition, Queensberry was free to pass a series of Acts ratifying the succession of Queen Anne, securing the Protestant religion and Presbyterian church government, and to nominate commissioners for negotiating a union with England. Why had the question of a union arisen at this point?

William had raised the matter shortly before his death. This was the first time the proposal had seriously come from an English quarter and it was as a direct result of the Darien fiasco. William was determined to ensure that none of his successors would have to repeat the experience of explaining to allies why a country nominally under his rule had established a colony to which he was opposed. Significantly, however, support for a union at this time was confined to the Crown itself – since Anne was determined to advance the wishes of her late brother-in-law – and by the two leading figures among the Ministerial bureaucracy of the English state, Godolphin and Marlborough. The Whig and Tory parties naturally supported the Hanoverian Succession for Scotland, but neither displayed enthusiasm for a union of any sort. The Whigs did so because, given the notorious servility of the Scottish Commissioners, any merger of parliaments would likely see them form a permanent phalanx of support for the Ministry – whichever Ministry it happened to be. The Tories did so because they had no desire to form closer links with a nation whose Presbyterian beliefs were so alien to their High Church Anglicanism. As long as it seemed to offer the path of least resistance, both parties preferred Scotland to remain a separate state under English influence.

Commissioners were therefore appointed from both countries to discuss terms, but the character of their negotiations can be judged from the fact that the commissioners sat in separate rooms and passed their proposals to each other on pieces of paper. They met for the first time on 10 November 1702 and for the last on 3 February the following year (although the Scottish Commission was not formally dissolved until 4 October). The problem was not, as is sometimes said, only the general question of admission to English trade, but the specific one of the Company Trading to Africa and the Indies. The English commissioners insisted that the Company be wound up before talks could proceed; the Scots refused, for although the Company was still of little positive economic significance, it remained a symbol of their last great national endeavour.

Queensberry had however dissolved Parliament on 30 June, long before the negotiators had even met, as the opposition was threatening to resume their seats and question the validity of legislation passed during their secession. Everyone was aware that dissolution could only be a holding operation. The last general election had been in 1689 near the opening of the Glorious Revolution and the majority of the commissioners elected at that time now no longer represented current ruling-class opinion. This would not in itself have persuaded Queensberry or his masters in London to call a new election, but the Succession had to be carried and, of more immediate concern, supply was desperately required to keep the state machine functioning at even minimal level. A general election was therefore called for the autumn, in the hope that the recomposition of Parliament would be more amenable to the wishes of the Crown. It was in these circumstances that the property-owning classes went to the polls to elect the last parliament while Scotland remained a sovereign state.

Class and Party in the Last Scottish Parliament

On 6 May 1703 the first commissioners to be elected since 1689 assembled in Holyrood Palace in Edinburgh to begin the ceremony of 'Riding the Parliament' up the Royal Mile to Parliament House on the High Street. Since Parliament was the focus for much of what subsequently transpired, it is important that we understand the nature of this institution. If it had been a genuinely representative assembly, cut short by the Treaty of Union, then we might echo the words of Charles Terry: 'Pathetic in other aspects, the Union is tragic in this, that it for ever closed the career of Parliament at the moment when, after long preparation, it was ready and able to play a fitting part in the nation's history.'[7] Yet even on the highly restricted definition of democracy prevalent at the time it is difficult to share this view.

The Parliamentary Roll consisted, at its fullest, of 67 burgess commissioners representing the Royal Burghs, 90 baron commissioners representing the shire or country constituencies and 67 peers representing themselves – although the only limit to the number of peers attending was the number in existence, and their preparedness to swear the Oath of Allegiance which would allow them to take their seat. How did particular individuals come to occupy their positions? To answer this question we cannot do better than to quote the words of Paul Scott, a writer who believes that the dissolution of the Scottish Parliament was a great loss to the Scottish nation:

> The lords were hereditary; the representatives of the burghs were appointed by self-perpetuating oligarchies; those of the shires, the lairds, were elected, but only by the other lairds [i.e. the lairds were also a self-perpetuating oligarchy – ND]. Only an infinitely small proportion of the population had a vote or any say in the matter. Parliament represented Scottish opinion only in a very general or theoretical sense.[8]

In England, over 4 in every 100 men could vote in Parliamentary elections.[9] In Scotland, the comparable figure was 1 in every 1,000.[10] The differences were more than simply quantitative. As Edith Thomson noted, in contrast with the English Parliament, which was divided into elected and unelected chambers, with the former chosen by property qualifications, the Scottish Parliament remained 'essentially a feudal Assembly: only those who held land directly of the king, whether as nobles, barons or royal burghs, were represented there. Technically and legally throughout the whole of its existence it was a "Baron Court".'[11] The commissioners themselves were quite aware of the social relations that brought them to their seats, although they were less eager to have it openly discussed. During the debate over Darien, Viscount Stair opined that any Act passed by the Parliament 'was but a Decreet of the Baron Court'. Asked to explain himself he said 'that none sat in Parliament but Barons, and the representation was feudal'. David Hume, whose account this is, then notes that: 'He was excused, but desired not to use the expression again.'[12] This does not of course indicate any reluctance to acknowledge the feudal basis of their representation, but an objection to being described as a mere 'baron court'.

The unicameral nature of the Scottish Parliament simultaneously prevented the Crown using divide-and-rule tactics to play one House off against the other as it did in England and facilitated continued magnate domination of the remaining Estates. 'It is interesting to speculate what would have happened had the shires and boroughs, in the years succeeding the Revolution, ploughed a common furrow,' writes Thomson, 'and refused to be cozened by the nobility. But such speculation is really futile since political education was as yet too much in its infancy for the Commons to be able to draw up an independent programme.'[13] The problem was not, however, caused by an absence of political knowledge or experience. Of course, the Parliament did not consist solely of feudal superiors and their nominees, but even the smaller lairds and burgesses who embodied both more advanced social relations and freedom from the influence of the great nobles – a rare combination – were present by virtue of the existing feudal means of representation which were maintained until the Treaty of Union brought the entire body to an end.

The reason for the character of the Scottish Parliament was not lost on the great thinkers of the Scottish Enlightenment, although it subsequently has been on some modern historians. As John Dalrymple wrote:

> The constitution of Scotland, till incorporated with that of England was in fact a mixture of monarchy and oligarchy: the nation consisted of a commonality without the privilege of choosing their own representatives; of a gentry entitled indeed to represent by election, but unable to serve the nation; and of a nobility, who oppressed the one, and despised both.

Dalrymple did not, however restrict himself to this brutally accurate description, but also proposed a commendably materialist explanation for it:

> The similar constitutions of parliament in England and Scotland, by the introduction of the commons and of the new nobility, ought to have had, it would be thought, similar effects on both countries; yet they had not. In England, the commons rose immediately to vast power: in Scotland, they never attained any power in the legislature, and it is only since the revolution they attained even common freedom.

The difference with England was that the 'commons' in that country possessed property as a result of trade and, as Dalrymple notes, in a passage showing how much Marx learned from the Scottish Enlightenment (and how much in turn Dalrymple learned from Harrington), 'power follows property':

> In Scotland ... we had little or no commerce; the land property was engrossed by the nobility, and it continued to remain so, as long as we had parliaments: the same cause then, which raised the commons in one country, depressed them in the other.[14]

It should come as no surprise, therefore, to find the 'Riding' of the last Scottish Parliament described in the following terms:

The procession, according to the old feudal usage, began diminutively, and swelled in importance as it went. The representatives of the burghs went first; then after a pause, came the lesser barons, or county members; and then the nobles – the highest in rank going last.[15]

Nor did the procession abandon its feudal ranking on arriving at Parliament House. The Estates then divided as usual so that the Dukes, Marquises and Earls hovered in that order over the shire commissioners, while on the opposite side of the hall the Viscounts perched above the Barons who in turn overshadowed the burgh representatives. Although the Parliament represented the dominant feudal class and their affinal groups, however, that class was by no means united as to the means of securing their continued dominance. Political divisions cut across membership of the feudal estates. What were they?

Courtiers and Countrymen, Whigs and Jacobites

One result of the bourgeois ascendancy in England was precisely to allow specific interests within the ruling class to affiliate to different and relatively stable party organisations. The agrarian and merchant capitalists who composed the English ruling class at this time were represented respectively, although by no means exclusively, by the Tory and Whig Parties – a political division coincident with and overlaid by the religious divisions between Anglican and Dissenter.[16] The composition of the Ministry (equivalent to the modern Cabinet) was not directly determined by party strength within the House of Commons, but by the monarch, who was still a significant political actor, despite being unable to determine policy. Sidney Godolphin remained Lord Treasurer (equivalent to the modern post of Prime Minister) throughout the period leading up to the Union, whatever the fluctuating fortunes of the Whigs and the Tories.

The fixity of party lines should not be exaggerated, since there was at least a partial disintegration and recomposition of both Whig and Tory parties between 1715 and 1760. Nor should the level of struggle between them be minimised. Paul Monod notes that neither party was strong enough to destroy the other: 'Consequently, party conflict had to be waged according to strict rules, so that it would not result in civil war.'[17] It is a mistake, however, to confuse the ferocity with which these groupings fought for a division of the spoils with separate class interests, since theirs were identical. Indeed, generally speaking, the more self-confident a ruling class feels itself to be, the greater the degree of internal division it can allow itself to display. Only in a situation of cumulative social and economic decline, such as that experienced in the Iberian Peninsula during the nineteenth century, are the ruling classes regularly pushed to the point of civil war as a means of resolving their differences.

And unlike the Spanish or Portuguese, the English ruling class was at the beginning of its ascent to world hegemony, not the end. Consequently, in England, opponents were bribed rather than executed. The organised hypocrisy of that ruling class was only possible because of the unity of interests which underlay their struggle for position.

Dominant classes are generally more aware of their collective interests than subordinate classes, that being a necessary condition of their remaining dominant. Nevertheless, it would be unrealistic to expect every individual member or political faction within these classes to achieve the same level of awareness. In early eighteenth century England the Whigs had a far greater collective understanding than the Tories of how English security required war to be waged against France, not least because their own interests as merchants and financiers lay outwith the territorial boundaries of the English state. As Adam Smith shrewdly remarked of merchants and manufacturers: 'Their superiority over the country gentlemen is not so much in their knowledge of the public interest, as in their having a better knowledge of their own interest than he has of his.'[18] The 'country gentlemen' of which the Tory Party was largely composed had, of course, to bear the burden of the Land Tax which was levied to fight these wars. This partly explains their lack of enthusiasm for English intervention overseas, but as John Brewer has noted: 'The domestic price of French hegemony in Europe was simply too great for even the most isolationist of MPs.'[19]

Attempts by historians to superimpose the structure of English party politics at this time onto Scotland are therefore profoundly misleading. At one level Scotland appeared little different in political structure – electorates were small, elections infrequent and organisational apparatuses impermanent – but the Scottish and English parties were as different from each other as the Parliaments in which they sat. There was no Whig Party in Scotland in the same sense as there was in England, just as there was no Jacobite Party in England in the same sense as there was in Scotland. This did not, of course, stop the English parties from deluding themselves to the contrary in the pursuit of allies in the Scottish Parliament. English Whigs confused either the Scottish Court Party or, more generally, the Presbyterian interest, with themselves. English Tories confused Scottish Episcopalianism with Anglicanism. In such self-deceptions they were, of course, aided and abetted by Scottish politicians seeking to strengthen their own interest with the Crown. What then was the real nature of Scottish party politics?

Above them all stood the full-time bureaucracy known as the Officers of State. These were a handful of officials – the Lord Commissioner, the High Treasurer, the Lord Justice Clerk, and so on – nominated by the Crown, in whose interests they were expected to act. In that respect they resembled the Ministry in the English Parliament, but with this difference. Whereas the English Ministry represented (at least theoretically) an independent interest from both the Whig and Tory Parties, the Officers of State were effectively the leadership of one of the Scottish parties: the Court Party, which was the largest of the parliamentary groupings with nearly 100 supporters. (All membership figures are approximate due to the loose nature of political organisation and shifts of allegiance by small numbers on the periphery of each party). One reason for this dominance was that the Lord Commissioner used the Court Party's powers of patronage to garner support:

> The court had intruded from the general election in the Autumn of 1702 a solid phalanx of carpetbaggers in the burgess estate, that is gentry who had failed to secure nomination as shire commissioners but were returned predominantly from lesser burghs in which they had no office or occupational interest.[20]

The Court Party appears analogous to the English Whig Party in that it proclaimed itself to be based on 'Revolution principles', but given the different meaning of the Revolution in the two countries it should come as no surprise to find that it also diverged strongly from the Whigs in two main areas. First, it was strongly in favour of the royal prerogative, largely because this was the only way to justify its acceptance of instructions from a monarchy based in England. Secondly, their class basis lay among not the mercantile bourgeoisie but the feudal magnates. The Lord Commissioner and consequent leader of the party, Queensberry, was, along with Atholl, Argyll and Hamilton, one of the four greatest members of this class. To refer to 'the Whigs' in relation to Scotland at this time is therefore – with the possible exception of Andrew Fletcher – to substitute a label for an analysis.

Where there is a Court Party there is usually a Country Party, and so it proved in Scotland. Formally the latter grouping was led by John Hay, second Marquis of Tweedale, but for all practical purposes the dominant figure was Hamilton. With a handful of additions the Country Party were essentially the bold 57 whose secession the previous year had provoked the general election. They claimed to uphold the mantle of patriotism against the Courtiers who were allegedly betraying Scottish interests – an attitude that carried a certain plausibility after Darien. It would be wrong, however, to imagine that these sentiments reflected anything comparable to modern nationalism. After 1689 the majority of Country members had tended to be nothing more than a new set of Courtiers in waiting, using the rhetoric of national emergency in order to propel themselves into the offices currently occupied by the existing Court Party. In one respect, however, their 1703 incarnation was different and reflected the reality of the situation after Darien, in which many of the leading members had lost heavily. They were set, therefore, on becoming not simply the Court Party, but a Court Party that held the monarch under their control, rather than the other way around. This was, of course, the traditional goal of the Scottish nobility as a class but, as things stood in 1703, it could not be achieved while the monarchy remained in England, since it was precisely this arrangement which allowed William to thwart similar attempts at control during the period of post-Revolution settlement. The Country Party comprised an unstable alliance of factions. Only one faction – and at 20 strong they had perhaps a third of the total membership – represented the intention to control the monarchy in the proto-national interest, rather than for the purposes of noble convenience. This was the faction around Andrew Fletcher, the one exception to the general non-Whiggism of Scottish Parliamentarians referred to earlier.

Fletcher has featured in this book before as an analyst of the Scottish class structure and a commentator on Scotland's economic plight during the 1690s. His most important role, however, and the one for which he is most famous, was as a commissioner in the last Scottish Parliament. Fletcher was not simply the opponent of union that he is sometimes represented as, but was committed to a programme of radical reform of the Scottish state and society which would have reduced the role of the Crown to a virtually ceremonial one and to the same degree strengthened the power of Parliament. The core of his programme can be found in his 'limitations' – the twelve points by which he argued that the Scottish Parliament could resist the imposition of arbitrary rule:

1. Annual Parliamentary elections.
2. As many barons as nobles to sit in Parliament.
3. Only commissioners and not the Officers of State to be allowed to vote.
4. No royal veto on legislation.
5. A council of 31 be empowered to act in place of Parliament during adjournments.
6. Only Parliament to have the power to declare war or make peace.
7. Only Parliament to have the power to confer offices or pensions of state.
8. Only Parliament to have the power to approve a standing army.
9. A militia of all able-bodied males to be created for national defence.
10. Only Parliament to have the power to issue indemnities or pardons.
11. The 15 members of the College of Justice to be ineligible to become members of Parliament.
12. The monarch to forfeit the crown on breaking any of the other conditions.[21]

Ironically, in the light of the position which he was shortly to take in opposition to union with England, Fletcher had been one of the few Scots to declare himself in favour of such an arrangement during the

Revolution of 1688, as his now famous letter of 8 January 1689 demonstrates: 'For my own part I think that we can never come to any settlement but by uniting with England in Parliament and Trade, for as for our worship and particular laws we certainly can never be united in these.' The point about this letter is not, as Paul Scott believes, that Fletcher is endorsing a 'federal' as opposed to an 'incorporating' union, but that his support for a union was on the assumption that it would be with a truly revolutionary England. His politics were therefore comparable to the extreme Whigs or Commonwealth Men who were to be defeated in the English Convention Parliament. Consequently, as William Ferguson has shown, when it became clear that William intended to agree to the most conservative settlement possible, the very reason for seeking union disappeared and the possibility of achieving his goals within Scotland alone became his main project.[22]

There was yet another party in Parliament – the Jacobites who, appropriately enough, referred to themselves as the Cavaliers. With around 70 members, they were the biggest gainers from the election, partly from winning contested seats but also through the adherence of 20 lords who had not previously attended, but who now took the Oath. Like Fletcher, the Jacobites had in mind a definite solution to the Scottish dilemma: a restoration of the Stuarts that would also have resulted in Scotland coming under the domination of France. It is worth considering this when reading their protestations of concern for Scottish sovereignty. Hypocrisy aside, however, it is possible to view the Jacobites as being nearer to the modern notion of a party than either of their competitors, not in the sense that they possessed a permanent organisation, but that they had a clearly defined programme, ideologically distinct from the inchoate shifting between Court and Country typical of the ruling class as a whole. Scotland was therefore graced with a counter-revolutionary party before it had given rise to a revolutionary one. The modernity of the Jacobites in organisational terms was a consequence of their need to establish an 'absolutism from below' by overthrowing the existing order, rather than imposing it from above, as had been done in the rest of Europe, through the concentration and centralisation of existing state power. Jacobitism had few practical implications in Scotland beforehand because it served no purpose for any significant section of the Scottish ruling class. They still had hopes of establishing their nation as an independent player within the state system. It was only after these hopes had been sunk in the swamps of Darien that Jacobitism, and the historical reversal of relationships between England and France that it would necessarily have involved, became an option. Charles, sixth Earl of Home, led the Jacobites, but Home was even less important in his party than Tweedale was to the Countrymen. For all practical purposes they too accepted the leadership of Hamilton.

There were also divisions within the Parliament which cut across party lines. The most important of these were religious. Most Jacobites were Episcopalians, but not all Episcopalians were Jacobites. The majority of the Court Party were Presbyterians, but so were their opponents in the Country Party. In addition, each of the great magnates had a personal following of dependants, largely, but not exclusively, composed of their kin. These could usually be relied upon to turn their coats when given the word, and some, as Byron wrote of a later political opportunist, would have turned their skins. It was in these shifting cross-currents of ambition and allegiance that the question of the Hanoverian Succession was raised.

A Class Divided

'Management' through the Officers of State had been a feature of Scottish political life since 1603, when the physical absence of the Crown from Scotland led absentee monarchs to seek some means of imposing their will. The disbursement of offices, titles and funds was combined with more direct administrative control through the Committee of the Lords of the Articles, but after the abolition of that body in 1690, buying support became virtually the only means at the disposal of the Court to ensure that required legislation passed through Parliament. The problem for the Court since 1690 had been that of having too little money to keep its supporters in line; but there was now a deeper difficulty. Management can be effective where there is a level of basic agreement about political goals and this had been the case in both the Scottish Parliament between 1660 and 1689, and – although on a different class basis – in the English Parliament after 1689. By 1703 the divisions within the Scottish ruling class were too deep to be accommodated by the usual methods of Parliamentary management. 'Factions rubb'd upon each other and with great severity,' wrote John Clerk of Penicuik, 'so that we were often in the form of a Polish diet with our swords in our hands, or, at least, our hands at our swords.'[23] The opposition had learned from the English Parliament the effectiveness of withholding supply from the Ministry in order to achieve their ends – previously this strategy had only been employed in Scotland during the brief existence of the Club between 1689 and 1690 – and Queensberry was therefore unable to gain funding, not least for the army. In desperation the Court introduced an Act of Security for debate on 26 May. For the Court this was probably unavoidable, but nevertheless it gave an opening to the opposition that they were quick to take. An orchestrated onslaught by the Jacobites and the Country Party transformed the Act of Security, through amendments and the addition of new clauses, from an anodyne original into an Act embodying the intransigence of the opposition stance. The Act of

Security was passed on 13 August and the opposition quickly followed through with the Act Anent Peace and War, based on the sixth of Fletcher's limitations. (In the Scottish Parliament the term 'Act' referred to both the initial bill and the eventual legislation.)

What were these Acts about? The Act of Security provided for the Scottish Parliament to choose the next monarch of Scotland, the only criterion being that whoever was chosen could not at the same time hold the Crown of England, unless certain conditions – which had still to be decided – were met. In the meantime all eligible males were to be trained to resist foreign invasion from an unspecified quarter. The Act Anent Peace and War additionally moved that only the Scottish Parliament could declare war on behalf of Scotland. Needless to say, Queensberry refused them both royal ratification, calling the sovereignty of the Scottish Parliament into question once again. Both Acts were the result of factional moves by different sections of the opposition rather than a coherent strategy and consequently could be interpreted in almost any way. The Jacobites wished to abort the Hanoverian Succession altogether and saw the Acts as a stepping stone in that direction. The majority of the Country Party saw them as a bargaining counter to secure the Hanoverian Succession on more favourable terms. The Fletcherite minority saw them as the beginning of parliamentary independence from monarchical control. Even the raising of troops could be presented as a defence against French as much as English designs. They were all deceiving themselves.

The Country Party majority represented what might be called the mainstream of Scottish ruling-class thought, in that they wanted the advantages of trade with England and English military protection, but without surrendering in return any of their privileges or freedom for political manoeuvre. As one author (probably George Ridpath) noted in a book dedicated 'To the Right Honourable the Estates of Scotland' in 1703: 'there will be no need of Foreign Auxiliaries except the Pretender come in with a Foreign Power, which England and Holland are able, and concerned in Interest to prevent'.[24] In other words: we want to be free of English influence, but still expect to be protected from Stuart and Bourbon meddling because it is in the interest of the English state to do so. It was Fletcher, however, who best understood the dilemma faced by the Scottish state. In a speech supporting one of his limitations on the Crown, and which his present-day admirers rarely quote, he made the position perfectly clear:

> For prerogative-men [i.e. both the Jacobites and the Hanoverians] who are for enslaving this nation to the directions of another court, are courtiers to any successor; and let them pretend what they will, if their principles lead necessarily to subject this nation to another, are enemies to the nation. These men are so absurd as to provoke England,

and yet resolve to continue as slaves of that court. This country must become a field of blood in order to advance a papist to the throne of Britain. If we fail we shall be slaves by right of conquest; if we prevail, have the happiness to continue in our former slavish dependence ... If we may live free, I little value who is king: it is indifferent to me, provided the limitations be enacted, to name or not name; Hanover, St. Germains, or who you will.[25]

The analysis is faultless. To accept the Hanoverian Succession would leave Scotland in exactly the same predicament as under William. To oppose it would involve either accepting another dynasty or being utterly subjugated by the English in response. Yet what does he propose as a solution? A set of paper limitations which, in the absence of any material force to back them up, would have been as successful in confining the powers of the Crown as the letters patent (under the Great Seal of the Kingdom of Scotland) waved by the Darien settlers had been in stopping the bullets of their Spanish opponents.

Significantly, Fletcher's limitations were opposed by both the Court and the Jacobites (both sets of 'prerogative-men') who wanted the Crown prerogative to continue, albeit in respect of different dynasties. Seafield, in a letter to Godolphin, referred to the limitations presented by Fletcher as representing virtually a republican programme. Strictly speaking this was incorrect, but from the viewpoint of the lords it was probably near enough to make no difference. Seafield's own reply to Fletcher had stressed the disasters of civil war and the stabilising role of the monarchy, but in a letter to Godolphin he was more candid as to the class basis for his opposition, writing that

... we had no reason to expect any advantage by overturning the monarchy, nor had we reason to think that even a republic would ever suit with our temper and inclinations, when we have so many nobility, superiorities and jurisdictions, and, in short, that our whole constitution was contrary to party.[26]

William Ferguson has summed up the problem that Fletcher embodies as being that 'the *tiers état* was unequal to its mission, and the revolution failed'.[27] But the revolution was not even attempted. For all the brilliance of his analysis, Fletcher had no social forces with which to impose his solution. The class of lairds to which he belonged were in general still too tied to the nobility, both economically and politically, and he had no intention of going to the rural tenants or urban artisans who stood below him in the class structure. Of course, if these classes had been pushing forward of their own accord, then Fletcher and his circle might have put themselves at the head of such a movement, as the Independents had done beforehand and the Jacobins were to do afterwards, but such a movement had not yet developed and would not do so until the 1790s. As it was, Fletcher's own faction within the Country Party was heavily based on a group of young lords – Haddington, Montrose, Rothes and Roxborough – who were more highly placed in the class structure than Fletcher himself and even less likely to look for plebeian support.

The Parliamentary session was adjourned on 16 September 1703, never to be reconvened. On the one hand, the opposition had demonstrated their ability to frustrate the Court, but had proved incapable of forcing the Court to give royal assent to their most important enactments. On the other, Queensberry could refuse royal assent, but had failed in his positive objectives of securing the succession and obtaining supply. Stalemate. Then, during the adjournment, an unforeseen turn of events was to lead to the replacement of the existing Officers of State and a partial recomposition of the parties.

Factional Regroupment

These events were set in motion by the activities of Simon Fraser of Beaumont. The incredible details of his personal history cannot be given here. Suffice it to say that by 1703 Lovat had been outlawed for the rape of the Dowager Lady Lovat whom he had forcibly 'married' in an attempt to lay claim to her family estate, which he considered his by right. Fraser had made his way to the Stuart Court-in-exile at St Germains where he became involved in an inconsequential Jacobite plot whose progress he was to facilitate back in Scotland. On returning, he found that there was little interest in a rising. Never one to let an opportunity pass, however, Fraser decided to seek the protection and gratitude of Queensberry by approaching him with a much-embroidered version of the existing plot. According to Fraser this had involved every major figure in Scottish politics including Atholl and Hamilton but excluding, naturally, Queensberry and his immediate circle. Queensberry rushed to London to inform Anne of the Jacobite treachery of his rivals. Meanwhile, Fraser was also in London giving the game away to Robert ('the Plotter') Fergusson, an ex-Williamite turned Jacobite and possibly the greatest exponent of political intrigue in the British Isles outside of Fraser himself. Fergusson, realising the damage that Fraser was doing to the Jacobite cause, warned Atholl and the others implicated in the plot what was being alleged against them, with the result that they too rushed to London to regale Anne in their turn with accusations against Queensberry.

'The Queensberry Plot', as it was known in Scotland, had two immediate effects. The first was to ratchet up the post-Darien level of anti-English hostility by a further notch as a result of the House of Lords conducting its own investigation into what they insisted on calling 'The Scotch Plot'. This was seen in Scotland as unwarranted and uncomprehending English interference into Scottish affairs. The second was that Anne dismissed Queensberry as Lord Commissioner. The 'Plot' was the occasion rather than the reason for Queensberry's sacking, since his stock had already irrecoverably sunk after his failing to carry Parliament for the Court.

The English Ministry was now faced with a difficulty. Queensberry and his personal faction (which was a large minority of the 'old' Court Party) were certain to cause trouble in their attempts to lever their way back into favour, and for obvious reasons neither the Country Party nor the Jacobites could be entrusted to form a government. The solution was provided by the formation, in May 1704, of the 'New' Party (i.e. the new Court Party) with Tweedale at the head. This grouping had a core membership of around 20, although it occasionally rose as high as 30, and largely consisted of renegade members of the Country Party – including the majority of Fletcher's 'cubs' – and a handful of Jacobites. The 'New' Party, whom I will henceforth refer to by their later nickname of the 'Squadrone Volante' (i.e. the 'flying squadron'), was entrusted with the ministry and told by the queen that their main objectives must be to secure supply and the succession, if necessary by giving royal assent to a diluted version of the Act of Security.

The granting of supply was the first priority because of the underlying military weakness of the Scottish central state. As we saw in Chapter 1, a British army already existed, the Scottish component of which was actually larger than the Scottish army itself.[28] A list drawn up on 15 May 1702 reveals the Scottish Army to consist of 2,934 men at an annual cost of £65,740 14s. In so far as its function was to provide defence against external attack it was clearly inadequate, being deficient both in men – there were only 321 men between the three main garrisons at Edinburgh, Stirling and Dumbarton – and in equipment. For the purposes of repelling internal rebellion the situation was no better: the entire Highland area was policed by one garrison at Fort William (367 men) and two regiments of foot with 772 men between them. The treasurer depute calculated in February 1705 that it would cost six or seven thousand pounds to rectify these deficiencies. The balance in the treasury was £1,900.[29] Even if we assume that the warriors of Clan Campbell and the feudal levies of the House of Argyll would also have been mobilised in the event of a French invasion, these would have been more than matched by the Jacobite Clans. It is clear, therefore, that the Scottish state was not well placed to defend itself – a fact well known to both the Jacobites and the French state.

When the session opened on 6 July 1704, the pressures on Tweedale and the Squadrone to deliver were therefore immense, but they were to prove no more successful at achieving their objectives than the old Court Party. Less than a month after the session began Tweedale was offering his resignation to Godolphin on the grounds of his inability to advance his legislative programme. Godolphin refused it, perhaps astonished that any Scottish politician would voluntarily offer to resign from a guaranteed source of income. It is a measure of the anxiety of the English Ministry and the Scottish Courtiers that, in return for six months' supply, Tweedale was forced to give assent to the Act of Security on 5 August, with almost every opposition amendment intact, after it had been passed yet again by a majority of 60 votes. Three days beforehand, Marlborough had led the British forces and their allies to victory over the French and the Bavarians at Blenheim. Had news of this triumph, which temporarily shifted the balance of power against Louis, reached Britain in time, the need for supply would have appeared less pressing and it is possible that Tweedale might have been able to resist the passage of the Act. As it was, when the session adjourned on 7 October, the Scottish Parliament had committed itself to a position which entailed accepting virtually any succession rather the Hanoverian, albeit for different reasons on the part of each opposition grouping. What was the English response?

A Union is Announced

The passing of the Act of Security seems to have been decisive in persuading the English Ministry, and a section of the Whigs, that an incorporating union was the only solution to the developing crisis between the two nations. It is worth insisting on this point, since two influential schools of thought have interpreted this shift in the English position very differently.

One school sees the drive towards union as the culmination of English attempts since 1296 to destroy Scottish sovereignty. According to Paul Scott: 'After centuries of effort, they [i.e. the English] had succeeded in neutralising Scotland and reducing her to control; they would be unlikely to allow Scotland to reassert her independence if they could help it.'[30] The reference here to 'the English' is perhaps a bit too capacious. The farm labourers, silk weavers and merchant seamen who generated the wealth for the English ruling class were not invited to give their opinion on constitutional relationships with Scotland, nor had they displayed any desire to subdue that nation to their own. Even leaving aside the difficulties of ascribing motive to entire nations, however, this assertion is wrong on at least two counts. On the one hand, relationships had never simply existed between the states, but between different social forces within those states. The Scottish Covenanters initially allied with the English Parliament, not 'the English' as such and this could scarcely have been otherwise, since the latter were engaged in a civil war. On the other hand, even where English policy was clearly determined by one faction or interest, it was by no means always directed towards the domination of Scotland. Elizabeth I intervened in 1560 to help the Lords of the

Congregation against the French-backed enemies, but then withdrew her forces and refused to become involved in internal disputes within either church or state, despite appeals for her to do so from various Scottish leaders such as Regent Morton in the 1570s. More importantly still are the actions of the New Model Army. After defeating the Engagers at Preston in 1648, Cromwell only stayed in Scotland long enough to ensure that an ostensibly anti-Stuart regime was installed in Edinburgh. There is no indication that either he or his generals wished anything further to do with the country. Indeed, when Charles I was executed the following year monarchy was explicitly abolished for England and Wales, but nothing was said about Scotland. As John Morrill has pointed out, this act effectively broke the Union of Crowns and allowed Scotland to go its own way – in the same manner as Portugal had separated from Spain in 1640 – with a Stuart king if it so wished. It was only the proclamation of Charles II as King of Great Britain, France and Ireland that provoked the second English invasion and the forcible incorporation into the Commonwealth.[31]

If the position of this first school is ahistorical, then that of the second is apolitical. Here, the attitude of the English state is explained, not as the final achievement of national aims stretching back for centuries, but as a short-term attempt by contemporary politicians to make factional gains within the English Parliament. According to Paul Riley, the main proponent of this view: 'In intention it [i.e. the Treaty] had little to do with the needs of England and even less with the needs of Scotland, but a great deal to with private political ambitions.'[32] Riley's reliance on the correspondence of the political actors to support this view has been correctly criticised by Rosalind Mitchison for ignoring the common assumptions which underlay such communications and which would not have needed restating on every occasion: 'On the same sort of material it would be open to scholars to decide that mid eighteenth century Britain had no economic policy, even though the country was pursuing an imperialist and exclusionist policy over trade and empire.'[33]

In fact, the alternative of an incorporating union embodied neither a long-standing ambition on the part of the English nation nor a short-term factional calculation by Westminster politicians. Rather, it was a strategy imposed on the English ruling class as a whole by the conflict with France. As Jonathan Swift wrote during the following decade:

... it was thought highly dangerous to leave that Part of the Island inhabited by a poor, fierce Northern People, at liberty to put themselves under a different King ... and so the Union became necessary, not for any actual Good it could possibly do us, but to avoid a probable Evil.

In summary, Swift thought that there were two reasons for making and retaining the Union:

First, that the Union became necessary for the Cause above related; because it prevented this Island being governed by two Kings, which England would never have suffered; and it might probably have cost us a War of a year or two, to reduce the Scots. Secondly, that it would be dangerous to break this Union, at least in this Juncture, while there is a Pretender abroad, who might probably lay hold of such an opportunity.[34]

Gilbert Burnet, in his reflections on this period, made a similar assessment:

Scotland lay on the weakest side of England, where it could not be defended but by an Army. The Collieries on the Tyne lay exposed for several Miles, and would not be preserved, but at a great charge, and with a great force, if a War should fall out between the two Nations, and if Scotland should be conquered ... it must be united to England, or kept under by an Army. The danger of keeping up a Standing Force in the hands of any Prince, and to be modelled by him (who might engage the Scotch to join with that Army and turn upon England) was visible, and any Union after such a conquest would look like a force, and so could not be lasting, whereas all was now voluntary.[35]

The Tory Swift disapproved of the Union on the grounds that it was disadvantageous to his native Ireland. The Whig Burnet approved of it on the grounds that it was advantageous to his native Scotland. Neither man felt it necessary to present the calculations behind the English Ministry proposing an incorporating union as anything other than – from their point of view – necessary *realpolitik*.

The first step which the English Parliament took to help induce 'voluntary' acceptance of the proposal was to pass a piece of legislation known as the Aliens Act, but whose purpose is better revealed in its full title – 'An Act for the Effectual Security of the Kingdom of England from the Apparent Dangers that May Arise from the Several Acts Lately Passed in the Parliament of Scotland'. This deprived Scots of the privileges of English citizenship, forbade all Scottish imports and, most importantly, decreed that all estates in England held by Scots were to be confiscated, unless the Hanoverian Succession was accepted by Christmas day, 1705. Some of the lords, including Hamilton, had estates in England, but more generally, what the Aliens Act offered was an uncertain economic future in which they would be excluded from English markets for the goods produced on their estates. Of no less importance, they would also be denied the prospect, however slight it might have been, of betterment, or at any rate escape, from the confines of Scotland through the avenues of the marriage contract or military service.[36] Yet an alternative to this dismal prospect was also on offer; the Aliens Act contained a clause appointing commissioners to negotiate a union between the two kingdoms. Events in Scotland had, however, now passed beyond the control of the Court. It is perhaps fitting that the episode that signalled this shift should have been directly linked to the failure of the Darien scheme.

A Lynching in Leith

The English Inland Revenue had seized the last ship owned by the Company of Scotland, the *Annandale*, early in 1704 at the behest of the East India Company, which was intent on pursuing the vendetta against its Scottish rival down to the very end. On 12 August officers of the Company seized an English merchant ship called the *Worcester*, which had docked along the Forth, in retaliation. While the captain and crew were awaiting a resolution of the affair in Leith, they were arrested and charged with an act of piracy against another Company ship, the *Speedy Return*, which had vanished in the East Indies during 1703. The evidence against the men consisted of nothing more than drunken boasting overheard in a Leith dockside tavern. Nevertheless, Roderick MacKenzie, Secretary to the Company, saw the opportunity of legal justification for his seizure of the *Worcester* and her cargo, and had them charged, not only with piracy, but with the murder of the *Speedy Return* crew. Between the arrest of the *Worcester* crew and their being brought to trial on 5 March 1705 in Edinburgh, the Aliens Act had passed and, in an atmosphere of rising tension they were found guilty and sentenced to death. All of the disappointed patriotic feelings produced by the Darien debacle, heightened by subsequent English high-handedness over the 'Scotch Plot' and the Aliens Act, now came to the surface. The Scottish legal system had in its power a group of Englishmen, Englishmen who had apparently been directly involved in attacking Scotsmen, Scotsmen who – if not actually Darien colonists – were at any rate employees of the Company into which so much hope and money had been poured.

The men were almost certainly innocent of the charges against them. Anne herself appealed for clemency and affidavits from members of the supposedly murdered crew of the *Speedy Return* were forwarded from London to Edinburgh, only to be ignored by a court in which the 'defence' seemed as willing as the prosecution to bring in a guilty verdict. In short, the Edinburgh crowd wanted blood and the politicians of the Squadrone were prepared to give it to them. The ferocity of the hatred directed against Captain Thomas Green and his crew impacted directly on the Privy Council. One Squadrone member, George Baillie of Jerviswood, recounted in a letter to another, John Ker, fifth Earl of Roxborough, that:

> ... it came to be unanimously resolved, that Green, Marder and Simpson should be carried to execution; and the rest reprieved till

Friday come seventh night; and it was good it went so, for otherwise, I believe, the people had torn us to pieces; for I never saw such a confluence of people, most of them armed with great sticks.

Of the 30 members of the Privy Council, only 11 turned up for the meeting which decided whether or not the men would be reprieved, the others pleading that they were prevented by such incapacitating complaints as sprained ankles and common colds. The Councillors who at least had the courage to attend proceeded to throw away the lives of Green and the others with brutal cynicism, as Baillie makes clear:

I shall not trouble you with every man's part in this affair; it were too long for a letter; only say that the authority of the Government is gone; for had these persons been never so innocent, the Council could not have saved them without endangering their lives, besides other inconveniences.[37]

It should perhaps be noted that the leaders of the Squadrone were major shareholders in the Company, which realised £2,823 from the sale of the *Worcester*.

On 11 April 1705, the day of execution, an estimated 80,000 people, many of them armed, lined the way from Edinburgh Castle to the gallows on Leith Sands chanting 'No Reprieve!' and howling abuse at the doomed men. The episode should, if nothing else, give food for thought to anyone who imagines that the actions of the pre-industrial crowd should always be retrospectively endorsed by modern socialists. There were times in the long history of the Edinburgh crowd when its violence was exercised in pursuit of a justice that would have otherwise have been denied. This was not one of those occasions.[38]

After the three men were hanged the public mood apparently changed to one of revulsion at what had been done. At any rate, the other prisoners were not executed, and there was no noticeable public demand for the sentences of the court be carried out. They were eventually released in September and the sentences quietly forgotten. But not everyone regretted the deaths. A poem written by William Forbes of Disblair published anonymously by the Jacobite James Watson took the view that, despite the lack of any evidence, the three men were guilty – must have been guilty – and that their demise was a justifiable, if inadequate, recompense for Scottish losses over Darien:

> Villains! Whose crimes to such a pitch were flown,
> And blackest Guilt to ripe for Vengeance grown,
> That Heaven itself no longer could forbear,
> Nor could they shun there own destruction here:
> ...

> Then *England* for its Treachery should mourn,
> Be forced to fawn, and truckle in its turn:
> *Scots Pedlars* you no longer durst upbraid
> And DARIEN should be with interest repaid.[39]

The death of Green and his comrades demonstrated the explosive nature of frustrated popular proto-nationalism in the Lowlands. One English visitor, Joseph Taylor, arrived in the aftermath of the Aliens Act and the lynching. He had left London in trepidation:

We had a great deal of cause to leave our Country with regret, upon account of the discouragements we received from every body, even upon the borders of Scotland, and by what I could gather from the discourse of all persons I conversed with, I concluded that I was going into the most barbarous Country in the world; every one reckoned our Journey extremely dangerous, and told us t'would be difficult to escape with our lives.

In the event, Taylor did escape with his life, unlike his unfortunate countrymen, but he has left us with a record of how English visitors to Edinburgh were treated in these months. Noting that the Darien debacle and subsequent English legislation 'has given their dull Bards an occasion to vent out some poetical malice, in barbarous satires, against the English', Taylor recounts how he purchased 'the most scurrilous' *A Pill for Pork Eaters*, which had already entered the language of popular culture:

... and the very boys would pull us in the street by the Sleeve, and cry a Pill for the Pork Eaters, knowing us to be Englishmen, and indeed its very observable that the children, which can but just speak, seem to have a national Antipathy against the English.[40]

The lynching also meant the end of any possibility that the Squadrone could continue as the replacement Court Party. They had given in to 'the mob' – bad enough under any circumstances – but had done so in such a way as to inflame public opinion in England and make the task of achieving a union that much more difficult. Godolphin had in fact already approached John Campbell, second Duke of Argyll, to take over from Seafield as Lord Commissioner. A young man of 25, Argyll was by virtue of birth the most powerful landowner in Scotland (although virtue is not perhaps the most appropriate word to use in this context) and was already a veteran of the French wars. It was from the latter aspect of his career, and not internal clan conflicts, that he derived his Highland nickname, 'Red John of the Battles'. Argyll set about his task in military style. For accepting this particular commission he demanded and got, among other things, the English Dukedom of Greenwich. He also insisted, much to the disgust of Anne, on the return of Queensberry as an Officer of State. By the time the session opened on 28 June 1705 the old Court Party had virtually been restored to power, but now with a brutally efficient leader and, for the first time in this Parliament, enough money to dispense patronage effectively – although, as I will argue in due course, this was not the most important factor in achieving the Union.

Divisions Within the Anti-Treaty Camp

By the late summer of 1705 Argyll had narrowly succeeded in getting Parliament to accept an Act for a Treaty of Union, largely through the support of the Squadrone. At this stage it appeared to the opposition that there might still be everything to play for. The nature of the union was left unspecified, and a federal union would still have allowed the radical restructuring of the Scottish state demanded by Fletcher, and left Parliament intact. The key tactical question was concerned with who would nominate the commissioners to conduct the Treaty, the Queen or the Scottish Parliament. If the former, then opposition tactics would be narrowed to resisting the ratification of the Treaty, since the Courtiers would invariably agree with English proposals. If the latter, then it was possible that the commissioners would be sufficiently independent to argue for a federal union, or, as the Jacobites hoped, to break off negotiations altogether if the English refused to compromise. The second outcome seemed more likely up to 1 September, when the issue was suddenly and unexpectedly resolved in one of the decisive moments of the entire affair. Hamilton was still the leader of the confederated opposition of Jacobites and the Country Party. Yet on this date he misled his supporters into believing that the issue would not be raised that day, and as soon as a majority had left the chamber, himself moved that the Queen should be responsible for appointing the commissioners. Significantly, perhaps, the Officers of State did not appear to be entirely surprised by this, and before any of the departed opposition members could be reached the vote was called and won by the Court.

Why did Hamilton behave in this way? In a letter to his brother (which he copied to Robert Harley) protesting that he 'meant good by it', his expectation that it would be well received by his own party apparently grounded in the fact that 'by its being a nomination large in itself and not confined to parties; it might have had the desired effect to unite them in interest'.[41] Paul Scott has assembled an impressive collection of contemporary claims that Hamilton was bribed by Court Party managers and the English Ministry.[42] This is certainly within the bounds of possibility, but is not the whole story, for even if he was not bribed directly, the contradictions of his position were enormous. In fact, it appears that Hamilton had ambitions to the Crown of Scotland, to which his family had a distant claim. These ambitions could only have been brought to fruition with the support of Louis XIV. Yet when it became clear in discussions with the French emissary in Scotland that Louis was only prepared to support the restoration of the Stuart line, Hamilton effectively switched his allegiance to the Court. Since his entire influence derived from his leadership of the opposition, however, that switch could never be openly acknowledged, with the result that he was able – no doubt with a great deal of pointed reminders from the Officers of State about the precariousness of his English estates – to provide a service greater than would have been possible had he openly changed sides.[43]

In spite of his sabotage, Hamilton remained leader of the opposition until the very end, his continued pre-eminence suggesting something of its weakness. Between the republican laird Fletcher and a great landowner and clan chief like Atholl there was little in common, but the very fact that the opposition harnessed together such different forces meant that they had to rely on a leader with no particular ideological convictions, but who could rally their forces – outside as well as within Parliament. Popular support for Hamilton remained strong, with William Forbes denouncing in verse suggestions that his patriotism might be for sale:

> Damned be that Hackney-pen that durst traduce,
> Great H———n, our Noblest Patriot thus:
> 'Gainst this Brave Patriot thou'st belched thy worst,
> Even what thy boldest Heroes never durst.
> Thy Country such a Patriot never could match,
> Whom no Preferments nor Baits can catch:
> Whatever the Court could bid, this Prince withstood,
> He sweats and toils to do his Country good:[44]

The dire consequences of these illusions for the opposition would shortly become apparent.

The session ended on 21 September 1705 after agreeing that 31 commissioners from each country would meet the following Spring to begin negotiations. Predictably, the 31 Scottish commissioners consisted of supporters of Queensberry (who took part) and Argyll (who did not), with the solitary exception of George Lockhart of Carnwarth, an active Jacobite whose memoirs provide many insights into the subsequent events.

On the eve of the talks there still had been no open proposal for an incorporating union on the part of the English; it was still a federal project as far as Scots are concerned. Yet some of the commissioners at least were aware of what was coming. In a letter to Carstares in March 1706, the Secretary of State, John Erskine, sixth Earl of Mar, made explicit the constraints under which they were about to enter the negotiations. He had tried to explain to the English Commissioners, he complains, that their refusal to consider anything but an incorporating union was lending strength to the arguments of those who opposed the succession:

> But this has very little weight with your friends here; and they tell me plainly, they will give us no terms that are considerable for going into their succession, if any, without going into an entire union; and, if we insist upon that, they will never meet us; for they think all the notions about federal unions and forms are a mere jest and chimera.

In short, the Scots were told that they had no alternative other than to refuse: 'You see that what we are treat of is not of our choice.'[45]

A federal structure had never been seriously considered in England. If Scotland could not be controlled at arms length then it would have to be incorporated completely. Federalism was the worst of both worlds, linking the fate of Scotland more closely with England while increasing the level of autonomy possessed by the Parliament. More generally, it would reverse the drive towards a centralised state that the Revolution and the subsequent wars had produced – a form of state consciously desired by the most advanced sections of the English ruling class.[46] Yet decentralisation was precisely the strategy behind Fletcher's federal solution to English dominance over the British Isles. As John Robertson notes: 'Fletcher frankly acknowledged that [a confederal union] would involve the break-up of the existing three Kingdoms of England, Scotland and Ireland into smaller political units.'[47] Marlborough in particular had seen at first hand in the United Netherlands the slowness of the decision-making process and the organisational incapacity to which such a structure tended. That was in no way to make war on the French, as he made clear to the officers under his command. 'All the people here show a greater fondness for it [i.e. the Union] than ever,' wrote Sir David Nairne, a rather naive courtier then serving in London as Deputy Secretary for Scottish Affairs, 'My Lord Marlborough made speeches to me on the subject before all the company.'[48]

Components of an Incorporating Union

The two sets of commissioners met in the Cockpit at Westminster for the first time on 16 April 1706 and thereafter matters progressed at great speed. The Scots were quickly disabused of any notions they might have entertained about the possibility of a federal union. As Paul Riley writes: 'Their only real negotiating position was the argument that if a Scottish parliament was to accept union then sufficiently good terms must be forthcoming.'[49] Agreement on the first set of proposals was reached by 25 April, the entire Treaty completed by 11 July and the text signed, sealed and delivered to Anne by 23 July. To what had the Scottish commissioners agreed? The Treaty that the commissioners carried back to Scotland with them had 25 Articles that covered three sets of issues.

The first set dealt with Scottish representation in the British Parliament and were the most obviously unsatisfactory for the Scottish political elite. Articles 22 and 23 established that there would be just 45 members (30 for the shires and 15 for the burghs) in the House of Commons – only one member more than the 44 who sat for Cornwall – and 16 peers in the House of Lords. There were currently 513 English MPs and 185 Peers, so the Scots were being asked to accept between an eleventh and a twelfth of the English representation. The number of representatives which Scotland was allowed was effectively a compromise between economic and demographic measures, since the Scottish population was then a fifth of the English, but the income which the Land Tax in Scotland was expected to raise for the Exchequer was calculated at less than a fortieth of that raised in England.

The second set dealt with existing Scottish institutions. Article 19 ensured the continuation of the main components of the Scottish state outside Parliament itself: the legal system – although the Article said nothing about which body would constitute a final court of appeal, the implication being that it would be the House of Lords, a gathering not renowned for comprehending the complexities of Scots Law. Article 20 specifically retained the Heritable Jurisdictions – a point to which I will return. The 'Rights and Privileges' of the royal burghs were preserved by Article 21. Contrary to what is sometimes supposed, the education system is unmentioned in the Treaty. Of far greater significance than this, however, is the fact that it also remained silent on the position of the Church of Scotland.

The third set dealt with economic issues. Article 4 conferred freedom of trade on Scotland and, although the importance of this to the Scots is a matter of dispute, it is worth remembering that it was a considerable concession – although probably an unavoidable one – for the English ruling class. They had, after all, been refusing precisely this measure for the previous 100 years. The corollary of equal access to English markets was of course equal contributions to the British exchequer, as detailed in Articles 6, 7 and 8. Whatever the enthusiasm, or lack of it, for free trade, these measures were always going to be unpopular. On the other hand, Article 9 set the level of the Land Tax, limiting Scotland to paying £48,000 p.a. as opposed to England's £2,000,000. In other words, a ratio of 1:42 or less than £50 per every £2,000 paid by England. Article 15 established the Equivalent, nicely calculated at £398,085 10s, for taking a share of the English National Debt. It specifically included compensation for losses incurred by the adoption of the English coinage and, more importantly, to repay Darien stockholders for their losses in the sum – again nicely calculated – of £232,884 5s 2/3d. Marchmont wrote of this that:

The equivalent, payable for what Scotland will be burdened with of the debts of England, did incline many of the meaner people, to whom debts are owing, to favour the treaty, because they did not see any ready way to come by payment.[50]

Only one thing now remained for the Court to accomplish: ratification in Scotland. There was little doubt that the Treaty would be passed in both English Houses of Parliament, but it was vital that it be passed by the Scottish Parliament first: in part because the result there was less predictable, but more importantly because if amendments had to be made, it would be easier for them to be incorporated before the Treaty came to Westminster. The vast majority of the Scottish people had, of course, no hand in electing commissioners to Parliament, nor were they going to be asked their opinion of the Treaty. Some of them would give it anyway.

The Struggle Over Ratification

Parliament reassembled on 3 October 1706. Argyll, having organised the Officers of State and the Court Party to his satisfaction, had long since returned to the French wars, leaving Queensberry in his previous position as Lord Commissioner, Seafield as Treasurer and Mar as Secretary of State. He was induced to return to Scotland and help carry the Treaty by the promise of a major-generalship for himself and an earldom for his brother Archibald, who was in due course to emerge as the greatest political manager of the eighteenth century.

Discussion of the Treaty began on 12 October in an atmosphere of high tension. Even before negotiations began, Mar had warned Carstares that the incorporating nature of the Union should not be divulged: 'I write this freely to you, though it is not fit this should be known in Scotland, for fear of discouraging people and making them despair of the treaty.'[51] Indeed, one of the first matters to be agreed at the negotiations was that they should be conducted in secret. Even before the commissioners had returned to Scotland, however, Lockhart made the contents of the Treaty public through his fellow Jacobites. The popular reaction was not, as Mar had anticipated, simply one of despair, but of anger.

Popular Opposition to the Treaty

Edinburgh began to fill with thousands of people from across the Lowlands intent on demonstrating their hostility to the Treaty and the politicians who supported it. Each day as the Officers of State and the commissioners neared Parliament House to begin the session they were met by the crowd. Queensberry and the 'Treater-Traitors' had abuse and other, more material objects hurled at them, while Hamilton and the 'Patriots' were cheered and lifted onto the shoulders of the demonstrators.

The process at this stage is often represented as being virtually concluded, with an all-powerful Court forcing the Treaty through in the face of an impotent opposition within Parliament and an irrelevant one outside. This is not how events appeared at the time. The Officers of State certainly employed all their resources of bribery, bullying and blackmail to consolidate the Court position and secure the votes of vulnerable individuals on the other side. However, with the exception of Hamilton – whose sincerity must already have been in doubt after his role in nominating the Treaty commissioners – these could not in themselves decisively affect the outcome. That hinged on the Squadrone, and its position was still unknown to the other parties. Strenuous efforts were made by the Court to bring the Squadrone leaders onside with assurances that they would be given the responsibility of distributing that part of the Equivalent earmarked for the Company stockholders, an offer which, given their heavy involvement in the Company, was virtually an invitation to reimburse themselves. But they had still not signalled their intentions when the session opened.

The opposition strategy was to delay the proceedings inside Parliament House while popular pressure built up outside, forcing intimidated commissioners to vote for wrecking amendments which would be rejected by the English Ministry and hence ruin the Treaty. The result would be the dissolution of Parliament and new elections, which would in turn produce a new balance of forces. The crowds who gathered on Edinburgh High Street were not simply a stage army brought on for the benefit of the opposition, however, nor were their objections to the proposed union the same as those of the Jacobite barons who comprised the majority of the remaining anti-Treaty commissioners. What form did popular opposition take and what were its objectives?

The forms taken by popular protest can be easily listed. Apart from the daily demonstrations outside Parliament House, opposition most commonly took the form of petitions submitted to Parliament signed ('subscribed') by the inhabitants of a particular parish or burgh, or by delegates to a particular institution like the Commission of the Assembly of the Church of Scotland or the Convention of Royal Burghs. Less frequently, the Articles of Union were publicly burned. On two occasions, once in Edinburgh and once in Glasgow, demonstrations turned into serious riots. Finally, in an extraordinary conjunction, an armed rising was organised uniting the Presbyterian sects of the south-west with the Atholl clans of the central Highlands. We have greater difficulty in assessing the aspects of the Treaty which were responsible for stimulating this discontent. Public meetings for the purpose of political discussion were banned and, although we can assume that private meetings took place – since any demonstration requires some initial organisation –

there are no records of what was argued or agreed. We are left, therefore, with the anti-Union pamphlets through which the case was put to the literate public, the texts of the petitions presented to the Estates, and the speeches made for public consumption in Parliament House. There are limitations in using these documents as evidence of popular demands. The pamphlets recorded the views of people who were both literate and financially able to express themselves in print. Similarly, the various petitions were not drafted spontaneously at revolutionary assemblies, but by individuals or small groups on the basis of demands (or requests or beseechments) which would gather the broadest support. To complicate matters further, many examples of both pamphlets and petitions were drafted by committed Jacobites who deliberately veiled their real political goals under a cloak of patriotic rhetoric. The very fact that they were intended to capture popular support means, however, that the content of at least some petitions and opposition speeches reflect, at one remove, popular concerns.

Pamphlets dealing with the condition of Scotland had appeared with increasing frequency from 1700 onwards, as realisation dawned about the extent of the Darien disaster. *The People of Scotland's Groans and Lamentable Complaints* (1701), for example, is a classic of this genre. The trickle began to gather strength in 1704 with the English response to the Act of Security. An attempt by the Whig lawyer, William Atwood, to prove that Scotland was a fiefdom of the English crown, *Superiority and Direct Dominion of the Imperial Crown of England Over the Crown and Kingdom of Scotland*, was answered by Scots lawyer James Anderson in his *Historical Essay Showing That the Crown and Kingdom of Scotland is Imperial and Independent* (1705). The Scottish Parliament ordered the first to be burned by the public executioner and awarded the author of the second £4,800 Scots. Undeterred, Atwood hit back with *The Scotch Patriot Unmask'd* (1705) which more or less accused the entire Parliamentary opposition of being in the pay of Louis XIV. This was an exaggeration, of course, only some of them were, but by now the floodgates had opened. The so-called 'pamphlet war' which accompanied the Union negotiations and the ratification process probably involved the greatest publication and circulation of political literature in the British Isles of the entire period between the English Revolution of the 1640s and the advent of a native Jacobinism during the 1790s. In this literary battle, the majority of the Scottish participants were to be found in opposition to the Union, with a minority of Scots and virtually every English contributor in support, although the only Irish contributor, Jonathan Swift, was also opposed. A survey of the anti-Union contributions gives the impression that the key issues were, in descending order, the integrity of the kirk (threatened by the corrupting influence of Episcopalianism), the sovereignty of the Scottish people (reduced to insignificance in a state where they would be a permanent minority) and some distance behind, the viability the Scottish economy (called into question by exposure to free trade with England). Reading the pro-Union arguments the order of importance is largely reversed. The difference in emphasis between the two camps was the result of a series of interventions by the one English contributor who requires special mention, since his role was considerably greater than might be supposed solely from his literary contributions.

Daniel Defoe ('that vile monster and wretch', as Lockhart engagingly calls him[52]) was sent to Edinburgh in September 1706 by the English Ministry with the twofold purpose of spying on the popular mood and propagandising on behalf of the Union.[53] His special contribution to the debate was to turn the emphasis of the pro-Union argument towards the advantages of free trade that Scotland would supposedly enjoy after ratification. Many commentators have argued that reliance on Defoe by historians has been deeply misleading, since his concentration on the question of trade was not a genuine engagement with the arguments, but an ideological justification for one side in the dispute. There is a great deal to be said for this argument – although free trade was not thereby of no consequence in the Union debate – but it is also important to remember that the 'pamphlet war' was to a large extent a shadow play on both sides of the debate. Pamphlets expressing concern for the likely fate of the kirk, for example, were chiefly generated by ministers with their own sectional interest to defend. The ominous lack of any reference to their constitutional position – in contrast to the guarantees offered to the legal profession – led many to suppose that their positions, or at least their authority, was once more under threat from bishops. The majority of the Lowland population shared their concern, but for reasons more to do with the possible removal of any form of democratic control over the kirk than the preservation of clerical benefices. Similarly, many of the works bemoaning the loss of Scottish sovereignty were produced by Jacobites, happy to invoke the names of Wallace and Bruce, but whose own fidelity to Scottish independence should be judged by their willingness to rely on support from France – a support which carried its own threat to the sovereignty of the Ancient Kingdom of Caledonia.

With these qualifications in mind, had the 'pamphlet war' any impact on events? Its significance has been played down by writers like Paul Riley, whose focus has been solely on relationships within the political elite: 'In the last resort the fate of the union would not be settled by the literature, but by the votes in the Scottish parliament, and of these the majority was predictable.'[54] There are reasons for considering this too dismissive. The literature gave expression – in however distorted a way – to popular concerns, but at the same time it also provided merchants, and literate artisans and shopkeepers, with arguments and slogans. This is of some significance since seventeenth century Scotland enjoyed relatively high levels of literacy, with only 25 per cent of craftsmen and tradesmen classified as illiterate, a figure which had fallen to 18 per cent by the following century. In particular, Edinburgh and Glasgow – where the major debates and disturbances over the Union took place – had higher than average levels of literacy. Edinburgh in particular was perhaps the most important town in Scotland for publishing and distributing printed material of all kinds, including chapbooks, newspapers, plays and sermons.[55] A relatively wide readership therefore existed and consisted in turn of the people who organised petitions and led demonstrations. The real question is whether these more collective forms of action had any influence on the outcome – the outcome being not simply the final vote for ratification, but the amendments made to the Treaty in its passage through Parliament.

From the moment the commissioners reassembled a stream of addresses began to flood into Parliament House. One third of the shires and a quarter of burghs submitted these petitions, the overwhelming majority of them against the Treaty. Argyll declared with patrician disdain that they 'served for no other use than to make kites', and many historians have reaffirmed this dismissal, albeit in more circumspect terms.[56] And at one level a degree of caution is justified. Noble pressure was still being exerted, since the lords used their power over tenants as a matter of course when organising petitions of opposition. Atholl wrote to his lairds complaining about the small number of Scottish representatives who would sit in the British Parliament:

This, and other things contained in the said Treaty, is so Dishonourable and Disadvantageous to this nation, that I doubt not that all Honest Scotsmen will concur to hinder it passing. It's very proper that the nation should Let their sentiments be known at this occasion by their Addresses, and petitioning the Parliament. I have sent with the bearer, my servant Robert Stewart, a Draft of an address which I hope will be satisfying to you, wherefore I expect that the whole parish will sign it, and those that cannot write Let a Nottier subscribe for them.[57]

His biographer and descendant notes that on 5 December, 'Leonard Robertson of Straloch wrote to his Grace … saying that he had accordingly acquainted his Grace's vassals within the respective parishes that had rendezvoused [i.e. to sign the address] not to do any more till they received further orders'.[58]

At a lower level in the ruling class hierarchy the Jacobite lairds also circulated a petition, which as Lockhart later admitted, was centrally produced. ('I shall not deny but perhaps this measure of addressing had its first original, as they report.') The text of the address encompasses most of the objections to the Union ('framed so as to comprehend everyone's wish') but is silent on the alternative – for good reason, since the Jacobites were unlikely to have met such an enthusiastic response with a petition calling for a Stuart Restoration. This in itself suggests, however, that the signatures were freely given and the view that there was genuine enthusiasm for the petitions is supported by the difficulties encountered by the pro-Union lords where they tried to raise petitions for the Treaty. Lockhart noted that the Court and Squadrone lords ('petty sovereigns themselves') attempted to force their tenants to give support: 'Yet they could not, though they endeavoured to, persuade their vassals and tenants to sign an address for the Union, and were obliged to compound [i.e. negotiate] with them not to sign against it.'[59] The last part of that sentence is astonishing, if one considers the power that the lords still had over their tenants. We see here then at least a partial break with the tradition whereby petitions were instigated by sections of the local ruling class, and tenants or indwellers expected to sign, regardless of their own views on the matter.

Nevertheless, the rural tenants had not generated their own petitions, but merely given unforced support to one produced elsewhere. Petitions which were drawn up in the burghs, where the influence of the great men was generally more circumscribed than in the rural areas, reflected popular demands more directly. The first of these, from Linlithgow, Dunkeld and Dysart, were presented before the vote on Article 1 on 4 November and thereafter they arrived on a regular basis until the end of the year. The same themes recur throughout. A petition from the burgh of Stirling attacked the Treaty on the grounds that it would 'bring an Insupportable burden of Taxation upon this Land, which all the Grant of freedom of Trade will never counterbalance, being so uncertain and precarious'. And once it had been passed, there would be no 'parliament to hear and help us Except that of a British one'.[60] Similar arguments are raised in the instructions of 23 October 1706 from the Lauder magistrates to their Burgh Commissioner, Sir David Cunningham, which:

... unanimously give as their Humble Opinion, that the Devolving of Power of the Scots Parliament into the hands of a small Number of Lords, Barons and Burghs allowed in the said proposed Articles ... is Disgraceful and Prejudicial to the Kingdom of Scotland, tending to the destruction of their Ancient Constitution, and all Rights and Privileges as a free People in general, and to every Individual Person and Society within the same, Especially that of the Burghs.[61]

The Unionist lords used their influence in the burghs to try and secure pro-Treaty petitions but, as Lockhart explains, with no more success than in the rural areas:

... they did attempt it, but could prevail in no place but the town of Ayr, where they got one subscribed, but by so pitiful and small a number that they thought shame to present it, especially when one a little thereafter, against the Union, was signed by almost all the inhabitants of that town. Neither did they omit any thing in their power to obstruct the addresses against the Union, but without success, except in the shire of Ayr, where the Earls of Loudoun, Stair and Glasgow prevailed with most of the gentlemen to lay it aside (though otherwise they expressed themselves as opposite to the Union as in any other place), and in Edinburgh, where, after an address was signed by many thousands, they prevailed with the magistrates to prohibit it by threatening to remove the Parliament and Judicatories from hence.[62]

The burgh of Montrose, one of the few with profitable trading links in England, was almost alone in instructing its commissioner to vote for the Treaty. Eight days before the Lauder petition was signed, the Montrose Burgh Council were recording in their minute book their intention to write to James Scott Younger of Logie, stating that:

> if the English Prohibitory Laws which were repealed last Session of Parliament in order to facilitate the treaty do again take place as undoubtedly they will, we shall be deprived of the only valuable branch of our trade, the only trade by which the balance is on our side and then one needs not the gift of Prophecy to foretell what shall be the fate of this poor miserable blinded nation in a few years.[63]

But Montrose was not Scotland and these burghers were not typical of the Scottish merchant class.

One of the few commissioners who might be said to have represented capitalist interests of a more advanced nature also opposed the treaty, but for opposite reasons to the majority of the burghs. William Stewart of Pardovan was the commissioner for Linlithgow, which, as we have seen, was one of the first burghs to submit a petition. Stewart was also entrusted by the Convention of Royal Burghs to present its address to the Estates, yet unlike his own burgh or the Convention he opposed Article 21 which preserved the status of the royal burghs precisely because he believed, correctly, that their feudal privileges were detrimental to a general expansion of trade.[64] But Stewart was as exceptional a burgess as Montrose was a burgh.

On balance, therefore, it is impossible to sustain the position held by Willie Thompson and his colleagues that the uniqueness of the Treaty lay in the fact that 'a bourgeoisie voluntarily renounced state independence in order to survive as a bourgeoisie'.[65] In fact, the bourgeoisie as such were, in their vast majority, opposed to the Union on the eminently material grounds that exposure to free trade would see their manufactures swamped by more competitive English rivals. As James Hodges wrote in 1703, 'there is no need of any other Argument to prove an Impossibility that the Scots can ever thrive by Free-Trade with *England* ... but a short View of the necessary Consequences of it'. Among the most important in this context were 'a multiplying of Demands' for 'all manner of Foreign Manufacture, as must quickly ruin all those advancements already made in Several Manufactories, especially being yet in their Infancy'. As a result:

> Scotland may then bid farewell to the Woolen, Stuff, Stocken, and many other Manufactures, especially now in so hopeful a way of Thriving among them, and by which so large a Number of the Poor are maintain'd, who then must go a Begging ... all Hope of Erecting New Manufacturies must be lost.[66]

The views of the Convention of Royal Burghs, and of the majority of its constituent burghs, were therefore perfectly in keeping with the conservative mercantile interests that they still represented. One of the reasons why Defoe in particular spent so much time stressing the beneficial effects of free trade was to persuade the mercantile bourgeoisie, whose timidity and fear of competition he was at a loss to understand, how it would act in their interest. He was neither the first nor the last to judge Scottish merchant capitalists by English standards and find them wanting.

One of the few representative thinkers of the Scottish bourgeoisie who did embrace the possibility of union was William Paterson.[67] He now argued that the Scots had to realistically assess their inability to establish a colony ('this Company fails in its attempts for want of sufficient support and protection') and draw the necessary conclusions:

> But since by this Union, Britain will become a formidable Government, its business and care will be effectually to support and encourage its subjects in their designs both at home and in foreign trade; to which monopolies, and exclusive and distinct companies, instead of being a help, would, in such a state, be the greatest hindrance.[68]

But Paterson saw a union as the basis for the empire which the Scots had been unable to achieve on their own behalf, writing of 'the opportunity the Union will give for further, and still much more, valuable possessions in America':

> Since it is an Union at home, and that only, which can make this island secure and comfortable in itself, and capable of improving its successes abroad, among which are so considerable as those which lie ready and open for it in the West Indies; since, by or before the conclusion of this

war, we now have a fair opportunity, either by force or by treaty, to secure the Isthmus of America – of which Caledonia is only a part – together with Carthegena and the Havana, either as cautionary places till our expenses of the war shall be refunded, or otherwise, upon our own account.[69]

But it would take another half century from the attainment of the Union for Scots to derive any significant benefit from, or make any significant contribution to the Empire.[70]

In terms of mobilising popular opposition, the attitude of the kirk was more important than the burgesses to subsequent events. The Reverend John Logan wrote to Mar on 27 August 1706 about the attitude of the majority:

> ... all of them I converse with in private are of a dissenting judgement from an incorporating Union, and do look thereupon both as sinful in itself and of dangerous consequence to the established government of this Church, it being (as is thought by some) to be contradictory to the covenants against prelacy in the three domains whereto this nation stands engaged, and are manifest exposing of their government to patent danger in regard the British Parliament may at after pleasure evert any fundament in our constitution without the consent of their constituents ... they are apprehensive of that in one nation two legally authorised forms of church government are unprecedented ... and so cannot be thought to stand long in Britain.[71]

Such attitudes evidently infected Logan himself, since on 27 October he preached a sermon before Parliament – subsequently reproduced as a pamphlet – on the need to value and protect the kirk.[72]

On 16 October the Commission of the General Assembly of the Church of Scotland (the leading body of the kirk when the General Assembly itself was not in session) presented its own petition. A week later the protests took on a more violent form. On 23 October, the crowd attempted to force its way into Parliament House, but was repulsed by the guards. Nevertheless, the proceedings broke up with Hamilton going to visit Atholl instead of allowing the crowd to carry him in triumph back to his 'lodgings' at Holyrood Palace. The crowd, denied the opportunity either to confront their rulers or to escort their hero, instead launched an attack on the house of Sir Patrick Johnson, once a popular Lord Provost, but now hated as one of the commissioners responsible for agreeing the Articles of Union. Fortunately for Johnson, he lived – as befitted a man of his station – on the top floor of one of the tall, narrow tenements in the Old Town, into which it was difficult to make a forced entry. Nevertheless, as Mar recounted to Nairne some days later: 'They assaulted his house, broke his windows, and did what they could to beat open his door, giving him names and calling out that they would massacre him for being a betrayer and seller of his country.'[73] They had failed to achieve their initial objective, but, as Lockhart reports:

> From hence the mob, which was increased to a great number, went through the streets, threatening destruction to all the promoters of the Union, and continued for four or five hours in this temper till about three the next morning, a strong detachment of Foot-guards was sent to secure the gate called the Netherbow Port and keep guard in the Parliament Close.

But the guards themselves were unreliable, saying: 'It is hard we should oppose those that are standing up for the Country, it is what we cannot help just now, but what we won't continue at.'[74] Despite this apparent display of sympathy, the guards remained in place for the duration of the Parliament without any noticeable breach of discipline. In part this was because the crowd itself had no long-term objectives which might have enabled them to win over the guards. One incident in particular throws an interesting light on the limits of their challenge to authority.

While these disturbances were going on, Mar, together with Argyll and Lord Lothian, were dining at Lord Loudoun's town residence. Rather than wait to be attacked they set off with their host, only to run into the very 'mob' they had sought to avoid. Mar recounts what happened next: 'We saw great numbers of the rabble with stones in their hands, but as soon as they saw us they dropped them and let us pass.' The crowd followed them, some cursing, 'some blessing us', but doing nothing:

> This expedition of ours, I confess, was hardly as wise. If one stone had been thrown at us there had been five hundred, and some of the mob were heard to say after we had passed the Cross that they were to blame for letting Argyll and Loudon pass unpunished. However we got free.[75]

The Edinburgh crowd were not famous for deferring to the lords but, threats to Johnston's life notwithstanding, at a crucial moment they were unwilling to strike at leading members of the political classes, even when they were completely in their power. Much to Mar's disgust, when Parliament assembled the next day some of the opposition were unwilling to condemn the riot, with Fletcher even arguing that the mob represented the true spirit of Scotland, and reminding the House that the people had been responsible for the success of the Reformation and the Revolution. Fletcher was familiar enough with Scottish history to know that this was, at best, a half-truth, and the very fact that a man so little enamoured of mob activity could advance this argument indicates a certain desperation on his part.

The Debate Opens in Parliament

Shortly after these disturbances Parliament finally moved to discuss the Treaty on an Article-by-Article basis. After several weeks of fencing around the issue, the Court called a vote on whether to proceed with consideration of the individual Articles, which they won by a majority of 66, although this in itself did not mean that the Treaty was bound to pass, since the vote may only have indicated that a majority wished to commence the struggle in earnest. The Court was certainly aware that clerical opposition was feeding disturbances outside the House, which in turn was pressurising a number of the commissioners inside. As Mar complained to Nairne:

> By the ministers preaching up fear and danger, and their carriage in the Commission, and the misrepresenting the Union by others, the humour of the commonality are mightily against us; and until the first Article of the Treaty be approven I doubt not that we will have more addresses against an incorporating Union; but they will signify nothing.[76]

Given that the vote on Article 1, which united the two kingdoms into the new state of Great Britain, would be important in determining the outcome of the overall debate, the arguments which were advanced for and against it are of particular interest.

William Seton of Pitmedden opened for the Court by outlining the uncertainties which Scotland experienced being the weaker state within a composite monarchy:

> Every Monarch, having two or more Kingdoms, will be obliged to prefer the Counsel and Interest of the Stronger to that of the weaker: and the Greater Disparity of Power and Riches there is, betwixt these Kingdoms, the greater Influence the more powerful will have on the Sovereign.

This much everyone agreed on. It was the solution to this problem that had divided Parliament for so long. Seton then outlined with stark clarity the alternatives left to the Scottish ruling class. They would have to ally with some other power, as they had always done, and this could only be Holland, France or England. Holland he dismissed right away on the grounds that both Scotland and Holland traded the same commodities. The fundamental choice lay between France and England:

> ... from France few advantages can be reaped, till the old offensive and defensive league [i.e. the Auld Alliance] be revived betwixt France and Scotland, which would give umbrage to the English, and occasion a War betwixt them and us. And allying the Scots, in such a venture,

with the assistance of France, to conquer England; Scotland by that conquest would not hope to better its present state; for it is more than probable, the conqueror would make his residence in England ...

Separation from England, Seton argued, would take Scotland backwards, 'returning to that Gothic constitution of Government, wherein our forefathers were, which was frequently attended with feuds, murder, depredation and rebellions'. The only real choice lay, not in whether to ally with England, but in the nature of the alliance. Here again Seton could draw support from the agreed inadequacies of the Regal Union:

... there's but one of two left to our Choice, to wit, That both Kingdoms be united into one, or that we continue under the same Sovereign with England as we have done for these 100 years past. The last I conceive to be a very ill State, for by it, (if Experience be convincing) we cannot expect any of the Advantages of an Incorporating Union; but on the contrary, our Sovereignty and Independency will be eclipsed, the number of our Nobility will Increase, Our Commons will be Oppressed, Our Parliaments will be influenced by England, the Execution of our Laws will be neglected; Our Peace will be interrupted by Factions for Places and Pensions, Luxury together with Poverty (though strange) will invade us, Numbers of Scots will withdraw themselves to Foreign Centres; and all the other Effects of Bad Government must necessarily attend us.[77]

It was a brilliant performance of compelling logic, with Seton incorporating many of the arguments against the existing condition of Scottish society – particularly with respect to the peasantry – which he had been advocating as a member of the Country Party since 1700. Fletcher had put forward many of the same arguments and done so from the same political position. One therefore wonders what he thought, listening to Seton use these arguments to support an incorporating union, and knowing that the lords whose mouthpiece he was had no intention of diminishing their own numbers, or of ceasing to oppress 'their commons'. Seton had given good reasons for supporting the Treaty of Union, but they were only in part the real reasons.

Neither was much honesty forthcoming from the opposition. Fletcher could have given an effective reply, but his views were shared by almost no one else in the Parliament, not the other members of the Country Party, and certainly not the Jacobites who formed the remainder and the majority of the opposition. Their choice was, as it always had been, to opt for the restoration of the Stuart line and hence for French domination. This could scarcely be trumpeted openly by those playing the patriotic card and so the opposition case was conducted in the vaguest terms possible, emphasising the depredations which the Union would bring to the common people of Scotland. The actual reply to Seton, by John Hamilton, second Lord Belhaven, embodied all these evasions. Between the Latin tags, rhetorical questions and theatrical sobbing with which his widely reproduced speech is studded, Belhaven does little more than give further ammunition to the pro-Unionists. In his vision of Caledonia under the Union, Belhaven presents as a serious argument the detrimental effect such an arrangement would have on Our Scottish Noble Families:

I think I see the Present Peers of Scotland, whose Noble ancestors Conquered Provinces, over-run countries, reduced and subjugated Towns and fortified Places, exacted Tribute through the greatest part of England, now walking in the Court of Requests, like so many English Attorneys, laying aside their Walking Swords when in Company with the English Peers, lest their Self-defence should be found murder.

For the majority of Scots, of course, the prospect that the Scottish nobility might at last be brought under control was one of the few unambiguous benefits which the Union seemed to offer, which was precisely why Seton had introduced the subject into his own speech. More importantly, however, Belhaven conceded the desperation of the Scottish situation, admitting that the Scots were:

... an Obscure Poor People, though formerly of better account, removed to a Remote Corner of the World, without Name and without alliances; our Posts mean and precarious: So that I profess, I don't think any one Post of the Kingdom worth the Bringing after, save that of being Commissioner to a long Session of a Factious Scots Parliament.[78]

Belhaven was instantly deflated by a dismissive intervention from Marchmont. (Summarised by Defoe as 'Behold, he dreamed, but lo! when he awoke, behold, it was a dream!'[79]) A more relevant assessment of Belhaven's vaunted patriotism has perhaps been given more recently by Rosalind Mitchison:

It was a patriotic declamation which would read better if Lord Belhaven's idea of patriotism had not allowed him to let his tenantry starve in the famine [of the 1690s] when he and the other heritors of the parish of Spott refused to fulfil their obligations in relief.[80]

Hamilton followed Belhaven in the debate, but did little more than evoke the sacred names of Bruce and Wallace, and the supposedly patriotic traditions of the nobility. The result of the vote was as follows:

	For	Against
Nobility	46	21
Barons	37	33
Burgesses	33	29
Total	116	83[81]

Two matters were clarified as soon as the result was announced. The first was that, of the three Estates, the nobility was the most committed to carrying the Treaty. The second was that the Squadrone had decided to cast their 25 votes with the Court Party, thus making eventual ratification much more certain. From this the two sides of the House drew different conclusions. The opposition realised that the only way the Treaty as a whole could be stopped would be by going beyond the confines of Parliament House to the population at large. Their only hope now lay in using popular pressure to intimidate the pro-Union commissioners into passing wrecking amendments which would in turn be rejected by the English and hence ruin the Treaty. The Court Party and their Squadrone allies drew a similar conclusion. Queensberry and his associates felt that the majority for Article 1 had not been high enough for safety and that concessions had to be made to the opposition outside Parliament in order to influence the votes inside. Mar wrote to Nairne the day after the vote that: 'What with the Addresses and the humour that's now in the country against the Union, several members left us, though I'm hopeful that many of them will come about again.'[82] They, at any rate, were under no illusions that the matter could be resolved within the confines of Parliament House.

Neutralising the Kirk

The Court introduced, on the same day Article 1 was ratified, an Act for Securing the Protestant Religion and Presbyterian Church Government. This move to ameliorate the kirk came not a minute too soon. Between the introduction of the Act of Security on 4 November and its approval by Parliament on 12 November, the Commission had called a fast, the traditional method by which the Scots made atonement for their various sins. On the appointed day, 7 November, James Clark, the minister at the Tron kirk in Glasgow preached a sermon (text: Ezra 8:21) at the climax of which, Defoe reports, he said that:

> Addresses would not do, and prayers would not do, there must be other methods; it is true prayer was a duty but we must not rest there; and closed it with the words, 'Wherefore up and be valiant for the city of our God'.[83]

The congregation then upped as requested and within two hours had grown into a crowd of several thousand which demanded that Lord Provost Aird and the magistrates sign a petition against the Union. Finding themselves repulsed they approached the Deacons of the craft guilds who were supportive and agreed to try and persuade the magistrates of their error. Denied a second time the crowd rioted, invaded the Provost's house (from where he had wisely fled with some of the other councillors to the relative safety of Edinburgh) and seized the supply of arms stored there. The subsequent arrest of one of the rioters for possession of these arms led to a second riot to liberate him from the tolbooth, a further attack on the Provost's house and another flight by the dignitary to the safety of the capital.

Defoe blamed the rioting on the influence of 'Jacobites, Papists and Episcopal people', and a Jacobite named Finlay was certainly involved in mobilising for the attack on the tolbooth. The day had yet to arrive, however, when events in Glasgow were decisive in shaping political events in Scotland. When Finlay set off for Edinburgh in an attempt to foment a rising, only 45 men accompanied him and they encountered no practical support as they rode east. Defoe speculated, with some degree of plausibility, that opposition to Jacobitism was a factor in the lack of support for Finlay: 'and I believe that is one reason the Cameronian people, though equally disaffected, would not join him, at least not so as to march from Glasgow or their other towns'.[84] Nor did Finlay draw support from higher up the social structure. Equally significant was the rebuff he encountered at Hamilton. Finlay and his comrades had approached Duchess Anne, mother to the Duke and herself a formidable anti-Unionist, but received only discouragement. The reason is not hard to find: 'Anarchy would have been even worse than the Union.'[85] Eventually they were dispersed by an advance detachment of 25 dragoons (out of a body of 400) who arrested the ringleaders. This did not end the matter. Finlay and his lieutenant, Montgomery, were taken under arrest to Edinburgh after which the dragoons withdrew from Edinburgh. 'As soon as they were come away,' wrote Defoe, 'the rabble rose again and took all the magistrates prisoner and declared that if their two men were not restored and set home again, they would treat the magistrates just in the same manner as they should be treated.'[86] Two magistrates were sent to Edinburgh to negotiate but were promptly ordered by the Privy Council to return to Glasgow and take control of the situation.[87]

As one would expect, the ministers of the south-western sects had taken a much harder line against the proposed union than the Church of Scotland. One pamphlet which appeared in 1706 was entitled *Protestation and Testimony of the United Societies of the Witnessing Remnant of the Anti-Popish, Anti-Prelatic, Anti-Sectarian True Presbyterian Church of Christ in Scotland Against the Sinful Incorporating Union*. Apart from providing a comprehensive list of their enemies, the title also announced that the network of activists who had once formed the core of the United Societies, now divided into several competing sects, had resumed a public role. One group (the 'McMillanites') chose as the site of their first intervention the burgh of Dumfries. This was not a random selection. Dumfries was one of the majority of burghs which voted against the Treaty in the Convention of Royal Burghs on the grounds that it would damage local trade. The parish representative in the Supreme Ecclesiastical Court of the Church of Scotland had also spoken against the Treaty on the grounds that it threatened the Presbyterian settlement. These sentiments were apparently in keeping with those of the majority of inhabitants, for on 20 November a crowd gathered, including 300 armed men: 'Near noonday this formidable band – made up partly of high-minded, well-organised men, and partly of the burgh mob – appeared menacingly in the High Street, and making their way to the [Mercat] Cross unopposed by the authorities, many of whom sympathised with them, in a calm deliberative manner, proceeded to their task; and so exciting was it that every other sort of work was abandoned in the town.'[88] 'Their task' was to burn a copy of the Articles of Union, followed by a list of the commissioners. A leaflet later distributed in the town describes how the Articles were carried to the Market Cross where 'with great Solemnity, in the audience of many thousands' they were burnt. The organisers were also concerned – in the traditional Cameronian manner – to explain their actions and, in particular, their contempt for the commissioners who had negotiated the Treaty:

> We must say, and Profess, That the Commissioners for this Nation have either been Simple, Ignorant or Treacherous, if not all three, when the Minutes of the Treaty betwixt the Commissioners of both Kingdoms are duly Considered; and when we compare the Dastardly yeildings unto the Demands and Proposals of the English Commissioners; who, on the contrar[y], have valiantly acquit[ted] themselves for the Interest and Safety of their Nation.[89]

The disturbances in Glasgow and the south-west had largely died down by 12 December when the Act of Security for the Church was passed with a majority of 74. Mar breathed an audible sigh of relief to Nairne in a letter later that day:

> You know the great rock we were most afraid to split upon was the Church; and notwithstanding all the pains and endeavours that have been taken to delude people on that score, yet we have this day carried the Act securing the Presbyterian Church government as now by law established in Scotland after the Union with very little alteration.[90]

Although separate from the Treaty itself, this Act must be considered as integral to it. The kirk ministers were not thereby won over to the idea of union with English Episcopalians, but the protection which the Act offered them effectively defused their opposition to the extent that they ceased agitating and started grumbling instead. Lockhart denounced them for their sectionalism, writing that 'no sooner did the Parliament pass an act for the security of their Kirk ... than most of the brethren's zeal cooled – thereby discovering that provided they could retain the possession of their benefices they cared not a farthing what became of the other concerns of the nation.'[91] Lockhart is too dismissive here. The lower kirk courts – the kirk sessions and presbyteries – were still hostile, but the defection of the General Assembly at the national level deprived their opposition of any focus or leadership. A mere two months before the Union came into effect, the Presbyterian attitude had hardened to such an extent that Seafield could write to Carstares from London: 'All the presbyterians, and you in particular, have been very happy of having this opportunity to testify your zeal and loyalty to her Majesty's person and government, and your fixed resolutions to withstand and oppose the popish pretender.'[92]

A Cameronian–Jacobite Alliance?

More serious than either of the momentary eruptions of collective disorder in Edinburgh or Glasgow was the possibility of insurrection in the south-west, where large-scale mobilisations were taking place for the first time since the Revolution. The burning of the Articles in Dumfries was their first public manifestation. Lockhart writes of the sects that they 'divided themselves into regiments; chose their officers; provided themselves with horses and arms'.[93] Is this the appearance, at last, of an independent radical movement committed to overturning the existing ruling class?

Our access to radical political thought is limited for this period, but one anti-Union contribution to the 'pamphlet war', *The Smoaking Flax Unquenchable*, addressed to 'the True Subjects of the Covenanted Kingdom of Scotland', certainly envisages a Godly regime modelled on the Cromwellian Commonwealth, and suggests both the extent of Cameronian radicalism and its limits. The proposals of the anonymous author are therefore worth considering in some detail. Elected rulers would be subject to a number of constraints which, given the venality of Scottish political life, had radical implications:

... we declare ourselves against all Hereditary Offices, either Civil or Military, as they shall pass from Father to Son, without the qualifications above mentioned, and the free Election of the People. ... We declare that we incline and intend to abolish all rents and Revenues given to any in public Office (either Civil or Military) more than will maintain an honest Christian life; as that Family and Children may be provided in a Christian way ...

In the administration of the law, a select panel of judges, similar to those operative in the 1650s, would assess the merits of particular cases without favouring the wealthy: 'And these Judges may Determine Causes and Controversies as the manner was at that present time, and thereby partiality and oppression may be removed, that thereby Justice may be Exercised towards all Ranks without Respect of Persons.' The author fully anticipated that the nobility would oppose these proposals 'as mountains in the way':

I doubt not, but that they shall have full Liberty (in the first place) to play their Game, in order to set up their Kings, that they are contending for, so that they may drink of the Cup that the Kingdoms of Europe are Drinking of, who are wasting and destroying one another, which Lot I fear will be Scotland's ere it be long: and then it shall be found that these great Mountains shall be removed.

Yet, radical though many of the ideas of *The Smoaking Flax Unquenchable* are, the key feature of the pamphlet – as the last quote suggests – is its passivity. The mountainous nobility may tumble and fall, but not through any active intervention by the author or his associates. This in turn seems to be a function of his pessimism about the likely effects of mere political activity:

Yea, they [i.e. the Scots] will rather join with the Citizens of Darkness (that is with the French), in receiving King James the eighth (as they call him) or else Hanover, or with the Prince of Prussia (as some has [sic] already proposed) before that they will Espouse that Government and these Governors, that's most for the propagating of Religion and Virtue in the Land.[94]

Why was this ideological radicalism ultimately linked to political quietism? At one level, the author of *The Smoaking Flax Unquenchable* was still locked into the fundamentally religious intellectual framework that had always characterised the plebeian conventiclers, even at their most extreme. (Indeed, in its reliance on Biblical precedent the pamphlet is in some respects a retreat from the position taken by Alexander Shields in his *A Hind Let Loose* of 1685, where historical examples began to vie with the word of God as a guide to action.) It may be, however, that beneath the quotations from the Old Testament, more secular considerations were also at work. During the 1640s, and again between 1660 and 1688, a millenarianism inspired the south-western plebeians to successive military challenges to the Engagers, the New Model Army and the Restoration regime. Why did this ideology, which once led them to conclude that God would be best served by these suicidal onslaughts on the state apparatus, now suggest that His will be done by surrendering to the powers and principalities of this world? The answer may lie in the reference above to 'join[ing] with the Citizens of Darkness'. For as Anonymous well knew, it was not only the Jacobites who were contemplating an alliance with France.

A lttle over a year earlier, in April 1705, a memorial to Robert Harley from William Houston contained a pro-conventicler account of the last years of Charles II and the reign of James VII and II. The main intention of this epistle was however to provide a political map of Scotland in terms of religious reliability. 'The five western shires, Ayr, Renfrew, Galloway, Nithsdale, Clydesdale and the Stewarty of Galloway' were where 'the people are all generally strict dissenters from popery, prelacy, erastian indulgency; exceedingly well armed and disciplined, zealous against the French or anything that smells of popery'. Houston claimed that the gentry would be unable to resist the will of the people: 'In fine, the common enemy cannot project any hopes here.' In the central shires adjacent to the Highlands: 'The commonality, being zealous Protestants, are obliged, especially in the winter season, to defend themselves against the ravagings of the Highlands, committing hardships, that's robbing all their cattle.' Finally, 'Relating to the army, it is very proper at this juncture that they have honest officers – men of courage, conscience, such as Colonel James Bruce, who came over with the late King William at the Revolution, and men of his spirit.' The reason why is of some interest: 'It would conduce much to the spirit of Britain.'[95] It is unlikely that Harley reacted with delight on being informed that sections of the population of south-west Scotland were prepared independently to take up arms, even if it was against 'the common enemy'. Nevertheless, Houston had confirmed what was widely known, even in the depths of Whitehall: the sectaries of the south-west were Phanatics in so far as their religious beliefs were concerned, but they could be relied upon to oppose Jacobitism and schemes involving the French monarchy. Or so everyone thought.

It now appeared that everyone may have been wrong. Of the situation in September 1706, Lockhart could write that the goal of the sectaries was 'the return of the King [i.e. James] as the most feasible grounds to go upon to save the country' and in their search for allies they:

> ... were so far reconciled to the northern parts (whom formerly they hated heartily on account of their different principles of religion) and episcopal party, that they were willing to join and concert measures with them for the defence of their common native country.[96]

The 'reconciliation' to which Lockhart refers involved a military alliance, arranged, at the instigation of local laird James Cunningham of Aiket, between clan warriors from the Perthshire superiority of Lord Atholl and the Presbyterian paramilitaries of the south-west. The strategy involved the former holding the main strategic pass by Stirling Castle while the latter took Edinburgh, dispersed the Parliament and then recalled James from exile to take up the succession. That an alliance was being negotiated had been registered by the English Ministry as early as September, when Mar had written to the English Secretary of State, Robert Harley: 'Great endeavours are made by some to unite those parties against us and the Union, but it is not very probable that it will be easily done, they being of so different principles.'[97] Mar almost certainly knew of these plans as a result of double agents who had infiltrated the Presbyterian wing of the alliance. What is remarkable is the fact that these agents constituted important members of the leadership. It is not known whether Cunningham had been in the pay of the Court from the start, or whether he was subsequently 'turned'. At one point he successfully denounced John Hepburn, leader of the sect known as the Hebronites, for warning against an alliance with the Jacobites, but this may have simply been a stratagem to gain trust within the movement as a whole. He was certainly paid £100 after the Treaty was ratified and made demands for further payments for his services in later years. Whatever the ambiguities of Cunningham's position, however, a second double agent, John Ker of Kersland, was definitely in the pay of Queensberry from the start.

Ker was correctly believed to have influence with the sects by virtue of the leading role played by his family, and particularly his father, in the struggles between 1660 and 1688. He was therefore sent by Queensberry to push his way into the leadership, a task that he successfully accomplished with remarkable speed. Given the pivotal role which the sectaries were expected to play in the intended rising, Ker was privy to several conversations in which leading anti-Unionists made their true intentions plain:

A Gentleman entirely in Duke Hamilton's Interest told me, that every Body was then sensible of my prevailing Interest with the Cameronians, and Believed that it was in my power to be very useful in relieving my bleeding Country from the Misery it was about to be plunged into from the Union; that it was better the Pretender should be our King, and we a free people than under the Notion of Liberty and Property live Slaves for ever ... I confess this shocked me ...[98]

Anti-Unionists naturally dismissed the threat of French influence (in the words of one) as 'the cobweb sophistry of hired Heads, or the waking Dreams of a Bribed Brain'. For, as the same author explains: 'In a word the French have neither Affronted, Injured nor falsely Reproached our Nation as the English have done, but on the contrary, have always proved more Courteous Friends, Kind Confederates, and more Mannerly Neighbours to us than the English.'[99] Yet whatever French relations with Scotland up to that point (and the assessment quoted above would scarcely have been considered credible in 1559 or 1690), a rising at the time would certainly have involved France, as Lockhart, who had helped negotiate the alliance between the sectaries and the Atholl Highlanders, himself makes clear in matter-of-fact terms, noting that 'Scotland might have defended itself for some time, till France had counteracted the troops that were to be sent from abroad'.[100] Indeed, the French regime was consciously trying to bring about such a conjuncture.

For Defoe was not the only foreign spy in Scotland at this time. Colonel Nathaniel Hooke, an Irishman who had fought with Monmouth before converting to Catholicism and committing himself to the Jacobite cause, was sending reports to the French regime on the possibility of a rising in Scotland against the Union and in favour of the Stuarts. Unlike Defoe, however, Hooke was not just a propagandist; he was engaged in trying to bring such a rising to fruition. To this end he entered into negotiations with, among other members of the Scottish Parliament, Hamilton. Hooke understood however that more than one set of forces would be necessary to overthrow the existing regime and defend Scotland against the inevitable English intervention:

> If arms and ammunition are sent only to the Presbyterians of Scotland to make them rise, as they have offered, the finest opportunity in the world will be lost; for the Presbyterians alone will not attack England, nor will be able to make themselves masters of Scotland; and the Scottish Lords will not put themselves at their head ... whereas if the insurrection be general, it will be out of the power of the English to prevent its taking effect.[101]

Could such a rising have succeeded? Bearing in mind that 'success' in this context would have meant holding out against troops loyal to the government and any English intervention until the French fleet arrived, it was certainly possible. Lockhart writes that:

> ... the nation was unanimous and cordial in the cause and [there were] not seven thousand standing forces in all Britain, of which those that were in Scotland were so dissatisfied with the Union that everybody knew, and the officers had acquainted the government, that they could not be trusted, nine parts of ten being inclined to join with those that opposed it.[102]

There are two claims here. First, that the Scottish state was militarily unable to withstand an insurrection. Second, that the majority of the Scottish population would have supported that insurrection.

On the one hand, Lockhart was undoubtedly correct to identify the absence of military power as the key weakness of the Scottish state. In this respect nothing had changed in the year since Tweedale had been forced to give royal assent to the Act of Security in order to gain supply. Nairne wrote to Mar late in November with a list of Lamentable Groans and Complaints:

> ... there is no powder almost in the magazine, and very little to be got in the nation. The castle of Stirling, of which I have the command, is mightily out of repair, and hardly a gun mounted, and there is not five barrels of powder in it. There's no beds within it for the soldiers to lie in, so they are forced to lie in the town, by all of which you may see how little secure it would be if there were anything to be done and how easily it might be taken. It is the great pass in Scotland, so no place is the more important. The Treasury here can do nothing to it for want of money, and I'm not to blame, for I have represented the bad condition of it again and again.[103]

Nor were the troops themselves reliable. Defoe reported to London in November that, 'if any insurrection come – which I must acknowledge is not unlikely – I crave leave to say the few troops they have here are not to be depended upon; I have this confessed by men of the best judgement'.[104] Could the English army have supplied the firepower that the Scottish state could not supply on its own behalf? Troops were indeed moved north to fortify the Border regions, but their use in the event of a rising would have been a high-risk strategy. English forces could not simply enter Scotland in response to a French attack; partly because the bulk of them were involved in the crucial struggle in Flanders, but even more because any move which smacked of an invasion of Scotland – even in response to a prior French invasion – could potentially have incited Scots within the British Army to mutiny, with unforeseeable consequences. As the century opened Scots held 10 per cent of all regimental colonelcies within the British Army. By the battle of Blenheim in 1704 they held 5 of the 16 regimental colonelcies.[105] More importantly, this disproportionate preponderance was not restricted to the officer level. During the course of the war in Flanders Scotland provided two regiments of dragoons, six battalions of foot (all paid from the English Exchequer) and the six battalions of the Scots Brigade. In addition to these 10,000 men, Scots also served in English regiments.[106] Against this, the French state had only recently sustained a serious defeat upon its own territory at Ramillies on 23 May. Presented with an open door, however, there is little doubt that Louis would have mustered an invasion force and entered it, to which the English state could have done nothing but reply with force, whatever the risks.

On the other hand, Lockhart seems to have been wrong over the crucial question of whether or not sufficient numbers of the Scottish people would rise in the first place in order to bring the other elements of the equation into play. The attitude of the sectaries was crucial, since they were the most motivated and organised of any group among the subordinate classes. These comments by Daniel Defoe, although condescending in the extreme to 'the poor deluded people of Glasgow and the West', nevertheless catch the nature of their quandary:

> ... will any man say, the men of Glasgow, famous for its zeal in religion, and the liberties of their country, even from the very infancy of the reformation, were now turned enemies to the Church of Scotland, and ready to fight against her, in the quarrel of their bloody and inveterate enemies, the Papists and Jacobites? ... will anybody think, that Glasgow men had so far forgot the history of twenty years ago only, that they could now join with the murderers of their brethren and fathers, and take up arms in favour of their mortal enemies?[107]

'Men are known by their friends,' noted another pamphlet (perhaps also written by Defoe) published after the Glasgow riots and the attempted rising: ' ... all the Jacobites are in League with you, the Papists are on your right Hand, the Prelatists on your left, and the French at your Back ... on what account do these people join with you?'[108] It was a point Defoe returned to again and again. He wrote gleefully to London on how the leader of the abortive Glasgow rising was conducting himself in Prison: 'Finlay, though a prisoner in the Castle, openly drinks King James the 8th's health – and 'tis as good a thing as he can do. I have made Mr J.P. write word of it into Galloway.'[109]

Mr J.P. ('Pierce') seems to have been Ker.[110] His activities are often credited – not least by himself – with having ideologically disarmed the sectaries by pointing out the inconsistencies involved in their alliance with the Jacobites:

> The Reader must know, that from the Confidence the Cameronians reposed in me, they laid aside their Resentments against the Union for some Time, and agreed to my proposal, which was to declare against the Pretender, and all that joined him, as Enemies.[111]

At the time, Defoe reported to Harley how 'Pierce' had gone into the mountain fastness of the Hebronites to meet with their leader:

> He has opened his [i.e. Hepburn's] eyes in several things, and he shows us he has been misrepresented in others, and he authorises me to

assure you that there is no danger from him unless some new artifices succeed to influence him.

We do not need to accept Ker's overwhelming powers of persuasion as the sole reason for the radical retreat, for he was not spreading black propaganda, but simply stating the truth. Indeed, a Scottish anti-Union pamphleteer, James Hodges, had to remind those among his countrymen who were contemplating the return of the Stuarts of the reasons for the Revolutions of 1559, 1637 and 1688: 'Can you think an Arbitrary and Absolute Monarch a fit Assessor and Supporter of Your Rights and Liberties as a Free People?'[112] The Hebronites seem to have contemplated a rising in conjunction with the Jacobites, but thought better of it. The McMillanites later denied having ever considered it.[113] It is difficult to see what else they could have done while still retaining their principles. For the sectaries to support a rising in conjunction with the Jacobite clans would have been like the Bolsheviks siding with Kornilov against Kerensky in September 1917.

In the event, Hamilton committed his second act of treachery against the opposition by sending out instructions to both sides of the alliance that the rising was cancelled. Although this dealt yet another blow to the Jacobites it removed the sectaries from the hook upon which they were impaled. We will never know the content of the discussions which took place among their ranks, but there is at least some evidence to suggest that, even if Hamilton had not reneged, they would not have proceeded with a rising which relied on Jacobite support. Radical Presbyterians were neither so unprincipled nor so unthinking as to imagine that the restoration of an absolutist regime, supported externally by Catholic France and internally by the Episcopalian clans, would benefit them in either religious or social terms. This was the conclusion that the author of *The Smoking Flax Unquenchable* had also reached and it must be supposed that similar considerations operated elsewhere in Scotland.[114] Nevertheless, it is just possible that some kind of insurgent movement could have arisen, even under Jacobite leadership, had it not been for the intercession of other, more general, factors depressing the level of popular unrest towards the end of the year.

Economic Concessions and the Decline of Popular Opposition

There were material reasons for the widespread suspicion of the Union. For the classes below the nobility and the merchant elite the Union offered, above all else, higher taxation. Moreover, although it was not mentioned in the Treaty, it was quite clear that a more rigorous Customs and Excise regime on the English model was to be imposed for the purpose of thwarting the smuggling operations which provided both illegal employment for many inhabitants of the east coast and access to cheap goods, especially wine, elsewhere. Yet many of these concerns were dealt with by amendments to the relevant Articles before the Treaty was ratified as a whole. The significance of these amendments has rarely been recognised. Paul Scott, for example, writes: 'Articles 6 and 8, on customs duty, regulations on trade and the duty on salt, had been referred to a committee because of the many objections which they provoked, and eventually led to detailed but comparatively trivial amendments.'[115] In fact, the vote of 20 December on Article 8, dealing with Scottish exemption from English salt taxes, was the only serious defeat suffered by the Court throughout the entire ratification process. Contemporaries were aware of the seriousness of the issue. Patterson, for example, wrote to London that he 'continue[d] to think the malt and salt exceptions the most material of the trade or money matters'.[116] Why this issue, above all others?

'Magnate wealth was not founded on coal, salt or black cattle,' writes Paul Riley.[117] That is right. Their wealth came rather from the feudal rents paid by their tenants (and not, as Riley believes, from the spoils of office – at least in the case of the majority outside of the Officers of State and their immediate hangers-on). But salt in particular was not for this reason insignificant. On Prestongrange estate shortly after the Union, for example, two-thirds of the estate income was derived either from rent or from the sale of agricultural produce. Sales of salt made up a quarter of total income in 1716–17 (63 per cent of the estate's non-agricultural income) and a fifth in 1717–18. More generally, salt production had two other beneficial economic effects for the landowners. Since their tenants were often involved in carrying coal to the saltpans and to the shores for export, the landowners were able to charge them higher rents in the knowledge that they were capable of paying. Moreover, although the majority of rents were still paid in kind, salt sales were generally conducted in cash – a commodity that was both absolutely necessary to the lords and otherwise in desperately short supply. It was not only the lords for whom the salt market was significant. If taxes on Scottish salt were kept lower than on English or other imported salt, then it would remain affordable by the mass of the population, for whom it was a necessity, both to preserve food during winter and to render their regular diet more palatable throughout the year.[118] It would be inadvisable to dismiss these as merely base material concerns. Given the highly circumscribed lives of most people at this time, a worsening of their material conditions in these areas was a serious matter. Therefore, far from the successful amendments being 'trivial' as Paul Scott believes, they were probably of major importance in defusing popular unrest. But Defoe was in no doubt that the amendments were a victory for the 'mob'; 'the rabbles and noise of the party have pushed them [i.e. the Commissioners] among amendments and there is no possibility to avoid it,' he wrote, shortly before they were passed.[119]

Is this not too dismissive of 'nationalist' resistance to the dissolution of the Scottish state? References to nationalism get us little further forward, however, unless we believe – as some modern nationalists evidently do – that it is a natural phenomenon requiring no further explanation. The inhabitants of the Scottish Lowlands were indeed beginning to develop a sense of national consciousness, but its transformation into political nationalism was never fully achieved while the Scottish state was in existence.[120] Nationalism involves at the very least some level of identification of the 'people' with the state, but such an identification was impossible for the vast majority of Lowland Scots. The Scottish state had failed miserably to achieve the goals it had set itself in Darien, and the functions that it did perform to any degree of efficiency were those of a feudal apparatus geared to aiding their exploitation. The crowds were provoked rather by a concern for the Scottish society in which they experienced not only oppression, but also the things that made their lives halfway bearable. Their 'nationalism' was a reaction to the specific ways in which the Treaty threatened to weaken the social fabric (through undermining the kirk – the only institution over which the plebeians exercised any democratic control) and worsen their material conditions (through increasing the cost of salt, ale, and so on). The combined effect of the guarantees offered to the kirk and the amendments which withdrew – at least temporarily – the economic cost of incorporation seem to have removed these immediate concerns. 'National identity is not people's *only* identity,' as Julian Goodare sensibly points out, nor is it always the most important one, and it is only from the ideological vantage point of nationalism itself that anyone could actually doubt this: 'While Scots went into union very much as Scots rather than as Britons, they were also mindful of their interests as Protestants, as capitalists, or as consumers.'[121] The majority of people did not, of course, become enthusiasts for the Union as a result, but they were more prepared to tolerate it.

Ratification Achieved

A recognition of the decline in active popular discontent, along with the realisation that a Parliamentary majority for ratification was secure, impelled the opposition to mobilise their class base in two last minute attempts to halt proceedings.

The first was launched during the final week of December. Fletcher and Hamilton jointly proposed that the various ranks of landowners should assemble in Edinburgh to petition Queensberry either to abandon the ratification process or to suspend proceedings while elections were called – their assumption being that a newly elected Parliament would have a majority against the Union. Queensberry seemed to have shared this assumption. The petition, however, never got as far as being presented. Although between 400 and 500 lairds descended on Edinburgh, their mainly Jacobite politics set them against Fletcher, who, consistent to the end, could not be induced to support a Stuart restoration. More seriously, it also set them against Hamilton, who refused to proceed with the petition unless a section was added accepting the Hanoverian succession. Needless to say this was unacceptable to the Jacobites in their turn and the entire enterprise became bogged down in fruitless wrangling over the contents of the address. While the demonstrators argued among themselves, Queensberry seized his opportunity to issue a proclamation banning assemblies convened to mount addresses and declaring them to be seditious. With the imposition of this final obstacle, the majority of the lairds packed up and went back to their estates. Defoe reported on 4 January 1707: 'I wrote you last week that the apprehension we were under here began to vanish ... the crowd of strangers lessens amain.'[122] And two days later:

> I have little to say today but to confirm what my last hinted, that all the fears of the matter are now over on this side and the Angus men and co. are most of them dropped away as silently as they came.[123]

The second attempt followed during the second week of January. Time was running out, as an increasingly confident Court oversaw the ratification of Article after Article. The opposition leaders therefore decided to concentrate their efforts on the last two Articles, which dealt with representation in the new British Parliament. Their tactic centred on the delivery of a 'protestation' declaring that Parliament was only a temporary custodian of the national will and that, consequently, it had no authority to dissolve the state. It was correctly assumed that Queensberry would be unmoved by this appeal. After its dismissal the opposition would therefore secede, leaving Parliament with less than two-thirds of its members, greatly reducing its authority and depriving the Treaty of any legitimacy which it might have possessed. In the meantime, the seceders would offer themselves to the nation as the basis of an alternative government. In effect, this was a resurrection of the tactic employed by Dundee in 1689 when he attempted to set up an alternative Convention in opposition to the Revolution Parliament. Like that proposal, it would have amounted to a declaration of civil war. And who was to present the protestation to Parliament? Hamilton – a fact which may lead the reader to guess the eventual outcome. On 9 January 1707, 'great numbers of gentlemen and eminent citizens flocked together that morning about the Parliament house to attend the separating members and assist them in case they should be mistreated as they came from the house'.[124] But Hamilton failed to appear. Eventually, some of his party were sent to inquire after him at Holyrood, only to be told that the Duke had toothache and was unable to attend. We have no record of what was said to Hamilton on this occasion, but he was nevertheless 'prevailed' (as Lockhart puts it) to go to Parliament House. On arrival, he found it necessary to inquire who would be delivering the protestation. On being told that, of course, no other person but himself was qualified to do so, he declined, saying that he would, however, be the first to adhere once it had been entered. After this debacle the heart went out of the Parliamentary opposition, with many leaving before the end of the session and those remaining barely bothering to continue their resistance. Surveying this farce, it is difficult to disagree with the verdict on the Country Party delivered by one correspondent, who may have been William Patterson:

> This party, though it be but small and upon the decline, is as little united itself as it would have this island to be. In short, as they have the foolishest cause ever was known, they manage accordingly; and serve the interest they are against more effectually by their opposition, than they could possibly by their concurrence.[125]

In the end, the same relative levels of support revealed during the vote on Article 1 were also present at the final vote on the Treaty as a whole on 16 January – or would have been had not some of the burgess commissioners not already departed in disgust:

	For	Against
Nobility	42	19
Barons	38	30
Burgesses	30	20
Total	110	69[126]

All that remained to be done after the final vote was to choose which Scottish MPs would sit in the new British Parliament. Given the level of discontent among sections of the enfranchised, Queensberry and Argyll refused to risk an election. So, true to form, the 'representatives' were nominated by the Officers of Court from the ranks of the Court Party and, to a much lesser extent, the Squadrone. Indeed, Squadrone members received much less than they considered their due in any respect. Queensberry and Argyll refused to acknowledge their part in carrying the Union and reneged on their promise to allow the Squadrone leaders to disburse the contents of the Equivalent. The resulting enmity between the two Unionist parties was to have unforeseen consequences in the ensuing period. It should not, however, divert attention from their underlying unity on the question of the Treaty itself. It is to the causes of that unity, which of course also prevailed among the classes they represented, that we now turn.

Explaining the Union

Why had the intransigent Parliaments of 1703, 1704 and 1705 now accepted an alternative which had only a few short years before seemed the least likely of realisation? Many historians have quoted Roxborough's letter to Baillie in late 1705:

> That a Union will do in the Scottish Parliament I think very probable ... The motives will be, Trade with most, Hanover with some, ease and security with others, together with a general aversion at civil discords, intolerable poverty and the constant oppression of a bad Ministry, from generation to generation, without the least regard to the good of the country.[127]

The attraction of this explanation is that it appears to offer a pleasing plurality of factors in some order of priority ('trade with most'), to which Roxborough might have added the prospect of his receiving a dukedom for delivering up the votes of the Squadrone for the Treaty. For his letter is not, of course, an objective assessment of the situation, but an attempt to persuade his fellow Squadrone member Baillie to throw in his hand with what – according to Roxborough – is anyway going to be the winning side. Revisionist historians of the Treaty are therefore right to urge caution when relying on this quotation.

Nevertheless, the fact that Article 6 on free trade had the most support of all the Articles, with only 19 votes against, scarcely indicates that it was of no importance. The problem here is that it is necessary to be more specific about for whom free trade with England was a reason for accepting the Treaty. As we have already seen, it was not for the majority of the burgesses. The English market was in fact much more important to lords such as Banff, Cromarty or Seafield, who were landowners in the arable lands of the north-east, than it was to urban manufacturing or rural extractive industries for whom the home market was of key importance. Since the noble Estate gave proportionally the biggest support for the Treaty, this might seem to resolve the issue. Unfortunately, matters are not so simple. The lord who would have benefited most from the continuation of free trade was the Earl of Galloway, on whose lands were raised the black cattle whose sale in 1703 amounted to 40.2 per cent of the value of all exports to England. Yet Galloway voted against the Article on free trade and every other except Article 1. The lord who would have benefited least was the Earl of Wemyss who, exceptionally among his class, derived the majority of his income from the sale of coal extracted from his estates. Given the superior quality of English coal he would inevitably suffer from competition. Yet Wemyss voted for every Article of the Treaty.[128] These apparent inconsistencies have led some historians, such as Paul Scott and Paul Riley, to argue that trade was irrelevant, or at least secondary, to the success of ratification. In so far as trade has been treated as the main explanation of the Union, there is no doubt that they are correct. This does not mean, however, that their own explanations are any more credible.[129]

Two Non-Explanations for the Union

Paul Scott, the leading Scottish nationalist historian of the Union, has argued that the threat of force and bribery were jointly decisive in carrying the Treaty. I have already argued that the English state would only have militarily intervened in response to a French invasion. The question of bribery is, however, a superficially more plausible explanation, and requires more detailed refutation. Accusations of bribery were first made by Lockhart in his memoirs, although they were given their most memorable literary expression much later in the eighteenth century by Robert Burns, who has the narrator of his poem describe the Court Party and the Squadrone as 'a parcel of rogues' responsible for the Scottish people being 'bought and sold for English gold'.[130] That the majority were a parcel of rogues is indisputable, at least from the point of view of the people over whom they ruled – although it is surely also true of those who voted against, since they did not become paragons of benevolence to their tenants, workmen and servants by virtue of preferring the House of Stuart to that of Hanover. The issue is surely not whether payments were made to certain individuals – this is undeniably the case – but first, whether they invariably voted the way they did as a result of such payments and second, whether the votes secured in this manner were what carried the Treaty. This is far less clear. Part of the problem is that a number of financial transactions and juridical enactments are lumped together under one heading as 'bribery', when in fact the recipients stood in quite different relationships to power. There are in fact three different types of activity involved.

The first type was where individuals were approached with offers of payment to secure their vote. In the case of at least one, Sir Kenneth MacKenzie of Cromartie, the offer of £100 Scots was combined with a threat to remove his name from the list of pensioners on the civil list. It was this type of transaction that Lockhart and Burns raged against. In other cases bribery is perhaps a less appropriate term than blackmail, since the £20,540 17s 7d supposedly advanced to meet arrears of salary was not distributed impartially on the basis of past service, but withheld until potential recipients had proved their loyalty by voting for ratification – at least in the majority of Articles. Nevertheless, over half the available money (£12,000) went to Queensberry, as payment for his expenditure as Lord Commissioner. Another £1,000 went to Atholl who voted against throughout. Are we seriously to believe that the Scottish state was abolished on the basis of how the remaining £7,000 was distributed? Most of the sums paid out were pitiful. The £60 paid to a messenger for carrying the Treaty to England was greater than five of the supposed bribes, the most ridiculous of which being that paid to the Earl of Banff who not only sold his vote for £11 2s, but also threw a conversion to Protestantism into the bargain. Given that this sum is in English currency and has to be multiplied 12 times to give the value in Scots (at the time 1 merk was equivalent to 1s 1d sterling and £1 Scots to 1s 8d sterling), the sum is less absurd than it first appears, although it does reveal something of the financial condition of the Scottish nobility.

The second type was where members of the ruling class, from Argyll at the summit to Seton of Pitmedden at the base, themselves approached the Court with a list of demands that they expected to be fulfilled before they would be prepared to support the Treaty. It seems to be stretching language to describe this as bribery, when it seems to be more a case of the individuals concerned, realising how desperate the English government was to achieve ratification, milking the situation for all it was worth – morally reprehensible, no doubt, but not an indication that they would have voted other than the way they eventually did. Indeed, as we have already seen, Seton's arguments remained remarkably consistent with those he had previously put as a member of the Country Party.

The third type of transaction was simply the terms of the Treaty itself, but here the language of 'bribery' and reality have completely parted company. The general inducements to comply with the English demand for union were not the trifling sums paid out to Banff and his ilk, nor even the £100 per annum guaranteed to Cromartie and Seton, but an astonishing series of concessions which effectively preserved many of the functions of the Scottish state. Indeed, if the English had been able to rely on bribery these would never have been included in the final Treaty. It is possible to consider the Equivalent as a bribe, perhaps, but measures intended to gain the acquiescence of an entire social class (such as the preservation of the heritable jurisdictions) or a profession (such as the preservation of the Scots law more generally) cannot be treated as such. One might profitably contrast the guarantees offered to the Church of Scotland with the conditions imposed on the Catholic and Presbyterian Irish after the Treaty of Limerick in 1691, notably the suppression of the Roman Catholic Church and persecution of its priests. Equally illuminating, however, are the conditions imposed on the Anglican land-owning class that actually ruled Ireland on behalf of the English. They were not to be admitted into Free Trade with the colonial power, and the difference between their situation and that of the Scots was one of which the latter were all too painfully aware. The Protestant Irish ruling class wanted a union with England, and were far more united on this point than their Scottish equivalents had ever been:

The Union of England and Scotland pointed to the contrast with the treatment of Ireland. Swift wrote, but did not publish, 'The Story of the Injured Lady', in which Ireland was cast in the role of a maiden ruined and laid aside by a gentleman who was prepared to marry her ugly and undeserving rival. ... In 1709 the Irish lords in an address to the viceroy expressed the hope that the queen 'will perfect this great work by bringing her kingdom of Ireland also into the union'. The viceroy replied that he had no instructions from her majesty to say anything on the subject.[131]

If my argument concerning bribery is correct then it also has implications for the second explanation, which has been advanced by Paul Riley. W. R. Scott gave the classic formulation regarding the respective English and Scottish reasons for accepting the Union long ago as 'a political necessity for England and an economic necessity for Scotland'.[132] Riley has reversed this orthodoxy and asserted instead the 'primacy of politics': 'There was a political struggle for the control of Scotland and there were Scottish economic problems; except in so far as the problems made excellent weapons the two were unrelated.'[133] Riley explains Scottish ratification of the Treaty as a consequence of the magnate struggle for position within Parliament and the quest for the ministerial position that would guarantee their salaries and those of their followers. One set of magnate interests had, for historical reasons, aligned themselves with the Court and, since the Court now wanted an incorporating union, they too found this desirable. Naturally, those who attached themselves to particular magnate interests followed the voting patterns of their benefactors. No other principles, beliefs or even interests need be considered. In fact, there is some doubt as to whether support or opposition to the Union always fluctuated according to party fortunes. Consistency was to be expected from Fletcher and the Jacobites, but for our purposes the important results are those relating to the pro-Union camp. Thirteen commissioners, comprising 15 per cent of party activists and 10 per cent of the combined Court Party and Squadrone membership, have been identified as supporting union consistently without securing any benefit to themselves during the course of the negotiations or ratification.[134] Even those pro-Unionists that had not always been so consistent had reasons that were not directly related to access to patronage. One of the most important of these was their position within the British Army.

A British state, unifying the ruling classes of England and Scotland, did not pre-exist the Union, even in embryo. 'Even in the diplomatic service, an area of government that was British rather than English,' notes Keith Brown, 'the numbers of Scots was low, seven among the one hundred and eighteen men employed by the crown between 1660 and 1688, three under William II and III, and six under Queen Anne.'[135] As we saw in Chapter 1, the army was the only exception. Out of the 44 nobles who supported Article 1, 18 were either in the army or had male relatives in the army; out of the 21 nobles who opposed the first Article, only two were in the army.[136] The vote on the Treaty as a whole produced a similar result: 18 out of the 19 commissioners who were military officers in January 1707 supported the Union; 21 peers out of the 27 who voted for the Treaty were either serving officers themselves, had held commissions since 1688, or whose eldest sons were officers, did likewise.[137] Of course the army was also a source of patronage. Argyll wrote to Godolphin in August 1705 naming an officer who had voted against the first reading of the act for a Treaty of Union and insisting that he be removed from his post, but not all officers were so junior as to be vulnerable to this kind of pressure. It is only if one shares Riley's dismally Naimierite view of human motivation that access to patronage must be assumed as their reason for supporting the Union. The existence of a large contingent of Scots in the British Army was not therefore simply a negative factor inhibiting English military intervention in Scotland. For the Scottish officers, the British Army prefigured what a future British state could mean in terms of their careers:

> As members of a British military elite loyal to the British crown, experienced in warfare against the enemies of the emerging British state, and functioning within an institution, the army, which was already British in its organisation and career mobility, they would be very unlikely to vote against a union of parliaments, particularly when national security (which was a British and not merely an English argument) was so fundamental to the union case.[138]

It was recognised within the state apparatus that the Scottish component of the British army would be generally supportive of the new state, and should therefore be treated carefully, regardless of the personal feelings of individuals towards the Scots. Consider the following exchange. In January 1707 Governor Parke of St. Christopher in the West Indies wrote to Secretary Hedges at Whitehall complaining of the shortage of munitions and warning of a French attempt to invade Nevis with a force from the American mainland. His solution was a proposal that he make a pre-emptive strike against the French colony on Martinique and settle it in order to secure the islands. And who would be responsible for carrying this out?

> Send me over ten thousand Scotch with oatmeal enough to keep them for 3 or 4 months, let them be well provided with arms, we will make what we can here, and [if] I might have leave, I will go to the Continent [i.e. America] and get some there, and let us try our fortune, if we take it [i.e. Martinique], we will have the plunder, the Scotch will have the

land, in time warm sun will exhale all the crudities that makes them so troublesome, and 'tis not impossible but it may have the effect to make them of a more sociable religion; if we have not success if you choose out those that are so zealous to maintain the Kirk and against the Union: if I get them all knocked on the head, I am of the opinion that the English Nation will be no great losers by it.

'I will dispose of the Scotch for you there,' he concludes, ''twill be a better settlement for them than their beloved Darien.'[139] These comments, with their contempt for the Scots and assumption that they are expendable, seem merely to prefigure the more famous remarks, equally offensive to Scots, of James Wolfe concerning the Independent Highland Companies in Canada ('no great mischief if they fall. How can you better employ a secret enemy than by making his end conducive to the common good?').[140] In fact, the reply which came, not from Hedges, but from the Earl of Sunderland, admonished Parke for his attitude towards the Scots:

I am to tell you that H.M. [i.e. Queen Anne] does totally reject your proposal of sending 10,000 Scots into your parts: perhaps the sentiments of these may differ from yours as to religious matters, yet H.M. looks upon them as good subjects and good Christians, too good to be knock'd on the head upon so wild a subject: I am glad your scheme did not appear before the Union was finished, for if it had, possibly it might have occasioned some delay to that which all Well-wishers to Great Britain think so great an advantage to H.M. Interest and the People of both Nations.[141]

These remarks clearly reflect a change in the official perspective, one signalled by a passing comment in a letter from the Council of Trade and Plantations to Thomas Handasyd, Governor of Jamaica, earlier in March. At one point it notes that 'your behaviour with relation to the Scotch and other foreigners, has been approved', but only a few lines later says: 'And as to Scotch men, that distinction will now cease, by an Act pass'd here for an entire union of the two Kingdoms.'[142]

The subsequent role of the Scots as the cadres of the British Army demonstrates that this was not mere rhetoric: 'During the first half of the eighteenth century 25 per cent of all regimental offices in the British army went to Scots, and the Scots captured 20 per cent of all colonelcies between 1714 and the end of the Seven Years War.'[143] Or take the career of Alexander Spotswood, Lieutenant-Governor of Virginia between 1710 and 1722, which illustrates what was possible. Spotswood was born in Tangier in 1676, son of the resident surgeon to the Governor, Middleton, then effectively in exile after losing an internal faction fight with Lauderdale in which he had pushed his royalist convictions too far in the

Privy Council. Spotswood became an ensign in the British Army in the infantry regiment of the Earl of Bath, rising to the rank of lieutenant-colonel, before being appointed to his post in Virginia by George Hamilton, the Earl of Orkney. In the same year as his appointment, Spotswood proposed that the exploitation of newly discovered iron-ore deposits should be carried out as a public enterprise for the benefit of the 'Mother Country', by which he, unlike most of his fellow Virginians, meant Great Britain, not England. Bruce Lenman comments: 'Spotswood's peripheral origins, shared by his German king [i.e. George I], made him assertively British and also made him identify with the metropolitan executive of a multi-national British world-state far more than most inhabitants of English America.'[144]

'An army is always a copy of the society it serves,' wrote Trotsky, 'with this difference, that it gives social relations a concentrated character, carrying both their positive and negative features to an extreme.'[145] Attitudes of the sort held by the Scottish officer caste reflected a more general shift within the ruling class. The issue is not the exercise of management, but why the underlying agreement on essentials which makes management possible, and which had been missing in the life of the Parliament up to that point, now prevailed. The divisions within Parliament House in fact reflected divisions within the feudal ruling class themselves about how best to preserve their existing place within Scottish society. The English response to the Act of Security had made it apparent that the options available to them were considerably fewer than they had previously thought. Party allegiance, and consequently voting, was therefore determined, for the majority of the Estates, not by calculations of what would result in short-term financial advantage to do so, but by a more long-term assessment of what a union was likely to offer them and what the alternative was likely to be.

The Dilemmas of the Scottish Ruling Class

The original Country Party position was for a federal union with a different monarch from that of England. Once it became clear that this option was unattainable, the choice was more starkly posed between three alternatives; the Stuarts and France, Hanover and England on a voluntary basis, or Hanover and England 'by right of conquest', as Fletcher put it. Some individuals, like Seton (and, for all practical purposes, Hamilton), moved their allegiance directly from Country to Court, but for the majority who were not Jacobites, the Squadrone acted as the means of transition. The correspondence between Roxborough and Baillie exemplifies the arguments which took place within the Squadrone from its fall from office in mid-1705 to the eve of ratification. In this connection there is a far more revealing letter than the one in which Roxburgh gives the list headed 'trade with most'. It is a reply from

Baillie giving some of the reasons why his own views are tending towards acceptance of the Union:

> It [i.e. the Union] would not be my choice; and what sticks most with me is that it will render the Session [i.e. the Court of Session] able to dispose of our estates at pleasure, when there shall be no appeal from their sentence but to the House of Peers [i.e. of Lords]. For the appeal that now lies to the Scots Parliament is the only thing that keeps them within bounds; and yet we cannot want the Session without an entire subversion of our laws about private rights, which must be a work of time, and may perhaps be attended with as many inconveniences as the other. Nevertheless, it is certainly preferable to our present condition, and of two evils the least is to be chosen.[146]

And what was their 'present condition'? Between the Restoration and the Treaty of Union the ratio between the tax yields in England and Scotland rose from 10.5:1 to 36:1, 'and several English counties were paying more in taxes than the whole of Scotland'. Julian Goodare asserts that this is less because of Scottish poverty compared with England than because the latter state was simply more successful in raising taxes: 'what we are seeing is not so much Scottish failure as English success in extracting resources'. These claims rest on an assumption – that 'the Scottish and English economies were comparable in structure' – which cannot, in my view, be sustained.[147] One figure reveals the extent of national economic weakness. Athol Murray has calculated that, on the most optimistic estimate, the Scottish exchequer raised £110,000 per annum on the eve of the Union:

> Yet if we set even £110,000 against the £66,000 required for the pay of the army alone under its 1692 establishment of approximately 3,000 army officers and men, apart from the cost of clothing and equipment and other charges of government, we must reach the conclusion that in 1707 an independent Scotland was not financially viable.[148]

Bruce Lenman dismisses this argument on the grounds that an independent Scotland would no longer have had to maintain the military establishment it needed to participate in the Williamite wars and that the funds thus liberated would have been available for other purposes.[149] This seems to me wrong on two counts. First, it assumes that an independent Scotland would not require a standing army of any size. But given that the circumstances under which the Scottish state would be reasserting its sovereign existence could only involve breaking with both England and France – if it were to be truly independent – then this assumption is highly implausible. Even Fletcher assumed that the militia he wished to see established would operate in a British, rather than purely Scottish context. Second, it ignores the fact that Darien did not simply show the inadequacy of a personal monarchy, but that of the Scottish state itself to sustain any large-scale venture, not just militarily (although that is certainly relevant to my first point) but financially. Nothing had changed in this respect by 1707 – if anything it had grown worse.

From this point of view it makes as little sense to talk about the 'treachery' of one faction of the ruling class as it does to talk about the 'patriotism' of another. As John Robertson writes: 'What mattered about any sovereignty was what it enabled its subjects to do.'[150] While Scotland certainly had formal sovereignty over its own affairs, what it lacked was the autonomy to put its sovereign power into effect. Realising this, the entire ruling class, with a handful of exceptions like Fletcher and Stewart of Pardovan, opted to abandon sovereignty altogether for incorporation into a greater power that would protect what they had. The only option, as Seton had correctly pointed out during the debate on Article 1, was which state they would choose to subordinate themselves to. Why did the majority choose England?

On the negative side, the return of the Stuarts could only occur under the same terms that Parliament had rebelled against in 1689 – at best they would become the comprador nobility of a French satellite, enduring absolutist encroachments on their social power and the imposition of Roman Catholicism on their Church – not to speak of the revenge which James might be expected to extract for what he would see as past betrayals of his family. Furthermore, since restoration in Scotland would inevitably mean war with England, the French option also held out the possibility of defeat and an English conquest that would reduce Scotland to the same condition as Ireland. Only the most desperate of the nobility could have contemplated this scenario. It is no accident that the commissioners who gave the most consistent opposition to the Treaty were the barons at the bottom of the ruling class ladder. They had least to lose. As John Dalrymple, first Earl of Stair, wrote to Harley when the Union still looked in doubt, 'the baulking of the Union at this time may be an irreparable loss to this nation, and to the liberty of Europe and our religion'.[151]

On the positive side, beyond personal bribery, beyond even the specific guarantees of institutional continuity and financial restitution, the Treaty contained an overall commitment to preserving the existing structure of Scottish society – with all its contradictions – within the new state. Shortly before the Treaty was ratified a correspondent of the English regime wrote of the opposition that: 'The parties most active here are discontented noblemen who fear their reign will be short in oppressing the commonality, as hitherto they have most shamefully done, their poverty and slavery here being little inferior to the negroes in Barbados.'[152] But what if they were to be allowed to continue 'oppressing the commonality'? In this respect the key clause in the Treaty does not maintain the educational system, nor does it preserve the Church of Scotland, nor does it even enshrine Scots law, although it is an aspect of that law. The key clause in the Treaty is the one which states:

> That all heritable Offices, Superiorities, heritable Jurisdictions, Offices for life, and Jurisdictions for life, be reserved to the Owners thereof, as Rights of Property, in the same manner as they are now enjoyed by the Laws of Scotland, notwithstanding of this Treaty.[153]

This Article alone would explain the extent of lordly support for the Union. Indeed, the very term 'superiorities', which had been omitted from the original Treaty, was added by an amendment to this article during the discussion on 6 January – obviously the lords were leaving nothing to chance.[154] In this respect the juridical element was infinitely more important than the pedagogic or confessional ones to which it is usually linked; and not as the bearer of some transhistorical 'national identity', but as a means of exercising class power. And these powers continued to be exercised even as the Treaty took effect. Ian Whyte notes that:

> ... in 1707 the baron court of Mey in Caithness fined tenants for travelling to Orkney without permission during July and August – they had probably absented themselves from labour services by doing so – and prosecuted another man for going to Inverness without notifying the proprietor, 'the laird having business to send with him'.[155]

In one of his many pamphlets opposing an incorporating union, James Hodges had asked: 'How are the *Scots* Nobility and Gentry to be satisfied about the particular Powers, and Privileges wherewith they are invested by the Tenures of their Lands, which are in *Scotland* very different from England.'[156] Indeed, supporters of an incorporating union used the same argument, but from a perspective that welcomed the potential destruction of noble power and the constraints it had placed on Scottish society. James Arbuthnot, who is perhaps best known today for inventing, or at any rate popularising, the figure of John Bull, was a Scottish Episcopalian working in London as a doctor during the run up to ratification. Unlike many of his fellow communicants, however, he was not a Jacobite and during a sermon in favour of the Union he made the following point:

> ... I will ask the greatest Zealot against the Union a few Questions, and let him answer me if he can. Whether the great Difference betwixt the Wealth of Scotland and England is entirely owing to the natural Advantages of England, as of Fruitfulness of Soil, Situation, etc. Or if it does not in some measure proceed from Political Causes?[157]

The question was a good one. Both sides had, however, under-estimated quite how anxious the English regime was to placate the Scottish nobility. Defoe noted in his history of the Union that continuing the superiorities 'gives too great a power to particular persons' and that 'it keeps the common people and tenantry of Scotland in a condition inconsistent with the liberty of a free nation'. The solution, he argued, would have been for the new British Parliament to buy out the superiors 'with full recompense'. 'Unfortunately', writes Defoe:

> ... this was a time of hurry, and people could not look about them as at other times; nor was the liberty of the poor people so near in view as to move that concern in men's minds, which, perhaps were it now to be done, might be otherwise: whether this or the fate of Scotland, I shall not determine as the cause of the omission: but it is evident the thing is, unhappily for Scotland, omitted and that great opportunity of extending the love of liberty, as well as the taste of it to all the people, is irrecoverably lost.[158]

This is among the feeblest passages in the whole of his *History of the Union*. It is as if, for once, the master propagandist found it impossible to argue his case convincingly. It was not that the English ruling class were unaware of the nature of the Scottish nobility. Charles Davenant was an Inspector-General of Exports and Imports who wrote to Godolphin, early in 1704, proposing that he journey to Edinburgh on behalf of the English government to report on activities and promote its position. The letter was ignored (although it may have inspired Godolphin to send Defoe on his mission shortly afterwards), but it contains observations on the 'Scotch [sic] Nobility and Gentry' which are of some interest:

> By their Sovereign's Absence for a hundred Years, they are now become a Sort of corrupt Aristocracy, and for a long Time have lived at the Stretch of, if not beyond their Fortunes, oppressing their Tenants beyond all Measure. The Great Ones may think that Peace, and a good Settlement, may not so much turn to their Account; but perhaps the People will wish to have the Succession settled, because it secures Religion. The Advantages accruing to the Vulgar are immediate, and apparent, they will increase in Shipping, their Poor will be set to work, and they may in a few Years gather such Wealth as shall exempt them from the Bondage they now lie under to their great Lords and Heads of Clans; and they have the Example of England before their Eyes, where the Nobility and Gentry had almost the same Power over their Tenants, as is now exercised in Scotland, until our Commons became enriched by foreign Traffic.[159]

I have quoted this at some length because it sets out both an extremely acute description of the Scottish ruling class and an explanation of how the Union might be the source of their undoing. Yet no section of the English ruling class showed the slightest interest in what could have been the real historical justification for Union – the completion of the task that Cromwell had temporarily carried out 50 years before. As Hugh Trevor-Roper wrote of the Union, in one of his few accurate observations on Scottish history: 'it contained no explicit provisions for social reform – that Cromwellian mistake would not be repeated'.[160] Scotland in fact saw the first application of a technique which the British ruling class as a whole were to apply with remarkable success almost from this moment on, that of ruling through existing local aristocracies without displacing or consciously altering the economic basis of the societies over which they ruled. The logic of this policy was demonstrated most clearly in the counter-revolutionary wars that the British state waged against revolutionary France between 1789 and 1815 in league with all the feudal absolutisms of Europe. The objection of the British ruling class to the French revolution was not only that it brought into being a more vigorous competitor, but that it involved for the first time in history the intervention of classes which had hitherto been excluded from political life – an intervention which set an unhappy example for the more developed British working class. 'After the domestic Jacobin scare of the 1790s and the threat of Napoleon's Continental System,' writes Mike Davis, 'the British bourgeoisie forsook any ambition to be revolutionary missionaries of capitalism in Europe itself.'[161] All that requires to be added to this assessment is that the reluctance of the British ruling class to foment bourgeois revolution in Europe (or Asia, or Latin America) after 1789 was already prefigured by the reluctance of the English ruling class to carry through the bourgeois revolution in Scotland 100 years earlier.

Can this alliance of convenience between the Scottish and English ruling classes therefore be described as 'progressive' in any way? For Marxists, this term refers, in the context of the bourgeois revolution, to an event or process which leads either to the development of the productive forces or which heightens the political consciousness and organisation of the bourgeoisie – or indeed the classes below them in feudal society. In neither sense can the Union be said to qualify for such a description. It should be clear that it was, literally, a conservative measure for both the English bourgeoisie and the Scottish nobility. The very most that can be said for it is that, unlike the only realistic alternative, it was not actually reactionary in the sense of throwing society backwards.

The implications of the Union did not remain in neutral for long. Rather than the results of the English Revolution radiating northwards to the benefit of the Scots, as has been claimed ever since, the opposite took place. The unfinished business of the Scottish Revolution was instead transferred intact into the new British state, bringing into its territorial framework the very source of counter-revolution itself. This is the paradox that lay at the heart of the Treaty of Union. The intention of the English regime was to prevent a Stuart restoration in Scotland opening up a second front for France (or any other hostile power) on its northern border through incorporation into a new state. The consequence of incorporation was precisely to increase the chances of such a front being opened, not as a short-term response to the immediate strains of adjusting to Union, but as the result of a long-term structural crisis in Scottish society. As Burns noted, in a poem which more accurately reflects our subject than 'Such a Parcel of Rogues in a Nation':

> The best laid schemes o' mice and men gang
> aft agley
> And lea'e us nought but grief an' pain for
> promised joy![162]

For Scotland did not enter the new state completely unchanged. The key difference was, of course, the absence of the Parliament, but this had different implications for different social classes. It is sometimes said that the removal of political representation from Edinburgh meant that the majority of the population without the vote now had no opportunity to influence the political classes through petitions, demonstrations or riots. This proposition informs one of Sir Walter Scott's greatest novels, *The Heart of Midlothian*, where, in the absence of a Scottish royal court or Parliament, Jeanie Deans has to walk to London to petition on behalf of her sister who is under sentence of death for infanticide. But this massively overestimates the role of Parliament before 1689 and the extent to which the crowd ever managed to force the leading politicians to do anything that they did not anyway intend to do. Ironically, the greatest influence which popular pressure may have had on political outcomes was forcing through the amendments to the Treaty that in the end made it more bearable, if not more popular. For the bourgeoisie too, Parliament was a most imperfect instrument, filled with its most conservative elements. For the lords, however, the absence of Parliament was decisive, and it is a measure of the crisis they felt themselves to be in that they consented to its dissolution by such a majority. For although their local power was left in place and, indeed, preserved as their private property, they could no longer command national politics in the same way. Reaffirming their power at the socio-economic base of society, the Union removed it from the political superstructure. Henceforth, any attempt to influence events by any faction of the nobility could only be violent and could only be conducted on an all-British basis.

It is appropriate that this should have been foreseen most clearly by one of the Presbyterian sects, the followers of John Hepburn. In an address to the Estates, printed towards the end of 1706, Hepburn himself pointed towards the real dangers posed by the Union:

Our Hearts do Tremble to think what bitter Fruits of Faction, parties and incurable Breaches the going into this Union may produce, and how easy an Access through this and the great Ferment of the Nation it may make for the pretended King *James* the Eighth to come to the throne.[163]

Despite the religious framework within which, inevitably, this viewpoint is expressed, the prediction was to prove remarkably accurate. The period between the Union and the last Jacobite Rebellion, when this threat was finally destroyed, is therefore the first British revolutionary epoch; and the site of this struggle was the territory which had once been the domain of the Scottish state. 'Now,' said Seafield as he engrossed the ratified Treaty, 'there's ane end of ane old song.'[164] The melody would linger on for a while yet.

Scotland and the British State: From Crisis to Consolidation (1708–1716)

The Treaty of Union was not intended to transform social relations in Scotland. Nevertheless, 40 years after Seafield's 'old song' came to an end, that transformation began to take place in earnest. It is sometimes implied that this was the result of a form of 'structural assimilation', in which Scottish institutions and social relations were gradually aligned with those of England.[1] Jacobitism, in these accounts, was unconnected with these social changes, and consequently an irrelevance which does not justify the attention hitherto lavished on it.[2] Understandable though this attitude is, given the nature of much of the writing on Jacobitism, it too readily consigns the movement to an earlier period in Scottish history. In fact, Jacobitism, as a popular movement at any rate, was a product of the Treaty of Union, not a political residue of the Scottish kingdom. There were two aspects to this. On the one hand, although the transition from feudalism to capitalism took several decades after the Union to gather momentum, the implications of the process were clear enough finally to provide Jacobitism with a social base in those sections of the ruling class which felt threatened by the emergent bourgeois world. On the other, opposition to the Union, provoked by breaches of the Treaty in the interest of English agrarian–mercantile capitalism, gave Jacobites an audience among the plebeians which their social positions would otherwise have denied them. Both aspects were to combine, with potentially explosive effect, in the rising of 1715.

Three Perspectives on Jacobitism

Historians have tended to explain Jacobitism as the political expression of one of two movements: a Highland movement for the self-preservation of the clans, or a British movement in opposition to the Revolution Settlements of 1689 which in a Scottish context aimed to restore a separate kingdom.

Jacobitism as the Political Expression of Highland Clan Society

In what is perhaps the most famous statement ever made on the subject of war, Carl von Clausewitz wrote: 'War is not merely a political act, but also a real instrument, a continuation of political commerce, a carrying out of the same by other means.'[3] If, by this, he had meant only that war was an aspect of politics, then the passage would scarcely have achieved its enduring fame. In fact, as the German military strategist makes clear elsewhere in his great work, *On War*, what he is in fact saying is that the character of any war is determined by the political character of the states involved, and that these states are themselves the product of a certain level of socio-economic development.[4] It is the question of civil war, however, which tests this theory to the limit; for if war takes place within, rather than between states, must we conclude that two different societies exist within that territory?

The question is relevant to our theme, since the means by which Jacobites hoped to regain the British throne was, precisely, civil war. Moreover, the successive threats to the Revolution Settlement, the Anglo-Scottish Union and the Hanoverian succession have tended to be treated as the expression of an unresolved conflict between two societies: one patriarchal, tribal and concentrated in the Scottish Highlands; the other commercial, individualistic and diffused throughout the rest of mainland Britain. From this perspective, Jacobitism was for all practical purposes a defensive political formation thrown up by the Highland clans in an attempt to prevent encroachments into their social order. In 1857, for example, Henry Buckle could write:

> The simple fact is, that the outbreaks of 1715 and 1745 were, in our country, the last struggle of barbarism against civilization. On the one side, war and confusion. On the other side, peace and prosperity. ... The result of such a contest in the eighteenth century, could hardly be doubtful.[5]

This was written at the height of Victorian Positivism (which does not necessarily indicate any great altitude on the part of either the discipline or the disciple). A hundred years later, George Pratt Insh could open his study of Scottish Jacobitism by declaring that his work 'represents the application to Scottish history of a Marxian – or, if you will, a Hegelian – technique'. Yet at the heart of his analysis was the same polarity which characterised that of Buckle: 'on the one hand the ancient civilisation of the Highlands leagued with the old scholarly Episcopalian civilisation of the north-east; on the other hand, the new commercial and industrial civilisation of Central Scotland'.[6] Pratt Insh at any rate recognised that it was not solely a question of the Highlands. Eric Hobsbawm, a considerably more orthodox Marxist, is if anything more reductive, writing that 'Scotland was a dual society and economy, in which the tribal Highlands coexisted with the entirely different and far more advanced Lowlands'. Hobsbawm then makes explicit the underlying theme behind all these interpretations of Highland–Lowland divide, whether they use Marxist language or not: 'The struggle for the equivalent of a bourgeois revolution in Scotland was also the struggle between two societies.'[7] Once this position is accepted it is easy to extend it to Britain as a whole: 'The divide lay not between the Highlands and the Lowlands of Scotland, but between the Highlands and the rest of Scotland *and* England.'[8]

The 'two societies' thesis is attractive for a number of reasons. By treating the rebellions not merely as Scottish, but as British civil wars, it disposes of the view that the Jacobite risings of 1715–16 and 1745–46 were national conflicts between Scotland and England.[9] By stressing that the majority of Scots had come to share the same economic, social and political characteristics as the English, it also exposes the inadequacy of the theory, advanced by John Pocock, that the risings were merely episodes in the history of an English frontier province.[10] Nevertheless, the thesis as a whole is profoundly flawed in the relationship it posits between, on the one hand, the Highlands and the rest of Scotland and, on the other, the Highlands and Jacobitism. David Cannadine exemplifies both flaws when he writes of the Jacobite risings that they were 'not built around collective social identities so much as geographical identities: the Gaelic, Catholic, highland clans in revolt against the modernising world of the south'.[11] I argued in Chapter 1 that society in the Highlands was based on the same feudal mode of production as that of the Lowlands, although important cultural differences divided them. Is there any more truth in the claim that a structural affinity existed between Highland clan organisation and Stuart absolutism?

The version of claim presented by Audrey Cunningham is markedly more sympathetic to 'Highland society' than most. Cunningham argues that the supposedly patriarchal relationship between the chief and his clan corresponded to that between the absolutist monarch and his subjects:

> The divine right of kings appealed to them [i.e. the Highlanders] in virtue of the great simplicities of life: the king stood to his people as the father to his children or the chief to his kinsmen, of common blood, sharing common interests, ready to give and take in a friendly spirit of co-operation for the common weal, and strong and prosperous only as long as they were united.[12]

Leaving aside the fantastically idealised versions of both absolutism and clan life which this account involves ('Here was an indefeasible hereditary right to which all good citizens consented, a conception appealing to the idealistic quality of the Celtic race,' etc., etc.), what still needs to be explained is why the alliance between the clans – or rather, their chiefs – and the Stuart dynasty was such a recent development when the latter fell from power. As George Pratt Insh once asked: 'Why was it that the Stuarts, flouted in the days of their prosperity, were cherished in the days of their adversity?'[13] Cunningham tends to argue that it was because of the promise of support which James seemed to offer the chiefs between 1681 and 1685: 'Yet the promise was enough to convince the Highlanders that James did desire and intend to secure fair treatment for those on whom the law and government pressed hardly.'[14] But even after the Stuarts lost power for the second time the clans did not leap to their defence. Of the three significant risings only the '89 was genuinely a Highland affair, although it was backed by none of the leading chiefs and made possible only by a combination of the administrative chaos attendant on the Revolution and the availability of Lowland leadership. The '15 drew support mainly from the north-eastern Lowlands and north-eastern England. The '45 had greater Highland participation, but even this was confined to a minority of the lesser chiefs. Nor was the relationship any closer on the other side. The clan chiefs, of all the lords, were generally the least amenable to royal control, and every attempt to construct an absolutist state had sooner or later been forced to confront the multiple problems contained in their domains: disregard for the legal authority, local power bases resistant to the military control and a subsistence economy which contributed nothing to the exchequer. James VI and I had, after all, subdued the Borders – an area comparable sociologically to the Highlands, but smaller, more accessible and consequently more vulnerable to royal power – and no doubt both Charles I and James VII and II would have conducted the same exercise in the Highlands had not the Civil Wars and the Revolution respectively supervened to make them reconsider that area in a more favourable light.

In short, the clans were not homogeneous in their interests, their chiefs were not historically linked to the Stuarts, they did not necessarily make this link after the Glorious Revolution and those that did were not the only social actors in Scotland to do so. Are we then dealing with a movement that could draw on support from a broader cross-section of Scottish society?

Jacobitism as the Political Opposition to the Whig Establishment

The inconsistencies of the 'two societies' thesis lends plausibility to a historiographical reaction which seeks to rehabilitate the Jacobites as the dominant political opposition in Williamite and Hanoverian Britain. In the vanguard of this movement is, not unexpectedly, Jonathan Clark, a writer to whom the term 'historiographical reaction' can be applied in more than one sense. Clark has made his reputation in part through arguing that between 1688 and 1832 Britain remained essentially an *ancien régime* comparable in all important respects to its European rivals. From this perspective, Jacobitism was a perfectly legitimate political contender and one, furthermore, which could not simply be dismissed as counter-revolutionary:

> Once Jacobitism ceased to be viewed through the romantic– reactionary filter as quintessentially a phenomenon of 'the right', it was possible to identify its dual nature as a vehicle for subversion as well as stability, proletarian dissatisfaction as well as patrician theological allegiance.[15]

William Ferguson has also taken issue with the identification of Jacobitism with reaction. Referring more specifically to Scotland, he writes that 'the Jacobites cannot be dismissed as mere divine right dotards at long last dispatched by "progress"'. How then should they be viewed? 'Instead, the Jacobites ... appeal[ed] to constitutional and legal arguments which showed that the only compact known to the laws of England was that of King, Lords and Commons, and that strict hereditary succession was an essential feature of the constitution.'[16] In a specifically Scottish context, the most serious revisionist discussion of Jacobitism is to be found in the work of Murray Pittock. He explains the existence of what he calls 'the myth of the Jacobite clans' by arguing that, after 1746, the victorious British state successfully marginalised Jacobitism as a historical movement through retrospective association with a backward society, historically doomed by the onward march of progress. This association fitted perfectly both with the romantic conception of the Highlands as a repository of lost primitive virtues and with the more recent construction of Scottish 'heritage', in which the Jacobite Clans play a significant decorative role. According to Pittock, this mythology has been accepted through a combination of confusion between the Highlands and the area north of the Tay, and ignorance over the extent of Lowland participation in the risings, particularly the '15 and the '45: 'Jacobitism is historically significant as an expression of Scottish national identity, a major military threat to the British state, and an ingenious, varied and socially diverse set of cultural images and values.'[17]

As with the 'two societies' thesis, there is much in the revisionist case that is valuable as a critique of other positions. In particular, all the individuals cited here, whatever criticisms may be levelled at their work in other respects, are correct to stress that Jacobitism was not an exclusively Highland phenomenon. Their failing lies in shifting the emphasis too far in the opposite direction, until Jacobitism becomes a ship that can be carried along by almost any political current whatsoever.

The period between 1707 and 1746 was a transitional one for popular movements in the British Isles. The last traces of the bourgeoisie as a class committed to democracy as a goal, and mass mobilisation as the means of achieving it, vanished with the 'True Whigs' after 1688. The Whigs in office, particularly after 1715, proved to be the more oligarchic and repressive of the two parties, but no working-class movement – in fact, no working class in any real sense – yet existed with its own objectives and organisational methods to oppose them. In the absence of such a movement, the English Tories, and in particular their extremist Jacobite minority, acted as a focus for popular discontent. Jacobite activity gave Walpole and the Whig oligarchy an excellent justification for the repressive legislation which increasingly filled the statute books after the Hanoverian Succession, but this anti-Jacobite propaganda, by misrepresenting every use of Jacobite imagery or slogans as a serious endorsement of the Stuarts, also had the effect of giving credibility to claims that the Jacobites were a viable political option with support among the people. The attention focused by the trial of High Anglican demagogue Henry Sacheverell in 1710 acted precisely to publicise Jacobitism to a degree that it would not otherwise have enjoyed. Dissidents of various types used Jacobite slogans in turn precisely because of the fury they provoked in the Whig oligarchy.[18] There were, however, structural limits to how far a movement dedicated to the restoration of absolutism across the British Isles could be a vehicle for plebeian insurgency. The artisans and apprentices who wore the White Rose in their buttonholes did not desire to be ruled by a local absolutism backed by Catholic France. Indeed, much of the public disorder characteristic of eighteenth century England was motivated precisely by the popular desire to defend English or Scottish 'liberties' against 'popery and arbitrary power'. The urban crowds felt that employing Jacobite imagery to infuriate their political masters was acceptable precisely because for most of the period a Stuart Restoration seemed so far from realisation. As Frank McLynn writes: 'The truth is that in an era of aristocratic politics the urban masses would follow whichever deviant political dispensation seemed to pose most of a challenge to their "betters".'[19] These comments are relevant to Britain as a whole. But did the Jacobites not embody at least some popular aspirations in Scotland? Their influence had always been greatest when they effectively concealed part of their programme, such as in the period immediately before 1707. After the Union had been attained, however, they faced two impediments to placing themselves at the head of a national movement.

The first was that aspect of their mythology for which they are most admired by contemporary Scottish nationalists: their apparent inclusion of the Highlanders into the Scottish nation. This is expressed best in the poems and songs written before 1746, while the movement was still a living force, rather than in political tracts or, indeed, in the poems and songs written after that date. For example, *A Pill for Pork Eaters* (1705), written to celebrate the juridical murder of the captain and crew members of the *Worcester*, evokes the Scottish victory at Bannockburn and 'Heroes like Douglas, Wallace and Bruce' before going on to imagine the clans overcoming their differences and overrunning London itself:

> But let our Chiefs all Factious Broils oppose,
> And join together in Common Cause:
> Insulting *England* to her cost shall know,
> What Brave united *Scotsmen* then can do,
> When our best Troops are at thy Border ranged,
> Then Caledonia's Wrongs shall be avenged;
> Our Highlanders thy City-walls shall greet,
> And *Gilliecrankies* rifle *Lombard-Street*.[20]

And in a Jacobite song of 1714 the 'national' imagery is even more pronounced:

> Let our brave loyal clans, then,
> Their ancient Stuart race
> Restore with sword in hand, then
> And all their foes displace
> All unions we'll o'erturn boys,
> Which caus' our nation mourn, boys
> Like Bruce at Bannockburn, boys
> The English home we'll chase.[21]

What is being evoked here is 'the kingdom of the Scots', the domain and the subjects of the Ancient Stuart Race, not any sense of modern nationhood. As one Highland Jacobite, Robb Don MacKay, wrote after the '45:

> Today, today, I recollect
> A date you should not leave forgotten,
> the birthday of this royal Prince
> Of the true royal house of Scotland.[22]

But even leaving this aside, the problem with such propaganda was that 'our Highlanders', 'our brave loyal clans' were not considered to be part of the Scottish nation in the Lowlands. The end result was compounded by the tactic of dressing Jacobite troops in Highland costume during the '15 – which, as we shall see, was a predominantly Lowland rising – and the '45, regardless of their place of origin, which simply recalled the atrocities committed by royalist troops in the Civil Wars of the 1640s. John Spalding noted of Montrose after the fall of Aberdeen in 1644 that 'The Lieutenant was clad in coat and trews as the Irish were clad.'[23] In 1745, Lord Lewis Gordon, Jacobite Lord-Lieutenant of Aberdeenshire and Banffshire, wrote to James Moir, fourth Laird of Stoneywood, in Aberdeen ordering him to ensure that his men were 'sufficiently furnished with plaids'.[24] Far from contributing to an all-embracing Scottish national consciousness, the appropriation of Highland culture by the Stuarts simply identified the region more closely with Jacobitism, with appalling consequences for the inhabitants.[25]

The second impediment was that the guiding principle behind Jacobite rhetoric was one sometimes wrongly attributed to Lenin, namely 'the worse the better'. Their popular appeal, in other words, was largely dependent on declining social and economic conditions to which they could provide a false, but coherent solution. One propagandist, attempting to stimulate support for the '15 late in that rising, argued: 'Thus miserable is our Nation, in much worse Condition, and in a worse State of Slavery to England than ever Ireland was.'[26] The difficulty with this line of argument was that Scotland was plainly not subject to the same oppressions as Ireland – oppressions for which the Scots colony in Ulster was at least partly responsible – let alone greater ones, as became apparent after the first decade of the Union was over. The contingent nature of the support gathered on this basis of Scotland's supposed oppression was exposed, as far as the southern Lowlands were concerned, by popular reaction to the '15 and – especially – the '45.

Jacobitism as the Social Basis of a Counter-Revolution

There are therefore two distinct positions on the question of Jacobitism. One anchors it almost exclusively among the social base of the Highland clans. The other sets it floating among the political superstructures, picking up various divergent forces on the way and quite possibly being an early form of Scottish nationalism. Each position feeds off the weakness of the other, but the reductionism of the former is not answered by adopting the indeterminacy of the latter. Instead, we must look for the material roots of Jacobitism throughout Scottish society as a whole and not merely beyond the Highland line. Equally, those roots must be sought in a specific social class, not an undifferentiated Scottish 'nation'. To identify them we must return to the unfinished nature of the Scottish, and hence the British Revolution.

Whatever their specific differences, all the Jacobite risings after the Union – 1708, 1715, 1719 and 1745 – were made possible by a combination of three distinct factors. The first was, of course, the exiled House of Stuart and its campaign to be restored to the three Kingdoms of the British Isles. Yet without the two remaining factors the Stuart cause would have been as futile as that of the Bourbons after 1830 or the Romanovs after 1917. One was the financial and military backing of an external power with an interest in limiting or reversing British expansion. The other was a social group internal to Britain whose dissatisfaction with the existing state was great enough to make them take up arms against it. In one sense the failure of Jacobitism was caused by the inability of these two factors ever to interlock at critical moments. Where the internal opposition was unprepared to rise in significant numbers then external powers were insufficient to force the issue, as can be seen from the relative seriousness of the different risings: the '08 was a fiasco brought about because both the French regime and the exiled house of Stuart mistook popular opposition to the Union as support for a restoration; the '19 was merely a tactical feint on the part of the Spanish regime, which did not even attain the dignity of a fiasco. Only two – the '15 and the '45 – had the indispensable element of relatively widespread backing within Scotland to bring them within striking distance of their goal, but these nevertheless still failed because foreign support could not be provided in time to influence events. Who were these internal and external forces?

The external force was absolutist Europe. The War of the Spanish Succession, which began in 1702 as a war between England and France, concluded in 1713 with the Treaty of Utrecht between Britain and France. The years from 1716 to 1741 saw an Anglo-French Alliance (although it might be more appropriate to describe the period as one of Anglo-French Cold War) and until the latter year opposition to British expansion was partially taken over from France by the Spanish Empire and other, lesser, powers such as Sweden and Prussia. Whichever of her rivals the British state was engaged in fighting at any particular time, however, the struggle was rarely conducted in the European heartlands themselves, but in North and Latin America, Southern Asia and ... Scotland. As Daniel Szechi has noted, the effects of the Military Revolution of the seventeenth century had been to force all the major European powers to adopt similar forms of organisation and structure in order to compete militarily at all. The main consequence of this transformation was to ensure that, where these states were set against each other in conventional battle, the result was almost invariably inconclusive. Marlborough's victories between Blenheim (1704) and Malplaquet (1709) were the exception, not the rule.[27] The fomenting of internal rebellion was therefore not an optional extra, but often the only way in which the balance of forces could be shifted in favour of one of the contending states. 'In the present state of things it seems impossible to re-establish the affairs of France without some great and important enterprise,' wrote the Jacobite agent Hooke to his French paymasters, shortly after the Union: 'The enterprise upon Scotland is distinguished from all others in the following particular, that the risk that France runs is very small, and yet, in case of success, the re-establishment of their affairs certain.'[28] Frank McLynn is therefore correct to write: 'At the profoundest level ... French support for the Jacobites made sense in the battle for global hegemony with Britain.'[29]

Scotland was certainly not the first choice among the absolutist supporters of Jacobitism. The words of the Spanish Cardinal Alberoni, writing to the Jacobite Duke of Ormonde in March 1719, could as easily be those of any French contemporary: 'only think of Scotland as a last resort because it will be difficult to obtain supplies there, especially as the British government has the means to fill the sea with ships ... to attack England is to attack the heart'.[30] Nevertheless Jacobitism dominated Scottish politics during the years between 1708 and 1746 in a qualitatively different way from that in the preferred terrain of England. Why? What social force within Scotland gave Britain's external enemies their internal leverage? The answer to this question must be tentative, given our current lack of knowledge. Nevertheless, the following hypothesis has, at the very least, the merit of explaining the unique ability of Scottish Jacobites to provide their cause with military support, in stark contrast to their English counterparts.

In a few celebrated cases the bourgeois revolution took the form of a direct onslaught on the feudal regime, leading to the reconstruction of state and society on a new class basis. More commonly it took the form of a gradual internal reconstruction driven by the need to compete with, and hence emulate, those nations which were already reconstructed on capitalist lines. But what if there was no longer a state to be either overthrown or transformed? In Scotland, the defunct state apparatus had embodied a transitional society in which feudal economic and military relations, although modified, still prevailed. Since these relationships had been carried directly over into a union with capitalist England, we might have expected them to disintegrate from within in the manner outlined by Georg Lukacs, where 'those parts of the feudal and absolutist superstructure that were not eliminated by "revolution from above" would collapse of their own accord when capitalism was already fully developed'.[31] But what if the 'revolution from above' never took place at all? What if 'those parts of the feudal and absolutist superstructure' were artificially preserved with outside support, so that they retained a social and political power far greater than their shrinking economic base would otherwise have justified?

The Scottish nobility escaped the consequences of successful revolution in England through a combination of their own geographical inaccessibility and the political expediency of all the English regimes from the Restoration onwards. The most recent manifestation of such support, Article 20 of the Treaty of 1707, seemed to guarantee them a preservation order in perpetuity, but whatever the intentions of the English government in this respect, a mere juridical diktat could not prevent the subtly corrosive influence of 'commercial' society from undermining the socio-economic basis of noble rule. In such circumstances the lords had three alternatives.

The first was to attempt to transform themselves into capitalist landlords. Only the most powerful were secure enough to make this decision confidently, and for these already great lords, the trappings of feudal power became increasingly decorative. 'The possession of five thousand fighting men as a personal following no doubt lent a certain romantic grandeur to the Duke of Argyll in the eyes of his peers,' writes Eric Cregeen, 'but the spending of five thousand pounds a year was more necessary if the Duke was not to feel down at heel among the Russells, the Stanhopes and the Pelhams.'[32] For lesser breeds than Argyll the risk of turning to commercial agriculture was simply too great, for it would involve dispensing with the military linkages and judicial authority which guaranteed them such power, status and even wealth as they possessed for the altogether riskier competitive world of the marketplace.

The second alternative was therefore to raise funds through greater exactions from their tenants. In 1750 one commentator looked back on the activities of the McKenzies of the Long Island:

> They have screwed their Rents to an extravagant Height (which they viciously term improving their Estates) without putting the Tenant upon a proper way of improving the Ground to enable him to pay that Rent, which makes the common people little more than Slaves and Beggars.[33]

The third alternative, which many of the second group eventually adopted, involved neither changing the means of exploitation nor intensifying the existing means, but looking instead for a political solution to the increasing economic pressures which they faced. That solution was, of course, the restoration of the Stuarts. In one of his contributions to the 'pamphlet war' over the Union, James Hodges had warned his English readers that 'Scotland pressed to an Extremity by England will certainly Declare for the Absolute Power of the Monarch of Both'.[34] But it was not 'Scotland' which was so pressed, nor 'Scotland' which was prepared to declare for absolutism, but a section of the ruling class within Scotland in the period of their decline – a decline which they assumed restoration would reverse, or at least stabilise more successfully than the Union. More immediately, they hoped it would wipe out both their debts and the Argyll empire to which so many of these were owed.

The internal force supporting Jacobitism was therefore a group of declining lesser lairds, together with a smaller section of the great magnate families, whose income and indeed survival, were threatened by their unwillingness or inability to transform the running of their estates on capitalist lines. It is always possible to find exceptions. Daniel Szechi has argued that George Lockhart of Carnwarth 'embodies a series of challenges to conventional assumptions about the kind of man who became a Jacobite':

> Our stereotypical Jacobite is a declining landowner, burdened with inherited debts left over from the civil wars of the mid-seventeenth century, jealous of his social position, suspicious of the local (prospering) bourgeoisie, hostile to innovation of any kind, agricultural, technological or religious, and with social connections only to other families of the same ilk. Basically a relic of an old order marked for destruction by the industrial revolution, Lockhart was a very wealthy, agriculturally improving laird who took a great interest in exploiting the coal reserves on his land, elegantly modernised and emparked his favourite country seat in the latest fashionable style and was closely (and fondly) connected to one of the most powerful Whig families in post-Revolution Britain. If nothing else, George Lockhart is an object lesson in the dangers of crude economic and social determinism.[35]

Let us attempt to draw out the implications of this pen picture of Lockhart for the case I have been making about the class basis of Jacobitism. Szechi, who inclines towards the second of the two perspectives on Jacobitism outlined earlier in this chapter, is effectively engaged in a similar project to those revisionist critics of Marxist historiography who claim that interpretations of the English Civil War or the French Revolution as bourgeois revolutions (or class struggles of any sort) cannot be sustained because of the presence of the bourgeoisie on the Royalist side. In this case, the claim could be made that interpretations of Jacobitism which identify it with counter-revolution cannot be sustained because of the presence of improving landlords like Lockhart among their ranks. There are three reasons why I find this position no more convincing than those of the revisionist historians of England or France.[36]

First, we must consider, in addition to the conscious intentions of political actors, the – perhaps unlooked-for – potential outcomes of their activities. Lockhart may have seen no contradiction between his own role as advocate of agricultural improvement on the one hand and supporter of Stuart absolutism on the other, but one existed nevertheless. A restored Stuart dynasty would ultimately have been forced to function as a comprador regime in thrall to an aspirant Universal Monarchy – the same Universal Monarchy which was busily engaged in persecuting Calvinists and frustrating agrarian capitalists who worshipped or accumulated capital within the territory of the French state. Lockhart might therefore have found that, on two counts at least, the realisation of his political programme would have actually been against his interests.

There is nothing in the least surprising in this type of contradiction. If individual members of social classes were always aware of where their own interests lay, then both past history and contemporary politics would be considerably simpler than in fact they are.

Second, the mere presence of capitalist landowners among the Jacobites is not in any case decisive in determining the nature of their movement. A desire among Scottish Jacobites to protect their economic position tended to find expression in certain forms of religious observance (which were usually Episcopalian) and support for certain forms of constitutional propriety (which were usually the rights and privileges of the Scottish Parliament). There are examples, however, where these religious or – in the case of Lockhart – constitutional concerns were themselves the motive for political action. The key issue is surely whether these extra-economic motives were integral rather than auxiliary for a majority of the movement. Lockhart's Jacobitism might be more of 'a challenge to conventional assumptions' had he represented a numerically significant group of improving landowners equally committed to the Stuarts for constitutional reasons. Yet Szechi presents no evidence to suggest that this was the case.

Third, although members of what I have called the declining gentry may not have been the only people to become Jacobites, they were a majority, at least of the active membership base. If a majority of the Jacobites had been like Lockhart, rather than Kilmarnock or Cromartie, then the movement would have been as irrelevant in Scotland as it was in England. It is true that, as George Pryde notes of the lords as a class: 'From about 1730, when they "walked abroad", they carried a cane instead of a sword.'[37] But the swords remained at home, and could be donned whenever necessary. This fact is of central importance. The link between the Stuarts and a section of the Scottish nobility stemmed, on the side of the former, from the absence of any other internal social base capable of conducting the necessarily violent struggle for restoration. The Scottish lords – particularly those north of the Tay – could raise their tenants to fight; English landlords – even those formally Jacobite in politics – could, at best, only raise their tenants to vote. As Eveline Cruikshanks notes: 'In England, the New Model Army had put an end to the chances of country gentlemen turning out their tenants.' In Scotland, on the other hand: 'The life expectations of a Fraser who defied Lord Lovat would have been short indeed'.[38] An example of this power is given by the behaviour of Donald Cameron Younger of Locheil, whose adherence to the Stuart banner in 1745 was the key determinant in ensuring that the rising got off the ground. According to John Home, Locheil rejected the possibility of abstention with a ringing declaration: '"No," said Locheil, "I'll share the fate of my prince; *and so shall every man over whom nature or fortune hath given me any power.*"'[39] Actually, no one knows what Locheil said to Charles, since they conducted their negotiations in private.[40] Nevertheless, the counterposition of 'nature' or 'fortune' catches the twin sources – clannic and feudal – of his social power. During the '15, Archibald Campbell, first Earl of Islay (and later third Duke of Argyll) expressed astonishment that men of such meagre income could command enough authority to challenge the state: 'The Captain of Clanranald ... has not £500 a year and yet has 600 men with him.'[41] In 1776 Adam Smith was equally bemused that such power had been exercised in Scotland as recently as 1746:

It is not thirty years ago since Mr Cameron of Locheil, a gentleman of Lochaber in Scotland, without any legal warrant whatever, not being what was then called a lord of regality, nor even a tenant in chief, but a vassal of the Duke of Argyll, and without being so much as a justice of the peace, used, notwithstanding, to exercise the highest criminal jurisdictions over his own people.

And in the case of Locheil, these feudal jurisdictions were also linked to his role as chief of the local branch of Clan Cameron. 'That gentleman,' Smith notes, 'whose rent never exceeded £500 a year, carried, in 1745, 800 of his own people into rebellion with him.'[42] 'Carried' is certainly the correct expression here, as many of Locheil's 'people' were less than enthusiastic about participating in the rising. A deposition made after it was crushed gives some examples of how the 'gentle Locheil' managed to raise his force. According to this account, on 15 August 24 men, led by the tacksmen, arrived in Rannoch where they:

... went from house to house on both sides of the Loch Rannoch ... and intimated to all the Camerons, which are pretty numerous on both sides of the loch, that if they did not forthwith go with them, they would that instant proceed to burn all their houses and hough [i.e. hamstring] all their cattle; whereupon they carried off all the Rannoch men, about one hundred, mostly of the name of Cameron.[43]

Even where military tenure was not the dominant form of tenure, the heritable jurisdictions preserved by the Union comprised a set of complex, interlocking territorial domains through which irresistible pressure could be applied to tenants. The north-east shows this most clearly. In a letter to his tenants written during the rising of 1715, Alexander Gordon, Marquis of Huntly, announced his intention of joining the Jacobite side. He also indicates in tones of quiet menace what he expects of them.

The present expedition [is] being undertaken by a great number of honest and brave men, who have for motive their Loyalty to the King. I cannot doubt but that you will cheerfully contribute your best endeavours in so good a cause. I do therefore Recommend to you to raise your men and provide them with arms, and Loan for nine days, to join with Me in My March, which I intend to begin in a few days. If your present circumstances do necessarily hinder your going in person, I recommend the raising and leading of the Men to Tillyfour. I expect your cheerful compliance in this matter ...

No doubt these unfortunate lairds knew what to expect from their 'affectionate Friend and Servant, Huntly' had their cheerful compliance not been forthcoming. In any event, Huntly was able to lead 2,300 men into the field, so his veiled threats obviously had the desired effect.[44] At the beginning of the '15, Mar sent a similar epistle to his baillie, John ('Black Jock') Forbes of Invergordon, complaining of his failure to appear with a sufficient number of men and offering veiled threats that he had 'used gentle means too long'. Mar instructs Forbes to tell his disloyal tenants that they might be treated as traitors should James be victorious; but in case this threat seemed unlikely to be realised, he also offered more immediate menaces:

> Particularly let my own tenants in Kildrummie know that if they come not forth with their best arms, I shall send a party immediately to burn down what they shall miss taking from them. And they may believe this only a threat but, by all that's sacred, I'll put it into execution – let my loss be what it will.[45]

No peasant faced with one of Locheil or Mar's tacksmen at their door, armed with fire and sword and suggesting that they share the fate of his Prince, could be in any doubt about the existence of the state, even if the word was not in their vocabulary. The territorially dispersed forms of local authority which oppressed them constituted examples of dual power – and on both sides of the Highland line. The concept was first used after the Russian Revolution of February 1917 to describe how the councils of workers – and later those of the peasantry and armed forces – came to constitute an alternative source of economic, social and political organisation to that of the state headed by the Provisional Government. 'Two powers *cannot exist* in a state,' wrote Lenin, shortly before one overthrew the other.[46] Trotsky also discerned similar experiences – involving different social classes and institutions – in earlier revolutions such as the English and the French: 'The two-power regime arises only out of irreconcilable conflicts – is possible, therefore, only in a revolutionary epoch, and constitutes one of its fundamental elements.'[47] He was careful to add, however, that this situation does not arise merely where there are divisions of interest within a ruling class, and he cited as an example the conflict between the Junkers and the bourgeoisie in Germany under both the Hohenzollern Empire of 1871 and the Republic of 1918. He might have added to this the struggle between Whig and Tory in England during the first half of the eighteenth century. In the English and the French (although not the Russian) Revolutions the centres of dual power opposed to the absolutist state were in territories seized through military onslaught or urban insurrection by forces opposed to the regime. In Scotland the situation was reversed, as feudal enclaves continued to function after the fall of absolutism within the overall territory of a state otherwise dedicated to the accumulation of capital. As an anonymous English writer whom we have already quoted notes, this co-existence of opposed power centres was 'a Thought our Constitution abhors' and which 'the present State of our Constitution can in no sense endure'.[48] This was with the benefit of hindsight, but even during the period between the '15 and the '45 the issue was sharply raised by a number of writers.

An anonymous open letter to the English Members of Parliament in 1721 pointed to the dangers which continuing lordly power posed to the British state as a whole:

Your Countrymen have always been afraid of a Standing Army, and opposed it from time to time with Vigour; we were therefore astonished at their not foreseeing that the Confirmation of these Superiorities laid the Foundation of a constant standing Army, even in time of Peace.

The author goes on to appeal that 'our Nation may be freed, as well as yours, from such senile Dependencies, either on the King or Subjects; and especially on such as have, from Time to Time, made too ill a use of them'. Such action would not be against the Union Treaty:

It may be objected, That this will be a Breach of the 20th Article of the Union ... but the Answer is easy, That it does not seem to be an unalterable Article, such as that which relates to our Church; since it is provided by the last Clause of the 18th Article, That an Alteration may be made in Laws which concern private Rights, for the evident Utility of the Subjects within Scotland, And that such a Law would be so, is too demonstrable to be controverted, and will appear to be more necessary, because of the great Oppressions which Vassals labour under by these Tenures ...

The author concludes with what he takes to be an unanswerable argument: 'And to what Purpose could these interposed Hereditary Jurisdictions in Scotland be continued? but to give Occasion to harass and oppress the poor People under them, with Fines and other arbitrary Impositions.' His final plea is for the completion of the Union:

I must also think, Sir, That our Scots may be encouraged to expect a Relief from the Slavery and Oppression of Superiorities and Heritable Jurisdictions, under which they labour and groan; and that not only from the Union that is now betwixt England and Scotland, Entitling Scotland to the same Privileges that you have, that the whole united Body may be uniform in Liberty and Property.[49]

Why then did the British state allow the heritable jurisdictions to continue after 1707, especially when a number of other Articles of the Treaty were broken? If they had originally been preserved as a contingent measure to sell the Union to the Scottish ruling class as a whole, then their continuation was the result of two different and contradictory considerations.

One was an awareness that some of the most committed supporters of the Revolution Settlement and the Union were themselves beneficiaries of these institutions and in a social crisis would employ them in support of the regime. The '15 gives examples of such behaviour. At the bottom of the ruling class hierarchy, Hugh Rose, 15th baron of Kilravock, who was also a clan chief (and as a commissioner had voted *against* the Union), 'stood firm in his loyalty to his Majesty [i.e. George I], and against Popery and arbitrary power'. When some of the neighbouring chiefs rose for the Stuarts: 'He armed a select number of above 200 of his clan, and preserved the peace of that part of the country.'[50] At the top, meanwhile, Argyll could write to Lord Townshend complaining of the lack of government supporters in Scotland, 'excepting our few friends in the North and those of my vassals in the West Highlands'.[51] To alienate these men was to risk depriving the state of their local military apparatus and even pushing them into support for the Stuarts.

The other consideration was also related to the question of state power. Neither the juridical nor the military aspects of the English state had been reproduced in Scotland; partly because it would in any event take time to overcome the uneven level of development between the states, partly because of the suspicion with which the English ruling class continued to regard their new partners. This weak nation-within-a-state was weakest precisely across the area north of the Tay, and successive administrations were prepared – indeed, were forced – to tolerate the continued functioning of local jurisdictions as a form of substitute. The situation was far from ideal, to the extent that an attempt to counterbalance the weight of the jurisdictions was made directly after the Union with the establishment of Justices of the Peace, who were intended to hold judicial and administrative responsibility for particular geographical areas. As a judiciary they were concerned with upholding law and order, and the collection of the new tax revenues introduced by the Treaty of Union. As an administration they were responsible for maintaining the means of transportation and incarceration, fixing wage rates, enforcing contracts and supervising weights and measures. Yet in spite of the state controls which theoretically existed over appointments to the Commission of the Peace, many Justices of the Peace were Jacobite in politics. Consequently, in the aftermath of the '08, members of the Commission responsible for testing the loyalty of suspected Jacobites were themselves supporters of the Stuarts. Even a purge following the '15 left in place many Jacobites who would later rise for Charles Stuart, such as John Gordon of Glenbucket and James Moir of Stoneywood, and they would shortly be joined by more of their comrades. The problem for the central state was that, since the justices were unpaid, there was a shortage of suitable candidates, the shortfall often being made up by the lesser landowners who sought the position to further their political ends.[52] In 1712 Lockhart wrote twice to Robert Harley, Earl of Oxford, a leading Tory and Lord Treasurer, pointing out that in some shires there were no Justices of the Peace and in others too few to be able to collect the excise effectively.[53] In short, the social influence of the class upon which Jacobitism was most reliant could not be avoided, at least in the northern half of Scotland.

The British State versus Scottish Society?

One of the main chains of arguments employed by the Jacobites after 1707 was that the Union had, as they predicted, resulted in dire economic consequences for Scotland, mainly in increased taxation and declining trade. But the Union itself resulted from, and was a Divine punishment for, the Revolution of 1688, when the rightful king had been deposed. (If in nothing else, the Jacobites were at one with later Enlightenment historians in seeing an intimate connection between these two events.) These arguments had little impact before 1700. As the Darien disaster had drawn to its inevitable conclusion and popular fury mounted, the Jacobites attempted to claim that this amounted to support for their cause. At the end of 1699 Marchmont was writing to Seafield:

> They would have it believed, that many of this nation concerned in the American undertaking are so dissatisfied by what has happened, that they are turned Jacobite, which is utterly false; and their trick is already begun to be discovered. ... I have made, and am making, as several others here do, all the inquiry that can be, and can find nothing, but that one madman, well enough known, Mr Andrew Darling, was heard to say to some little boys in the street, 'Come lads! Let us go drink King James's health,' but had not a drop to give them; and there was no more about it.[54]

Despite Marchmont's characteristic over-optimism his concluding sentence contains a striking metaphor for the Jacobite failure to gain influence among the wider population; they had 'not a drop to give them' in the way of any positive social programme. After the Union, however, they had a definite and entrenched target which allowed the movement to act not only as a repository for general political and economic discontent, but also as the expression of a bruised proto-national consciousness now denied institutional expression. Every action by the British government that placed pressure on these sensitivities tended to lead to temporary support for the Jacobites who, whatever else they may have been, were the only party committed to the abolition of the Union.

If the Union had brought the much-advertised benefits in its wake then it is possible that other grievances would have produced a more muted response, but it did not; and although the Union was not responsible for the continued decline in Scottish trade, it nevertheless received the blame. Apart from the exceptional and short-lived profits made by some merchants in the period between ratification and the Treaty coming into effect – they imported goods at the still relatively low Scottish duty then sold them in England at a massive profit – there were no immediate perceptible economic benefits at all. On the contrary, the most noticeable effect – and it was immediate – was the arrival of 'shoals' of additional excisemen to strengthen the authority of a state openly mocked by the participants in the smuggling industry. This did not go unopposed: 'From virtually every part of Lowland Scotland comes evidence of quite extraordinary disorder, mainly in the form of assaults on customs and excise officers and the warehouses in which they locked seized goods.'[55] These incidents continued until the 1730s, although with diminishing frequency and intensity after the initial post-Union explosion.

Adam Smith later admitted that many of the complaints voiced at this time were initially justified: 'The immediate effect of [the Union] was to hurt the interest of every single order of men in the country.'[56] Just because individual 'hurts' were perceived as national humiliations did not make them so, but perceptions have their own impact on politics. In the prevailing atmosphere of popular hostility to Westminster and its entire works, unconnected political events seemed to form a sinister pattern. Some of these were episodes in the inter-party struggle between the Whigs and the Tories, others were the result of jockeying for position by factions within Scotland, still others were attempts to introduce uniformity within state institutions across Britain as a whole – but all breached the Union to the detriment of the Scots. What aspects of life in the new state provoked such hostility that the Jacobite movement stood a chance of coming to power? Five breaches in particular seemed to bear out all the warnings about the likely consequences of the Union.

The first was the abolition of the Privy Council. As might have been expected, given the differences between them in terms of class base, the Scottish parties made uneasy bedfellows with those in England. The Court Party, as the Whigs had feared, became the mainstays of the

Ministry. The Squadrone, as ever, sought to supplant it in ministerial favour, although it is fair to add that some members of the Squadrone – particularly those with a mercantile interest – were growing nearer to the Whigs in questions of ideology. In 1708, however, the main thoughts of the Squadrone were of revenge on the Court Party for refusing to recognise their role in carrying the Union, and for reneging on their promise to entrust disbursement of the Equivalent to Squadrone leaders. With the dissolution of the Scottish Parliament the only remaining means of dispensing patronage left to the political managers was through the Privy Council – the body which had historically carried on the business of state when Parliament was in recess. The Squadrone were determined to stop Queensberry and Argyll from using this institution to strengthen their hand, and moved that it be dissolved – not on these grounds, of course, but ostensibly because it was no longer needed, now that the Parliament it had served was gone. Their case, in the cant phrase which would be uttered often – albeit with differing degrees of sincerity – over the next 40 years, was that abolition would 'make the Union more complete'. The Privy Council was duly sent after the Parliament into oblivion on 1 May 1708, but far from strengthening the British state in Scotland, this episode in the internecine struggles of the two Unionist parties in Scotland effectively removed the one institution which could exercise central control over that territory. The political consequences of this would soon become apparent.

The second breach was the passing of the 'Treason Act'. Even before the Treaty came into effect on 1 May 1707, an alliance of the Jacobite lords had written to Louis requesting that he invade Scotland in order to support an intended rising. By the end of the year the French agent Hooke had completed a tour of the country collecting signatures from lairds who were prepared to commit themselves to such an enterprise. Finally, on 6 March 1708, 5,000 French troops, accompanied by the putative James III and VIII set sail from Dunkirk with the intention of landing in south-west Scotland and combining with the thousands of Scots who, according to Hooke, were prepared to rise against a British state whose military strength was concentrated on the European mainland. The strategy did not involve marching on London, but rather seizing the Tyneside coalfields which supplied most of English domestic and industrial fuel, thereby provoking a run on the pound (which in fact took place even before the fleet had completed the Channel crossing) and forcing the withdrawal of British troops from the Netherlands.

If we exclude the abortive attempt of 1744, this was certainly the most serious attempt by the French state to mount an invasion of Britain. But on this occasion the French relied on their own external military resources to bring about victory, not on an internal rising in Scotland, since the French commander, the Comte de Forbin, rightly suspected the ever-optimistic Hooke of exaggerating the level of support they could expect. In fact, the same considerations that had prevented a rising in 1706 were still operative in 1708. The Presbyterian sects had withdrawn from their proposed alliance with the Atholl clans to overthrow Parliament because they feared that their actions would potentially have opened the door for the Pretender and his French allies. Are we to believe that they would have risen now to support an actual French invasion? It is even uncertain whether the clans would have aided the French. Atholl their chief, despite his opposition to the Union, was a Presbyterian and a supporter of the Revolution of 1688, characteristics that made him an unlikely supporter of a restored Catholic Stuart monarchy. If this was true of non-Jacobite opponents of the Union like Atholl, how much more so was it for the other great lords, the majority of whom had not yet repented of their support for the Treaty? Even the magnates who were prepared to contemplate a restoration hedged their bets. The only Jacobites to come out openly for the Pretender were among the lairds, several of whom could be found gallivanting about Stirlingshire toasting his health. Whether they would have been capable of mustering serious levels of support at this stage is doubtful, but the matter was never put to the test. Bad weather, the presence of the British Royal Navy and the scepticism of the expedition's own leadership combined to prevent a landing taking place, and by 7 April the battered expedition was once more in port at Dunkirk. In the aftermath various people of suspect loyalty were arrested. Ludicrously, these included Belhaven and Fletcher, whose hostility to Jacobitism could not have been in doubt to anyone with the faintest knowledge of Scottish politics – a criterion which of course excluded most members of the Ministry. No one was executed, but the Jacobite lairds who had openly demonstrated their support for the Pretender were put on trial in Scotland and, despite being transparently guilty, were released after the jury returned a verdict of 'not proven'. In part the leniency with which these potential counter-revolutionaries had been treated was due to a certain indifference on the part of the Privy Council, which was then in its final days.

The majority of the British ruling class were shocked that their Scottish contingent had proved so forgiving, perhaps even so complicit, with treason. In response the outraged Ministry successfully introduced a Treason Act – or to give it the full title, 'An Act for Improving the Union of the Two Kingdoms' – into Scotland to help prevent such self-evident traitors escaping justice in future. This enactment imposed on the Scots those aspects of the English Treason laws which they had previously been spared: the use of torture to secure confessions, the admissibility of evidence obtained from co-defendants, the power of judges to select membership of a jury and to convict on the evidence of one witness, rather than two, as the law currently stood in Scotland. Above all, the English penalties for treason – hanging, drawing and quartering of the traitor and forfeiture of their estates – were now applicable in Scotland.

Unlike the abolition of the Privy Council, this was clearly an attempt by the new state to extend control over its Scottish territory, albeit in response to a foreign-backed attempt at counter-revolution.

The third breach was the passing of the Toleration and Patronage Acts. The General Election of 1710 returned a Tory majority committed to bringing the war with France to an end. The Scottish Jacobites, who had posed as 'Cavaliers' in the last years of the Scottish Parliament, now styled themselves as 'Tories', but changed nothing in their political orientation. James Greenshields, an Episcopal minister, had been found guilty by the Edinburgh magistrates of using the English liturgy, and sentenced to imprisonment, a decision upheld by the Court of Session. Supported by the Scottish Jacobites, Greenshields appealed to the House of Lords, where the Court of Session verdict was overturned in March 1711. Their ruling effectively demonstrated that an English court had superiority over any Scottish one as a court of final appeal, but the intention of the Jacobite petitioners was not primarily to demonstrate this for propaganda purposes – although they did do so, of course – but to strengthen their Episcopalian base in Scotland. In this they were successful beyond their wildest dreams, for, emboldened by the apparent presence of co-thinkers in Scotland, the Tories pushed through two Acts in 1712 the combined effects of which were to weaken Presbyterianism dominance in civil society.

The Toleration Act granted the legal right of Episcopalians to worship, providing they used the Anglican prayer book. In a concomitant move, it also removed the power of the Church of Scotland courts to enforce penalties on anyone who did not voluntarily submit to them. The Patronage Act restored the right of the patron to nominate a minister where a vacancy arose, although it also allowed for the matter to be decided by the presbytery in a case where the heritors or elders objected to a nominee. The effect of these Acts was to withdraw the last remaining attribute of a state within a state, social control over parishioners from the kirk, while its autonomy in relation to the landowners was greatly reduced. Despite Presbyterian outrage, particularly over the Toleration Act, the immediate effects of the legislation should not be exaggerated. The role of the kirk as repository of religious conviction on the one hand, and as the central organising force in parish communities on the other, made it strong enough to prevent congregations walking away simply because ministerial pronouncements no longer had the force of Law. Nor did every minister automatically become a mouthpiece for the local laird. Nevertheless, the direction in which events were moving was clear and, by mid-century, the kirk had suffered more than one split at the hands of those for whom the position of that organisation was now intolerable. Indeed, it could be argued that the greatest impact of the Toleration Act was not the negative effect it had on the Church of Scotland and the sects, but the positive effect it had on the Episcopalians. Robert Wodrow, along with many of his Church, had long complained of 'the legal toleration given to the Episcopal party' and saw the Act as contributing to the Jacobite movement not only by legitimising its ideological wing, but also by providing opportunities for organisation:

> By this the prelatic preachers recovered strength, openly, under the colour of right and law, made their intrusions, set up the English forms [i.e. of worship], and declared in favour of Papists, closely hedged with them, and their meeting were daily rendezvouses for the Jacobites.[57]

The fourth breach was the exclusion of the Scottish peers from the House of Lords. On 20 December 1711 the House of Lords decided that Hamilton had no right to sit in the House on the basis of his English title (i.e. the Duke of Brandon). This was a successful attempt by the Whig opposition in the Lords to stop the Tory administration from filling the Other Place with Scottish peers, since the latter could be expected – on the basis of their notorious servility to whoever was in power at Westminster – to vote with the Tories for peace with France. The effect was to prevent all of the Scottish peerage outside the 16 allowed by the Treaty from participating in the formal political process. The Jacobites suffered most through this ruling, which was applicable to all peers with English titles, and began a half-hearted boycott of the House, which had to be called off in order that they be present to vote in the Second Reading of the Toleration Bill. Of all the factors listed here this was the one most driven by purely short-term considerations.

The fifth and final breach of the Treaty was the extent of increased taxation. The first four breaches, with the exception of the religious legislation, affected the ruling class to a far greater degree than they did the mass of the population. Taxation, however, impacted on the latter to a far greater extent than their masters. By 1713, the government was near to achieving the goal for which it had been elected, securing peace in Europe. During the negotiations which were to result in the Treaty of Utrecht, which took place during March and April of that year, it was announced that the duty paid on malt would be equalised across Scotland and England. As Bruce Lenman points out, there were three 'excellent' reasons why this was bound to infuriate the Scots:

> First, the Treaty of Union exempted Scotland from contributing to the costs of the war, but the new tax was expressly designed to meet those costs. Secondly, the Treaty specifically exempted the Scots from a tax on malt during the war, which was not yet at an end. Thirdly, the Act of Union specified that future taxes be fairly apportioned, yet the annual value of the Scots barley crop was a mere fraction of the English one, so an equal tax was unjust.[58]

Ironically, it was this measure which finally provoked sections of the Scottish ruling class to reconsider their position. On 2 June 1713, Seafield, now the Earl of Findlater, moved a motion in the House of Lords for dissolution of the Union, listing as reasons the accumulated grievances of the previous six years, including 'the dissolution of the Council, the Treason Act, the incapacity of Peers – but above all our many Taxes, especially the Malt Tax Bill, and the ruin of our trade and manufacturies'.[59] It was a symbolic gesture. Although defeated by only four (proxy) votes in the Lords, the motion stood no chance of succeeding in the Commons. The government was, however, sufficiently shaken to make a tactical withdrawal over the Malt Tax, for, although the Act went unrepealed, it was not put into effect. Nevertheless, the implications of these successive enactments were unmistakable.

The period of maximum popular dissatisfaction with the Union was therefore concentrated in the decade following the Treaty. The level of popular discontent which characterised these years gave Jacobitism the appearance of a movement with a broader base of support than it in fact possessed. The depth of that support would be put to the test in rising of 1715.

1715: Dress Rehearsals for the End

By the death of Queen Anne on 1 August 1714, then, the conditions for a Jacobite rising with widespread popular support were as good as they would ever be. And there was also an additional reason for believing that a rising at this time had a better-than-average chance of success for, quite exceptionally, it could rely on a degree of support from England. This may appear to contradict our earlier assessment of the situation in England as being inherently resistant to civil war; but the events which propelled some of the English Jacobites into rebellion were an unrepeatable combination of crises: the effect of the Hanoverian Succession on the Tory Party and the impact of a severe economic depression on the Catholic gentry in the north-east of England.

Even before their electoral victory in 1710, the Tories had been, as an expression coined 250 years later has it, 'the natural party of government' in post-Revolution England. Yet there could be little doubt that George I would favour the Whigs, whose aggressive foreign policy in Europe was most likely to offer protection to his home state of Hanover from French depredations. Following the accession of George and the subsequent Whig electoral victory, a concerted onslaught was mounted against the Tories, whose despair at being excluded from office and the fruits of patronage, particularly after the seeming invincibility of their position the previous year, pushed a minority towards a Jacobitism which otherwise seems to have been the creed of a radical minority. As Henry

Saint John, Viscount Bolingbroke, noted in the aftermath: 'The violence of the whigs forced them into the arms of the Pretender.'[60] As it did Bolingbroke himself. The main foci for the proposed rising were the towns of Exeter, Bristol and Plymouth in the West Country. Yet, in the end, pre-emptive arrests by the government and a failure of nerve on the part of the leadership prevented the call to insurrection being made. The main focus for rebellion in England therefore became, not the Tory heartlands of the south, but the north-east, where sections of the ruling class had quite specific difficulties unconnected with the collapse of Tory influence in the state.

The rising in the north-east of England was quite different in social content from that in Scotland. Paul Monod writes: 'It is tempting to envision the Northumbrian rebellion as a sort of feudal parade, led by a host of squires, followed by a crowd of retainers, with a few artisans and craftsmen in the rear.'[61] Monod rightly rejects this vision, which is far more relevant to Scotland. The real roots of the rising lie in the religious complexion of the north-east. The region had a high concentration of Roman Catholic gentry, who were coming under financial pressure as a result of falling agricultural prices. More specifically, the Tyneside coal industry, in which many of them were owners, was in crisis. Many seams were exhausted and it would have involved high levels of investment to dig deeper into existing seams or mine new ones altogether with any guarantee of a return.[62] Leo Gooch has argued that the economic situation was irrelevant, as 'the Fifteen was a national rising aimed at the restoration of a dynasty, not a remedy for some regional economic grievance'. According to Gooch, all gentry families suffered 'perennial indebtedness' – we simply know more about the Catholic gentry because of the laws concerning the registration of estates.[63] While this is true, it ignores the fact that non-Catholics in straitened circumstances could seek to raise their incomes through public office. Catholics, on the other hand, were forbidden by law from occupying state positions and consequently had no possibility of relief from this source.[64] Discrimination against Catholics was a popular cause in England at this time, not least because of the widespread perception that their religion necessarily involved support for the French state. It might be said, therefore, that the particular constraints which operated on English Catholics made them more than usually vulnerable to economic recession, and consequently made some of them – but still a small minority – more likely to consider rising in insurrection as a remedy.[65] Given this fundamental motivation, the greater concentration of Catholics among the landowning classes in the north-east than elsewhere in England provided better opportunities for organising and the mutual reinforcement of their beliefs – a situation similar, from the opposite side of the religious and political spectrum, to that of the con-venticling bonnet lairds of south-western Scotland. But a rising which depended on Catholic support – and a narrowly regional Catholic support at that – had no possibility of drawing in wider social forces. It was a commonplace among Tories that the refusal of James Stuart to abandon his faith was the biggest obstacle to his gaining the support of larger sections of their party. In the end, the numbers who rose in the north-east of England were insignificant. On Gooch's own estimates, only 271 Northumbrians were 'out' in the '15. He describes 187 of these as 'plebeians', two-thirds of whom took part involuntarily because they were servants, tenants or otherwise in positions which left them open to pressure at the hands of their masters or landlords.[66]

The '15 in England was therefore an extremely marginal enterprise from the start. If the rising was to have any hope of success then events in Scotland, where vast reserves of post-Union discontent were waiting to be tapped, would be decisive. The key figure in Scotland was Mar. From being one of the men most responsible for ratification he had moved, along with others of his class, to viewing the entire arrangement as a failure. As early as 1711 he wrote to his brother: 'If we saw a possibility of getting free of the Union without a civil war we would have some comfort, but that I'm afraid is impossible.'[67] From admitting the necessity of a civil war he then went on to organise exactly that, but for reasons which were rather more personal than his correspondence might suggest. Financially insecure, like many of the other lords, Mar had nevertheless kept himself afloat through his hold on office. He failed, however, to gain preferment at the hands of the new monarch; indeed, George pointedly turned his back on him at a reception shortly after his arrival in Britain. It was as a result of this snub that Mar returned to Scotland and, under the cover of a hunting party, raised the Jacobite standard on the Braes of Mar on 6 September 1715. He was quickly joined both by clan warriors (e.g. the MacKenzies) and feudal levies (e.g. those of the Marquis of Huntly). In effect, this was the anti-Union rising which failed to happen in 1706 or 1708; it therefore provides us with some measure of what degree of opposition actually existed.

By the beginning of October an army of 8,000 had established itself at Perth and was preparing to strike at the government troops who were gathering near Stirling. Who were they? One minute written in the aftermath of the rising, probably by Patrick Haldane, MP for Forfar District of Burghs, divided prisoners into four groups according to the reason for their participation. The first were those who were pressed:

> It is certain that the Rebellion breaking out of a sudden, when there was no army in the country, the people on the North side of the Tay were soon under the feet of the rebels, and many were forced not only to submit to them as a government, but in many places men who had not any time before shown the least marks of dissatisfaction were directly forced into their service, and were dragged to the rebels army

from their houses and families, and even from the churches where his Majesty was publicly prayed for.

The second were 'boys under age, from fourteen to twenty-one', who had not yet come 'to the maturity of their judgement'. The third were 'parents who went out with their fathers into the Rebellion, and menial servants who followed their masters'. The fourth were those 'who hastily joined the Rebels', but who 'did leave them when the Rebellion was yet subsisting'. Haldane, if it was he, speaks in mitigation for the first three groups by virtue of the reason for their presence in the Jacobite army (military impressment, youthful folly, submission to patriarchal authority) and for the fourth by virtue of their behaviour after joining (they deserted before it became apparent that the rising would fail).[68]

Scotland had been virtually defenceless at the start of the rising, with only 1,500 men spread between the three great Lowland fortresses. Argyll had returned from London to take command, but even on the eve of battle, he had at his disposal a maximum of 3,000 men, and although a section of the Jacobite army had crossed the Border to link up with the English rising, it still outnumbered the government forces by two to one. Even given that Argyll was, next to Marlborough, the greatest British general of his age, Mar had overwhelming numerical superiority and should have won on these grounds alone. At the Battle of Sheriffmuir on 13 November, however, the armies fought out an inconclusive draw after which, although the government suffered higher casualties, Mar retreated back to Perth and refused to re-engage with Argyll. From this point on the rising began to collapse. No help was forthcoming from England. The Scottish Jacobites who had earlier crossed the Border succeeded in linking up with fewer than 100 mainly Catholic gentry in Northumberland. Marginally strengthened by the adherence of a force raised by Catholic lords from the Scottish Borders independently of Mar, they advanced south to Lancashire where they were resoundingly defeated at Preston on 14 November – the same day as Mar retreated to Perth. Prince James Francis Edward Stuart arrived in Scotland on 22 December, but it was already too late to influence events in his favour.

These had been the most favourable conditions under which any Jacobite rising had taken place up to that point, or would subsequently do so. This was not simply a function of the inadequacy of government forces available to defend Scotland. The failure of the Union to deliver what had been promised in the short term and the breaches of the treaty by an English-dominated Parliament gave the rising a potential level of popular support outwith the lords and their followers, and, unlike every other Jacobite rising, the '15 had the potential to succeed without French intervention. It is important, therefore, to understand why the Jacobites failed to realise this potential. Two reasons stand out.

The first was the nature of the Jacobite leadership. The ineptitude of 'Bobbing Jock' Mar has often been commented on, particularly in respect of his failure to turn the draw at Sheriffmuir into victory by continuing the attack against Argyll. Obviously this was not treachery comparable to Hamilton's in 1705-07, but it does suggest that Mar had failed to consider exactly what victory would involve. It was as if he had hoped that an armed demonstration would restore his fortunes without the necessity of forcing the matter to a conclusion by attempting to conquer state power.

The second reason was the lack of support in the southern Lowlands. We are unlikely ever to uncover the deepest intentions of Mar at this distance in time; nevertheless, had even a Montrose or a Dundee been available to lead the rising, they would still have had to deal with the fact that support was minimal south of the Tay. The heartland of the rising was in the north-eastern Lowlands and the adjacent Grampian Highlands. It was the largely Episcopalian lords in Banffshire and Aberdeenshire who raised the majority of the Jacobite forces, yet in the two largest burghs benorth Tay, Aberdeen and Dundee, and all points between, Mar gained overwhelming support. Why?

As I have already suggested, the reasons were overwhelmingly economic.

> The east-coast towns were ripe for disaffection as they were not only Episcopalian strongholds, but were also suffering economically through the long-term trend initiated by the Union which moved Scotland's economic axis to the west and imperial trade away from the traditional European links of the major ports on the east coast.[69]

Aberdeen itself was Jacobite in sympathy and, when the magistrates refused to recognise James as King, a crowd deposed them then proceeded to elect a suitably loyal set of officials. Nevertheless, it should be noted that although Aberdeen was the main source of finance for the Jacobites, a demand that the town provide a troop of 30 horse did not meet with a favourable response as 'there were apparently no volunteers'.[70] Dundee had barred its gates to Claverhouse during the rising of 1689, but by 1715 matters were quite different. 'Over the years,' writes Annette Smith, 'the Town Council had become predominantly sympathetic to the deposed dynasty, possibly for reasons similar to those over Scotland as a whole – poor economic conditions and dissatisfaction with the Union.'[71] When the Pretender entered Dundee on 16 January 1716 with a mere 300 armed men, at a time when the rising was clearly on its last legs, he was nevertheless greeted enthusiastically by the assembled burgesses and proclaimed at the Market Cross by the Town Clerk.

The reception granted the insurgents in the two great burghs of the north-eastern Lowlands constituted the apogee of popular Jacobitism.

Edinburgh remained loyal, although this may have been partly due less to conviction than to the accessibility of the capital to English military retaliation and its economic dependence on government-related expenditure. Even before the rising had broken out, however, rumours of the forthcoming attempt had led some of the burgesses to form two associations offering military and financial support to the city fathers. The crucial area, however, was Glasgow and its south-western hinterland. The inhabitants of Glasgow had rioted and demonstrated against the Union almost up until the moment of ratification. If they supported the Jacobites, they might well have gained a Lowland base of far greater significance than among the disconsolate lairds of Fife. In fact, the town held militantly for the regime. Following a Town Council meeting of 26 August in that year, the magistrates wrote to their King:

> The City of Glasgow, being deeply affected with the certain evidences of a designed invasion from abroad in favour of a Papish Pretender, and of the preparations of a restless Papist and Jacobite faction at home ... we the magistrates of the said city, for ourselves and in the name of our burgesses and inhabitants, humbly present to offer to your majesty a regiment to consist of five hundred sentinels, with ten captains and other subalterns needful for such a regiment, to be paid by us for the space of sixty days for defence of this city and country ...[72]

Despite receiving a polite brush-off from the Lord Secretary Townshend, the regiment was raised and defended Stirling during the battle of Sheriffmuir. And this response was typical of the whole region.[73] As William Law Mathieson writes:

> Almost all the principal towns from Glasgow to Kirkcudbright, and from Kirkcudbright to Kelso, raised companies; parishes were mustered by the minister, who in many cases actually took arms; and throughout this district a spirit was evoked which had hardly been seen since the days of the Whiggamore Raid.[74]

This author touches on one important element in Lowland resistance to the Jacobites – the unremitting hostility of the kirk to their cause.

The careers of the Presbyterian ministers and the very existence of the Church of Scotland were at stake and threatened with destruction in the same way that Episcopalianism had been after the Williamite victory of 1688. This was the one issue on which the ministers could be guaranteed to oppose the will of the local lairds, regardless of whether they exercised patronage or not, as they certainly did in parts of Fife. This position was not without its tensions, which the correspondence of Robert Wodrow catches in stark relief, as in this letter of December 1714 after the publication of a Jacobite Address against the Union:

I was and still am against the Union, in this shape we have been burdened with now more than seven years, and I reckon it is the great fountain of many of the grievances this Church groans under, and if mercy prevent not, is likely to [be] an inlet to more. And yet I would be very unwilling to give any countenance to any thing that may embarrass the King [i.e. George I] in the entry of his government, when he hath his hands so full with the Jacobites in England, or to do any thing which may strengthen the Jacobites among ourselves.[75]

Wodrow elaborated his position in a further letter early in the following year, where he explains his opposition to addresses against the Union:

I own unless the Union be broken by whigs and not Jacobites, and till we have, if I may call them, limitations even in a Scots Parliament, and conditions of England which we might have had, if the Jacobites had not driven England and some of our Presbyterian and Revolution party into the Union, I am not in favour of addressing.[76]

Hostility to Jacobitism was not restricted to the Presbyterians within the Church of Scotland, but also extended to the post-Cameronian sects. 'For any thing I can learn,' wrote Wodrow:

... there is not one who ever was reckoned Presbyterian who is with him [i.e. James]; yea, even Messrs Hepburn and McMillan pretend they will act in separate bodies against this rebellion, and are pretty well armed and do much service, if their counsels and meetings were steadfast and fixed; but one day they are one way and the next another.[77]

The dismissiveness of this judgement is partly justified, since the Hebronites and MacMillanites refused, of course, to defend the 'sinful' Union as such, but nevertheless mustered outside Dumfries – where they had once burned the Articles of Union – in order to defend the burgh should it come under attack.[78]

By the time that Mar and his royal master set sail from Montrose for France on 4 February 1716, the Union had clearly survived its first major crisis. In the aftermath the principal features of the British state in Scotland had been established in the forms they would retain until the end of our period. The key feature was a political void. The problem was that 'politics', even in the restricted sense characteristic of the pre-Union Parliament, had virtually ceased to exist, even at the official level. The reduction of Scottish politics to manoeuvring between elites, wrongly identified by Paul Riley as characteristic of the period between 1688 and 1707, was in fact only now realised for the first time. As Daniel Szechi notes:

The net effect of government control of Scotland resting on the support of a minority (albeit a growing one) was that for the next half century Scotland became a client state administered on semi-colonial lines by a select inner group within the traditional ruling class.[79]

Shortly after the rising one of the 'inner group', Duncan Forbes of Culloden, wrote to Robert Walpole, then in the role of Paymaster General, drawing attention to the issues which had allowed the attempted counter-revolution to gain momentum and complaining that although 'it is undoubtedly his Majesty's interest to cherish England, as being the most valuable part of his dominions, it is by no means prudent to disoblige Scotland by open injuries, which may create general dissatisfaction, not to be ended but with the ruin of that part of the United Kingdom.'[80] The disobligements largely faded away after 1716; indeed, the London government took little active interest in Scotland, as long as it remained quiet. Lockhart gave an interesting assessment to George Keith, tenth Earl Marischal, in 1719:

> Though the King [i.e. James] does not want some friends in the western shires, yet the gross of the people, both gentry and commons, are either presbyterians favourably disposed towards the present Government, or pretty indifferent as to all Governments whatsoever. But as far as the greatest part of both have an hearty aversion to the Union, if once they were thoroughly convinced that the King's prosperity would terminate in the dissolution thereof, there is reason to believe a great many of the first would be converted, at least so far as to be neutral, and most of the others declare for him.

His conclusion was that the Earl Marischal should publish a manifesto on James' behalf, highlighting the iniquities of the Union ('decay of trade, and the violation of the Scots' liberties and ancient rights') and emphasise that James, if restored to the throne, would reassemble the Scottish Parliament and re-establish the state.[81] Yet beneath the stagnant political surface of Scottish life, subterranean changes were taking place which would simultaneously strip away the layers of conjunctural post-Union support for the Stuarts and force the exposed inner core of the Jacobite movement into action on its own behalf. David Hume (the philosopher, not the commissioner who attended the last Scottish Parliament) wrote, shortly after the '45 that 'we never had any Tories in Scotland, according to the proper signification of the word, and that the division of parties in this country was really into Whigs and Jacobites'.[82] For the period after 1716 there is no doubt that Hume was two-thirds right. There were certainly Jacobites in Scotland, and there were equally certainly no Tories. The English Tories were a post-revolutionary party, the party of a conservative landed capitalist class; but for conservatism to become entrenched it is first necessary for reaction to be crushed. In Scotland, as scarcely needs repeating by now, this had not yet taken place. Where Hume went wrong was in his claim that Scotland had a Whig Party, at least if the term means a radical bourgeois faction intent on transforming feudal property relations on their own behalf. It would take another 30 years for this process to complete, by which time the Union had assumed a different aspect from that which prevailed between 1708 and 1716.

Social Transformation and Agricultural Improvement (1717–1744)

Scotland was still relatively backward after 1716, in comparison not only with capitalist England, but also with the more developed feudal absolutist states of the European mainland. Yet the implications of this backwardness are not exhausted simply by invoking the mainly descriptive concept of uneven development, where all states undergo the same stages of development, in the same order, but at different times. In this perspective, which can be traced back to the beginnings of the capitalist system, development is characterised by an unevenness which is overcome as the backward gradually attain the same level as the more advanced. Shortly before he was sent to Scotland during the ratification of the Treaty of Union, our auld acquaintance Daniel Defoe wrote cautioning his English readers against holding foreigners in contempt:

> From Hence I only infer, That an *English* Man, of all Men, ought not to despise Foreigners, *as such*, and I think the Inference is just, *since what they are to-day, we were yesterday, and tomorrow they will be like us.*[1]

Marx later wrote in the 'Preface' to *Capital*: 'The country that is more developed industrially only shows, to the less developed, the image of its own future.'[2] He was not, however, suggesting that all countries would reach the future by the same route, or that arrival there would have the same implications for late developers. Crucially, the prior development of some states cannot but affect the conditions under which later developers enter the world system, not least through imperialist domination which prevented the latter from becoming independent centres of capital accumulation in their own right.[3] Scotland was affected by uneven development in both senses. In the case of the Glasgow merchants during the seventeenth century, for example, their English equivalents were both in advance of them (thus showing 'the image of their own future') and used that position to prevent their achieving parity (thus affecting the conditions under which the late-developing Scottish merchants enter the world system).

The Consequences of Combined and Uneven Development

The theory of uneven development alone, however, even in modified form, is inadequate to explain the pattern of Scottish development. We also require the concept of uneven and combined development, first developed by Leon Trotsky in an attempt to explain what he called 'the peculiarities of Russian development' in the early twentieth century, but capable of application to other historical periods. Trotsky argued that in relation to the advanced countries, the backward are condemned neither to repeat their experience, nor to find their progress towards development blocked by them, but under certain conditions could adopt their technological, organisational and intellectual achievements. 'The privilege of historic backwardness – and such a privilege exists – permits, or rather compels, the adoption of whatever is ready in advance of any specified date, skipping a whole series of intermediate stages.' Often this process of assimilation takes place within an overall socio-economic structure still characterised by archaism: 'Savages throw away their bows and arrows for rifles all at once, without travelling the road which lay between those two weapons in the past.'[4] The reference is to the Native American response to the European colonisation of their continent, and this is the most extreme example possible.

In certain circumstances it is possible through this process for a hitherto backward economy to equal or even surpass those previously in advance of it, but in the absence of such circumstances, combined and uneven development also has a downside which affects the very organisation of production itself. As Trotsky wrote: 'The [backward] nation ... not infrequently debases the achievements borrowed from outside in the process of adapting them to its own more primitive culture.'[5] In the Russian context the 'debasement of borrowed achievements' took the form of an industrialisation programme principally undertaken to strengthen the ability of the Tsarist autocracy to participate in military competition with rival (and more advanced) states, but which at the same time had the unwanted effect of producing a working class which threatened the state from within. Subsequent research supports this analysis. As Clive Trebilcock notes: 'The paradox was not resolved: from 1861 until 1917 Russian industrialisation was pursued always in part for military purposes and always within a framework rigidly defined to minimise domestic upheavals.'[6] Clearly, no direct comparisons between Russia and Scotland are possible, given the territorial disparity between the two states and the chronological difference in the relevant historical periods. Changing what needs to be changed, however, a similar process of 'debased adaptation' can be discerned in both. As in Russia, process in Scotland was not confined to the type of picturesque juxtaposition beloved of Hugh Trevor-Roper. ('Francis Hutcheson was lecturing on Locke and Shaftesbury in Glasgow while carts were unknown twelve miles away.'[7]) Take, for example, the Scottish coal industry.

We noted in Chapter 1 how feudal labour laws were used to obtain workers – technically, serfs – for the mines, and how the heritable juris-dictions were then used to discipline them. The technology and techniques with which these workers were expected to extract the coal were, with one exception (Culross), more primitive than those used in the northern English coalfields of Durham and Northumberland. After 1707, however, more advanced English methods began to penetrate at the instigation of the owners. In 1709 John Erskine, sixth Earl of Mar, asked the English hydraulic engineer George Sorocold to inspect his mines, which were in danger from flooding. Sorocold recommended replacing the existing bucket and chain drainage system with a waterwheel-driven pumping engine, but his advice was never implemented since no one in Scotland was capable of actually building and installing such a machine. This false start was soon overcome. The first use of steam technology in mine pumping took place in England during 1712; by 1719 an engine had been installed at Tranent Colliery in East Lothian followed by another four before the end of the decade. From this point on the Scottish adoption of English methods was unabated. Clerk of Penicuik, at the same time as imposing labour discipline through his baron court, was also a particularly assiduous student of English (and Belgian) techniques, preparing a dissertation on mining technology which he circulated privately among his acquaintances.[8]

Yet the increasing modernity of the technology used in the mines contrasts strongly with the conditions of the labour-force employed to use it. Workers in the extractive industries embodied a transitional form of labour that embodied both feudal and capitalist methods of surplus extraction. What is decisive here is not the extent to which the colliers and panners were strictly comparable to agricultural serfs, but the extent to which the industry in which they laboured was the source of supple-mentary income for lords or merchants rather than of capital accumulation. For the majority of the landowners, mining operations tended to fall into the former category. Baron Duckham notes that, had they been prepared to make extractive operations the central source of their income, these landowners might have been at forefront of the indus-trialisation process; but this was never their intention: 'The very size of the plant and their "new" concepts of management and work discipline represented a challenge to and a disruption of a traditional way of life never previously called into question.' Not only did mining ruin their estates, in some cases it even threatened the foundations of their houses. 'Estate mining,' Duckham notes of James Bruce of Kinnaird, 'was one thing; systematic and large-scale exploitation of coal was another.'[9] In short, by the first quarter of the eighteenth century Scotland had a coal industry where the most advanced forms of imported English technology were operated by men who were, at least formally, judicially bound to their masters as serfs.

Yet these workers were not only industrial serfs, as a consequence of the restrictions on their freedom, but also wage labourers, and even in 1716 their wages were by no means simply imposed by the mine owners. Their very scarcity gave them a bargaining power to which mere peasants could never aspire. By the time the Acts of Parliament of 1775 and 1799 abolished servitude in the mines and related industries, the coal miners had developed forms of trade union organisation by which they secured relatively high wage levels.[10] Indeed, the reason for the abolition of servitude was not to raise wages in order to attract more workers to the industry, but in part to reduce them over time by breaking the labour monopoly that the colliers had established by the changed circumstances of the late eighteenth century.[11] In other words, in what is virtually a text-book example of the base–superstructure relationship, changes in the forces of production (introduction of the new mining technology to increase output) led to long-term changes in the relations of production (gradual transition to wage labour to ensure workforce availability) leading to still longer-term changes in superstructure (the law both recognises and formalises in juridical terms the shifts in relations of production).

The coal industry eventually experienced quite spectacular expansion. Christopher Whatley has argued that, contrary to what most economic historians have assumed until recently, annual output during the 1690s was not of the order of 475,000 tons, but the considerably lower figure of 225,000 tons, and that it fell still further by the turn of the century. Rather than coal output in the eighteenth century rising to four times the 1700 level, as was previously thought, it may have risen by as much as eight or ten times – a rate nearly double that for Britain as a whole. The industry continued to use the most advanced forms of technology:

For the [eighteenth] century as a whole, Scottish collieries accounted for 17 per cent of all steam pumping engines erected in Britain (including the improved and more efficient Boulton and Watt engines) – at a time when Scotland accounted for only 13.3 per cent of British coal production.[12]

By the last quarter of the eighteenth century the class position of the men operating this machinery had, however, undergone a decisive change: they were no longer legally bound as serfs to the coal they dug, but were wage labourers, whose terms and conditions were at least partly determined by their collective organisation.

But these successive changes took time, decades stretching into nearly a century. And although the type of adaptability displayed in the coal industry was also demonstrated in other aspects of Scottish social and economic life, it was with equally limited short-term impact on the overall structure.[13]

The Pivotal Role of Agriculture

The process of socio-economic transformation was therefore slow and, as Thomas Devine has written: 'By any reckoning the impact of Union up to the early 1730s was peripheral.'[14] Even supporters of the Union agreed that the promised rewards had not manifested themselves. Take, for example, the testimony of a minor ruling-class figure, whom we have encountered before in his role as mine-owner: John Clerk of Penicuik. As one of the Court Party commissioners who negotiated the Union Treaty, Clerk cannot be suspected of deliberately underplaying the beneficial effects of union. His comments of 1730 are therefore valuable in so far as they show an honest Unionist confessing how little structural change had taken place. Clerk notes that a short-term boom had taken place immediately after 1707 as a result of three factors: the import of foreign commodities at the existing low duties before the new levels were imposed, the payment of the Equivalent and the bringing up of the value of the Scottish coinage to the value of the English – despite the significantly lower gold and silver content of the former. On a longer-term basis he also notes the increase in exports of cattle and the expansion of linen manufacture, and the potential for growth in corn and the extractive industries of lead and coal. On the debit side, however, must be set the stagnation of wool manufacture and fisheries, retrogression in tobacco exports and the continuing import of French wine and brandy, much of it smuggled. Clerk then goes on to summarise ('as if I were my self a real Grumbletonian') the political and economic reasons for the problems experienced by his nation since the Union. It is a formidable list. The political aspects will be familiar to the reader from Chapter 4 (the absence of a parliament or Privy Council, the inability of the majority of the peerage to sit in the House of Lords and the disproportionate increase in appeals to the House of Lords over relatively trivial matters after the Greenshields case of 1711), but the economic aspects are in some ways more important. They include: the high levels of tariff on imported goods, particularly those of French origin; the prevention of wool exports; the lack of hard currency (not least because money earned from exports tended to be spent on foreign luxury goods); the lack of manufacturing industry; the departure of those with money to London and the destructive rivalry between the Bank of Scotland and the Royal Bank of Scotland. Clerk concludes with two observations:

> The first is that if since the Union of the Kingdoms we have not improved our opportunities of increasing in trade and riches as we might have done, it is entirely owing to a want of industry or perhaps honesty amongst ourselves, and to the obstinate neglect of the welfare of our country. The second is that considering our mismanagements, 'tis a very great wonder that we are not in a much worse condition than we find ourselves.[15]

On the other hand, almost every commentator not blinded by adherence to Jacobitism could see that Scotland had the potential to match English capitalist development. During his tour of Britain between 1724 and 1725, Daniel Defoe returned to the Scotland he had last visited nearly 20 years before. On this occasion, however, he ventured further than the taverns of Edinburgh High Street. Pausing briefly in the south-western coastal town of Kirkcudbright, he noted the paradox that it presented:

> Here is a harbour without ships, a port without trade, a fishery without nets, a people without business; and, that which is worse than all, they do not seem to desire business, much less do they understand it. ... They have all the materials for trade, but no genius for it; all the opportunities for trade, but no inclination to it. In a word, they have no notion of being rich and populous, and thriving by it. ... It is true, the reason is part evident, namely, poverty ... People tell us that slothfulness begets poverty, and it is true; but I must add that poverty makes slothfulness, and I doubt not, were two or three brisk merchants to settle in Kircudbright, who had stocks to furnish out ships and boats for these things, they would soon find the people as industrious, and laborious as in other places; or, if they did not find them so, they would soon make them so, when they felt the benefit of it, tasted the sweet of it, had boats to fish, and merchants to buy it when brought in; when they found the money coming, they would soon work ... 'tis the poverty of the people makes them indolent.

Yet later in his journey Defoe enters Stirling where matters are quite different. Here are manufactures:

> This manufacture employs the poor very comfortably here, and is a great part of what Scotland might soon be brought to by the help of

trade and manufactures; for the people are as willing to work here as in England, if they had the same encouragement, that is, if they could be constantly employed and paid for it too, as they are there.[16]

John Cockburn, the innovative but ultimately unsuccessful agricultural improver, made virtually the same point in a letter to his English gardener during 1735:

All the people in Scotland are not so void of taste or their other senses as you incline to think them. It is not being able to get good things which makes people not have them, and if they whose business should lead them to furnish good things, were at more pains in supplying with good at all seasons and to introduce them to some Customers, it would soon take.[17]

Let Patrick Lindsay, the one-time Lord Provost of Edinburgh, stand for all those who were frustrated at the apparent stagnation of Scottish society. Writing in 1733, Lindsay attempted to catalogue the difficulties facing the Scottish bourgeoisie. Lindsay makes a general polemic against 'idleness', of the sort which was to become all too familiar in coming years, and which itself is suggestive of a hardening bourgeois world-view in relation to work. ('Persons of all Ranks misemploy too much time on expensive Pleasures, or fruitless and unprofitable Diversions.') The specific problems which he identifies begin with the by now familiar complaint against forms of military feudal tenure: 'While our old Aristocracy subsisted, all our lands were held by Ward-tenures; the Power of the Country was possessed by the great Families, and the Property by their Vassals, who served them in the War.' He argues that these forms had eroded by the time of writing – a judgement that was by no means wholly accurate even for the Lowlands – but that removing the heritable jurisdictions or wardholding would not in itself result in a transformation of agriculture:

The Case is now altered, and yet we have received small benefit by the Alteration. The Tenants possess indeed their Farms upon Leases, and the Stocking of the Ground is their own; but should they attempt any considerable Improvement, their leases would be out before they can be fully repaid of their Experience and Labour; therefore they trade on the old beaten Path, without ever forming any Project of enriching themselves by their Industry, while they justly imagine their masters are to reap more Benefit by their Labour than themselves.[18]

Lindsay echoes Belhaven, Donaldson, Fletcher and Seton at the end of the previous century in his attacks on agrarian stagnation. Why was the transformation of agriculture of such importance to economic development?

First, it was the largest sector of the economy, not merely in terms of employment but in GNP, and was to remain so until after the Revolution recounted here had been completed – at least until the last quarter of the eighteenth century. The significance of agriculture was shared across the political spectrum. William Mackintosh, a Jacobite writing in jail during the 1720s for his part in the '15 and the '19, claimed that agriculture was 'the main body source from whence all the rivulets run and water the body, the main and first spring that must give motion and life to all the parts and branches of improving the nation'.[19] Fifty years later, the arch-Whig, Adam Smith, wrote in *The Wealth of Nations*:

> The ordinary revolutions of war and government easily dry up the sources of wealth which arises from commerce only. That which arises from the more solid improvements of agriculture is much more durable, and cannot be destroyed but by those more violent convulsions occasioned by the depredations of hostile and barbarous nations continued for a century or two together, such as those that happened for some time before and after the fall of the Roman empire in the western provinces of Europe.[20]

Even those sectors of the economy which did show signs of economic growth also connected to agriculture. On the one hand, cattle, which were themselves raw material products of agriculture. On the other, the woollen and linen industries, which were still largely dependent on locally produced raw materials – wool and flax – which were the by-products of agricultural production.

Second, and more important still, it is in agriculture that the origins of capitalist development lie, at least in England and Lowland Scotland – a point first recognised by the thinkers of the Scottish Enlightenment during the later half of the eighteenth century. Chris Harman has argued that there is a dialectical interrelationship between the four elements which, according to Marx, acted to produce capitalism: 'the growth of trade ... the use of free labour in manufacturing ... separation of the peasantry from the land and ... the "primitive accumulation of capital"'.[21] But these are in fact three elements, not four, since without the expropriation of the agricultural population ('separation of the peasantry from the land') free labour will not exist in sufficient numbers for manufacturing to become the dominant sector within an economy. In fact, Marx complemented Sir James Steuart for noticing precisely this fact: 'He examines the process [of the genesis of capital] particularly in agriculture; and he rightly considers that manufacturing proper only came into being through this process of separation in agriculture.'[22] Although manufacturing industries had existed for centuries, it was only

after the driving of the rural population off the land and into the 'manufactories' that the economies of which they formed part were able to enter
self-sustaining growth. As Marx writes of the methods used: 'They
conquered the field for capitalist agriculture, incorporated the soil into
capital, and created for the urban industries the necessary supplies of free
and rightless proletarians.'[23] Without this, and the relations of
production which it implies, the mere stockpiling of wealth from either
trade, plunder or slavery (the latter two being the principle sources of the
'primitive accumulation of capital') would not lead to any transformation of the mode of production. The Spanish and Portuguese ruling
classes had access to vast wealth from these sources, but nevertheless
remained mired in decaying feudal economies which this influx of wealth
helped sustain beyond the point where they would otherwise have
collapsed.[24] Only in England had the final element become available to
complete the combination.

As Lindsay was aware, the process of separating the peasants from
their land had scarcely begun in Scotland, but neither were the peasants
themselves engaging in industrial activity in addition to farming. Two
factors tended to make tenants do so. One was excess population leading
to increasingly smaller plots which were less and less able to sustain
tenants and their families on their own. The other was the possession of
a degree of free time, which in itself implied a greater degree of efficiency.
In Scotland neither of these factors applied. Population levels, depressed
by the impact of war and disease in the 1640s, and by famine in the
1690s, were probably no greater in 1755 than they had been when the
Civil Wars began. And, although holdings were nevertheless small,
tenants did not generally have the time to supplement their income,
because of the need to perform labour service for their landowners.[25]
Indeed, where they had any connection to manufacturing it was usually
in the course of preparatory work on raw materials like wool and flax as
part of these labour services: 'Once prepared [the raw material] was later
worked up by hands obtained from the ranks of agricultural labour, or
from those who, if not strictly agricultural workers, yet relied for part at
least of their livelihood upon the products of the soil.'[26]

The problem was that no systematic qualitative change, as opposed to
quantitative expansion, had occurred in the nature of tenure or the
organisation of agricultural production.[27] The expansion of the cattle
trade is one example of this process. Hailed by Adam Smith as one of the
successes of the Union – a judgement which, although qualified, has never
been refuted – it involved an increase in the numbers bred to meet new
markets in England and, to a lesser extent, Edinburgh and its environs,
but no fundamental change to the ways in which the beasts were
reared.[28] Yet some changes, although still too scattered and unsynchro-
nised to be described as a movement, had occurred. As might be expected,
these took different forms in the Lowlands than in the Highlands.

The Lowlands

Some straws in the wind followed on hard after the '15. In 1717 Atholl tried to commute the labour services owed by his vassals into cash payments in line with an Act passed after the rising which attempted to loosen the influence of the feudal superiors over their tenantry. The tenants objected, presumably on the grounds that, without the means to increase their income, a fixed cash sum was actually a greater burden than even the existing labour services. Atholl met them at Logierait, the site of his regality, only to be presented with a memorial that, as he complained to his son, Lord James Murray, was 'full of scandalous reflections on my predecessor and more on myself'. Later he confided to Murray:

> I have been so harassed and fatigued by some of my undutiful vassals that I have not been able to write to you or anyone else. I have been near three weeks past in Dunkeld and Logierait treating with them as the Act directs for an annual duty in lieu of their services of hosting, hunting, watching and warding, and their personal attendance, But to no purpose, for besides the scandalous Memorial they have presented to me ... they have entered into a band of association to stand and support one another in this affair and all other causes whatever ...[29]

In the end, the tenants backed down, apparently after taking legal advice to the effect that they had no grounds for refusing to comply. All that Atholl was attempting to do here was change the form in which feudal rent was paid. Elsewhere, however, changes were being made to the very nature of the landlord–tenant relationship, many instigated by members of the Honourable Society of Improvers in the Knowledge of Agriculture in Scotland, founded in 1723. One of the leading figures among the experimenters was the now familiar one of Clerk, who, perhaps more than most, epitomises the shift from feudal to capitalist agriculture within the life and activity of an individual landowner. Clerk funded his initiatives from his salary as a baron of the Court of Exchequer, an advantage he had over many of his contemporaries. In 1730, at the same time as he was setting down on paper his thoughts on the economic consequences of union, he was insisting that his tenants abandon the runrig system for individually defined land holdings. 'This I found a most difficult matter,' he wrote in his *Memoirs*, 'for that a few Tenants could be induced to alter their bad methods of Agriculture.'[30]

A more successful attempt to impose Improvement occurred in Aberdeenshire, where Sir Archibald Grant, second Baronet of Monymusk, began to enclose his estates and introduce new crops such as turnips and clover in the 1720s. The majority of these innovations were, however, carried out after 1732, when he was expelled as an MP from the House of Commons for financial irregularities. He expected his tenants to carry out the enclosures and the related work of clearing the fields of stones; innovations which were met by hostility on their part, as Henry Hamilton recounts:

> ... the clearing of fields of boulders and other obstacles hitherto accepted as unalterable, the levelling of ridges and the more careful ploughing and harrowing of the soil seemed to them to be undermining ways of farming hallowed by centuries of practice. Grant had often to scold his tenants and on many occasions he used the authority in the Baron Court to punish them for obstructing his efforts and destroying his plantations and dykes.[31]

Two points are of interest here. First, unlike Atholl, Grant was seeking to alter the nature of tenancy on his estates to one in which longer-term leases were offered on a commercial basis, but was still using his superiority to enforce agreed terms – 'a combination of feudal power with capitalist appetite', as Victor Keirnan wrote of the landowning class as a whole after the Treaty of Union.[32] Second, contrary to what Hamilton suggests in this passage, the tenants were not uncomprehending children who failed to appreciate the improvements devised by Sir Archibald; for the subtenants in particular, the process ultimately pointed towards their expulsion from the estate or their retention as mere wage labourers. Like the Atholl tenants, they were prepared to resist. During the 1730s the factor wrote to Grant about his difficulties in removing some of the families:

> Our tenants are such lawyers and they tell me that I dare not poind our Baillie's decreet [i.e. conduct a forced auction of the tenant's property] unless he and the clerk were qualified, which they are not, so that you see I have need to be cautious how I proceed with them, for I remember my predecessor was threatened to be porteous rolled for an illegal step in poinding, but it was submitted and even that way he was fined.[33]

The combination of legalistic obstruction and threats of violence delayed, but did not stop, the process of enclosure and re-leasing. And the financial success that Grant obtained was a greater incentive to imitation than the propaganda of the Society of Improvers. The total rent for the Monymusk estate in 1733 was £299; it had almost doubled by 1757 and rose by a further 40 per cent to £809 over the next ten years.[34]

Why was there so little effective resistance? On the one hand, enough of the tenants were given greater security through long-term leases to divide them from the subtenants who were the main victims of enclosure. On the other, the lords advanced with extreme caution onto the terrain of commerce. It took decades for the changes introduced by Cockburn, Clerk and Grant to be properly established and, more to the point, their profitability demonstrated. Cockburn himself went out of business in 1748 after overextending his investments, which was scarcely an encouragement to the others. There was also another reason for their caution. One area where agrarian change had been introduced with great speed, Galloway, had in 1724 seen an organised and violent response from the tenants. Although this movement was ultimately defeated, it may well have persuaded other landowners to hold their hand until it was clear that similar outbreaks would not occur – Grant himself was well aware of events in Galloway and had a copy made of an order issued by the local magistrates for the dispersal of 'mobs'. The events themselves are full of interest.

In England, the process of enclosure began in earnest after the Tudor accession of 1485 and had been accomplished in three-quarters of England and Wales by 1700.[35] It was against this that the original Levellers had risen in the Midland Revolt of 1607.[36] The absence of commercial agriculture in Scotland meant, however, that whatever other depredations were suffered by the peasantry, clearance had not yet been one of them, as the time lag between 1607 and 1724 suggests. The Gallwegian economy was largely geared towards cattle rearing and in that respect was closer to the economy of the Western Highlands than to that of Aberdeenshire or Midlothian. With the expanding markets for cattle opened up by the Union, many of the landowners attempted to consolidate unprofitable smallholdings occupied by their tenants or subtenants into large estates which could then be wholly given over to pastoral farming. The first notices to quit were issued on Whitsunday 1723, the tenants duly ejected and the territory of the consolidated estate enclosed by a series of dykes. In March 1724 two tenants refused to vacate their farms and they, along with a number of those previously ejected and their families, banded together to 'level' the dykes – it seems to have been because they were engaged in the same activity as the rebels of 1607 rather than a conscious adoption of their name that the Gallwegians came to call themselves the Levellers. They later explained why they had been driven to take this action with reference to:

> ... tenants being to be driven out in order to inclose the ground, their grievous cries who did not know where to put their heads or what to do with their stocks, together with the fear of others of us who expect the same fate in a short time, did alarm us so that we thought it our duty by the laws of God and self-preservation to do whatever we could to show the world not only our own distressed state but the dangerous consequences of inclosing the lands and turning out the inhabitants ... We therefore judged that the best way of declaring our grievances was to assemble in a body together, by which means we could have an

opportunity to declare first to the gentlemen themselves our great grievances, and if they refused, to lay the same before the Commander of the Troops whom we expected to be sent here ...[37]

The action of the Galloway landlords was not only unexpected; it seemed, in terms of the moral economy of the Scottish peasantry, in many respects unnatural. And it was not only the displaced tenants who suffered through the process. Even those who retained their occupancy lost access to what had once been common lands, as they too were marked off by the man-made barriers of stone and turf. There was, however, another reason why this area should produce a militant response to these changes. As we saw in Chapter 1 and Chapter 3, Galloway was part of the south-western heartland of the later Covenanters and, in particular, was the area from which the post-Cameronian sects which succeeded them had drawn their highest levels of support. Some of these sects, like the Hebronites and the MacMillanites, who had been active in opposition to the Treaty of Union, were still functioning and provided the insurgents with an ideological and organ-isational framework within which to mobilise; their justification refers to both 'self-preservation' and 'the laws of God'.[38]

In April their first manifesto was pinned to the door of the kirk in Tongland and several other parishes, a method of public address which recalled several earlier manifestos pinned to the Cross at Sanquar and elsewhere. There followed an intensive campaign that involved not only the destruction of dykes but also the injuring or slaughter of the cattle that had replaced the tenantry. First notices would be posted, advising participants of where the next attack would take place. Then for three nights – usually between Wednesday and Friday – the landlord would be subjected to attacks on his property, although not – unless he attempted to resist – his person. At the height of the insurgency, during May and June, the Levellers mobilised over 1,000 people, many of them women and boys. According to the census drawn up by Alexander Webster 30 years later, the entire population of Galloway (Kircudbrightshire and Wigtonshire) was 37,671. These numbers therefore constitute a large activist minority which must have enjoyed at least a degree of passive support from other peasant families.[39] Local landowners and state officials displayed their unease in their private cor-respondence. James Clerk, Collector of Customs in Kirkcudbright, wrote to his brother, Clerk of Penicuik, early in May:

... the country people are now wholly loose and resolute, threatening the persons, as well as the enclosures of the gentlemen. They have already thrown down 12 or 14 gentlemen's enclosures, and are still going on. The damage they reckon £1,000 will not repay and the gentlemen are very much out of temper ... Yesterday a party of them [i.e. the Levellers], about 1,000 in number, assembled at the Steps of Tarf, 4 miles from this town ... at which place they drew up armed in front with 300 good effective flintlocks, the rest with pitchforks and clubs and all with resolution enough.[40]

Neither the local state, in the form of the Sheriff Depute, nor the landowners themselves were capable of suppressing the movement. By June, the dragoons had been sent for and, by October, a combination of military repression and legal judgements that invariably found against the evicted tenants had effectively put an end to the entire episode. Although played out in one of the most socially distinctive areas of Scotland, the Leveller rising nevertheless throws two aspects of the rural situation, post-Union, into sharp relief.

The first was the attitude of the Church. In 1648, 1666 or 1688 the majority of the plebeian Covenanters had considered themselves to be part of the Church of Scotland; only the Cameronians after 1680 had set themselves up as an alternative to it. The Cameronians and the sects which emerged from their disintegration were never more than a few hundreds at most, though this was often disguised by the fact that, in moments of actual or potential social crisis, such as 1688 or 1706, much larger numbers of mainstream Presbyterians were described in this way by concerned government officials. Yet the rabblings of 1688–89 could not have been carried out without the participation of people who had either remained with the Church of Scotland throughout the Restoration period, or who had rejoined it after the Revolution. In the situation of 1724, where the only voices urging a more militant road came from the sectaries, it was always debatable whether a majority of activists would continue to follow their advice rather than that of the ministers of the Kirk By Law Established. In fact, although it professed sympathy with the Levellers, the kirk did all it could to discourage their activities. On the one hand, on 6 May the Presbytery of Kirkcudbright noted 'the grievous and extensive enclosures that hath been made in the bounds to the straightening of several families'; but on the other hand, 'the Presbytery do unanimously judge it their duty to warn and admonish these gentlemen [i.e. the Levellers] to desist from their offensive and grievous practice in prejudicing the interest of the people'.[41] This was also the position taken by the General Assembly on 27 May. The last comment may strike a familiar note to anyone who has ever been involved in trade union activity that goes beyond the wishes of the officials. As John Leopold has pointed out, the ministerial relationship to the congregation is analogous to that of contemporary trade union officials to their membership. The officials generally try to hold their members in check, but occasionally they have to approve some action, so that the latter feel it is still worth belonging to the union (and the employers know that the officials are still worth negotiating with):

Thus Rev. Falconer of Kelton could be both the prime target of Laird Murdoch's attacks on the ministry and the man who persuaded the Levellers not to level the dykes of Captain Robert Johnstone at Gallows Slot as it was a march dyke and not an enclosing one.[42]

It would be wrong, however, to imagine that the ministers were a reformist layer holding back a revolutionary peasantry.

For the second aspect of Scottish society illuminated by the revolt is the changed attitude of the tenants themselves. In one of their explanatory manifestos, *An Account of the Reasons of Some People in Galloway, Their Meetings Anent Public Grievances Through Enclosures*, the authors stress their loyalty to the Hanoverian regime, as displayed during the '15, and indeed write of the enclosing lairds that their actions are:

> ... like the accomplishment of the Jacobites at the late rebellion, that they would make Galloway a hunting field, because of our public appearance for his Majesty King George at Dumfries, and our opposition against them at that time in their wretched designs.[43]

The same issue arises in an important letter from the Levellers to Major Du Cary, the commander of the dragoons sent to repress them. Here the anonymous author claims that depopulation attendant on the enclosures threatened the security of the realm in two ways. On the one hand, 'his Majesty's troops, who ought to be recruited out of the best and most loyal subjects, can expect none of this country'; on the other, 'that the turning of a country desolate will be no small encouragement to foreign enemies landing if there should happen a rebellion to bring in to Britain'. The letter explains that the Levellers' grievances were economic and directed at the gentlemen who had refused to attend to their complaints. Continuing the theme of loyalty, the author argues that the Levellers had upheld the law against breaches by the landowners, who had been illegally importing Irish cattle: 'we did, in obedience to the law, legally seize and slaughter them to deter the gentlemen from the practice of importing or buying Irish cattle, to the great loss of this poor country as well as the breeders in England'. Nevertheless, a solution was possible:

> ... if the gentlemen should enclose the grounds in such parcels that each may be sufficient for a good tenant and that the Heritors lay as much rent on each of these enclosures as will give him double the interest of the money laid out on the enclosure.[44]

This displays a high degree of tactical intelligence: stressing loyalty, legality and offering a solution to their grievance against the implied Jacobitism, illegality and unreasonableness of the landowners. No doubt the loyalism and legalism are heightened for the consumption of Major

Du Cary, but there is no reason to suppose that they were completely invented. Christopher Smout has argued that this was the first rural movement where the issue was not 'political, personal or religious' but 'determined by an economic grievance with the combatants clearly split along class lines'.[45] Smout is wrong to suggest that economic issues had not previously contributed to peasant insurgencies, but right to point to the greater significance which they now acquired. It might be more accurate to say that, for the first time since the Whiggamore Raid in 1648, it was possible for Scottish peasants to enter into an economic conflict with their landlords which, although violent, did not involve an attempt to overthrow the state. In other words the Levellers were seeking change – or rather, seeking stability against the forces of change – within the existing system.

Such a defence of customary relationships was different in degree, but not in kind, from those enacted elsewhere in Scotland. If the landlords in Galloway had not been more concerned with extending the area devoted to a particular profitable activity – which only required expelling their tenants – than in improving cultivation, which required that at least some of their tenants be convinced of the necessity to adopt new tenurial relationships and farming methods, then it is possible that the response to commercialisation would have been nearer to that experienced in Aberdeenshire or East Lothian. As it was, even in Galloway some of the larger tenants, whom Leopold calls 'potential cadres' for the movement, were pulled into the cattle-raising business and thus aligned themselves with the lairds rather than the lesser peasants.

The Highlands

The Highlands remained largely unaffected even by the limited changes that occurred in the Lowlands. Attempts to transform the area – with the important exception of the Argyll domains in the west – were either directed at the culture of the peasants or were military operations designed to subdue lawlessness; neither directly confronted the system of class power embodied in rural social relationships.

The Society in Scotland for Propagating Christian Knowledge (SSPCK), successor to the Society for the Reformation of Manners of 1696, was formed in Edinburgh during 1709 with the aim of educating the Gaelic-speaking inhabitants of the Highlands in the English language and Presbyterianism. This was the first conscious attempt to roll back the frontiers of the Gaidhealtachd among the majority of the population and, since the SSPCK provided the only schools in many parts of the region, it was of considerable significance. To begin with, although Gaelic books were forbidden, students were permitted to speak their native language until they learned sufficient English for the lessons to be conducted on that basis. From 1716, however, even this concession was withdrawn. 'From that date,' writes Charles Withers, 'the Gaelic language was denied an effective place in the education of a population whose only language it was.'[46] It is probably no accident that the year in which this policy was introduced was the year that saw the first significant Jacobite rising suppressed. A statement issued by the SSPCK on 7 June announced:

> Nothing can be more effectual for reducing these counties to order, and making them useful to the Commonwealth than teaching them their duty to God, their King and Country and rooting out their Irish language, and this has been the case of the Society so far as they could, for all the Scholars are taught in English.[47]

Gaelic was held to be a contributory factor to the supposed degradation of those on the Highland side of this line. An anonymous 'Highland gentleman', who had clearly assimilated Lowland attitudes towards his 'people', wrote in 1736:

> Our poor People are from the Cradles trained up in Barbarity and Ignorance. Their very language is an everlasting Bar against all Instruction, but the barbarous Customs and Fashions they have from their Forefathers, of which they are most tenacious, and having no other languages, they are confined to their own miserable Homes.[48]

Some indication of the success enjoyed by the SSPCK in combating these 'barbarous Customs and Fashions' can be gathered from the praise heaped on that organisation by Patrick Lindsay in 1737 for their success in overcoming the irreligiousity of the benighted natives:

> In the remote and thinly inhabited Highlands and Islands, the Society for The Propagation of Christian Knowledge have already done great Good, in reclaiming the poorer sort from Pagan Darkness, and the more dangerous superstitious Rules and ecclesiastical and foreign Bondage of the Church of Rome.

However, Lindsay also makes clear that, as long as this missionary work remained at a purely religious level, its impact would be limited, but:

> ... if the Managers of that Fund would, in Concert with the Gentlemen of those Countries, introduce some Kind of Work amongst them, and teach the People to labour, they would soon become practical Christians as well as professed Protestants, when taught how to provide Things honest, and to labour with their own Hands, without purloining or being a burden to any.

In a terrifying passage, Lindsay identifies what type of instruction is desirable for such as these:

> No Writing or Ciphering ought to be taught there; we are already overstocked with this Kind, while we want Hands for our hard and necessary Labour, and carrying on Manufacture, upon which chiefly the Wealth and Power of every Nation Depends.[49]

Yet nothing was done at the level of the state to transform the Highland peasants into proletarians. As we saw in Chapter 4, the '15 ended inconclusively, with the Jacobites being defeated more by inadequate leadership than by the military power ranged against it. An indication of how the Highlands were already being turned into a scapegoat for Jacobitism can be found in the way that the legislation passed in the aftermath of the rising was aimed almost exclusively at this region rather than at social relations in Scotland as a whole. Two moves stand out, both superficial in their conception; both ultimately to backfire on the state which introduced them.

The first was a piece of legislation passed in 1716 called the Disarming Act that forbad clan warriors to carry their weapons. This was later amplified by a further enactment of 1724 that forbad even their possession. As might have been expected, the only clans to obey either law to any extent were the Unionist clans already 'well affected' towards the government. Hostile clans simply ignored them, and the state had insufficient authority in the Highlands to compel them to do otherwise. George Lockhart of Carnwarth wrote to the Old Pretender shortly after the Disarming Act came into force:

> No doubt the Government will be at pains to magnify and spread abroad their success in disarming the Highlands, but depend upon it, it is all a jest. For few or no guns and swords are or will be delivered, and only guns as are of no value, so that a small recruit of good arms will put them in a better state than before.[50]

The consequence was that, at the time of the next, and last, rising in 1745 those who might have acted in defence of the Hanoverian state found it more difficult to do so, while the disaffected had at least enough arms to begin their campaign.

The second was no more successful. From the mid-1720s General George Wade was sent to the Highlands to extend the territorial reach of the state apparatus by constructing a network of roads across the Highlands, connecting the military outposts which had been constructed intermittently since the Revolution at Fort William, Fort George and elsewhere. The intention was to provide the means for troops to move more easily into the heart of what was still considered enemy territory.

Wade earned the gratitude of civilians who now had alternatives to the generally impassable Scottish roads, but without adequate numbers of troops, which the government were unwilling to provide, the use of this network for counter-insurgency was strictly limited. Indeed, the first serious use of the roads for military purposes was not by government forces at all, but by the Jacobites on their march south during the '45. Wade himself highlighted the problem in the second of two reports to the King, where he states that 'in my humble opinion, the greatest Inconveniency that attended the frequent use of Arms in the Highlands was their being ready and proper Instruments of the Pretender or any foreign Power to give Disturbances to the Government'. The question of the standing army was paramount:

> And I hope Your Majesty will pardon my Presumption, if I here Insert a saying of the Jacobites; abroad, as I have been assured from Gentlemen well affected to Your Majesty's Government ... They always owned that their greatest Hopes were from the Highlands of Scotland, and when it was said that these hopes were in vain, since His Majesty had an Army of 12,000 Regular Forces at Command (The Establishment at that time for Great Britain) their usual Answer was, We have also a Standing Army of 12,000 Highlanders, as Resolute, as well Armed and as much under Command, as the Regular Forces you so much depend on.[51]

Captain Burt, then serving with Wade, expressed concern at the power of the chiefs, not so much to challenge the state, as to dominate their own tenants. He recounts the following story from his travels during 1726:

> I happened to be at the house of a certain chief, when the Chieftain of a Tribe belonging to another Clan came to make a Visit. After talking about some indifferent Matters, I told him that I thought some of his People had not behaved towards me, in a particular Affair, with the Civility I might have expected from the Clan. He started; and immediately, with an Air of Fierceness, clapped his Hand on his broadsword and told me, if I requested it, he would send me two or three of their heads.

Burt first attempted to take this offer as a joke, but was told by his host that '"*he was a man of his word*"; and the chief who sat by made no manner of Objection to what he said'. It is possible that this was a performance for the benefit of an English visitor; one chief anxious to demonstrate his authority in front of a fellow lord, the other unwilling to suggest that these powers were not still enjoyed by all of their class. Burt reflected after this display of lordly authority: 'The heritable Power of *Pit and Gallows*, as they call it, which is still exercised within their more proper Districts, is, I think, too much for any particular Subject to be entrusted withal.'[52]

A detailed analysis of Highland conditions, bringing together both elements of the critique, was carried out between the '15 and the '45 by an anonymous writer who was most likely Duncan Forbes of Culloden, Lord President of the Court of Session and also business manager to John Campbell, second Duke of Argyll. After carefully surveying the fighting strength of the clans (which he calculates to be 21,650 in total), distinguishing between whether the men could be raised under clan or feudal jurisdictions, the memorialist concludes that only a minority of 4,900 – mainly MacDonalds – are still capable of actual violence: 'These families are Now the only people whose Chieftainries and Capabilities of Giving Disturbance Still Subsists, and are not in the least touched or Diminished, by all the Acts and Laws as Yet Made.' The writer is over-optimistic as to the extent to which the legislation passed after the '15 had already liberated the mass of the Highland population from their clannic and feudal obligations. Consequently he concludes that if another rising were to take place the majority of clans would sit it out and, seeing this, even those which would previously have participated would refuse to become involved. As an additional precaution, however, the government should establish villages at various points throughout the Highlands where the population could be employed in woollen manufacturing (this proposal makes the author almost certain to be Forbes, the subject being one of his obsessions) or fishing, thus inculcating the habits of labour discipline and self-reliance in the erstwhile clansmen:

And if these poor Miserable people (who would willingly take any Employment in their own country) were once fitted and used to earn their bread by their Labour, it would utterly eradicate all beggary and Starving Dependence upon any person whatsoever. So that it would give a final Blow and dead Stroke to all dependence and would Make the poorest, and most despicable part of the Kingdom, Amongst the Richest.

There would be another beneficial effect: 'Beside that, it would Convert that torrent of Lawless power, which lay always as thorns in our Sides, to disturb our peace at their pleasure To a Society of very Useful and Necessary Members of the Commonwealth.'[53] The reader may feel that the urgency with which these recommendations are made undermines the supposedly small-scale nature of the problem identified earlier. In any event, the memorial, along with that of General Wade, was ignored. As long as the compromise of 1707 continued undisturbed, the British state had no interest in changing the nature of social relations in the Highlands or Scotland as a whole. As in so many other aspects of Scottish life, where such changes were initiated, it was from within civil society that they came.

The first indication of what might be forthcoming occurred in 1726, less than two years after the rising in Galloway, when James Erskine, brother of 'Bobbing Jock' Mar of the '15, attempted to evict tenants from the family estate at Glenui. These tenants were, of course, among those who risked their lives for his wretched sibling ten years before. 'The Directions firmly given as to the ejection are so particular that we need only refer to them,' he wrote to his clearly unenthusiastic factor, 'and we desire you to act accordingly to them and eject those people after their harvest is over.' Erskine gives two reasons for seeking the eviction. First:

> ... that the possession of the land be no longer usurped and, the possession being restored, that the due management of the Woods may meet with no destruction, and that the Land may be ordered so as is proper for carrying on the Improvement and the sale of the Timber.

Second, 'that people may see that they are not to be suffered in their illegal Insolence, nor dream that by such doings they can continue their usurpations'.[54] Erskine was a Hanoverian, but his object here was simply to remove the existing tenants in order to make the property more attractive on the marketplace; he was not interested in restoring the family fortunes through the slow work of Improvement, but from raising cash from a quick sale. Yet his use of the insecurity of tenure typical of the Highland peasantry was an indication of what was to follow.

As we saw in Chapter 1, the first serious attempt before 1688 to alter tenurial relationships between landlord, tacksman, tenant and subtenant took place in the lands of the House of Argyll. The expansion of the Argyll empire was a matter of continuing concern for the Jacobite gentry of the western Highlands. In 1718 Colin Campbell of Glendarule wrote to Mar in exile of his concern that 'Argyll is resolved to increase his land estate and to make all the purchases he can in the Highlands,' by buying up the lands of 'Highland gentlemen' who were currently indebted before they had a chance to improve their financial position: 'To accomplish his designs, Argyll has money and credit that may answer, for, small sums go a great way in that country.' But money gave Argyll political power, 'for its plain his family is the natural leader and head of the Whigs in Scotland, so that the Whigs will never despair so long as their leader and head subsists in his greatness'.[55] What is more significant in this context, however, is the extent to which tenurial changes were made in the new territories. Forbes of Culloden, perhaps seeing the opportunity to put into effect locally the changes which the government refused to contemplate on a national basis, was deeply involved in the process in his capacity as Argyll's business manager. Like events in Glenui, however, these changes were not initially conscious attempts to impose the agrarian capitalist structure of landlord, tenant farmer and landless labourer. In this case they emerged as a by-product of the clash between Argyll as a feudal superior and Clan Cameron as inhabitants of his superiority.

The tacksman system was central to the effective running of class society in the Highlands. As Eric Cregeen writes:

> It had been designed not only for the collection of revenue but for the reduction of hostile districts to order, for the settling of loyal colonists, for the administration of justice and policing of wide areas, and for political and strategic purposes that went beyond the simple collection of rent.[56]

Since the tacksmen required military and labour services from their subtenants, they may have been more restrained about evicting them than might have been the case had a purely commercial relationship existed – this is the 'rational core' of the argument which holds that clan relationships were less exploitative than those of capitalism. Yet from 1715 onwards the system in the western Highlands had come under increasing strain. Argyll, in search of greater income, had raised the rent of his tacksmen, increases which were then passed on to the subtenants. In Morven the tacksman was Ewan Cameron of Locheil who had been deeply involved in the '89 rising and was no friend of the Argyll interest. On Locheil's death in 1732 a group of subtenants petitioned Argyll that they be allowed to pay rent directly to him in return for leases giving them security of tenure. Instead a compromise was implemented whereby no tacksman was appointed, but a Campbell (Donald Younger of Airds) was made factor with authority to let out tenancies on an annual basis, but without leases. Meanwhile, Campbell colonists were settled in areas that had traditionally been the territory of the Camerons.

The situation was unsatisfactory to almost everyone. The Camerons, outraged that one of their number had not been given the tacksman position after the death of Locheil, now found themselves under pressure from Campbell intruders whom they attacked and whose animals they destroyed in an attempt to stop the colonisation process. For the existing tenants, however, the new arrangement was even worse than the old, since they did not have the security it provided and, consequently, neither could they attempt the improvements that might have increased their income. As Cregeen notes:

> From the standpoint of a modern man like Duncan Forbes it must have appeared beyond doubt that the time had come to sweep away all the confusion and inconsistencies of the existing system and to produce a purely commercial landlord–tenant relationship which, would open wider opportunities of productivity and trade.[57]

Forbes had a principled objection to the continuation of feudal relationships in the Highlands; his master was presumably more swayed by the possibility of increased productivity and increased revenue: the two positions are not necessarily incompatible in any case.

Whatever the precise motivation, in 1737 Forbes himself was instructed to go to the estates concerned and negotiate leasing out the tenancies. The resulting agreements were usually for 19 years, the tenants were freed from all forms of military or labour service (except 'repairing harbours and mending highways') but forbidden to sub-let, at least on a formal basis. On the other hand, in anticipation of increased revenues, rents were increased by 40 per cent across most of the area and by 60 per cent in Mull and Tiree:

> The assumption on which the new system was based was that the land should produce a revenue for the landlord like any other capital asset and that it should therefore be allocated, not as a token of kinship, as a reward for allegiance or as a means of maintaining a following, but in response to the operation of the market.[58]

As Cregeen has stressed, this was the unlooked-for outcome of a struggle between two different forms of feudal organisation; if Forbes had not been there to offer a solution then the outcome might have been different. In the event, the anticipated effects were longer in coming than expected. Before the tenants could make the necessary changes to their farming practices many of them were hit by catastrophic weather conditions which meant that, instead of the revenues growing, many were unable to pay their rents, much to the discomfiture of the Duke. Equally, because the tenancies were leased out without concern for kinship, the military feudal power of both Clan Campbell and the House of Argyll was reduced. Nevertheless, the first serious breach in pre-capitalist economic organisation and the accompanying bonds of social solidarity had been made by one of the great lords. It was not to be the last.

The End of the British Revolution (1745–1746)

The difference between the period 1692–1707 and the period 1707–45 – particularly the years after 1716 – can be summarised in this way. In the former, although the obstacles to economic development were recognised by a handful of thinkers, no social force existed which could force the Scottish Parliament to implement the changes necessary, or put such legislation as it did implement into practical effect. In the latter, that social force was in the process of formation, but the central institution of the Scottish state no longer existed to be influenced one way or the other, while the British Parliament was unwilling, in the absence of a major crisis, to disturb the status quo. A major crisis was, however, now about to unfold.

When Charles Edward Louis John Casimir Silvester Xavier Maria Stuart anchored *Le Du Teillay* off the coast of Barra in the Hebrides on 23 July 1745, he also set in train the final stage of the Scottish and British Revolutions. It was a stage that many on both sides of the political divide assumed had already been reached at the Battle of Sheriffmuir.[1] On the one hand, George Lockhart of Carnwarth concluded his memoirs of the Union with a melancholy reflection on the fate of King James:

> And thus whilst no party is acting in his interest, no projects formed, nothing done to keep up the spirits of the people, the old race drops by degrees and a new one sprouts up, who have no particular bias to the King, as knowing little more about him than that the public newspapers bear, enter on the stage with perfect indifference, or at least coolness towards him and his cause, which consequence must daily languish and in process of time be totally forgot.[2]

On the other hand, Charles Delafaye, one of the Duke of Newcastle's under-secretaries, wrote, complacently, but at any rate more briefly, in

1733: 'Jacobitism must, in the nature of things, be rooted out by the long continuance of a government under which no man can say that he has been injured in his liberty or his property.'[3] Having cynically exaggerated the extent of the Jacobite danger for electoral purposes at the time of the Hanoverian Succession and the '15, the majority of the dominant Whig Party in England appear to have convinced themselves, not only that the threat was extinguished, but that it had always largely been of their own invention. Consequently, most contemporaries, faced with the '45, thought that the only possible explanation for anyone rising on behalf of the House of Stuart must be an irrational attachment to the principle of the Divine Right of Kings.

Henry Fielding, who conducted a notable propaganda campaign against the Jacobites during the rebellion, included an episode in *Tom Jones*, set around the time of the '45, which expresses this belief well. At one point in the novel, Tom encounters the character known as The Man of the Hill, who knows nothing of events in Britain since the Glorious Revolution. Informed by Tom of the existence of the Jacobites, he exclaims:

> 'You are not in earnest!' answered the old man: 'there can be no such party. As bad an opinion as I have of mankind, I cannot believe them infatuated to such a degree. There may be some hot-headed papists led by their priests to engage in this desperate cause, and think it a holy war; but that protestants, that are members of the Church of England, should be such apostates, such *felos de se*, I cannot believe it.'[4]

It might be protested that, as an Englishman, Fielding was unaware of the complexities of the Scottish scene, but the same argument was put by the Scottish legal theorist and agricultural improver Henry Home, Lord Kames, during the '45 itself: '[The Jacobites] can have no other Motive but Principle, when they risk their Lives and Fortunes in the service of their Idol Prince, as their prospect of success can never balance the Hazard.'[5] There is, however, no reason for us to share the astonishment of these two great, if very different, Enlightenment figures.

Two Sources of the '45

In fact, both of the elements which I identified in Chapter 4 as being necessary for the Stuart dynasty to act – external opposition to the expansion of the British state and active internal opposition to the nature of the British state – were again present by 1745.

The Resumption of Open Anglo-French Rivalry

By the early 1740s the relationship between Britain and France had changed again – or perhaps it would be more accurate to say that there was a recognition on both sides of the true relationship between the states, which was one of systemic antagonism. As Robin Blackburn has noted:

> To postulate an alternative vision [to that offered by Marx] in which the feudal lion and the capitalist tiger would have lain down together, and both agreed to stop molesting the colonial lambs, would be not merely 'counterfactual' but deeply at odds with the nature of the power-holding classes and states competing for dominance in Europe and the New World from 1640 to 1815.[6]

The fast-declining Spanish Empire had never posed a serious threat to British expansion, and the resumption in 1739 of hostilities over trade routes to the West Indies was soon relegated to the status of a side-show by the renewal of war in Europe. The ostensible issue, as in 1688 and 1702, was the succession to one of the major European states – Austria. The War of the Austrian Succession is usually dated from the invasion of Austrian territory in Silesia by Frederick the Great on 16 December 1740 against the successful candidate, the Habsburg Marie Theresa, who was supported by George II in his capacity as Elector of Hanover. England and then Britain had in any case been intermittently allied with Austria against French expansion since 1688, and, since the other main contender for the Austrian throne was Charles Albert, Elector of the French satellite state of Bavaria, a renewed clash between Britain and France was only a matter of time. Over the next three years France and Britain gradually became ever more directly involved in the resulting conflict on the sides of their respective allies. At first this was in the capacity of auxiliaries, although this designation had become meaningless by the Battle of Dettingen on 27 June 1743, when George personally led a largely British 'auxiliary' force to victory over the French. Accordingly, by the beginning of 1744, the French were drawing up plans for an invasion of Britain. A fleet was assembled at Dunkirk with the objective of carrying a force of 15,000 men across the Channel; 12,000 to be landed along the Thames Estuary at Maldon in Essex and 3,000 in the Western Highlands. The expedition was to be commanded by the most prestigious of all French military leaders, Marshall Maurice Comte de Saxe – a sure sign that the invasion was being treated seriously – but the figurehead was the aforementioned Charles Stuart, the 24-year-old eldest son of James.

What did the French hope to gain from raising the stakes in this way? Louis XV had an interest in reviving the alliance with Britain that had prevailed between 1660 and 1688, and again between 1716 and 1741. It had become apparent to the French Court, however, that these two periods were different in character. The first had been one in which the aspirant Stuart absolutists had been at least partially reliant on France to maintain their independence from Parliament. The second had seen a purely tactical alliance against Spain and Austria, when those states had temporarily posed a more immediate threat to British international interests than France. Consequently, for Britain to become a permanent ally of France, it would have to be turned into a satellite, and this could only be done by replacing the House of Hanover with that of Stuart. This had short-term advantages in that the Stuarts had no territorial interest (unlike the Elector of Hanover) in assisting Austria. More fundamentally, however, it would also reverse the British rise to world-power status which had begun with the wars of the Spanish Succession and been consolidated at the Treaty of Utrecht in 1713. Only the death of Louis XIV had prevented the French state aiding the Jacobite attempt of 1715. As Robert Wodrow noted at the time, 'had Louis lived to have supported it ... the prize was great, the universal monarchy for him, and the ruin of our liberty and reformation'.[7] If the Stuarts were restored then land titles acquired since their expulsion would be in question, but the real threat would be to the Whig financial and mercantile interest through the cancellation of the National Debt and concessions which the French state would require by way of restoring lost colonies and trading privileges. In the end, bad weather conditions at the end of February scattered the fleet and made the Channel impassable, but the idea of an invasion supported by internal rebellion had now been seriously raised as a strategic option. Early in March France formally declared war on Britain.

For Charles, who had largely taken over from his father as the active leader of the exiled Court, it was imperative that he take action while the war continued and the French had the most pressing need to intervene directly in Britain. The very successes of the French army made it appear that peace might be secured through military victory before another attempt could be made. On 11 May 1745 the French were victorious at Fontenoy over British troops led by George II's youngest son William, Duke of Cumberland. Their forces then began a march across the Austrian Netherlands (present-day Belgium) taking one town after another before the climactic seizure of Ostend on 12 August. The significance of this for Britain was immense. The Austrian Netherlands had been partially subdued, but more importantly, the United Provinces, the only state in Europe to which Britain was allied through a comparable socio-economic structure rather than military convenience, was now threatened with conquest. As a result of this crisis the vast majority of the British Army – over 34,000 men – was on the European mainland. In Britain there were fewer than 4,000 men scattered across Scotland and fewer than 6,000 in England, most of them concentrated in London.[8]

On 5 July, while the French were making their triumphal progress across the Low Countries, Charles Edward Stuart set sail for Scotland with around a dozen companions, the majority of them Irish Jacobites. The extent to which the French Court was aware of his intentions is unknown – his father was certainly ignorant of them – but Charles expected support in Scotland. A Jacobite group known as the Association had been in existence since 1739 and had been in contact with the both the French and Stuart Courts since then. Yet the backing that they sought from France always included at least 6,000 regular troops together with sufficient money and weapons to guarantee support once a landing had been made. Charles had some money, but no weapons and not even the promise of manpower from His Most Christian Majesty. Prospects for a rising therefore depended on whether the second element needed for a serious attempt – internal support – would be forthcoming.

The Crisis of the Lesser Lords

The first news to greet Charles after landing on Eriskay in the Outer Hebrides was not encouraging. A number of chiefs whose adherence he might have expected sent word that they refused to join him, not because they had abandoned the Cause, but because without the type of support previously asked for by the Association, they considered that any rising was doomed to failure. Charles sailed for Arisaig on the mainland where for 10 days he waited, meeting the local chiefs and trying to persuade them that success was possible. What seems to have swayed a sufficient number to get the rising under way was the adherence of Donald Cameron Younger of Locheil. As I noted in Chapter 4, no one knows exactly what passed between Charles and Locheil in their discussions. Nevertheless, the decisive factors for the latter appear to have been, on the one hand, the argument that Britain was so poorly defended it would be criminal to let the opportunity slip and, on the other, the promise that, even if the attempt failed, Charles would guarantee that Locheil's current income would be maintained – a promise which, unlike many others, he seems to have kept. On 19 August Charles raised the Jacobite standard at Glenfinnan and waited. By the end of the day the Jacobite chiefs had arrived with between 1,000 and 1,500 men, enabling the rising to begin with a march across country to Edinburgh recruiting and raising 'contributions' from the burghs. He was joined by a number of Lowland lords en route. Frank McLynn estimates that, at the time of its maximum strength of 5,500, the Jacobite army contained 'fourteen peers, including two countesses ... and over three hundred knights, lairds and landowners great and small with members of their families'.[9] What motivated the lords – from both sides of the Highland line – who joined it?

David Stevenson has found the participation of the Highland chiefs in particular to be both a 'tragic miscalculation' and a result 'almost inevitable'.[10] Such a view is untenable. Miscalculation may explain the participation of individuals in a particularly inept rising like the '08, but inevitability suggests that the historic process had dramatically narrowed their options as a class – and the latter is nearer the truth. Those who had lived through the events certainly saw the impoverishment of the lesser lords as an important factor in the rebellion. John Dalrymple suggested in 1764 that the 'late disorders' were the result of allowing 'men of family' to fall into distress, resulting in their becoming 'either the meanest, or the most desperate of mankind'.[11] In a sermon delivered in Gaelic to the Hanoverian First Highland Regiment prior to their leaving to fight the Jacobites, Adam Ferguson, himself a Highlander, expounded his view of rebel motivation:

> For what purpose rebel against one [i.e. George II], whose Clemency and equitable Government they have experienced, in favour of another, about whom nothing further is known, but that he has been bred in the Schools of Tyranny and Superstition? The Madness of such a procedure is open and palpable, or looks rather like the daring attempt of desperate Men, to Advance their own Fortunes at the Expense of their Country.

But their reliance on France would prove their undoing; for should the Stuarts succeed in regaining power: 'They [the Jacobites] will feel the Consequence, that they are only made Tools to serve Purposes very different from the ends they propose to themselves.'[12] Duncan Forbes of Culloden, another Highland Whig, and one of the few figures in the state apparatus to have any understanding of the situation in Scotland, expressed similar sentiments. In a letter to Tweedale, after hearing the first news of the rising, he first expresses his disbelief: 'I consider the report to be improbable, because I am confident that Young Man cannot with reason expect to be joined by any considerable Force in the Highlands.' He then allows that the Pretender may elicit some support:

> Some loose lawless Men, of desperate Fortunes, may indeed resort to him, but I am persuaded that none of the Highland Gentlemen that have ought to lose will ... unless the undertaking is supported by an Arm'd Power from Abroad, or secured by an invasion in some other part of his Majesty's Dominions.[13]

This was astute on both counts. The majority of the hitherto loyal clan chiefs – Munro, McKay, Sutherland – refused to support the rising, some – MacLeod and MacDonald – doing so for the sound tactical reason that without a firm commitment of French help it stood no chance of success. Who then were these 'men of desperate fortune' who were prepared to risk all?

One was Donald Cameron of Locheil, who had been technically bankrupt for at least 15 years before 1745:

Personal debts were to a wide variety of creditors, to his brothers, to neighbouring lairds, to his tailor and his saddler and so on, and came to close on £2,000 Sterling, an uncomfortable encumbrance when the annual rental of his whole estate was little over one third of that amount.[14]

A tenant of the estate, who had also been employed by the family, gave evidence at the trial of John Cameron, some years after the '45, as to their financial condition at this time. According to his testimony:

Donald Cameron of Locheil was understood to be in straited circumstances, borrowing money wherever he could find it, and particularly that the Deponent lent him 6,000 merks upon a Wadset; and the Deponent believes, that this was occasioned by his Experience about his House, by building Parks, a Summer-House, and making a fine Garden, and by his great Expense, when he went from home.[15]

Another desperado was George MacKenzie, third Earl of Cromartie, who was as near to bankruptcy as Locheil but, unlike the latter, was also a feudal baron and consequently could not be sued in his own court. Faced with his debts to the state, however, not even his class position could protect him:

By the fateful year 1745 the Earl of Cromartie was almost swamped by debt. He and his managers, with some difficulty had managed to stave off the demands of the Crown since he inherited his lands in 1731. ... But, by 1745, the Crown Debt had accumulated to the huge sum of £5498.9.3 sterling. This was a five times the gross rental income of the estate: rents were about £1103 sterling per annum: Cromartie's personal estate was worth about £3770 sterling (mostly in the form of houses on the estate). He was clearly very close to bankruptcy, not in itself a new thing for his family, but in 1745 connected with more threatening circumstances. In fact, in June 1745, Cromartie's 'Petition for a stay of execution on the Crown Rents' was rejected by the Lords of the Treasury.

In short, 'Cromartie was profoundly, and, perhaps irretrievably in debt to the crown at the very moment when Jacobitism emerged in such spectacular confrontation with the Hanoverian crown in the West Highlands.'[16]

Nor did motivations vary greatly among supporters who joined up after the Jacobite army crossed the Highland line. During the '15 the north-east was the area of greatest support for the Jacobite cause, but even in these Episcopalian heartlands the response was not now encouraging, for there too numbers were well down from 30 years earlier. In one memoir of the '45 in Aberdeenshire, written anonymously, but evidently by a Presbyterian minister of staunchly Whig sympathies, the author discusses the composition of local support for Charles:

> In 1715 they were supported by most of the Nobility ... Whereas now only Lord Pitsligo was the only [sic] nobleman that joined them ... As to the landed gentry the difference is full as considerable. Though the most be from Banffshire and Buchan, yet even there they are not one fourth of what they were in the 1715 ... Only five on Deeside from the head to the foot. And though there were several gentlemen of small estates on Deeside, yet of all of them put together were not equal to the Lord of Invercauld who engaged in the former rebellion ... There were several merchants of note appeared from the towns in the 1715, but now but a few smugglers and a very few tradesmen.

Their reasons for joining seem to have been similar to those of their class who joined in the Highlands proper. John Gordon of Glenbucket, aged 72 at the time of the rising,

> ... sold the estate at Glenbucket, from whence was his designation, a good while ago, and at the breaking out of this Rebellion, had not a foot of property, and yet those creatures in Strathdawn and Glenlivet were so attached to him that they rose voluntarily with him.

He was not alone. James Moir of Stoneywood joined Charles, but this attachment was not entirely born of principle either, for 'his fortune was also greatly embarrassed, so that his going off was no great surprise'. A very different type of man appeared to join later: 'Carnusy was esteemed a wise solid man and not at all wedded to Kingcraft [i.e. absolutism].' In one respect, however, he was like Stoneywood: 'But as many debts of his never heard of formerly are appearing, this somewhat unravels the mystery.'[17]

The link between the threat of financial collapse and support for the Jacobite cause – or more precisely, this particular Jacobite rising – can never be definitively demonstrated. The authors of a study of Cromartie write: 'The fact that the Earl of Cromartie was terminally insolvent at the time of his defection to the Jacobite Prince may, of course, have no connection with his decision to follow such a course.'[18] Perhaps not, but we can surely infer a connection if the same combination of circumstances reappears time and time again among the participants. Few of the Jacobite lords were willing to admit that their motives were anything other than the highest, particularly when justifying themselves as a prelude to execution or a life in exile. One – who in public took the same line as his comrades – nevertheless did confess in private that his financial state contributed directly to his decision to join the insurrection, and these statements by William Boyd, fourth Earl of Kilmarnock, are completely unambiguous. To the chaplain who attended to him while awaiting execution he confided:

> That the true root of all was his careless and dissolute life, by which he had reduced himself to great and perplexing difficulties, that the exigency of his affairs was in particular very pressing at the time of the rebellion; and that, besides the general hope he had of mending his fortune by the success of it, he was also tempted by the prospect of retrieving his circumstances, if he followed the Pretender's standard.[19]

Speaking to Argyll in his death cell he was even more explicit:

> My Lord, for the two kings and their rights, I cared not a farthing; but I was starving, and by God, if Mohammed had set up his standard in the Highlands I had been a good Mussulman [i.e. Muslim] for bread and stuck close to the party; for I must eat.[20]

But what of the rank and file of the Jacobite army? For Kilmarnock and his ilk the choices may have been limited, but for their tenants there was no choice at all.

Victims of a Dying Feudalism

It is customary to divide the Jacobite forces into three groups: those raised under a clan levy, those liable to military service under feudal land tenure, and a residual category of 'others' (Irish mercenaries, French regular troops, Hanoverian deserters, Mancunian Roman Catholic volunteers).[21] Of these groups, the first two are by far the most significant, since they formed the bulk of the army and were never less than half its number, but two points need to be understood regarding their composition. First, by this stage the supposed difference between 'clan' and 'feudal' levies is less significant than it appears, since many of the clan territories in fact corresponded to the areas where the members held their tenure. Second, the distinction between those who went willingly and those who were forced out is irrelevant – those who 'chose' to go would have been forced even if they had not so chosen.

Even among those who did go willingly the need for economic survival took precedence over cultural deference. It is instructive in this context to contrast the response of clansmen in the western Highlands who experienced this final push into willing rebellion and the Atholl clansmen in Perthshire – on the very border of the Lowlands – who did not and consequently had to be forced out, at least in the majority of cases. Many chiefs had responded to their need for revenue by increasing the rents due from their tacksmen, who in turn passed these on to their subtenants. This pressure was compounded in the western Highlands by severe climatic conditions that produced a run of bad harvests from 1741 onwards, particularly in 1743 and 1744, and to starvation among the cattle herds. The consequent absence of stock to sell at the markets induced a precipitous decline in income among the tenants and subtenants for whom cattle-grazing was the main non-subsistence economic activity. Inevitably these peasants had difficulty paying their rent:

> Arrears of rent in 1743–4 for the whole Argyll estates in Scotland, with a gross rental of about £7,500 Sterling, were approximately £2,000, which was much more than the Duke's earlier years. By 1744–5 arrears cannot have been less than £4,000; in 1745–6 they exceeded £5,000 and were still larger in 1746–7; they declined to a little under £4,000 in 1747–8.[22]

The debt of many a Cameron therefore mirrored that of their Chief, Locheil, but so too did those of the Campbell tenants whose link to their one-time chief and feudal superior was now mainly through the cash nexus.

'Forcing out' was not confined to the Highlands. One anonymous report to the Duke of Newcastle notes, somewhat surprisedly: 'Moreover persons who had no Clans and were not of the Highlands by the power which their regalities and superiorities gave them, raised their vassals and drew them into the rebellion, e.g. the Duke of Perth and Ogilvie.'[23] The pressure applied on behalf of the latter was direct. Although the fourth Earl of Airlie was cautious enough not to enter the field himself, his son, Ogilvie, did so and his obliging father got his agents to 'beat up recruits in the country for Lord Ogilvie's regiments; being reported as ordering all tenants and servants on the Airle estates to take up arms, saying, "They maun dae [i.e. must do] or be destroyed"'.[24] In the north-east, the Jacobite Lord Lieutenant, Lord Lewis Gordon, wrote to Stoneywood late in 1745:

> No pains shall be spared to raise the men, as proposed, from the valued rent, and for that end, so soon as I finish this [letter], [I] am to make out letters to the several gentlemen, in ten or [a] dozen parishes round, to have their different quotas of men here [i.e. at Huntly] and at Keith, against Friday and Saturday next, under power of military execution, which I am resolved strictly to execute against every deficient heritor, though I have reason to believe they not will bring things to that extremity ... [25]

Not all the Jacobite lords were successful in anything but the short term. Desertion was common. The Hanoverian James, second Duke of Atholl, fled his estate during the rising, only to have it seized by his Jacobite brother William, Marquis of Tullibardine. The chief factor on the estate, Commissary Bisset, who remained loyal to the Duke, wrote of the Jacobite attempts to raise troops:

> [Tullibardine] proposed one man out of each merk land, which would have raised 1100, which was to be divided in two regiments, one for Lord Nairne, the other for Mr Mercer of Aldie, and, although the greatest force and violence was used, he got only about 500 raised for Lord Nairne, who mostly deserted.[26]

The following month Bisset was able to report to Atholl that although:

> ... my Lord Tullibardine expected, seeing the harvest was over, to raise men out of each merk land, which would have made 2200, and set up a standard, he could not get a man to join it, until after two weeks labour, with the help of the McKinnons as they passed through last week, pressed 2 or 300, whom I am positive will desert as formerly.[27]

Sometimes the penalties exacted for defying the will of the lord took the form of economic pressure rather than physical violence. In the case of Lawrence Oliphant of Gask:

> This enthusiastic Jacobite was, it seems, so extremely incensed at the resistance he received from his tenants, that he actually laid an arrestment or inhibition upon their cornfields, in order to see if their interest could not oblige them to comply with his request.[28]

Frank McLynn has argued that much of the outrage at 'forcing out' is synthetic as it also occurred on the Hanoverian side in, for example, the regiment raised by Lord Loudon.[29] This is correct, but merely emphasises the extent to which these feudal levies were still generally operative throughout Scotland, regardless of political affiliation. The point is also intended metaphorically, however, in that while the majority of British troops were not forced out in the technical sense, they were usually compelled to join the forces by economic compulsion and sometimes even by the press gang. Again, this is correct, but misses the most significant aspect of the comparison, which is that while the alternatives may have been almost equally grim for those concerned – although there is no record of even the press gang burning down the family homes of their victims – the difference between 'unfree' compulsion and the 'freedom' to starve is almost a text book example of the difference between a feudal and a capitalist labour market.

The evidence for the extent both of 'forcing out' and of attempts to evade it might seem to rule out any attempt to describe the rising as 'popular', in the sense that large numbers of the subordinate classes voluntarily joined it in order to advance their own interests. Murray Pittock has made the strongest case for the Jacobite army as a popular force.[30] Pittock makes the perfectly correct point that the size of an army in rebellion is not in itself necessarily indicative of the support which it had in the country, but then goes on to weaken the force of his point by arguing that the size of the Jacobite army has in any case been systematically underestimated by historians. The maximum number of troops – not at any particular time, but counting everyone who was ever in the ranks – was, he claims, around 14,000. If this is true – and let us grant that it is possible – it compares favourably with the number of troops raised by the Covenanting regimes between 1638 and 1651, which, Pittock argues, would have been a maximum of 25,000; and the Covenanters had the advantage of being in control of the state, not in rebellion against it. The comparison with the early Covenanters might be expected to carry a special resonance, given the way in which they are seen as the leadership of an early national movement. But if the core of the Covenanting movement between 1637 and 1648 was essentially the revolt of a regional nobility against absolutism, then the comparison has other implications altogether. For the Covenanters also raised the majority of their forces through clan and, more commonly, feudal levies in which those levied had little choice in the matter. Pittock is no doubt aware of this and therefore makes much of the fact that half of the Jacobite force were raised in the Lowlands, a fact obscured by the fact that their campaign dress was a version of the Highland costume, regardless of their place of origin. This was not a momentary aberration on the part of Charles, of course, but a move wholly consistent with the Jacobite idealisation of the Highlanders as the real representatives of Stuart Scotland. The key issue for us, however, is whether or not these Lowlanders were volunteers who had taken up arms through political conviction.

It is true that a minority of men, both bourgeois and – stretching definitions a little – proletarian, did volunteer. What of it? Were the character of Confederate war aims during the American Civil War determined by the fact that the majority of their forces were composed of farmers and farm labourers – of whom a far higher percentage were volunteers than in the Jacobite ranks?[31] The point is surely that Confederate soldiers fought on behalf of the slave-owning plantocracy, whatever individual volunteers may have thought they were fighting for.[32] Similarly, the Jacobite risings were fought on behalf of a faction of the landowner class and, at one remove, the French monarchy. Those who enlisted voluntarily may have done so for many reasons, not least a desire to be on what appeared the winning side, but they had no programme of their own nor any means of imposing it on their commanders even had one existed. In any event the emphasis placed by Pittock on volunteers is highly misleading. We have already noted that feudal relations remained in place in the Lowlands, mainly – but not exclusively – in the north-east; but even where they did not, force was applied, not directly to the tenants by their landlord, but indirectly through the landlord by the Jacobite army as an occupation force. Most of the Lowland recruits joined after the Jacobites were victoriously ensconced in Edinburgh. These were mainly fencibles or militiamen whose enthusiasm for the Cause was highly debatable. As Stuart Reid writes: 'Using the existing tax records, the Jacobite authorities demanded that land-owners should supply an able-bodied man, suitably clothed and accoutred, for every £100 [Scots] of valued rent.' Some Jacobite officers were prepared to accept money (£5 for every man), but not all; and the normal methods of 'persuasion' (burning property, injuring livestock) were employed on recalcitrant landlords. Some avoided handing over their tenants by the expedient of hiring mercenaries instead. In Banff, for example, a third of the local Jacobite forces were men employed to go in place of tenants.[33] Whatever else the '45 may have been, it was not a popular rising.

This lack of popular support tends to cast doubt on attempts to portray the '45 as the expression of a nationalist movement. Nevertheless, several writers have done precisely this. Bruce Lenman writes: 'There is no doubt one of the emotional supports of the '45 was a streak of unreconstructed Scottish nationalism.'[34] Pittock writes: 'If it would be too much to claim that the '15 and the '45 were truly national risings, they nonetheless possessed a national quality.'[35] One of the first Proclamations by Charles on taking Edinburgh was certainly the dissolution of the Union:

> With respect to the pretended Union of the two Nations, the king [i.e. 'James VIII and III'] cannot possibly ratify it; since he has had repeated Remonstrances against it from each Kingdom; and since it is incontestable, that the Principle Point then in view was the exclusion of the Royal Family from their undoubted Right to the Crown, for which Purpose the Grossest Corruptions were openly used to bring it about.[36]

As both Lenman and Pittock note, the dissolution of the union was scarcely avoidable for Charles if he was to continue to enjoy the support of the lords, such as James Hepburn of Keith, who had advanced up the steps at Holyrood Palace in front of him with sword drawn, symbolising the precedence which Scottish sovereignty took for them over the Stuart claims on Britain as a whole.[37]

Were these lords exhibiting 'a narrow kind of Scottish nationalism', as Eveline Cruikshanks believes?[38] Leaving aside the pejorative tone of this remark (was the Duke of Cumberland later to exhibit 'a narrow kind of British nationalism'?), such a position confuses the loyalty to the Scottish crown displayed by Hepburn – what Susan Reynolds calls regnal solidarity – with a modern form of nationalist consciousness which would have been quite alien to him and his fellow-nobles.[39] In so far as the latter had begun to develop in Scotland, it was precisely against the kind of feudal particularism that they represented. The Jacobite lords correctly regarded the Union as a symbol of the socio-economic forces undermining them, and gambled on counter-revolution to preserve their territorial privileges. The irony is that, had they succeeded, the restoration of the Stuart dynasty across the British Isles, subject to French hegemony, would have rendered the formal abandonment of the Union completely irrelevant, since power within Britain would still have lain in London, only now reinforced by the very French state which had once acted as a counter-weight to England in Scottish politics.

In the Hour of Civil War

What did Charles do with the still relatively small army he had assembled? 'The incredible fact,' writes Bruce Lenman, 'is that the army of Prince Charles conquered most of Scotland by the process of walking from Glenfinnan to Edinburgh.'[40] Sir John Cope was sent with a force of 2,000 men to intercept the Jacobites before they could break out of the Highlands. These had been assembled from the 4,000 available in Edinburgh, most of whom were 'invalids' (i.e. too old or unfit for active service) or new recruits who had not yet been in battle. Cope marched north expecting to be met by reinforcements from the Whig clans. None were forthcoming. In particular, Argyll's embrace of the market in land had already begun to undermine the Clan Campbell military machine. The Campbells were not prepared to risk death for their landlord. Cope had intended to head his opponents off at the Pass of Corrieyairack, at the mouth of the Great Glen, but decided against on the eminently sensible grounds that the Jacobites held the strategic advantage of the high ground above the Pass and could have shot his force to ribbons as they negotiated the hillsides. The much-maligned General therefore veered east for Inverness and from there south to Aberdeen where his troops were shipped back towards Edinburgh.

Consequently, the Jacobite army faced no opposition as they marched south-east to the capital along the roads so carefully constructed by General Wade 20 years before. By 4 September they had taken Perth where they were joined by, among others, Lord George Murray, the greatest military leader to support the Cause since Viscount Dundee. By 16 September the rebels had arrived at the suburbs of Edinburgh and in the early hours of the next morning a contingent of Highlanders successfully rushed the main gate. There had been a great deal of debate within the city walls as to whether or not the invasion should be physically resisted. These discussions had not led to any definite conclusions, although the Lord Provost, Archibald Stewart, had sent a letter to George II asking for his authority to raise troops. Historians have been bemused by politicians whose observance of bourgeois legality was such that it required them to seek permission from the state to organise resistance to possible counter-revolutionary violence, and some have concluded that this was merely a front for secret Jacobite sympathies. It is at least as plausible to argue that the burgesses simply realised the extent to which Lowland society had moved beyond the days when it was possible to mobilise the citizenry for a defensive struggle against absolutist restoration – a position with which the bulk of the population evidently agreed. A small group of Edinburgh Defence Volunteers had earlier been assembled – 400 men out of 40,000 inhabitants – but when the time came to march out and face the approaching Jacobites their number quickly dropped to vanishing point.

Cope arrived at Dunbar on the same day that Edinburgh fell and marched his troops to Prestonpans on the east of the city. At daybreak on 21 September they were attacked by the Jacobite army using the Highland charge for the first time since Killiecrankie, and to similar effect. Although the opposing armies were roughly the same size, there was no way that the exhausted Hanoverians, most of whom had never expected to see serious combat, could face an onslaught of this nature. Most broke and ran after ten minutes, leaving behind the broadsword-mangled corpses of their comrades, although, contrary to what was later claimed by Hanoverians, there is no evidence that the Jacobites killed prisoners or mutilated bodies after the fighting had ceased. Charles found himself with Scotland at his feet, and without a serious confrontation with the enemy. The unexpectedness of this outcome was caught at the time in a manuscript written during the occupation of Edinburgh by Patrick Crichton, a saddler, ironmonger and Presbyterian based in the Canongate. To record the events of the rising, he confided in his journal, was 'to write of wonderful things':

> A poor Italian Prince C Stewart, from Lochaber in the obscurest corner of Britain, with an ill-armed mob of Highlander and bankrupt Tweedale laird his secretary, and bagpipes surprising Edinburgh, overrunning Scotland ... penetrating into the heart of England, seizing garrisoned towns, proclaiming a King in spite of a mighty King some six million in hand, with powerful armies and fleets and many generals, and the Parliament of Great Britain now sitting to support all.[41]

How was this possible? It was not due to high levels of popular support, since the majority of the Lowlands population were, like Crichton, unremittingly hostile. Kames, who may be taken as representative of contemporary Enlightenment thought, saw the opposition between the Jacobite movement and the Hanoverian state in the starkest terms: ' ... are we to follow the Rules of *England* or *France?* Are we to be guided by the Law as at present established, or as it was three Centuries ago?' This sense of crisis allowed him to reassert the case against Divine Right in terms unheard since the eclipse of the Radical Whigs and Fletcher after 1688, writing that 'hereditary Right may be laid aside altogether without any Crime; since the Good of the Society is an Object of much greater Importance than the Right of any particular Family can be'.[42]

More important, because they were assured of an audience among the poorer and middling sort, were the views of the Presbyterian ministers. The kirk had long since turned away from supporting agrarian resistance to enclosure, as the Galloway Levellers had discovered to their cost, but counter-revolution was another matter altogether. A Jacobite victory would not only lose them their individual posts – in the same way that the Williamite victory of 1689 had lost those of the Episcopalians – but would in all likelihood spell the end for the Kirk By Law Established as an institution. Ferguson, an even greater Enlightenment figure than Kames, was a minister by profession and, in a speech to Hanoverian Highland troops, from which we have already quoted, gave reasons both political and religious for opposing the rising:

> But even let us suppose the French only meant to seat this Pretender on the Throne of Britain, and leave him afterwards the free Management of the Kingdom. What can we expect in our civil and religious Concerns from a Popish King, but the Subversion of our Liberty, and the entire Corruption of our Religion?

Under the present regime, he argued: 'your Persons and Liberty is [sic] secured, your Religion is established pure and undefiled, according to the Word of God. What Change for the better this Rebellion would bring, is not easily conceived.'[43] The last point was the most convincing, since it did not require listeners to believe that the Hanoverian world was the best possible, simply that a Jacobite one would be worse. Similar arguments, no doubt less eloquently expressed, were being put in parishes across the Lowlands and even in those areas of the Highlands where the SSPCK had established itself. In many places they continued to be put even under Jacobite occupation. The Jacobites themselves certainly saw the ministers as one of the main sources of opposition. 'I have one more thing to recommend to you,' wrote Gordon to Stoneywood in October,

> ... which is that I am informed by the Prince's best friends in this country, that his affairs have suffered by the vile and malicious

behaviour of the Protestant ministers, who abuse his Highness's goodness by irritating the minds of the common people by telling them a parcel of infamous lies.

Gordon goes on to recommend that Stoneywood warn the ministers in his jurisdiction to stop attacking Charles and his followers or be 'punished as the law directs'.[44]

In addition to Politics and Religion, there was, of course, Economics, consideration of which involved a somewhat less elevated, if more fundamental, objection to Jacobitism than that offered by Ferguson. During October, Commissary Bisset wrote to Atholl complaining of 'our present arbitrary and military government in this country': 'No mercats [i.e. markets], no trade, all business is at a stand, no administration of Justice, no travelling of the highway, except such as are in the Jacobite Interest and who have their passes.'[45] Similar views were expressed in the towns. Days before Bisset put pen to paper, Lord Provost Cochrane of Glasgow wrote:

There is an absolute interruption of business; our manufactories at a stand for want of sales and cash to pay their servants, and an entire stop to payments; the rebels harassing the boroughs, distressing the collectors of public revenues, and endeavouring forcibly to get all they can without regard.[46]

And these words were written even before Glasgow was occupied. The same complaints were voiced by the town council in Aberdeen, in a letter to the Duke of Cumberland's Secretary, Sir Edward Falconer, towards the end of the rising: 'You know that there has been a total interruption of trade of the place ever since the commencement of this wicked Unnatural Rebellion, whereby all trading people have suffered greatly.'[47] The distressed burgesses were sufficiently outraged at these impositions to raise subscriptions for two regiments of 600 men. All in all, seven Lowland towns between Stirling and Berwick – including those which were occupied by the Jacobites – proclaimed Loyal Addresses when to do so still involved an element of risk.[48]

But hostility was not solely the preserve of those – Enlightenment intellectuals, Presbyterian ministers, Whig dignitaries – with most to lose. There were a number of occasions in which some form of resistance was mounted against the Jacobites by the citizens of the conquered towns. In some cases this took a mainly passive form. After Glasgow was occupied in December, the people whom Cochrane condescendingly refers to as 'our mob' remained unimpressed by Jacobite posturing: 'They [the Jacobites] attempted to huzza two or three times as he [Charles] went to his lodgings, but fell through it, our mob with great steadiness declining to join in.'[49] The Aberdonian magistrates were as hostile as they had been during the '15, but this time there was no popular support to act as compensation and even money was not forthcoming. The Reverend John Bisset, one of the 'vile and malicious' ministers complained of by Gordon, noted in his diary on 1 November:

> Stoneywood is also at Aberdeen recruiting; they come [with] little speed. I am ravished to hear that, when the drum beats, not a few of the boys cry 'God save King George'. I love an early seasoning against the spirit of Jacobitism.[50]

In general the school students seem to have been less susceptible to Jacobitism than their teachers:

> Although the masters of the Grammar School drop King George['s] name at the prayers, it rather aflames many of the young people, who, when Mr Howson was praying this week upon his omitting the King's name, cried out 'King George'; and one of the boys, after prayer was ended cried out: 'None pray for King George'.

Nor was this some peculiarity of Aberdeen Grammar schoolboys. These events took place on 30 October, George's birthday:

> The cries throughout all the streets, that afternoon and evening were: 'King George for ever'; 'down with the Popish Pretender'; 'back to Rome with him'. This with many men through the town firing guns and pistols; and a convention of them on the Castle Street, before the place where Stoneywood was drinking, did, in the open street, drink all the royal healths, with a discharge of such arms as they had.[51]

Confirmation of this account is given in a letter from Gordon commiserating with Stoneywood and tacitly upbraiding him for failing to use the necessary force:

> I am sorry the town people continue so backward, especially that those people who were intended for the council should show so much unsteadiness. As for those violent people, who threaten mobbing, and have insulted the guard, I wish that they had been proceeded against with a little more vigour: for, although leniency and moderation is commendable in most cases, yet, in the present conjuncture of affairs, it may only tend to fortify those zealots in their obstinacy, and make them persevere in their tumultuous practices.[52]

A more extreme change of attitude from that displayed in 1715 was apparent in Dundee and Perth. While Charles was occupying Perth, between 200 and 300 Highlanders had captured Dundee on 8

September. The town was defenceless, and the magistrates declined to offer resistance. On this occasion there was, however, no joyful proclamation of the Pretender. The Highlanders arrived on Saturday and during church service the following day Presbyterian ministers continued to argue support for the Hanoverian regime. The council swore allegiance to George on 26 September and on 30 October his birthday was celebrated with the usual fireworks and bonfires, after which the crowd chased the Jacobite-imposed governor out of town. A similar pattern is visible, in even more extreme form, in Perth. After the bulk of the rebel army had marched on to Edinburgh, the crowd similarly turned on the notorious Jacobite zealot, Lawrence Oliphant of Gask, who was acting as treasurer and deputy governor of the town:

> On the Elector's [i.e. George's] birthday, the 30th November [sic] ... the Perth folks set the bells a-ringing, set on bonfires, and did all that was in their power; all of which Gask took no notice of, as he had not force for them. Luckily, there came to town 15 of Lord Pitsligo's men that day and 2 Frenchmen; at night 12 of the guard went to patrol, when the mob fell on them and wounded and disarmed them. They then wrote a letter to Gask to deliver up the arms and ammunition to save the effusion of Christian blood. This was signed by 4 of the ringleaders. Gask upon this with 19 men went directly to the council house where the arms was, and was there till 8 next morning. About 12 the fire bell began to ring, which was the signal to gather. As they were coming down the street, Gask and his men fired on them, and killed and wounded a great many; but when they came near, they stood behind forestairs, and shot out at windows upon them above 300 shot, and killed one of the French gentlemen.

At this point 300 members of Clan MacIntosh arrived to save Gask and his supporters.[53] The rising against the Jacobites seems to have brought a response, since the Town Council minutes are silent from 11 November to 8 February, suggesting that the magistrates were prevented from meeting. What is certain is that, in response to opposition by the kirk, services were halted from mid-December.[54]

The inhabitants of Perth were not alone in showing a level of opposition to Charles extending to physical resistance.[55] The Jacobites laid siege to Stirling from 4 January 1746, to be met by opposition from the inhabitants as well as a lesser number of militia:

> The inhabitants, to the number of three hundred, joined with two hundred military forces, with eight companies of militia, extending to three hundred and twenty, all well armed from the castle; when hearing of the rebels coming to St. Ninians, and other parts about us,

were daily expecting a visit from them, were fully resolved to stand it out, and all in top spirits.

The spirit of the magistrates, on the other hand, left something to be desired, since they wanted to surrender the town and, accordingly, on the morning of 8 January the militia were ordered to hand in their weapons at the Castle. Some of the civilian defenders, however, refused to concede defeat:

> Notwithstanding whereof, the townsmen took to their arms, elected new officers in place of such as deserted and placed their guards as usual ... The General [i.e. Blackeny], observing the bravery of the inhabitants, gave orders that whosoever of the militia intended to go out to their assistance should have allowance; whereupon one Mr McKillop, one of the captains of the townsmen, came out with some of the militia about twelve o'clock at night, who all kept their parts that night.

In the end the burgh surrendered several days later, after receiving assurances that it would neither be sacked nor would taxes be raised from the inhabitants.[56]

It is frequently argued that the Scottish population below elite level were neutral with regard to 'the two kings and their rights' and as far as the Highlands were concerned this may well have been the case, as Cope discovered in his vain search for support from the supposedly Whig clan warriors. The evidence from the Lowlands, however, suggests that at least a large minority in some of the bigger burghs were prepared to physically oppose the Jacobites when they had the chance. It was not a matter of indifference to them who won. As Bob Harris and Christopher Whatley have noted of the riots and demonstrations which took place on the anniversary of George II's birthday on 30 October:

> They highlight the fact that Scotland was greatly divided during the crisis, not between a minority of active supporters of the young pretender and those who were indifferent to the fate of the Hanoverians, but between two minorities, made up of Jacobites and the supporters of George II, and a further group or series of groups, who probably made up the majority.[57]

Despite the widespread unpopularity of the Stuart cause, however, it is untrue that there were more Scots on the Hanoverian than on the Jacobite side at the battle of Culloden, contrary to what is often claimed by over-enthusiastic debunkers. Indeed, since the vast majority of the Jacobite army was Scottish and the Hanoverian army was twice its size, it is difficult to see how this could be true, unless it is being suggested that the majority of the Hanoverian army – i.e. the army of the British state – were also Scottish, which is plainly absurd. What can be said is that proportionally there were more Scots on the Hanoverian side than would have been the case had the national composition been relative to the size of their respective populations. Elcho put the total number of Hanoverian Scots at 2,400 and as two historians of the campaign have noted that 'of Cumberland's 15 regular battalions, no fewer than three regiments – 1st, 21st and 25th Foot – were Scottish, and to these must be added the companies of Lord Loudon's regiment and those of the Argyll Militia'.[58] The point would in any case only be significant if both armies had been based on volunteers, rather than conscripts.

If Jacobite success was not a result of popular support, then was it because of the qualities of the troops that they had assembled? This too is implausible. Why would an army of raw peasants, the majority of whom would never have raised a sword in anger, automatically be transformed into an efficient fighting force? Alexander Carlyle – admittedly not an unbiased witness – attended the rebel camp as a doctor after Prestonpans and saw the condition of their men. His class prejudices apart – the men are of 'low stature and dirty, with a contemptible appearance'; the officers were 'gentlemanlike'; Locheil was 'polished and gentle' – his report is of some interest:

This view I had of the rebel army confirmed me in the prepossession that nothing but the weakest and most unaccountable bad conduct on our part could possibly have given them the victory. God forbid that Britain should ever again be in danger of being overcome by such a despicable enemy, for, at best, the Highlanders were at that time but a raw militia, who were not cowards.[59]

The reasons for Jacobite success were in fact largely negative. The letter written by Forbes to Tweedale at the beginning of the Rebellion identifies two of the difficulties under which the regime laboured:

First, tho' the Government has many more friends in the Highlands than it had in 1715, yet I do not know that there is at present any Lawful Authority that can call them forth to Action ... In 1715, Lieutenancies were established in all of the Counties. If any such thing now subsists, it is more than I know. Secondly, In that unlucky year, the King's friends, tho' few in the Highlands, were armed; whereas at present they are not; tho' the loose Banditti of that Country are; and there can be no doubt that, if any enemy from abroad land, plenty of arms will be brought along.

To the lack of any central mobilising authority and the failure of the Disarming Act to force compliance on clans other than those already supportive of the government, Forbes conjoins a third, more direct complaint against the attitude of the Government:

> Want of money in the year 1715 was a great obstruction to the progress of those who Arm'd on the side of the Government; and that Difficulties got the better of by the Zeal of private Gentlemen, who out of their own Pockets advanced large Sums for the Public Service; but as due care was not taken ever to repay, far less to reward, the Gentlemen who made those advances, it is highly probable, that at present men will not be so ready to put their hands in their Pockets; and thereby occasions of doing essential Services may be lost.[60]

To this excellent summary two further reasons can be added.

First, the Jacobites had a tactical advantage in having a small mobile army of irregulars whose officers at least were ideologically committed to their cause. The very archaic militarism of the Jacobites gave them an initial advantage in a society now geared to making money rather than making war, at least at home. They did not have to be a tremendously efficient fighting force – merely the fact that they were a fighting force in an otherwise demilitarised society was enough, as the good burghers of Edinburgh had realised. As Douglas Cole and Raymond Postgate wrote of Charles: 'He was marching, in the language of Marxian economists, with a feudal army into a bourgeois society.'[61] Twenty years later Adam Smith sadly told his students of how 'In the year 1745 four or five thousand naked unarmed Highlanders took possession of the improved parts of this country without any opposition from the unwarlike inhabitants.' This was one of the regrettable consequences of the development of civil society on a commercial basis:

> 200 years ago such an attempt would have roused the spirit of the nation. Our ancestors were brave and warlike, their minds were not enervated by cultivating arts and commerce and they were ready with spirit and vigour to resist the most formidable foe.[62]

There are obvious parallels with the initial successes of the Covenanting armies 100 years earlier; but just as the victories at Berwick and Newcastle would turn to ashes at Dunbar, Preston and Worcester, so too would Prestonpans be shadowed by Culloden.

Second, the men who staffed the state apparatus suffered from overwhelming complacency. It may have been that Whig overestimation of Jacobite support up to the '19, and the knowledge that this had been artificially inflated for electoral purposes, now resulted in their disregarding any potential threat from that quarter. Having deliberately exaggerated the significance of Jacobitism after the '15 for electoral purposes, they now seemed to regard it as a relic. Fielding wrote as the Jacobite armies were poised to enter England that:

> ... so accustomed were they to treat this Rebellion as imaginary, that even when it was impossible to doubt longer of its Reality, they made it still the Subject of Contempt and Ridicule, saying it was only a company of wild Highlanders got together, whom the very Sight of a Body of Troops, However small, would infallibly disperse.[63]

This was not simply an attitudinal problem. There very few troops in Scotland; the majority were on the continent attempting to stop the French advance into the United Netherlands.[64]

The Jacobite position was therefore precarious. They had not yet been fully tested in battle and the Highland charge which won the day at Prestonpans would not be effective in all conditions – a fact which was recognised by Murray, who began conventional drilling of his troops in preparation for the coming struggle. The key issue was whether to advance into England or consolidate the position in Scotland. There was little doubt which alternative Charles would choose. 'The mind of the Prince,' recalled the Chevalier de Johnstone, 'was occupied only with England, and he seemed little flattered with the idea of possessing a kingdom to which the family of Stuart owes its origin and its loyalty.'[65] Most of the lords, including Murray, opposed the invasion and it was only carried by one vote in the Council of War on 30 October 1745. Crucial to winning even this slim majority was a promise by Charles that his counter-revolution would be joined by both a supportive rising in England and an invasion from France. Many writers have subsequently endorsed Johnstone's scepticism and concluded that all would have been well had the Jacobites remained in Scotland. Alexander Youngson has concluded that had they done so the London government might have washed their hands of the entire business and allowed Charles to retain an independent Scottish kingdom.[66] It should be clear from the argument of the preceding chapters, however, that in the context of international Franco-British rivalry, this was the one outcome that was absolutely excluded. In fact, as Charles correctly saw, the Jacobites had no choice but to invade England. Every day they remained in Edinburgh saw their funds diminish and any attempt to raise money through the systematic collection of the Malt Tax could have turned passive resentment into active hostility. The threat of desertions would increase and the chances of a Hanoverian counter-attack become more likely. But there was also a deeper logic at work. They required to strike 'at the heart' – as Cardinal Alberoni had correctly designated England – because only with French aid could Charles hope to retain power, and the only way to persuade the French that it was worth their while committing troops was to aim for London, to offer them the prize of removing the greatest rival of the French state from the international arena.

On 31 October, 5,000 foot soldiers and 500 cavalry left Edinburgh for the march south. Almost as soon as they had gone the Hanoverians retook the town with troops from the Castle with a minimum of difficulty. The Jacobite territorial base in Scotland now gone, much depended on the level of support which would be forthcoming in England. Contrary to what Charles had claimed at the Council of War, this was minimal. The strategy of beginning a rising in the Highlands had always been regarded with caution by the more intelligent Scottish Jacobites. Shortly before his death in 1727, Lockhart had written to James pointing out that 'the Highlanders breaking out singly by themselves' raised two problems with his English supporters. The first was that the majority 'have a national antipathy to Scotsmen, and are particularly jealous of their having the honour of being too active and instrumental in your restoration'. His remarks on the second and more serious problem deserve to be quoted in full:

In the next place, though over a bottle or even in their most serious consultations, they are enough sensible of their unhappy state and seem willing to enter into measures for their deliverance, yet many of them are to so intoxicated with the love of ease and plenty that they are backward to enter into action, and would willingly cast the brunt onto Scotsmen, and wait and declare and take a part, till they see how matters are like to go, and that betwixt the different views of these two sets of men, the game has been and may again be lost, and therefore it would appear absolutely necessary that the English should know that they have no staff to lean on but their own.[67]

Lockhart was right. During the preparations for an abortive French invasion in 1744 a Jacobite emissary called James Butler – actually the Pretender's equerry – was sent to England to assess the situation. Sir James Hynde Cotton, a man thought correctly by the French to be one of the most important English Jacobites, and who had promised his full co-operation in the event of an invasion, first declined to meet Butler, and then protested about January as the proposed date on the grounds that it would be too cold to conduct a campaign. No doubt Hynde Cotton was concerned lest such conditions prevented him from consuming his customary six bottles of claret a day. As Frank McLynn observes: 'A more sagacious observer than Butler could have inferred a lot about the English Jacobites from this.'[68] As indeed could some modern historians.

It is sometimes said that had Charles reached London he would have been greeted enthusiastically by a population only too glad to be rid of the unpopular Hanoverian regime and its corrupt parliament. There is little support for this contention in the reception his army received in the north of England. No matter how many toasts had previously been drunk to the King Over the Water, or how many members there were of the Cycle of the White Rose, practical support was not forthcoming. John Maclean, a Highland captain in the Jacobite army, noted in his journal that several towns, the majority in Lancashire, gave the Jacobites an apparently supportive reception. On entering Derbyshire 'a Jolly hearty man met us who wished us good Success and Said we would see him on the Morrow with five hundred [men] not one of them worse than himself'.[69] 'It was needless to add,' comments the editor of this journal, 'that he was not seen again.'[70] And this was generally the case. Only 50 Welshmen and 300 Englishmen joined south of the border. 'Manchester greeted him not by supplying firearms but by discharging fireworks.'[71] And Manchester provided the most men – 200 – of anywhere in England. Nothing could therefore demonstrate the exceptional nature of the '15 better than the lack of support for the '45 in England. As Ian Gilmour puts it, in his best Tory–Marxist mode: 'Whatever their words, the actions of the English Jacobites were in favour of the [Hanoverian] regime.'[72]

A similarly materialist analysis might be applied to another academic growth industry of recent years – the question of how far the Tory party, or at any rate, individual Tories, were committed to the Jacobite cause. There is no sure way of knowing this, since there was no formal organisation with membership lists that would reveal such information. Assessments are therefore little more than guesswork: 'Possibly a majority of the tory M.P.'s were loyal [i.e. to the Hanoverian regime]; but clearly a large number were not, and that majority was not, as has sometimes been suggested, an overwhelming one.'[73] This, it has to be said, is not a great deal of help. There is, however, one relatively foolproof way of assessing the strength of their convictions, and that is, as with the English Jacobites per se, by a survey of what they were prepared to do. And, as Gilmour notes: 'No prominent Tory did anything at all.'[74]

Murray Pittock has argued that the strength of Jacobite support cannot be judged simply by the number of people prepared to take up arms on behalf of the Stuarts: 'The prevalence of Jacobite culture illuminates the extent of Jacobite support, even where such support was limited in time of crisis from moral principle, personal cowardice, or the sheer impossibility of organising effectively.'[75] Since Pittock has argued elsewhere that, in Scotland at least, there was popular support for the rising, this seems to be a case of having your cake and eating it: claim where possible that the Jacobite army was a volunteer force (as in Scotland); but where this is demonstrably not possible (as in England), argue that the issue is anyway irrelevant. In fact, as I have tried to demonstrate, voluntary support was considerably less than Pittock supposes, even in Scotland, at a time when it was not only possible to 'organise effectively', but to achieve several victories over the Hanoverian army. The loyalty to the Stuarts expressed by Hynde Cotton and his ilk is sometimes described as 'sentimental Jacobitism', but even this is to overstate the level of their commitment. For English and Welsh 'Jacobites' of the ruling class, the movement was already an occasion for indulging in nostalgia, rather than organising for action. Pittock argues that this type of argument fetishises violence as more 'real' than other forms of activity: 'It is insulting to term an Irish Republican opposed to the IRA a "sentimental nationalist",' he writes, pursuing an analogy with 'sentimental Jacobitism', but the comparison is of limited value.[76] The choice for Republicans in the north of Ireland was never restricted to support for the guerrilla war waged until 1999 by the Provisional IRA, but there were no political alternatives to civil war for supporters of a Stuart restoration. Consequently, if only insignificant numbers of those claiming to be Jacobites were prepared to take that road, then the same can be said of them that Gilmour says of the Tory Party: '... in the sole sense in which it is here relevant – readiness to use violence, the only possible way of restoring the Stuarts – it clearly was not Jacobite'.[77] Jacobite slogans were raised and its emblems displayed in a number of plebeian riots and demonstrations in England between 1715 and 1745 – many of which involved the use of violence, at least against property – yet there were none in 1745–46, at the moment when such displays could have actually transformed the political situation. This suggests that, although the relationship of the plebeians to Jacobitism was different to that of the patricians, both were equally uncommitted to its political goal – the restoration of the Stuarts.

In fact, given the unpopularity of the Hanoverian regime, its military weakness and the apparently unstoppable Jacobite advance, Colley is surely right to say that: 'If large numbers of Britons had really wanted to throw in their lot with the Jacobite cause, it is difficult to see how they could have been stopped.'[78] Contrary to what Colley sometimes implies, this scarcely indicates a positive endorsement of the Hanoverian regime, but as our anonymous 'English Gentleman' points out, the Jacobites' biggest mistake was to imagine that everyone 'who wrote or talked against this General Corruption, would join with them in rooting it out,' for instead, 'the People preferred the lesser Evil to the greater, and by preferring Fools to Knaves, united to save the Nation.'[79] This judgement is borne out by the conduct of the English opposition periodicals, which had before Prestonpans maintained relentless criticism of the Hanoverian regime and the Ministry, and now urged loyalty on their readership in the face of the crisis. On 21 October, *Old England, or The Constitutional Journal* declared: 'The Dispute now is not who shall set the sail or handle the rudder, but whether rudder, sails, and all shall sink or swim.'[80]

The Jacobites reached Derby, 130 miles from London, on the afternoon of Wednesday, 4 December. On the way they had avoided engagement with the enemy except for a successful, if largely irrelevant, siege of Carlisle. Now they were faced with the prospect of being caught between three separate forces, many of whose soldiers were veterans recalled from Flanders as an earnest that government was finally taking the situation seriously. His own Council of War forced Charles to retreat from Derby. The main arguments for turning back were put by Murray who, according to Lord Elcho, pointed out to Charles:

> That they had marched into the heart of England ready to join any party that would declare for him, that none had, and that the Counties through which the Army had passed had seemed more Enemies than friends to the Cause, that there was no French Landed in England for him, and that if there was any party in England for him it was very odd that they had never so much as Either sent him money or intelligence or the least advice what to do, but if he Could produce any letter from any person of distinction in which there was an invitation for the army to go to London or any part of England, that they were ready to go. But if nobody had either invited them or meddled the least in their affairs, it was to be supposed that there was either no party at all, or if there was they did not choose to act with them, or else they would have let them know it.[81]

According to the Chevalier de Johnstone, who also witnessed the scene, Murray continued by arguing that even if they won the battle with Cumberland, this would not suffice:

> Especially was this so as a second battle must soon be fought against a second English army on Finchley Common, before we could enter London; and that, supposing that by some miracle we should arrive at this capital without losing a man, what sort of figure would four thousand men make amidst a population of a million of souls?[82]

These arguments alone would cast doubt on the view expressed by Kames that noble participation in the rising was the result of their attachment to an 'Idol Prince'.

While Charles sulked in his tent, the Jacobites began the retreat from Derby on 6 December. Murray staged a brilliant tactical operation which brought them back to the Highlands, winning a minor encounter at Clifton in the north of England and engaging the Hanoverians in a serious but indecisive battle at Falkirk on the way. None of this mattered, for the real balance of forces now began to reveal itself. Jeremy Black has argued that: 'Had the French landed in 1745-6 they would have been able to defeat whatever irregular forces the local authorities had raised and they would have outnumbered the regular troops in and around London.'[83] This is probably correct, but conflicts within the French Court over the prospects for the rising had delayed the launch of a supportive invasion until December, at which point it had to be postponed as the result of bad weather. The French never regained the initiative and thereafter British naval superiority ensured that neither military nor financial aid crossed the Channel.

The Hanoverian army, commanded by George's youngest son, William, Duke of Cumberland, now moved deep into Scotland, deeper than any army had done since the days of Cromwell, burning as it went. One medical officer serving with Cumberland described in a series of letters home the targets of their repression: 'I stayed at Blair Castle in Atholl near a month, in which time our detachment plundered all the houses which were concerned with the rebels for five or six miles compass.' And these were not peasant huts, but the homes of the gentry. 'I believe most of the country about here deserved the same treatment,' opined this correspondent, 'for I fancy there were few that were not rebelliously inclined.'[84] These actions foreshadowed the events to follow.

Endgame

The Jacobites were exhausted, hungry and below full strength when Charles chose to confront the Hanoverians on Culloden Moor near Inverness on 16 April 1746. Could they have followed an alternative strategy of withdrawing into the mountains and waging a guerrilla war? Their military leader up to that point, George Murray, later reflected on the possibility of 'dispersal', but rejected the view that this could have brought victory by itself. In his view it could merely have gained time until 'perhaps such succours would have come from France as would have made the Highlanders to have made an offensive instead of defensive war'. Everything turned on France. Murray claims that the Scottish Jacobite officers (and the implication is that this included him) were aware of 'the consequences of losing a battle' and in particular, of what it would mean in terms of the attitude of the local population: 'They [the officers] knew well that few of the Highlanders would join heartily against them so long as they continued entire, but would do it upon a defeat.' This speaks volumes for the supposed 'popularity' of the Jacobite cause. Why did Charles ignore the advice of his officers? Apparently the Irish officers and Lowlanders 'could not endure the fatigue of a Highland campaign' and the French officers and troops, to whom this presumably also applied, had the option of surrendering; the Scots, as traitors, did not: 'But any proposition to postpone fighting was ill received, and was called discouraging the army.'[85] So the battle went ahead, on the 'ill-chosen ground'. The decision to make a stand at this point was not, however, simply because of the incompetence of his mainly Irish advisers; the blockade of France had prevented money reaching the rebels and this meant that the situation was unlikely to improve. The Hanoverian troops were supported by artillery and equipped with flintlock muskets and bayonets. And, even though they outnumbered the Jacobites by something like 9,000 to 5,000, the majority of the government troops were not even required to fight, for to compound the military imbalance still further, the site was flat boggy terrain (the Gaelic name for the moor translates into English as 'Yellow Bog') which deprived the Highland contingent of any element of surprise, but provided their opponents with unprotected targets for their mortars and cannon.[86]

We noted in Chapter 4 that during this period military equivalence among the leading powers made decisive victories difficult and internal revolts necessary. Outright victory was still theoretically possible, however, where the opponent was at so low a level of comparative development that the military techniques and technologies of the more advanced side gave it an overwhelming advantage. In practice, of course, these situations occurred most often in the colonial territories of Asia and the Americas where the native inhabitants derived a tactical advantage over the metropolitan powers through familiarity with what, to the latter, was unfamiliar and unpredictable terrain. None of these advantages was available to the Jacobites. As Jeremy Black has pointed out, although the Military Revolution is usually dated between 1560 and 1660, it was in fact largely the product of the following century.[87] No previous Jacobite rising had been faced by a British army shaped by this Revolution: the '89 was halted at Dunkeld by ideologically committed Cameronian irregulars and the '15 was checked after an indecisive draw at Sheriffmuir against equally feudal forces over which the Jacobites actually had numerical superiority. It was only during the latter stages of the '45 that the full military might of the British state was brought to bear on internal rebellion for the first time. Several non-Highland Jacobites had previously expressed their uncertainty over the usefulness of Highland troops except in very specific conditions. The Master of Sinclair, for example, recalled after the '15:

> I freely own, that no man of the party [i.e. the Jacobites] has so bad an opinion of Highlandmen as I; and that what they are capable of doing, in a plain field, against regular troops, depends on accident, or the irregularities of the troops, and that they will never be brought to attack any who have the least cover, nor will the wit of man bring them to stand cannon, which has an astonishing influence over them.[88]

Now the Jacobites no longer had a choice. Charles waited for Cumberland to attack, but the Hanoverian cannon instead subjected his army to bombardment at close range – latterly with grapeshot – for at least a quarter of an hour, at men who were neither given orders to retreat nor to advance, but were simply left presenting themselves as targets until Charles and his advisers decided what strategy to follow. When the order to charge finally came the Jacobite forces ran first straight into the rifles and bayonets of the Hanoverian troops. Few even made it as far as the enemy lines and those that did fared little better. As a soldier on the Hanoverian side recalled:

> The battle was now entirely fought between swords and bayonets. Our soldiers, by a new practice of using the latter, became much too hard for the swords; and the rebels, as they pushed forwards, fell on certain death. ... Ours at least killed ten men to their one in this kind of fighting, besides what fell by the musketry and cannon.

As the Jacobites understandably turned to flee they were pursued by dragoons and horse, 'and then followed a general carnage,' by the end of which: 'The moor was covered with blood; and our men, what with killing the enemy, dabbling their feet in the blood, and splashing it about one another, looked like so many butchers.'[89] In such circumstances it is no surprise that the outcome was decided in less than half an hour. 'No other battle that ended a civilisation was so brief,' wrote Cole and Postgate.[90] A comparison of the respective casualty lists tells its own story: 60 Hanoverian dead; over 2,000 Jacobite. Yet many of the latter were killed, not on the battlefield, but on the road from Culloden to Inverness.

With the Jacobites in full flight, the Hanoverians began a systematic sweep of the moor, clubbing, stabbing, bayoneting and shooting the wounded as they lay on the ground. Donald Maclean, a survivor on the Jacobite side, wrote in his journal:

> In this Battle the greatest Barbarities was committed that was ever heard to be done by Either Christians, turks or Pagan, I mean by our enemies who gave no quarters, killed our men that was wounded in cold blood and continued so doing for three or four Days.[91]

As Maclean indicates, the slaughter did not stop on the day of battle itself. One dragoon in Lord Ker's regiment recounted that:

> ... he himself went into the field of battle the day after the engagement in the forenoon; that on coming to the place he found that the noise he heard was several of the wounded rebels who had crawled together bemoaning one another's condition; that in a short while he saw some small parties of the King's troops with officers on their head go through the field and shoot the wounded rebels; that six or eight of the soldiers fired together at different rebels, but did not receive the word of command from their officers, though they stood by and saw the service performed; that they went through the field thus; that some of the rebels seemed pleased to be removed of their pain by death, while others begged of the soldiers to spare them, which, however, was in no ways regarded.[92]

Only one group among the rebels was spared, since 'such severity would not have been exercised against a foreign enemy, and at this time the French were treated with great humanity, as they are said to be remarkably human when conquerors'.[93] 'The enemy,' confirmed the Jacobite Sir John Macdonald, 'who treated the Highlanders with every imaginable cruelty, were extremely polite to the troops which had come from France.'[94] Of all the troops who fought at Culloden, the only ones who were allowed to surrender were the French, who were, in the eyes of the Hanoverian state, fellow civilised Europeans, and not dirty savages like the Highlanders, little better than American Indians – who were in due course treated in much the same way. Indeed, as Alan Guy has emphasised, the interplay between the colonial experience of the British army and their intervention in the Highlands was close. The fortress and road building programme of the 1720s was adopted in Jamaica during the following decade in a series of fortified barracks established along the boundaries of Maroon rebel areas. In return, the counter-insurgency tactics used against the Maroons – which included the use of free blacks against the rebels and the destruction of their villages – were adapted for use in Scotland in more intensified form: 'Methods employed included the bayoneting of rebel wounded, summary executions, the burning of settlements, the confiscation of livestock, and even the threat of mass deportations.' And, although the latter were not actually carried out in the Highlands, they were subsequently used in Canada against the French inhabitants of Acadia during 1755.[95]

The fate of those who were not summarily executed varied. Of the 3,463 listed, 88 died of wounds or illness in prison, 120 were executed (including 40 deserters from the Hanoverian army), 936 transported, 348 banished (including 126 who were allowed to go to America), 1,287 set free (including 387 French and Spanish) and 684 whose fate is unknown, although a large percentage of these must also have died of neglect in the prison hulks to which the prisoners were taken.[96] Beyond these recorded casualties, however, hundreds, perhaps thousands, of civilians suffered for a cause which was never theirs. The testimony of Lady Inches gives some indication of how savage the repression was. Unbearable though these passages are to read, they make clear the extent of the cruelties visited on the combatants:

> On Friday after the battle, April 18th she [i.e. Lady Inches] went home to her house called the Lees, within a mile or so of the field of battle. Upon the road as she went along she saw heaps of bodies stripped naked and lying above ground. When she came to the Lees she found sixteen dead bodies in the Closs [i.e. the lane leading to the house] and about the house, which as soon as possible she caused to bury. When she came into the Closs some of the soldiers came about her, calling her a rebel-bitch, and swearing, that certainly she behoved to be such,

or else so many of these damned villains would not have come to get shelter about her house. Then pulling her by her sleeve they desired her to come along with them, and they would show her a rare sight, which was two dead bodies lying in the Closs with a curtain laid over them. They took off the curtain and made her look upon the bodies, whose faces were so cut and mangled that they could not be discerned as faces. They told her that the party that had been formerly there had cut and mangled these villains, and had left them in the house in their wounds; but when they themselves came there they could not endure to hear their cries and groans, and therefore had dragged them out of the Closs and given them a fire to their hinder-end. 'For', said they, 'we roasted and smoked them to death, and have cast this curtain down from the side of one of your rooms over them, to keep us from seeing the nauseous sight'.

The treatment that this woman received also shows that the repression was conducted without regard to the property rights, class position or even political affiliation of anyone who got in the way:

The house of the Lees was all pillaged, the doors of the rooms and closets, the outer doors, the windows and all the lining being broke down to pieces. The charter-chest was broke open, and the papers scattered up and down the house; all her horses and cattle were taken away, though Inches was not in the least concerned in the affair, save only that he was a great Whig, and had a son out with the Duke of Cumberland.

Most of all, however, her testimony shows the indiscriminate nature of the violence: 'On the day after the battle ... one of Inches's tenants and his son, who lived at the gate of the Lees, stepped out at the door to see what was the fray, and was shot by the red-coats.' Nor was any greater discrimination shown in terms of gender: 'Much about the same place they came onto a house where a poor beggar woman was spinning, and shot her dead on the spot.'[97] The Hanoverian Commissary Bisset confirmed as much in a letter to Atholl written late in June: 'Whatever part the Military fall upon, they make no distinction, the innocent suffer alike with the guilty.'[98]

The destruction was not entirely random. At least in part it was consciously directed at the ideological supports of Jacobitism:

We journeyed this six miles, when we came to Port Soya [i.e. Portsoy], and in our way were presented with many non-juring meeting houses burning, which our soldiers (very deservedly) took no small pleasure in destroying, they being seminaries for training up Roman Catholics and Rebels.[99]

Nor was the onslaught restricted to the summary justice described above. The theft of cattle, oxen, horses, sheep and goats was in the medium term an even more destructive act. As one participant, and a medical officer at that, recounts:

> Whilst our army stayed here, we had near twenty thousand head of cattle brought in, such as oxen, horses, sheep and goats, taken from the rebels, (whose houses we also frequently plundered and burned) by parties set out for them, and in search of the Pretender; so that great numbers of our men grew rich by their share of the spoils, which was bought by the lump by jockeys and farmers from Yorkshire and the south of Scotland; and the money was divided amongst the men, and few common soldiers were without horses.[100]

As John Prebble writes:

> Neither fire nor sword, bayonet nor hangman's hemp, was to have so terrible an effect on the clan system as this great robbery ... The primary purpose of driving off the cattle was to break and destroy the economy of the Jacobite clans, but he [i.e. Cumberland] quickly saw a secondary value. The money received from the sale of stock to Lowland or English dealers was distributed amongst his soldiers. It kept morale high, and their rebel-hunting enthusiasm in good fettle.[101]

Lady Inches recalled of the Hanoverians that 'they were really mad; they were furious, and no check was given them in the least'.[102] What was the cause of this savagery?

The Hanoverian army did not 'lose control' – the favourite excuse for British atrocities from Culloden itself down to Bloody Sunday in 1972 and beyond. Nor will it do to blame the remnants of the Jacobite leadership for refusing to submit immediately after the battle, as if the atrocities would somehow have remained uncommitted had they not briefly reassembled at Ruthven in Baddenoch in the days immediately after the battle.[103] In fact, the ferocity of the Hanoverians was both licensed and encouraged from the top. The brutal behaviour of systematically brutalised men – schooled in both the lash and the rigours of continental service – was deliberately fostered by black propaganda concerning Jacobite ill-treatment of prisoners after Prestonpans and orders to give 'no quarter' before Culloden. These allegations had little substance. Nor did the Jacobite rank and file commit atrocities unsanctioned by their officers. Even the most bitter critics of the Jacobite army conceded their self-control:

> The rebels approached with good discipline for, to give them their due, never did 6,000 thieving naked ruffians with uncouth weapons make

so harmless a march in a civilised country, and the discipline was so severe they hanged up one or two at Lithgow for pilfering.[104]

In fact, the Hanoverian High Command decided on these tactics for two reasons. The first was to avenge, but also retrospectively to justify, their previous defeats by portraying the Jacobites as superhuman savages against whom any actions were permissible. The second was the grim logic which said that the only way to prevent any regrouping of the enemy, or any future rising, was to unleash such a tidal wave of violence that no one who survived it would ever again consider rising against the new order.

'Barbarians and Enemies of All Civil Society'

The ferocity displayed by Lowland Hanoverians like Major Lockhart or Captain Caroline Scott towards Highland Jacobites, both on the battlefield of Culloden and in the subsequent harrying of the Highlands, has been a major factor in fixing the war as a cultural – or as we would say nowadays – 'ethnic' clash. There is no need, however, to employ such useless metaphysical notions. There is always a danger when using terms like 'ethnic cleansing' from a position of support, or at least of sympathy for those being 'cleansed', that the historian comes to accept that there were indeed real 'ethnic' differences between the groups involved.[105] In fact, as we saw in Chapter 1, there were no 'ethnic' differences of an essential nature between the Lowlanders and the Highlanders, only cultural differences that had steadily grown during the preceding century, and which increasingly led Highlanders and Lowlanders respectively to describe themselves (and be described by the other) in terms of 'Celtic' and 'Saxon' racial characteristics. This racism reached its climax in the aftermath of Culloden. The issues involved were, as is usually the case, political.

The rising in England had produced a ferocious xenophobia towards the 'Rebellious Scots' whom the National Anthem, written at this time, enjoins George II to crush. It is important to note, however, that this was a relatively new development. Burt had observed in 1726 that in England little distinction was drawn between the Scots: 'In England the name of Scotsman is used indiscriminately to signify any one of the Male Part of the Natives of North Britain.' It was, however, the Lowlanders who were generally taken as typical Scots: 'to the People of England, excepting some few, and those chiefly the Soldiery, the Highlands are hardly known at all: for there has been less that I know of, written upon the subject, than either of the Indies'.[106] What the rising had done was temporarily to reverse this identification; the Highlanders were now taken to stand for the Scots as a whole, and the Highlanders, as several outraged English subjects now came forward to testify, were barbarians, or worse. As William Speck notes: 'They became dehumanised, "animals", "monsters", "beasts in confusion", "vermin", fit only to be "hunted down" and destroyed.' After one captured Jacobite was hanged at Cheadle a local apothecary surgeon bought the body for 4s 6d, so that it could be flayed and the skin tanned into leather. It is ironic, in the light of this obscenity, that the Highlanders found themselves described as 'barbarians, enemies of all civil society'.[107]

The Jacobites themselves could scarcely credit what the English believed them capable of doing. The Chevalier de Johnstone recounts one episode concerning Locheil:

> The terror of the English was truly inconceivable, and in many cases they seemed quite bereft of their senses. One evening, as Mr Cameron of Locheil entered the lodgings assigned to him, his landlady, an old woman, threw herself at his feet and, with uplifted hands and tears in her eyes, supplicated him to take her life but spare her two children. He asked her if she was in her senses, and told her to explain herself. She answered that everybody said the Highlanders ate children, and made them their common food.[108]

Johnstone was not exaggerating the extent of English credulity. In the pages of that invaluable gazetteer of contemporary London periodicals, *The Gentleman's Magazine* ('Edited by Silvanius Urban, Gent.', i.e. Edward Cave), we find one self-proclaimed 'gentleman' of Derby, who had Jacobites quartered on him during their occupation of that town, expressing every existing prejudice possible about the Highlanders in the space of one brief letter. First, their appearance:

> Most of the men, after their entrance into my house, looked like so many fiends turned out of hell, to ravage the kingdom and cut throats; and under their plaids nothing but a various sort of butchering weapons were to be seen.

Even though these fiends in human form proceeded to eat and drink this gentleman out of house and home (although unaccountably failing to cut either his throat or those of his family), he could still find amusement in their religious observance:

> ... what did afford me some matter for an unavoidable laughter, (though my family was in a miserable condition) was, to see these desperadoes, from officers to the common men, at their several meals, first pull off their bonnets, and then lift up their eyes in a most solemn manner, and mutter something to themselves, by way of saying grace – as if they had been so many primitive Christians.

As if, indeed. His greatest abuse, however, is reserved for their language:

Their dialect (from the idea I had of it) seemed to me, as if a herd of hottentots, wild monkeys in a desert, or vagrant gypsies, had been jabbering, screaming, and howling together; and really this jargon of speech was very suited to such a set of banditti.[109]

The conflation of 'hottentot', 'monkey' and 'gypsy' is suggestive and horrifying, but such feelings were by no means unique to the English.

The Highland Jacobite poet, Robb Don MacKay, rhetorically asked the Lowlanders after Culloden:

> O Scotland! art thou not ashamed
> At the part thou'st played
> Leaving a handful of Gaels
> to face the foeman's blade?[110]

But the Lowland Scots were amongst those wielding the blade, or at least willing the foemen on to wield it. In an area like Ayrshire, which had suffered the worst excesses of the Highland Host in the previous century, a tradition of hostility to Highlanders acting in the service of the Stuarts was reawakened by the Jacobite attempt.[111] But some of the most violent Lowland reactions were in areas which had no previous experience of the Highlands as a military threat. Patrick Crichton, who at some points in his diary of events in Edinburgh is prepared to acknowledge the disciplined behaviour of the Highlanders, elsewhere exudes the hatred felt for them by members of the Lowlands petty bourgeoisie:

They robbed some butchers on our Linton Road and came to Bread House and took all they could lay hands upon from Mrs Brown, and October 12, came this road and did all disorders of plunder and robbery that lawless wandering wasters (such as they are) could do.[112]

An account of the Jacobite presence in Hamilton later in the retreat described them as 'an undisciplined, ungoverned army of Highland robbers, who took no more notice of their nominal Prince or Commander than a pack of ill-bred hounds'. And what was this writer and his family forced to endure? 'We were freed from these troublesome neighbours upon Friday morning the 27th [December]: who left us nothing but an innumerable multitude of vermin and their excrements, which they left not only in our bed-chambers, but in our very beds.'[113] It was easy to persuade men who held such opinions to see the Highlanders as the main source of Jacobite disruption, and correspondingly difficult to stir them into any sympathy for the Highlanders in the fate that now befell them, for they had made it possible for some Englishmen to accuse all Scots equally of treason. The Reverend John Bisset noted in his diary, early in the rebellion, that: 'The very mob in London are high against the Pretender, and a Scotchman is looked ill on, because of our rebellion, and no wonder.'[114]

There were, moreover, rather more specific reasons for such accusations to be levelled. The surrender of Edinburgh without a fight had reinforced English perceptions of inherent Scottish Jacobitism. As Andrew Mitchell, the Under-Secretary of State for Scotland, wrote to the Solicitor-General, Henry Dundas:

> But this Act declaratory of the prerogative after a long usurpation, can never be extended to deprive the subject of the right of self-defence, and in this country such principles are turned into open ridicule, as tending to cover something that must not be openly avowed.[115]

The Commander-in-Chief of Scotland after Cumberland, William Anne Keppel, second Earl of Albermarle, revealed the same attitude of suspicion towards Scotland as a whole while writing to Newcastle of his 'inexpressible joy' at leaving:

> Upon the whole I think that this Kingdom can never be kept in awe but by a sufficient military force, and at the same time I think it a shame that the pay of so many men should be spent amongst them, for it is enriching this country at the expense of England.[116]

The classic example of Scot-baiting, however, occurred in December 1746 when one author ('Aretine'), writing in the appropriately entitled *Old England*, complained about three Scottish judges being appointed to the English bench:

> We ought to remember the late odious attempt to subvert our constitution, for it was all their own, and sprung from the innate animosity they have always entertained and invidiously shown against us; as well in the brutal ignorance of the barbarous Highlander, as in the politer treachery of the false Lowlander, ever faithful allies of France!

The conclusion of this tirade, so painful to the majority of Scots, was that: ''Tis observable, that a Scot is a natural Jacobite, and incurable by acts of generosity.'[117]

The double identification of the Highland Clans with Jacobitism as a political movement on the one hand and with the Scots as a nation on the other made it easier for those at the top of the Hanoverian state apparatus to adopt the attitude they did towards the Scots as a people. On some occasions Scots fought back against such assumptions. According to the Chevalier de Johnstone, English and Scottish Hanoverians, camped at Inverness after the battle, came to blows when an English officer had a Scottish deserter hanged, and accused the rest of the Scots of being 'traitors and rebels': 'the soldiers, of their own accord, beat to arms and drew up along the streets, the Scots on one side and the English on the other, beginning a very warm combat with fixed bayonets'. It required the intervention of Cumberland himself to mollify the Scots and restore order.[118] For the Scottish ruling class and their ideologues, however, it was of paramount importance that those areas that had remained loyal turned the distinctions between themselves and the rebels from matters of degree into those of absolute difference. Sir James Ferguson, Second Baronet of Kilkerran, wrote to Lord Halifax late in 1745 to thank him for arranging a commission for his son, John, in the Halifax Regiment. He was careful to add this explanation:

> I can assure your Lordship that but a small number of the low country other than persons of desperate circumstances have joined the Highlanders, and that the greatest, the far greatest and best part of this part of the United Kingdom are firmly attached to our present happy constitution and ardently wish success to the measures for preservation of religion and liberty.[119]

Arguments such as these were carried right to the summit of the state apparatus. In an interview with George II towards the end of 1745 the then Earl of Marchmont put the line to George and, as he no doubt intended, had it helpfully relayed back to him by the monarch: 'You have factions amongst yourselves; there are the Highlanders against the Lowlanders and others; but one must do the best one can.'[120]

The separation implied here was taken to its logical conclusion in a report on the forfeited estates by a Lowlander, Edward Bruce, after the suppression of the rising:

> That the disaffected and Savage Highlanders need to be Bridled and kept in awe by Garrisons and Standing Forces, 'till the present Generation wears out is Evident to all Men of common understanding, and that these unhappy and infatuated People will still Continue Savages if nothing else is done to recover them from their Ignorance and Barbarity seems as Evident; but as the rest of the People of Britain who are now Civilised were once as Wild and Barbarous as the Highlanders, I think it is not to be doubted but that proper Measures would Civilise them also.[121]

The same astonishing comparison with the English tribes before the Norman, or perhaps even the Roman conquest was made by an English correspondent, who nevertheless felt that exemplary punishments would be both 'cruel and impolitic':

> But cool reflection will suggest a great deal of the common Highlanders, who are but little removed from a state of nature ... The South Briton, when the Romans first landed here, were not a very different people from the present Highland Scots, who want only property, trade, and an intercourse with the more civilised part of mankind, to bring them nearer to a resemblance of the present English.[122]

One James Pringle wrote to the Hanoverian Earl of Marchmont shortly before Culloden:

> We were surprised today with a story of a [pro-Jacobite] mob at Edinburgh in the Gazette when there was not the least foundation for it, that has been a damned English fiction, for I dare say no good Scotsman would be such a traitor to his country.[123]

The Highlanders were not 'good Scotsmen'. Also in Edinburgh, a young orphan, John MacDonald (one of the 'poor children, of whom, after the Rebellion there were a great many'), wrote in his memoirs that 'the poor Highlanders were more despised at that time by the Scots in general, of the other party, than the devils in hell'.[124] Many literary Scotsmen took up the pen to prove their adherence to the British state just as their military compatriots were raising the sword in the same cause. As one polemicist pointed out, in direct response to *Old England*: 'There have been Two [sic] Rebellions since the Union, and both were happily quelled, But were they not quelled by Scotsmen?' At any rate, he hurriedly continues, the English did not play the major part: 'We had an Army in the Field it is true; but it was found, by Experience, that English Troops alone were no match for the Highlanders.'[125]

The ideological manoeuvre whereby the Highlands were to be regarded as completely distinct from the Lowlands was later theoretically enshrined by the great Enlightenment thinkers for whom the Highlands represented everything from which they wished to escape. It should be added, however, that this was a retreat from the earlier clarity regarding the feudal nature of the Highlands expressed by the numerous pamphleteers we have quoted throughout this book, a retreat which was compounded by the later romanticisation of the (largely mythical) Highlanders which became fashionable from the 1760s onwards. The theory of social development bequeathed by the Scottish Enlightenment is one of the great intellectual achievements of the modern epoch, but the fact that they identified the inhabitants of the Scottish Highlands as examples of the first and most primitive stage of that development helped contribute towards an obscurantism – the supposedly absolute social difference between the Highlands and the Lowlands – whose dismal effects are with us still.[126]

The End of Feudalism in Scotland

The historic misconception which sees 'Highland society' as different and inferior to that of the Lowlands only became fully entrenched at the very point when the former was about to be destroyed. 'As exposure to the atmosphere reduces all mummies to instant dissolution,' wrote Marx during the Crimean War, 'so war passes extreme judgement on social systems that have outlived their vitality.'[127] Even at this stage, 'dissolution' was far from being wholly automatic. Robert Forbes, the Episcopalian chronicler of the repression, received one communication from a correspondent suggesting that the very brutalities imposed by the Hanoverians upon the inhabitants of the Highlands might have the effect of strengthening Jacobite support:

> In the North of Scotland I happened to fall in with a venerable old gentleman, an honest Whig, who, looking at me seriously in the face, asked if the Duke of Cumberland was not a Jacobite. 'A Jacobite!' Said I, 'How comes that in your head?' 'Sure' (replied the old gentleman), 'the warmest zealot in the interest of the Prince could not possibly devise more proper methods of sowing the seeds of Jacobitism and dissatisfaction than the Duke of Cumberland did.'[128]

The old gentleman was surely being ironic. Jacobitism in the Highlands – in so far as it had ever been a popular force – was now completely dead in political terms, although it was to have an afterlife in Gaelic culture as an emblem for the Highland society whose destruction Jacobitism had helped bring about. Nevertheless, Cumberland and his associates were taking no chances. On 23 May 1746 Newcastle proposed that the clans might be transported 'not as Slaves, but to form colonies in the West Indies'. On 5 June 1746 we find Cumberland replying in support of 'the only sure remedy for establishing Quiet in the country':

> I mean the transporting of particular Clans ... This Scheme might be put into Execution, either by a Citation to every individual of the Clans to appear under penalty of Outlawry, as the most open Acts of Treason may be proved against every one of them, or by a Law passed for their being transplanted ... for, I am sorry to be obliged to say, that in my opinion, was there the least Occasion, they would rise again tomorrow.[129]

This is usually cited as an example of the Butcher living up to his nickname, but lest anyone imagine that it was a uniquely barbaric suggestion, it should be recalled that this was not the first time it had been made. As we saw in Chapter 2, Andrew Fletcher made his famous – or perhaps one should say infamous – proposal to reintroduce serfdom as a solution to the problem of unemployment in 1698. The point here is that those are the views of the most advanced and radical thinker of the preceding period. We can assume, therefore, that if Fletcher had achieved his Utopia of an Independent Scottish Republic and (stretching counterfactual history to the limit) it had not been dominated by the very lords to whom he was opposed, something similar to the aftermath of Culloden would have been demanded by the state, and probably sooner than was allowed by the compromise of the Union. In the event the schemes of the Patriot proved too drastic even for the Butcher and no more was heard of transportation.

Five days after Cumberland's initial proposal, Thomas Sherlock, Bishop of Salisbury, was writing to Edward Weston, Under-Secretary in the Northern Department:

> The forfeited country being put under a proper government, supported by a sufficient military force, will not only be kept quiet itself, and in time civilized; but it would be a barrier against the *now* well affected clans, should they ever alter their mind; to which there wants nothing but an alteration in the affection of the chief.[130]

Lord Justice-Clerk of Scotland, Andrew Fletcher (no relation), in a memorial to Newcastle, went further:

> Could we but at once get rid of all the Chiefs of Clans in these barbarous and disloyal parts of the Highlands, it would facilitate all other operations both in point of difficulty and time; And therefore, so far as we can get rid of them, we ought; and where we cannot get rid of them, That such Regulations be made and carried into Execution as make the common people as free and independent of their chiefs as the nature of their case can admit.[131]

These were not new proposals either. In fact, most of the events we have surveyed in this book can be traced to the tragic inability of the Commonwealth regime permanently to break the power of the lords. As Lord Justice-Clerk Fletcher noted: "'Tis true that Cromwell Reduced The Highlands by the force of an Army, But as soon as the Army was Removed, They Returned to their Natural Barbarity.'[132] Now that reduction was to be permanently accomplished, but it was scarcely the 'common people' or 'meaner sort' whom Cromwell and John Jones had wished to raise up that were to benefit. Attention had, however, shifted from the clansmen themselves to their chiefs and the socio-juridical basis of their authority. During the Rebellion, Kames wrote in the Introduction to his *British Antiquities* that he:

> ... has at Heart to raise a Spirit among his countrymen of searching into their antiquities, those especially which regard the Law and the Constitution; being seriously convinced that nothing will more contribute than this Study, to eradicate a Set of Opinions, which, by Intervals, have disquieted this Island for a Century and a Half.[133]

Other men, more concerned with the practicalities of exercising power than he, now turned to the social relationships which had allowed that Set of Opinions to end in armed struggle once again.

After the initial repression had died down, it became apparent to at least some members of the British ruling class that merely driving off the peasants' herds might bring them to starvation – a matter which caused them no great concern – without necessarily breaking the power of the lords. As late as 1812 John Craig noted that the forms of law had lagged behind social development: 'the Feudal law, adapted to a state of society which has long ceased to exist, still continues to regulate the landed property of Scotland.'[134] But this is to confuse form with content. The measures that were to ensure that the '45 could never be repeated therefore took the form of a barrage of new laws, which effectively disabled the old. William Ferguson has written of the first, the Tenures Abolition Act of 1746: 'In its day this was a notable reform, but it may now be regretted that the opportunity was not taken to make a St Bartholomew of feudalism in Scotland along the lines foreshadowed by Cromwell.'[135] In fact, this was exactly what happened, if not in the manner that we associate with the Great Protector. The Tenures Abolition Act itself abolished wardholding, whereby personal and, more importantly, military services were performed in exchange for grants of land, and replaced it with nominal cash payments. The Disarming Act of the same year reasserted earlier legislation forbidding the possession of arms, and this of course complemented the abolition of military service. Equally significant were two other clauses. The first banned the bagpipes and all outward expression of clan identity, old (the plaid) and new (the kilt), as weapons of war. The only groups excepted from these prohibitions – and they were very important indeed – were the Highland Regiments, some of whom had already seen service against the clans at Culloden. The second struck at the heart of the Episcopalian ideology which had sustained Jacobitism since 1688, by insisting that all tutors, masters and chaplains in private schools or households publicly take an oath of allegiance to George II and 'his heirs and successors' in order to qualify to teach at all. The penalties for unqualified preaching or teaching, or for employing someone unqualified to do so, extended to transportation.

Interestingly, not all English commentators saw the connection between the banning of Highland dress and disarming the population. As one noted at the time: 'As to the other Regulation for stripping the Highlanders of their usual Clothes, I do not know what to think of it, at least I shall not say what I think.' Fortunately, he relented:

> Surely the Highland Garb, or a Party-coloured Plaid or Stuff does not infect People with Jacobitism, because many of those that wear it have upon all Occasions, particularly the last, taken Arms in favour of the Government: It cannot be looked on even as a badge of Jacobitism, because his Majesty's Officers and Soldiers are by this law Expressly allowed to wear it.

The sanity of these sentiments demonstrate that not all had been seduced by the myth that the Rebellion was a product of some distinctly Highland culture. The same author did, however, propose a more serious solution:

> ... the most effectual, and indeed the only effectual Method for preventing any future Rebellions in Scotland, is to abolish all hereditary Jurisdictions and all Casualties and Personal Services, and to make the People in Scotland as free and Independent of their Superiors or Landlords, as the People now are in England ... Unless something of this Sort be done, and effective Methods be taken for having the People in Scotland educated in right political Principles, and Employed in Trade and Manufactures, a numerous Army of mercenary Troops must always be kept up in that Country, which, I hope, the British Parliament will never agree to ...[136]

His hopes were to be rewarded. The most significant legislation of all, the Heritable Jurisdictions Act of 1747, was significantly titled 'An Act for taking away and abolishing the Heritable Jurisdictions in that part of Great Britain called Scotland ... and for rendering the Union of the Two Kingdoms more complete'.[137] The way in which heritable jurisdictions had been used to mobilise support for the rising meant that their relative usefulness to the British state was well and truly at an end. Now they were all to be swept away, with the exception of the baron courts, which Duncan Forbes managed to have retained for the purposes of enforcing payment of arrears and adjudicating on small claims. Compensation was paid, of course, but scarcely at the levels requested. The Duke of Hamilton submitted a claim for £38,000 for the loss of his four jurisdictions: he got £3,000.[138] The Act came into force on 24 March 1748, and as Bruce Lenman writes: 'Arguably this is a date which should rank with the Union of Crowns in

1603 and the Union of Parliaments of 1707 in the slow destruction of the traditional Scottish polity.'[139] There is no argument here. Abolition covered the entire country, and no exceptions were granted, even for those who had been the most loyal supporters of the regime.

The previous August, when it was obvious that a rising was in progress, but the scale was not yet apparent, Argyll wrote to Norman Macleod of Dunvegan expressing the view that even a rising confined to the Highlands would have repercussions across the whole of the country because, unlike the aftermath of the '15, the matter would be taken out of the hands of the Scottish section of the ruling class.[140] The Duke was right. When the House of Lords first instructed the Court of Session to prepare a Bill on this subject, the motion was passed unopposed:

> The question for ordering the Lords of Session to send up the draft of a Bill was first put, and then that for the Report of the Regalities, and both were carried without any division, but without the least support from the Duke of Argyll, who sat in a corner silent, and complained of the headache.[141]

As well he might, for alone of all the jurisdictions held in Scotland, his vast empire was specifically referred to:

> And it is hereby further enacted that the county or shire of Argyll, and all the islands, places, districts and lands lying within or subject to jurisdiction of the justiciary now vested in or belonging to the most notable Archibald Duke of Argyll, shall be and be deemed and taken to be within the limits of circuit called the Western Circuit.[142]

There is no need to waste sympathy on the notable Archibald, however, since he received £21,000 in compensation – three times as much as anyone else – and was still the most powerful man in Scotland. The shadow cast by the House of Argyll, which has fallen over this entire history, was not to be lifted yet.

The test of these measures was to come in 1759, when the French state attempted the last invasion of Britain it was to make while the *ancien régime* persisted. As a prelude to the reconquest of Canada and India, French troops were to stage simultaneous landings in both England and Scotland, the expectation being that Jacobite supporters would rise on their arrival. 'It was,' wrote Sir Alexander Peter Mackenzie Douglas of the Stuart Court-in-exile, 'essential to have their support, especially in Scotland.'[143] In fact, the only Jacobites to participate in the attempt were exiles like Mackenzie Douglas himself. The destruction of the French fleet by the British navy at the Battle of Quiberon Bay on 25 November ended their hopes, but even had the descent been accomplished, no support would have been forthcoming in Scotland: the social basis for it no longer existed.[144]

Epilogue

The Scottish Path to Capitalist Development (1747–1815)

The most helpful comparisons with the end of the revolution in Scotland, and the events which followed it, can be found over 100 years later, in nations which did not exist during the period between the Glorious Revolution and the '45. During the 1860s, the unifications of Italy, Germany and the USA marked the climaxes of their respective bourgeois revolutions. In each case these were mainly imposed from above by the state power of the more advanced geographical area – Piedmont, Prussia, the North – expanding its control over the backward adjacent regions and incorporating them into a new nation-state. Despite the resulting internal unevenness, each was then set irreversibly on the road to capitalist industrialisation.

In his writings on the Italian Risorgimento, Antonio Gramsci wrote of the importance of the Piedmontese state in the unification – indeed the creation – of Italy, over the head of the local bourgeoisie:

> This fact is of the greatest importance for the concept of 'passive revolution' – the fact, that is, that what was involved was not a social group which 'led' other groups, but a State which, even though it had limitations as a power, 'led' the group which should have been 'leading' and was able to put at the latter's disposal an army and politico-diplomatic strength.[1]

Prussia played a similar role to that of Piedmont in Italy during the unification of Germany. As Eric Hobsbawm notes:

> The Prussian way to capitalism was through the combination of a bourgeoisie reluctant to make a bourgeois revolution and a Junker state prepared to give them most of what they wanted without a

revolution, for the price of preserving the political control of the landed aristocracy and the bureaucratic monarchy.[2]

Of the three examples, however, the American experience, although on a much greater scale than that of Britain, provides the closest parallel. The Piedmontese and Prussian states came to dominance by defeating, intimidating, bribing or even persuading smaller states, as a prelude to incorporating them in new political formations. The North initially entered the American Civil War to prevent the secession of a major part of the existing nation-state. Of course the Jacobites were not merely involved in an attempt at secession for Scotland, but in overthrowing the existing state throughout the territory of the British Isles. Ultimately, however, this was also the goal of the Confederacy in relation to the United States. Once battle was joined, the aims of the Confederacy were to expand slave production northwards to areas where it had never previously existed, retarding the advance of industrial capitalism and free wage labour, and, as a result, placing the United States as a whole under the informal control of the British Empire, for whom most of the Southern cotton exports were destined. The analogy cannot be pursued too far – Scotland was itself divided by civil war in a way that the Confederate states never were – but it nevertheless indicates the pattern of 'revolution from above' into which the Scottish Revolution falls, or rather, which it foreshadows.

By some point in the second half of the eighteenth century, even before the French Revolution, the capitalist system had taken on a purely economic momentum which made bourgeois domination unstoppable and irreversible, regardless of the temporary political setbacks suffered by individual revolutions in, for example, 1848 and 1849. Gettysburg in 1863 did not therefore have the same significance as Culloden in 1746. For, even if the Confederacy had won that battle and gone on to win the Civil War, the ultimate victory of industrial capitalism across the entire territory of what is now the United States of America would sooner or later have followed, either through a renewed attempt by the North or adaption by the Confederate plantocracy to the new order, in the manner of the Prussian Junkers or Japanese Samurai.[3] This was not yet the situation in Britain during 1745 and 1746. Had the Jacobites, and through them, absolutist France, been victorious, Britain, the most dynamic economy in the new system and the only significant state geared to capitalist accumulation, would have been severely weakened and its greatest opponent given a further lease of life. The Jacobites would have been incapable of reimposing feudalism over the whole of Britain – the relative economic weight of Scotland was still too slight, and the development of capitalist agriculture elsewhere too great for that to be possible – but they could have established a regime more subservient to French absolutism than even that of Charles II during the previous century. In practical terms this would have removed the main obstacle to French hegemony in Europe, allowed France to inherit British colonial possessions and, at the very least, reversed the land settlement – particularly in Ireland – that resulted from the Revolution. Britain would have necessarily been reduced to a satellite of France; for, even assuming that the seizure of London had miraculously restored the convictions of wavering Jacobite supporters, their very lack of a firm social base in England would have forced the new regime to rely on the force of French arms for its existence. The '45 was therefore far from being the historical anomaly, inevitably doomed to failure, that is so often portrayed. This violent irruption of the old world into the new finally bestirred the British bourgeoisie into performing its final act as a revolutionary class. For this was a war fought by them, not only to defend the achievements of the revolutions that brought them to power, but also to preserve the independent existence of their state. For that reason alone, Culloden was not a minor event, significant, if at all, only to the Scots, but one of the most decisive battles in British and world history.

Nevertheless, the suppression of the '45 did have a particular significance for the Scots. The removal of the counter-revolutionary threat had different implications in England and Scotland. In England, it meant safety from forced retrogression for a territory over which capitalism was already established as the dominant mode of production. In Scotland, it meant the removal of institutional obstacles to the process of capitalism becoming the dominant mode of production, but that process still had to be undergone. All bourgeois revolutions presuppose a certain level of prior capitalist development, without which no new ruling class would exist to lead, or at any rate, benefit from the overthrow of the feudal state. But equally, no bourgeois revolution has inherited an economy completely geared to competitive accumulation, for without the continuation of feudal social relations in at least some areas, the old regime would have no internal basis of support and the revolution would therefore be rendered unnecessary. The extent to which these relations required to be superseded has varied from case to case, but in Scotland it was more considerable than it either had been in England or would be in France. As a result of the Union the Scottish bourgeoisie had been able to call on a British army to destroy the internal counter-revolution, but the very fact that this had been necessary indicated how weak the indigenous forces of Scottish capitalism remained, compared with those of England. As we saw in Chapter 5, local changes to tenurial relation-ships had taken place before 1746, but as long as these were not generalised across Scotland, the possibilities of increasing productivity and proprietorial income, let alone of feeding a growing population, or accumulating capital for the purpose of investment, would remain unrealised. Capitalist agriculture was the necessary precondition for any wider transformation of economy and society. It was necessary, in other words, to bring the Scottish economic base into alignment with the British political superstructure.

Between 1747 and 1815 an extended epilogue or coda to the Scottish Revolution finally saw the Lowland economy wrenched into line with that of England, with the result that both countries began industrialising from approximately the same level – an outcome inconceivable in 1707, or even in 1746. The process of uneven and combined development, which had previously involved members of the Scottish feudal classes borrowing enough from England to maintain the existing social structure, now involved members of a new class borrowing not to preserve, but to transform. Who were they?

Theoreticians and Practitioners of Passive Revolution

In Chapter 1 we identified a series of disparate groups – south-western bonnet lairds, Glasgow tobacco merchants, Edinburgh lawyers, Church of Scotland ministers, the House of Argyll and its tacksmen – some of whose members had the potential to coalesce into a bourgeoisie, given certain conditions. Post-1746, those conditions now existed. In the context of the decisive agricultural sector, the relevant sections of this class fell into two distinct but overlapping groups. One consisted of the intellectuals, the social theorists, whose names we associate with the Scottish Historical School and whose professional lives were generally those of university professors, Church of Scotland ministers or lawyers. These were the theorists of capital; they were not, in most cases, its owners. The other was the class of landowners, the majority of whose members had hitherto been the biggest obstacle to the introduction of capitalist agriculture. These were the practitioners of reform and, as such, are comparable to the much longer-established 'agrarian bourgeoisie' discussed in an English context by Edward Thompson.[4] Writing in 1964, when direct state intervention in the economy was at a far higher level than it is today, Christopher Smout noted of the activities of the Scottish landowners that 'it was the sort of work which in an underdeveloped country today could be undertaken by the state'.[5] Although I distinguish below between the distinctive contributions of these two groups, it would be wrong to conceive of them as mutually exclusive, since they inter-penetrated each other at every point.

The Intellectual Cadres of Improvement

'A distinctive feature of the overall Scottish experience,' writes James Young, 'was the absence of a bourgeois revolution through which the middle classes and *philosophes* might have experienced their *own* authentic confidence, mission and pathbreaking role.'[6] I have tried to demonstrate that, among other things, the bourgeois revolution is not an absence in Scottish history, but simply invisible to historians expecting parallels to the Putney Debates or the September Massacres. But if Scottish history has no Revolutionary Seizure of State Power, what of the supposedly necessary precondition of that event, Class Consciousness of the Rising Bourgeoisie? If this was absent, as Young believes, then what were Messrs Dalrymple, Ferguson, Hume, Kames and Smith doing if not expressing 'their own authentic confidence, mission and pathbreaking role? One answer falls readily to hand: far from mapping out their own path, the great intellectuals of the Scottish Enlightenment were following one laid down by the English state after 1707. Their work was done, so to speak, in the wrong historical period: after the end of Scottish statehood, rather than in the run up to its attainment. That is no reason, however, to lament the supposed poverty of the bourgeois experience. If, as I have argued, the process of bourgeois revolution was not cut short in 1707, but – with all the unexpectedness of real history – simply changed its form, then the writings of the Scottish Enlightenment must also be reconsidered in this light.

The specific national form taken by the Enlightenment in each nation depended, at least in part, on its relationship to the bourgeois revolution. In England, the bourgeois revolution preceded the Enlightenment and was conducted largely under religious banners. Indeed, those who can be described as the standard bearers of proto-Enlightenment were, like Hobbes, aligned with the Stuart regime rather than with those who sought to overthrow it.[7] By the time Enlightenment thought became (with John Locke) the province of those committed to commercial society and constitutional monarchy, 'England,' in the words of John Pocock, 'was too modern to need an Enlightenment and was already engaged upon a quarrel with modernity itself.'[8] The new propertied classes had greater power and freedom to discuss how it should be exercised than any other national group in Europe. 'In these circumstances,' writes Roy Porter, 'enlightened ideologies were to assume a unique inflection in England: one less concerned to lambast the status quo than to vindicate it against adversaries left and right, high and low.'[9] In France, on the other hand, the Enlightenment preceded the bourgeois revolution and provided the political ideology which guided it. Although superficial similarities with aspects of the English Enlightenment can be found, their context renders them quite different in implication.

Only in Scotland, however, did the Enlightenment emerge neither before nor after the bourgeois revolution, but during it.[10] The uniqueness of this situation may explain why the thinkers of the Scottish Enlightenment were more concerned in their writings with the attainment of economic dominance over society than with the conquest of political power within the state. In his discussion of the progressive role played by absolutism, Adam Smith wrote that 'the power of the nobles has always been brought to ruin before any system of liberty was established, and this indeed must always be the case'.[11] The nobility – or at least the section still prepared to use their powers against the central state – had now been 'greatly crushed', as he recommended. The 'revolution after the revolution' which followed the '45 was therefore one of the purest bourgeois revolutionary experiences in history. Unconstrained by feudal lords behind them (since they had been destroyed by the military and juridical apparatus of the British state), unafraid of a working class before them (since it had not yet come into existence in significant numbers, and would only do so as a result of their activities), the Scottish bourgeoisie was free, as no other bourgeoisie had been before or would ever be again, to reconstruct society in its own image.[12]

As Tom Nairn has written: 'Scotland was the country where the transition from feudalism to capitalism was undertaken not only successfully but *self-consciously*.'[13] In the first instance this involved a scientific assessment of how other societies, particularly England, had made the transition in the past, as a necessary precondition for Scottish society to make the transition in the present. An important aspect of the Enlightenment was therefore the theory of Improvement; and Improvement was in many respects the practice of Enlightenment – not simply the introduction of better techniques, or even the changes to tenurial agreements which allowed these techniques to be implemented, but the conscious and systematic transformation of an entire society in which agriculture was still the most important single sector of the economy. As Eric Hobsbawm has pointed out, *The Wealth of Nations*, perhaps the greatest product of this movement, was regarded by the contemporaries of Adam Smith as 'a handbook of development economics': 'This theory sought to identify not only the nature of the historical process which led to economic development, and of the obstacles that stood in its way, but also the conditions that would allow them to be overcome.'[14] For whom were these 'handbooks' written?

The Self-transformation of the Landowning Elite

Ironically, their core audience was among the lords, the majority of whom had previously been the greatest obstacle to capitalist agriculture. In one respect, therefore, the Scottish experience after the '45 prefigured that of Europe as a whole during the following century. Some Marxists, in reaction to exaggeratedly heroic depictions of the rise of the bourgeoisie, have tended to overstress the voluntary self-transformation of English feudal landowners into agrarian capitalists by 1648, while others have argued that this was in fact a general tendency throughout Western Europe by that date. The case is overstated even for England and completely misleading for the rest of Europe, with the possible exception of the Netherlands.[15] In so far as 'self-transformation' was a common European experience, it was one which can be dated from after 1815 and, more specifically, from after 1848 when the surviving absolutist regimes attempted, with widely differing degrees of enthusiasm and consistency, to reconstruct the state machine so as to compete more effectively against their modernised British and French rivals. Prussia, or rather, Imperial Germany, had by 1871 clearly emerged as the most successful of these. Similarly, their predominantly agrarian ruling classes were sufficiently impressed with the productivity of English and Lowland Scottish agriculture to seek to emulate its achievements. Yet the means by which they could do so were limited. No other nation would ever again have the luxury of the prolonged emergence of agrarian capitalist relations which characterised English history between the Black Death and the passing of the Enclosure Acts. The alternatives were either to make minimal adjustments and run the risk of peasant revolts comparable to those which accompanied the French Revolution – which was ultimately the fate of the Russian autocracy – or to replace the existing methods of exploitation with those which prevailed in Britain.

As with the recasting of the state, it was Prussia which was at the forefront of this process. So much so that, looking back from his vantage point at the beginning of the twentieth century, Lenin discerned two distinct paths towards capitalist agriculture in Europe and its overseas extensions, which he defined respectively as the 'Prussian' (or reformist) and 'American' (or revolutionary) paths. In the first, the landowners of the great estates would gradually replace feudal methods of exploitation with those of capitalism, retaining feudal instruments of social control over their tenants (at least in the medium term), but ultimately transforming themselves into large capitalist landowners. In the second, the landowners are overthrown, feudal controls removed and the estates redistributed among the previous tenants, who now emerge as a new class of medium capitalist farmers.[16] In an important historical study comparing these two paths of development, Terence Byers has charac-terised the 'Prussian Path' as a form of 'capitalism from above' in two senses, not only because the feudal landlord class transformed itself into a capitalist class, but also because they consequently controlled the process, 'in a manner which stifled any development of the peasant economy...whereby a capitalist agriculture might emerge from an increasingly differentiated peasantry'. Byers contrasts both aspects with developments in England, where the feudal landlords became capitalist landlords rather than capitalist farmers and where the latter class did emerge out of class differentiation among the peasants.[17] In fact, the American path was exceptional; the Prussian path typical (except in France, where the victory of peasant smallholding during the Revolution established an enduring obstacle to rural capitalist concentration and centralisation).

It is in this context that the earlier experience of Scotland is important. The Scottish Lowlands were not only a component of the admired British model, but had been the first region to undergo what became known as the 'Prussian' path and which should be more accurately referred to as the 'Scottish' path instead. There are two ways in which the Scottish experience prefigures that of Prussia.

One is the 'external' event which precipitates the reform process. In the case of Prussia, defeat by the Napoleonic armies at Jena and Auerstadt in 1806 seemed to demonstrate the superiority of free peasants over serfs as a source of manpower, while the indemnities imposed by the victorious French demanded an increase in revenues which was unlikely to be produced as long as serfdom endured. In the case of Scotland, defeat of the Jacobites at Culloden and the subsequent destruction of its social base removed forever the possibility of stopping, let alone reversing the advance of capitalist relations of production. Consequently, landowners who had hoped to subsist through feudal super-exploitation of the peasantry or, at best, by supplementing their feudal rent through the sale of coal or timber, now found that they had no option but to enter the marketplace, or to fail in competition with their more commercially orientated rivals. From the 1740s – and the 1780s in the case of the Jacobite estates once their forfeitures were revoked – the landowners' influence began to be measured, not in terms of the antiquity of their lineage or, of more practical importance, the size of their following, but more prosaically, as with their English counterparts, by the value of their rent rolls. They had in fact no remaining alternative to making this change – assuming of course that they wished to retain their social positions.

The other parallel between Prussia and Scotland was that, because of the very primitiveness of economic relations in both countries, the landlord class appropriated the peasant surplus in the form of labour rent. As Byers puts it, a class in such a position is 'more likely to be poised for possible transformation to hirers of wage labour than one which appropriates surplus via kind or money rent', not least because the taking of labour rent involves a 'direct relationship with labour' and a consequent link 'with the process of production'.[18] Even after the legislative onslaught of 1746–48 all property in Scotland remained feudal in the technical sense; that is to say it was either held directly from the Crown or indirectly from a Crown vassal. Within this overall framework the uses of feudalism could extend to the power to force tenants into performing particular actions. These feudal services were now conscripted into the cause of capital accumulation and 'many proprietors continued to exact ancient rights of service in leases alongside clauses prescribing the most advanced rotation systems'.[19]

Scottish agriculture in the aftermath of the '45 was therefore still transitional in character. What Lenin wrote of Russian agriculture after the abolition of serfdom in 1861 is suggestive of the Scottish situation 100 years earlier: 'With all the endless variety of forms characteristic of a transitional epoch, the economic organisation of contemporary landlord farming amounts to two main systems, in the most varied combinations – the *labour-service* system and the *capitalist* system.' These were not absolute differences. 'Life creates forms that unite in themselves with remarkable gradualness systems of economy whose basic features constitute opposites. It becomes impossible to say where "labour-service" ends and where "capitalism" begins.'[20] 'Labour service' took a number of different forms in Scotland. Even outwith the economic aspects of the landlord–tenant relationship, occupiers who held land within the feudal superiority of the local lord were still subject to his baron court and, in many cases, were required to take their corn to his mill for grinding – a monopoly situation which was of course virtually a textbook example of how to violate the Principles of Political Economy. More important than the retention of economically peripheral labour services was the continuation of the law of hypothec, which allowed the landowner a lien (i.e. first claim on the goods of his tenants) on unpaid rent. In 1748 this was interpreted by allies of the landowners among the legal profession in a way which exceeded even the intentions of the original law, by forbidding tenants from 'touching the crop' until the rent had been set aside.[21]

Many reformers were deeply unhappy with the continuation of the practices which had facilitated the process of feudal exploitation before 1746, and perplexed at the failure of the proprietors to abandon them. The Reverend Mr Walter Chambers wrote that: 'It is astonishing that heritors, in many respects liberal-minded and indulgent to their tenants, still continue this vestige of feudal slavery.'[22] Perhaps we find this less astonishing. In 1774 Lord Kames noted that the owners of the great estates were becoming a 'united body of ambitious oppressors, overawing their sovereign as well as their fellow-subjects', and reminded his readers that 'such was the miserable condition of Britain, while the feudal oligarchy subsisted: such at present is the miserable condition of Poland; and such will be the miserable condition of Scotland, if the legislature afford not a remedy'.[23] But he and the other reformers had, in a sense, missed the point. A new tyranny was indeed being established; it was not a feudal resurgence, however, but the specific form taken by capitalist landownership in Scotland. If the latter only bore an approximate resemblance to the model of capitalism devised by the reformers, it must be recalled that they were grappling with a new phenomenon and can for that reason be forgiven for not anticipating the discrepancy between their models and reality. There is perhaps less excuse for such misrecognition by their epigones today.

The Revolution After the Revolution

Yet what was decisively different about the use of these powers was that they were now harnessed to quite different ends than had generally been the case before the '45. The Scottish reformers could adopt both the men (as estate managers) and the methods which in England had taken centuries to develop, but which in Scotland could be applied immediately in their most advanced form. As Angus Calder writes:

> England had no 'Agricultural Revolution'. The term is misapplied to a country where novel techniques came in gradually from the seventeenth century onwards. But it suits eighteenth-century Scotland. The rallying cry of the revolutionaries was 'improvement'. Their new methods were called 'English husbandry'.

Calder draws an illuminating parallel with a later, and equally precocious example of economic transformation:

> An equivalent to the Lowland Scottish self-colonisation of the eighteenth century may be found in the Japanese self-westernisation in the late nineteenth, which was still swifter and equally successful – but the Scots helped to pioneer the industrial revolution which the Japanese adapted wholesale.[24]

The precise means by which this transformation was accomplished must be the subject of another history. It remains here simply to give an indication of how successful, in capitalist terms, it proved to be. In 1776, the same year in which *The Wealth of Nations* was published, Lord Kames asked: Was it too much to expect 'that our progress may be rapid; and that agriculture will soon be familiar among us, and as skilfully conducted as in England'?[25] The very way in which the question is posed suggests that Kames did not expect such progress to occur any time in the near future. It is therefore instructive to compare his very tentative optimism with the following verdict from an anonymous supplement to the sixth edition of his book in 1815:

> ... it may suffice to observe in general, that there never were greater agricultural improvements carried on in any country than there have been in Scotland during the last thirty years; that the progress of the most correct systems of husbandry has been rapid and extensive beyond what the most sanguine could have anticipated; and that, in short, when we contrast the present state of agriculture in the south-eastern counties with what must have been its state about the middle of the last century ... the efforts of several centuries would seem to have been concentrated in the intermediate period.[26]

Anonymous was right. Let one measure of economic buoyancy – the increase in rent – stand for all those which could be cited. In 1792 Patrick Stewart reported of Kinneff in Kincardineshire:

> The rent has been rising for these 20 years past. Of late it has been astonishing. For example, an estate of this parish was lately bought for £7,000 that 25 years ago offered to be sold for 2,000 guineas: that estate, however, now pays nine times the rent it paid at that period.[27]

Nor was this an isolated example. If we take 1660 as our base year and adjust for inflation, by 1740 the national average of rent had doubled, by 1770 it had tripled, by 1793 it had increased 7.6 times and by 1811 it had increased 15 times. When the rate of increase finally began to stabilise at the end of the Napoleonic Wars in 1815, the total increase in real terms from 1660 may have been of the order of 15.6 times.[28] This sharp upward trajectory of landlord income, which in turn depended on the increased ability of the tenant farmers to pay higher rents, was important in two ways.

One was that, along with the profits of the tobacco trade, for which imperial markets and Caribbean slave labour were both essential, it laid the financial basis for the industrialisation of the Lowlands. This occurred in two ways. On the one hand, the landlords lent their deposits to other capitalists for investment, notably through the British Linen Bank which was founded in 1746. In this respect they were primarily passive sources of funding, although since many landowners were also shareholders and directors of banks they can be supposed to have had some influence over who received the loans. On the other hand, the landlords also participated more actively in manufacturing, extraction and construction. The extent of their involvement varied across these three sectors. Manufacturing proper mainly involved industries whose purpose was profitably to burn up excess coal, such as soap boiling or sugar refining, although some also became involved in brewing or papermaking. The three textiles which successively dominated the Scottish economy – linen, wool and cotton – saw a fall in landowning investment with each shift, and in the case of the iron industry there is scarcely any record of direct investment at all. Extraction mainly involved coal, as it had always done, but to which were now added slate and limestone. Construction may have been the landowners' most important, albeit indirect contribution to industrialisation. The harbours, canals and – especially – roads which they commissioned were initially designed for the transportation of their own produce and, more generally, to connect their estates more effectively to the outside world than could be done through the decrepit statute roads. Once constructed, however, these roads became available for wider use. Between 1750 and 1840,

350 Turnpike Acts were passed for the construction of new roads, most of them between 1770 and 1800.[29]

Let the example of Ayrshire, on the other side of the country from Edinburgh and the Lothians, and consequently far from where the greatest intellectual and agricultural advances were being made, demonstrate the wide-ranging nature of landowner involvement. At one level the interventions of the local landlords were typical for their class: 'In the agrarian revolution, the most extensive renovations were on the estates of the six earls who had their principal seats in the shire.' In addition to this, however, they became involved in all three industrial sectors:

> As part of their improvements, the great landowners exploited the mineral resources of their estates, developing the coal industry with deeper pits which required steam engines – at least five were locally installed before 1750 – and with waggonways to the coast, where early next century new ports served by railways would be constructed by two Ayrshire peers. ... The need for general improvement in transport facilities persuaded the country gentry to obtain Turnpike Acts in 1767 and 1774. One member of the Ayrshire Turnpike Trustees was John Loudon McAdam of Sauchrie, who would later win fame bringing English roads up to Ayrshire standards. ... The landowners were also initiating manufacturing enterprises: McAdam and the 9th Earl of Dundonald with their tar works at Muirkirk; the Earl of Cassillis with a paper mill at Doonfoot; the Earl of Dumfries with a pottery at Cumnock and his countess with a woollen mill; and the dowager countess of Eglinton – to whom Allan Ramsay had dedicated his *Gentle Shepherd* – had a brewery at Ayr.[30]

The other way was more fundamental. The massively increased levels of return in both profit and rent had been possible, not simply because of improvements in technique, but because of the extension and eventual domination of capitalist relations of production across the Lowlands. As Robin Blackburn writes: 'The simple amassing of wealth is a secondary aspect of "primitive accumulation", since capitalist industrialisation required an appropriate framework of institutions and production relations capable of converting wealth into capital.'[31] It was in the agricultural sector of the rural Lowlands that 'an appropriate framework of institutions and production relations' was first established in Scotland on a basis that could then be generalised throughout the economy, most importantly in the emergent manufacturing industries of the south-west. These relations involved, most importantly, dispossessing peasants of their land and transforming them into a workforce deprived of property and – although this took longer where they actually remained on the land – unencumbered by feudal constraints.

'A Different Class of Beings'

The Napoleonic Wars ended on 7 April 1814 with the abdication of Bonaparte. As the allied armies closed in on Paris at the opening of the year, *The Scots Magazine* of 1 February carried an advertisement for a novel entitled, *Waverley; Or, 'Tis Sixty Years Since*, which was to be published the following month.[32] Published anonymously, Walter Scott's first novel recounts the adventures of the eponymous hero during the '45. In a famous passage near the end of the novel the omnipresent narrator looks back from his vantage point in 1805 at the changes which had taken place in Scotland over the preceding 60 years:

> There is no European nation, which, within the course of half a century, or little more, has undergone so complete a change as this kingdom of Scotland. The effects of the insurrection of 1745, – the destruction of the patriarchal power of the Highland chiefs, the abolition of the heritable jurisdictions of the Lowland nobility and barons, – the total eradication of the Jacobite party, which, averse to intermingle with the English, or adopt their customs, long continued to pride themselves upon maintaining ancient Scottish manners and customs, – commenced this innovation. The gradual influx of wealth, and extension of commerce, have since united to render the present people of Scotland a class of beings as different from their grandfathers, as the existing English are from those of Queen Elizabeth's time.

The 1815 edition of *The Gentleman Farmer*, which we quoted above, extols both the extent of the transformation in agriculture and the speed with which it occurred. Scott generalises this across the whole of Lowland Scottish society. Yet only sentences later, as if terrified by this vision of the Promethean power of capitalism, Scott is emphasising the evolutionary nature of it all: 'But the change, though steadily and rapidly progressive, has, nevertheless, been gradual; and like those who drift down the stream of a deep and smooth river, we are not aware of the progress we have made until we fix our eye on the now distant point from which we have drifted.'[33] Here, within a single page of Chapter 93 ('A Postscript, Which Should Have Been A Preface'), the Enlightenment historian and the Tory politician who co-existed within Scott's consciousness are visibly at war. The former was right. The changes which had taken place in Scotland after 1746 amounted to the thing which Scott the Tory dreaded above all else – a social revolution, albeit a revolution from above.

As Scott was painfully aware, industrial capitalism did not come alone. The deeper pessimism which lies underneath the surface optimism of the famous passages from *Waverley* are a response to the changes which capitalism was bringing to Scottish society. At the beginning of 1820 he was consoling himself in a letter with this thought: 'The poor ARE to be trusted in almost every situation where they have not been disunited by circumstances from their natural superiors.' But as he goes on to say in the same letter, these circumstances of disunity were becoming the norm, as the very nature of industrial capitalism was undermining the sense of obligation which had supposedly regulated the attitude of feudal superiors to their tenants or even the relationship between master and man that had been a feature of manufacture before the coming of the factory.[34] In the spring of 1820, as the first general strike in history erupted along the western Central Belt, he extended his analysis: 'The unhappy dislocation which has taken place betwixt the Employer and those under his employment has been attended with very fatal consequences. Much of this is owing to the steam engine.' In the days when manufacture was dependent on the watermill the employer had no choice in his location, but had to recruit workmen from the nearest village and consequently spent time trying to influence their behaviour. 'This is now quite changed':

> The manufactures are transferred to great towns where a man may assemble 500 workmen one week and dismiss them the next without having any further connection with them than to receive a week's work for a week's wages nor any further solicitude about their future fate than if they were so many old shuttles. A superintendence of the workers considered as so many moral and rational beings is thus a matter totally unconnected with the Employer's usual thoughts and cares. They have now seen the danger of suffering a great population to be thus separated from the influence of their employers and given over to the management of their own societies in which the cleverest and most impudent fellows always get the management of the others and become bell-weathers in every sort of mischief.[35]

Scott was a Tory, yet his insight here is greater, his connection closer, to the great Enlightenment figures like Ferguson and Smith than most of his contemporary Whig opponents. He understood, as I think they did not, that the dialectic of history did not offer the conquering Scottish bourgeoisie an untroubled progress towards ever greater economic prosperity, but one fraught with contradiction and conflict. Only weeks before Scott wrote this letter, around 60,000 of those 'beings as different from their grandfathers, as the existing English are from those of Queen Elizabeth's time' struck in Paisley, Kilmarnock, Glasgow and all around the new Scotland of the industrialising south-west. It is not too paradoxical to say that the success of this most obscure, but in many ways most complete of the bourgeois revolutions, should be measured, not in terms of enlarged rent rolls, but by the speed and intensity with which it conjured up its own class nemesis.

Conclusion

I began this book by arguing that the decisive turning point in Scottish history did not occur in 1707, but across the entire historical period between 1692 and 1746, which I have characterised as the epoch of the Scottish bourgeois revolution. The Introduction dealt with the theoretical objections to such a characterisation. The Conclusion will look at another set of objections. These do not represent a failure to recognise the Revolution because of a deficient theoretical model, but rather a refusal to recognise it because the Revolution does not play the role expected as emotional centrepiece in a national tradition of popular radicalism.

The attitude of socialists to what Walter Benjamin called 'the tradition of the oppressed' is necessarily a complex one.[1] Eric Hobsbawm has questioned whether 'the search for ancestors' among pre-capitalist revolutionary movements has any relevance to modern revolutionaries:

> What precisely did or do modern Marxists gain from the knowledge that there were slave rebellions in ancient Rome which, even supposing their aims to have been communist, were by their own analysis doomed to failure or to produce results which could clearly have little bearing on the aspirations of modern communists?[2]

Hobsbawm is, however, being unnecessarily dismissive of what he calls the 'emotional satisfaction' the oppressed and exploited derive from belonging to a tradition of rebellion. Since the birth of the modern socialist and labour movement – to go no further back – men and women have felt the need to situate themselves within a tradition of popular revolt, including revolts from earlier historical periods which have no direct bearing on contemporary struggles. For Benjamin, both 'hatred' and the 'spirit of sacrifice' are necessary for the working class in 'the task of liberation in the name of generations of the downtrodden', for 'both are nourished by the image of enslaved ancestors rather than that of liberated grandchildren'.[3] The point was well made, in a Scottish context, by Lewis Grassic Gibbon, through his character Ewan Tavendale in *Grey Granite* (1935):

Passed in a minute, that flaming savage sickness, and you got to your feet and went on again: but the same everywhere, as though suddenly unblinded, picture on picture limned in dried blood, never painted or hung in an art gallery – pictures of the poor, folk since history began, bedevilled and murdered, trampled underfoot, trodden down in the bree, a human slime, hungered, unfed, with their darkened brains, their silly revenges, their infantile hopes – the men who built Munster's City of God and were hanged and burned in scores by the Church, the Spartacists, the blacks of Toussaint L'Ouverture, Parker's sailors who were hanged at Nore, the Broo men manhandled in Royal Mile. Pictures unceasingly of the men of your kin, peasants and slaves and common folk and their ghastly lives through six hundred years – oh hell, what had it to do with you?

And you bit your lip to keep something back, something that rose and slew coolness and judgement – steady, white-edged, a rising flame, anger bright as a clear bright flame, as though 'twas yourself that history had tortured on, trodden on, spat on, clubbed down in you, as though you were every scream and each wound, flesh of your flesh, blood of your blood.[4]

In Scotland supporters of the Radical movement between 1792 and 1820 honoured both William Wallace and the later Covenanters as forerunners, but they did not confine themselves to honouring figures from Scottish history, however, as is demonstrated by their evocation of near contemporary American and French revolutionaries, including Napoleon himself.[5] As a far from friendly witness, William Aiton, the Sheriff-Substitute at Hamilton, noted of the commemoration organised by the inhabitants of Strathhaven in June 1815, with all the contempt that he could muster for the classes to whom he represented the state:

And the proposal was no sooner known than it was highly approved by all the democratical people in that and neighbouring towns, whose hopes were much elevated by the return of Bonaparte from Elba to France. These people with the schoolboys, idlers and fools, turned out in a body, to 'celebrate the victory gained by the Covenanters over the King's troops at Drumclog, 1st June, 1679'. They went first to the place where the Covenanters defeated Claverhouse, and from thence to a cairn of stones or tumulus, on the farm of Allanton, Ayrshire, about two miles from the field of Drumclog, where they imagined Sir William Wallace had fought his first battle with the English.[6]

Almost as soon as the labour movement emerged from its initial insurrectionary phase, however, and entered that of institutionalised reformism, the notion of the tradition underwent a twofold metamorphosis, making it an impossible one for Marxists simply to celebrate. First, rather than one international tradition, to which different national movements made their own greater or lesser contributions, what began to be upheld was a series of discrete national traditions. The German revolutionaries of 1919 who called themselves the Spartacists were internationalists even down to their very name, but the dominant reformist wing of the socialist movement has always operated within the confines of the existing nation-state, in matters of historical legitimisation as much as in the search for political office. Second, and even more damaging than the nationalisation of the tradition, was its declassing. Instead of the successive struggles of slaves, peasants, artisans and workers against their respective ruling classes, variations arose of 'the People's Story', in which historical periodisations and the different class configurations present in each were suppressed in favour of an amorphous national populism. This has been true regardless of whether the reformists in question have adhered to the Second International or the Third International in its Stalinist phase.

The individual bourgeois revolutions are central to the resulting national populist traditions. For Scottish socialists, however, the Scottish Revolution cannot occupy the same place that comparable events do for socialists in England and France – or even socialists in Italy and the USA. On the one hand, unlike 1642 in England or 1792 in France, at no point in the Scottish Revolution were popular interventions decisive in shaping the outcome. The key turning points do not involve the revolutionary crowd storming Edinburgh Castle or a *levée en masse* overwhelming Royalist armies against all odds, but deals struck in snuff-filled rooms off Edinburgh High Street and Royal troops hunting down defeated peasants across Culloden Moor. On the other hand, unlike 1870 in Italy or 1871 in Germany, the end result was not the establishment of a modern nation-state, but the dismantling of its foundations and their absorption into a new state dominated by a historic enemy. Whichever way the matter is approached, both 'the people' and 'the nation' are absent, and such an absence tends to feed into one of two positions (although it is not unknown for individuals on the Scottish Left to hold them both simultaneously). These are not so much alternative interpretations of the period 1692–1746, however, as alternative histories – expressing how events should have resolved themselves as opposed to how they actually did. One position questions the necessity for the process of capitalist consolidation in Scotland to have taken the form that it did, particularly in respect of the Union, and looks instead for a more revolutionary alternative, which might have involved greater popular participation and produced a more democratic state (but unaccountably did neither).

The other position questions not the process but the outcome, throwing doubts on the very necessity of capitalism itself as a historical precondition for socialism.

A Revolutionary Alternative from Below?

According to Alan Armstrong, 'forward movement in history comes through the clashing of social forces'. Few Marxists would disagree with this somewhat diluted paraphrase of the opening sentence of *The Communist Manifesto*. Nor would they deny the relevance of his subsequent question: 'What have been the forces at work in Scotland and what policies have they adopted?' Doubts begin when Armstrong follows it with another which introduces a quite unnecessary and untenable assumption: 'In particular, what were the politics of the popular classes which could take the majority of people forward at a particular point in history?'[7] But what if the 'popular classes' in Scotland had neither the politics nor, more to the point, the structural capacity to take the nation forward between 1692 and 1746? In order to be any sort of socialist, it is necessary to know the history of the oppressed and exploited, and the circumstances in which they have struggled against successive ruling classes. For a Marxist, however, it is also necessary to situate these histories and struggles in their context in order to understand the material conditions which either allowed the oppressed and exploited to emerge victorious or which prevented them from so doing.

Let us revert briefly to the slave revolts referred to by Hobsbawm, before focusing on the more specific question of bourgeois revolution. Marx famously admired Spartacus, the leader of the greatest movement against the Roman slave empire, but he also repeatedly expressed his appreciation for Aristotle, a thinker who was both a beneficiary and a defender of Greek slave society. Jeffrey Vogel has suggested that this may be less of a contradiction than it first appears:

> ... Marx intends his praise for ... Spartacus to indicate the sort of historical values he acts on. But he also intends his admiration for ... Aristotle to indicate other values. ... Marx is 'on the side of' the oppressed in the sense that he traces his lineage back to Spartacus, an inspiring example. But this does not mean that Marx would support the victory of Spartacus at the cost of future human development, for which large-scale exploitation is indispensable.[8]

Marxists must therefore view history from a dual perspective: that of the toiling majority at all times, but also that of the classes whose role has been to force socio-economic development forwards. These have rarely been the same people. Indeed, only the working class under capitalism occupies both the first position and has the potential simultaneously to occupy the second.

Forerunners and Equivalents

It is while considering the bourgeois revolutions that a failure to distinguish between the agents of historical development and representatives of the oppressed is most disabling, for there are many cases in which the only forces capable of transforming society were not those with which contemporary socialists would wish to morally identify themselves. In England during 1640 or France during 1789, sections of the oppressed not only opposed the existing feudal exploiters, but also were themselves members of a new, if more economically advanced, exploiting class. The resulting dilemma for modern socialists is often expressed in disagreements over the most appropriate choice of revolutionary ancestry. Did the Independents take the English Revolution as far as possible? Or did they form an obstacle to even greater advances? Conversely, were the Levellers or Diggers the real radicals? Or were they mere utopians, whose ambitions, if implemented, might have prevented such gains as were achieved? Christopher Hill recounts a story that nicely expresses the problem:

> The dispute [over Cromwell] was summed up after a speech made not so long ago by an eminent Liberal member of the Cromwell Association. 'The question we must all ask ourselves,' he thundered as he reached his peroration, 'is, On which side would I have stood at Naseby'? 'Yes,' said a voice from the audience; 'and on which side would you have stood at Burford?'[9]

The paradox contained in this story – that Cromwell is 'progressive' in his victory over the Royalists at Naseby, but 'reactionary' in his victory over the Levellers at Burford – can be resolved, but only if we separate out two different sets of actors. Those who, like the Independents or the Jacobins, represented the revolutionary movements appropriate to their time (the bourgeois equivalents to modern socialists); and those, like the Levellers or – more to the point – the Diggers, who were nearer to socialist politics but incapable of realising their goals in their own lifetime (the plebeian forerunners of modern socialists). To recognise the achievements of Cromwell does not mean dismissing the Levellers or their equivalents in other revolutions. People can scarcely be expected to postpone fighting for their interests until the time is 'historically appropriate' – by which point they will more than likely be dead. And even though such struggles are defeated, they can leave a wealth of experience, a memory of self-activity, which can be brought into play in future struggles. Most importantly, however, popular interventions in pursuit of unrealisable goals have sometimes driven bourgeois revolutions farther than they would otherwise have gone and, indeed, produced the very outcomes that we know as historical fact today. As Engels noted of the English case:

> ... had it not been for that yeomanry and the plebeian element in the towns, the bourgeoisie would not have fought the matter out to the bitter end, and would never have brought Charles I to the scaffold. In order to secure even those conquests of the bourgeoisie that were ripe for gathering at the time, the revolution had to be carried considerably further – exactly as in 1793 in France and 1848 in Germany. This seems, in fact, to be one of the laws of evolution of bourgeois society.[10]

Yet to elevate the structure of what were in fact quite exceptional events into a 'law of evolution of bourgeois society', can prove profoundly misleading. This an example of what Gareth Stedman Jones calls:

> ... a quasi-Hegelian way of writing about revolutions, in which, by pushing the revolution to the left, the pressure of small producers unwittingly takes the 'bourgeois revolution' to its logical conclusion. Thus, by a formidable feat of ventriloquism, measures pushed through in the teeth of bitter opposition from the grande bourgeoisie become essential 'hallmarks' of the 'bourgeois revolution'.[11]

The result can prove profoundly misleading, as the Scottish experience convincingly demonstrates. The Cameronian sects are certainly the most plausible contenders for the role of the plebeians identified by Engels in respect of the English revolution. Armstrong, one of their most vociferous advocates, argues that:

> Without an understanding of the significance of the Cameronians and the potential for outcomes, other than 'The Glorious Revolution' Settlements from 1688–90, and the Act of Union, a proper understanding of subsequent Scottish and U.K. history is not possible. As long as the two alternatives appear to be the Whig and Jacobite, the Left (or more properly liberal) and the Right versions of Unionism, then Scotland's popular history will remain buried.[12]

There are two issues here. First, 'the significance of the Cameronians' is open to multiple interpretations. Lewis Grassic Gibbon has Ewan Tavendale say of those 'funny chaps the Covenanters' that 'he had always liked them – the advance guard of the common folk in those days, their God and their Covenant just formulae they hid the social rebellion in'.[13] But this was not the only tradition sustained through their example. The year after the publication of *Grey Granite*, Lewis Spence, a founding member of the National Party of Scotland, recalled another aspect of Covenanting ideology during an attack on Glasgow Corporation, the majority of whose members he denounced as 'pro-Irish and pro-Muscovite', for being 'aggressive and offensive to the Scottish minority' and for deliberately keeping the rates high in order to support the unemployed 'Irish' population: 'Yet with a supineness which ill becomes the seed of the Covenanters, it bows patiently before the ebullient and contemptuous alien.'[14] It should be clear from the evidence presented in this book that racist hatred of the Catholic Irish (and Scottish Highlanders) invoked by Lewis Spence is as much a part of the Covenanting inheritance as the disguised social rebellion identified by Ewan Tavendale.[15] This is as good an example as one might wish for of why modern socialists cannot uncritically lay claim to the history of pre-working-class radicalism.

Second, in spite of these problems, a properly contextualised view of the Cameronian sects might nevertheless still leave us with much to admire in their beliefs and actions – that is my own position – but it cannot, without massively distorting the evidence, confer upon them a significance which they did not possess. Elsewhere in the same article Armstrong asks: 'What is at Stake – a History to Take us Forward or Backwards?', and this indicates the nature of the problem.[16] For socialists, history is not – or at any rate, should not be – simply a source of consolatory myths or inspirational legends 'to take us forwards'. During some historical moments, of which the situation in Germany between 1918 and 1933 is perhaps the most important in the last century, decisive alternatives have been possible. But to pretend that this is always the case, to imagine that every situation always contains potential 'other outcomes' of a more radical nature, is not only to ignore the material constraints under which actors at the time had to make history, but to abandon history altogether for the realms of the 'useful myth'.

The purpose of historical writing is not to provide inspiration or consolation, but understanding. History is not therapy. If your purpose is primarily to provide the latter, then it is likely that the historiography you produce will distort reality in order to produce the necessary effect. I noted above the importance of recognising the alternative courses of action available to historical actors. The existence of alternatives does not mean, however, that all of them were equally capable of realisation. The Treaty of Union was not inevitable, but the alternatives were either the domination of Scotland (and the British Isles as a whole) by French absolutism or the colonial subjugation of Scotland to England on the model of Ireland, not the re-emergence of an independent Scottish kingdom or the establishment of a republic of smallholding peasants and artisans. If there is one approach which causes even more distortions than the worship of the established fact, it is to imagine that our own preferred historical outcomes were feasible no matter what the weight of material circumstances.

It is worth noting, in this connection, that in England during the 1640s, the Levellers – whose members represented numerically significant sections of the petty bourgeoisie, whose organisation had roots in both the army and urban society, and whose beliefs were relatively unencumbered by religious ideology – were nevertheless unable to move the English Revolution to a more democratic conclusion. Yet we are expected to believe that the Cameronian sects, who had none of these advantages, could have done precisely this in the considerably more backward conditions of Scotland. Here we see the difficulties of a 'national' approach to the tradition of struggle: not all nations have an equivalent to the Levellers in their history. Many do not even have equivalents to the Independents. The 'bourgeois equivalents' of the Scottish Revolution, with a handful of ambiguous exceptions like Fletcher of Saltoun and Forbes of Culloden, are not individuals who invite inclusion in the pantheon alongside Cromwell or Robespierre. The point was well made by the Scottish Radical James Callender in 1792, while comparing the Glorious Revolution of 1688 with the French Revolution of 1789:

Does anybody compare the packed convention Parliaments of the two kingdoms, in 1689, with the democratical members of the first national assembly of France? As well we might parallel Charles Jenkinson with the Duke of Sully, or the assassin of Culloden with the conqueror at Bannockburn.[17]

At one level Callender was right: the comparison is absurd. Yet at another level there is no doubt that the activities of the tenth Earl of Argyll and 'the assassin of Culloden' were – no doubt unintentionally – far more important in the destruction of feudal Scotland than any potential 'socialist forerunners' of the period. Indeed, it might be argued that bourgeois revolutions are more typically represented by figures like the Duke of Cumberland than by Cromwell, Lincoln or even – in our context – Fletcher of Saltoun. For, as I have argued throughout this book, the majority of bourgeois revolutions have, in fact, involved change which was forcibly imposed from above rather than seized from below: 'The "Bismarckian" path was not the exception for the bourgeoisie, but the rule, the exception was the French revolution.'[18] Ultimately, no bourgeois revolution can simply be absorbed into a socialist tradition of struggle, no matter how much popular intervention was involved, because the very nature of the process is ultimately to establish another, albeit more economically and culturally advanced, ruling class. As Walter Makey expressed the point, in the closing sentence of his great work, *The Church of the Covenant*: 'The castle gave way, not to the cowshed, but to the mansion.'[19]

Culloden, the Highland Clearances and Capitalist Development

There is a second argument, however, which is not so much concerned with identifying a failed revolution from below as with opposing the outcome of the successful revolution from above. Many Scots see the Highland Clearances – rightly, in my opinion – as a historical crime. But, since these events could not have taken place without the changes to the Scottish ruling class that followed Culloden, there is an associated tendency, which I do not share, to regard as obscene any notion that the Hanoverian victory at Culloden was progressive. James Young has expressed the dominant structure of feeling on the Scottish Left towards the subject: 'How can Marxists argue that the extermination of the Scottish Highlanders was necessary for the growth of capitalism, and yet morally criticise the historical actors who brought this about?'[20] The question is deliberately formulated so as to conflate two separate if related issues. Does 'extermination' refer to the killings during and immediately after Culloden? Or to the long process of clearance which did not enter the phase of forcible eviction until the following century? Let us deal with the question of Culloden first.

The 'progressiveness' of the Hanoverian victory does not lie in the fact that 'the extermination of the Scottish Highlanders was necessary for the growth of capitalism', but in the fact that it destroyed the social basis of the counter-revolution in Britain and thus prevented a reversal of such capitalist development as had already taken place. Even then, the repression levelled at the Jacobites directly after Culloden was less important to this process than the subsequent legislative enactments against their leaders. Could the destruction of Scottish feudalism not have taken place without the former? Theoretically perhaps, but given the attitudes of the men who were responsible for the practical suppression of the rising, particularly their ideological need to find an 'other' upon whom revenge could be extracted, I think this extremely unlikely. The tragedy of the Union of 1707 is therefore revealed, not as the loss of Scottish sovereignty, but the failure to destroy Scottish feudalism in time for the people most oppressed by it to experience that destruction as liberation. When the long-postponed settling of accounts did take place, it was the oppressed themselves who were handed the bill and many of them paid it with their lives.

Ray Burnett has attempted to situate the events during and after the battle of Culloden within the history of imperialism on a global scale, arguing that their uniqueness lies only in that they occurred on the British mainland:

Within the historical time referral points of global 'development', the cultural genocide, state terror, and ethnic cleansing and displacement of the post-Culloden Gaidhealtachd have a resonant continuity right into the present. In this framework, the '45, Culloden and its aftermath are more usefully perceived in a matrix of wider co-ordinates which would extend from Drogheda to Amritsar, Wounded Knee to Mai Lai, Srebrenica to the 'French' Pacific.[21]

There is much truth in these observations, but in the context of this discussion the key issue is not the one with which Burnett is concerned – the similarity between events during and after Culloden and later acts of imperialist brutality – but the relationship between the bourgeois revolutions and the events he lists. The English Revolution cannot be separated from the massacre at Drogheda. The French Revolution cannot be disassociated from the slaughter of the Chuans. The American Revolution cannot be cordoned off from the genocide committed against the Native Americans. The Scottish Revolution cannot be envisaged without the aftermath of Culloden. These events are the other side of the coin to the popular insurgencies that characterised the first cycle of bourgeois revolutions. Given the type of exploitative system that capitalism is, however, could we expect it to have come into being in any other way than, as Marx put it, 'dripping from head to toe, from every pore, with blood and dirt'?[22]

The Place of the Highland Clearances in the Scottish Revolution

But what of the Clearances? Were they also a necessary part of the bourgeois revolution? Let us return to the question asked by Young in this context, rather than that of Culloden itself: 'How can Marxists argue that the extermination of the Scottish Highlanders was necessary for the growth of capitalism, and yet morally criticise the historical actors who brought this about?' The term 'extermination' is not accidental, but betrays a calculated ambiguity also present in the expression 'cultural genocide' used by Burnett. How appropriate is it? The comparison between the Clearances and the Holocaust is, perhaps understandably, one which inhabitants of the Highlands themselves are sometimes tempted to use. During his pursuit of the Highland diaspora David Craig encountered one woman on Barra who described the local Clearances in precisely these terms:

Morag MacAuley likened the forced exodus from Barra and South Uist to 'when they shipped off the Jews' and cited a television treatment of that, presumably the American series *Holocaust*, although paradoxically she felt the Nazi genocide – so much worse than the Scottish – had been made too much of.[23]

The implied anti-Semitism of these remarks is disturbing enough; for our purposes, however, I wish to concentrate on the fact that Craig can only concede that the Jewish experience was 'so much worse' than that of the Highlanders, rather than one qualitatively different in kind.[24] Craig is a more serious historian than Young, but the rhetoric of genocide which both employ in this context is profoundly inappropriate, to say the least. Near to the examples of slavery and genocide lie such events as the Irish potato famine of the 1840s; but it should be clear after this recitation that the Highland Clearances, while unquestionably examples of the exploitation and oppression attendant on capitalist development, were historical events of a different order. Nothing like the Irish famine, let alone these other examples, took place in Scotland. The rhetoric of genocide and extermination forces those who disagree with it into the distasteful business of trying to establish a scale of human social catastrophe, as I have done here; but even more seriously, the exaggerated parallels involved can have one of two profoundly damaging effects on historical understanding. First, they diminish the specific horrors associated with the conquest of the Americas, New World slavery and the Holocaust, by associating them with others which, however illustrative they are of the sufferings imposed by capitalist development, do not fall within the limits of any objective comparison. Second, they produce precisely the opposite impact from that intended, and diminish instead the impact of the Clearances. Since they cannot realistically be compared with the catastrophes inflicted on Native Americans, African slaves, European Jews or Irish peasants, the suspicion is likely to remain, at least among those ignorant of what took place, that the reality of the Clearances might be less than it actually was.[25]

There is, however, another problem with what Young writes, not so much concerned with exaggerating the suffering involved in the Clearances as with misinterpreting their significance. He is not alone in doing so. Christopher Harvie, for example, writes: 'Marx violently attacked the Sutherland clearances in *Capital*, vol. II, but the Duke only seemed to be carrying out his own prescription.'[26] Leaving aside the fact that Harvie will search in vain for any reference to the Scottish Highlands in Volume 2 of *Capital*, the fact is that Marx did not regard the Clearances as, in the words of James Young, 'necessary for the growth of capitalism'. Many socialists, particularly outside Scotland, take their view of the Clearances from the discussion in Chapter 27 of *Capital* Volume 1, 'The Expropriation of the Agricultural Population From the Land', where Marx demonstrates how the expulsion of the rural population from their holdings, the enclosing of common land and the turning over of arable land to pasture were crucial components of the 'primitive accumulation of capital'.[27] The process described so eloquently by Marx is characteristic of the origins of capitalism; indeed, he traces it in England back to the period after the Tudor accession in 1485, then asks the reader to observe the 'clearing of estates' in action in the Highlands of Scotland, 'the promised land of modern romantic novels'.[28] Reading about the Clearances in this context, many socialists have assumed that they were equally necessary for the establishment of capitalism and, indeed, were the last episode of the process in Britain, although certainly not in the world as a whole. James Holstun has argued that the term usually translated as 'primitive accumulation' – *ursprüngliche Akkumulation* – should in fact be rendered as 'original division' or 'expropriation' or just plain 'theft', in order to better emphasise what Marx intended the phrase to mean.[29] Yet his own use of the term contradicts this usage. Hulston sees the 'original theft' taking place wherever agrarian natural economies are being destroyed by capitalist development, from St George's Hill in Buckinghamshire during the 1640s to the Brazilian rainforest 350 years later: 'A single "phase" like capitalist primitive Accumulation may recur as agrarian accumulation again and again in different places.'[30] Naturally this includes the Highlands:

> In Scotland, the disruption of traditional agriculture by improving enclosure did not reach its height until the Highland Clearances of the eighteenth or nineteenth centuries. They disrupted the patriarchal economies of the clans, as scientific improvers from England or the Lowlands worked with Highland nobility and landowners to evict crofters and convert their communal smallholdings into pasture and deer parks.[31]

Such assumptions quite unnecessarily provide Scottish nationalists such as Young and Harvie with a licence to accuse Marxists of apologetics, retrospectively endorsing the Clearances in the name of historical progress, and thus supposedly exposing their authoritarian or even totalitarian propensities. Even if the Clearances had been necessary for capitalist development, the solidarity of socialists would still be with the dispossessed peasants rather than with their oppressors, but the Clearances in fact had nothing whatsoever to do with the primitive accumulation of capital: the entire argument is based on a misunderstanding.

The introduction of capitalist agriculture was so long delayed in the Highlands that the process was concentrated into a much shorter timescale than the original English pattern of enclosure and eviction. Consequently, as Marx noted, 'the clearing of the land proceeded more ruthlessly'.[32] Not only did the Highland Clearances have a different duration from that of, say, East Anglia, they also took place at a different time in the historical development of capitalism. The Highland Clearances are conventionally dated between 1760 and 1860, but the vast bulk of the enforced migrations fell within the latter half of this period and the outrages which accompanied them were being closely reported, particularly as the process reached its climax in the 1850s.[33] The newspapers during the period in which *Capital* was written seemed to show Marx what he had previously only observed in the writings of Sir Thomas More or Sir James Steuart. By the time the Clearances were taking place – and certainly by the second phase of clearance – capitalism was absolutely dominant throughout Britain and the working-class movement had begun to organise against it. While soldiers were helping expel tenants from their homes in Ross-shire during 1848, considerably greater numbers of them were mustering in Edinburgh to repel the Chartist challenge. If there is a parallel to the English 'primitive accumulation' in Scotland it is not to be found in the Highlands, but in the transformation of the Lowlands between 1750 and 1780. The Highlands, far from being crucial to the development of British capitalism in any economic sense, were peripheral to it, which is where they remain to this day.[34]

What Marx was actually doing in *Capital*, apart from expressing his own moral revulsion at the Clearances, was drawing an analogy between the events then taking place in the Highlands and the original process of primitive accumulation, as if to say to his readers: 'If you want to see what the process was like, this is the nearest parallel in the contemporary world.' But clearing the land of people in the first half of the nineteenth century had different implications from doing so in the sixteenth, seventeenth or eighteenth centuries. An existing, and thoroughly rapacious, capitalist landowning class seeking to increase their income as efficiently as possible carried out the Highland Clearances. Far from being 'necessary' to the development of capitalism, the Highland Clearances were an example of an already triumphant capitalist class whose disregard for human life (and, indeed, 'development') marked it as having long passed the stage of contributing to social progress. Precisely because these events were not a consequence of the transition to capitalism, but of its established laws of motion, the successful displacement of the Highlanders should not be seen as inevitable, but as an unnecessary political defeat. This failure did not reflect a continuation of the semi-racial hatreds which manifested themselves during and immediately after the '45. As I have tried to demonstrate elsewhere, the Highlanders were accepted as members of the Scottish and British nations by no later than 1815, as the different state responses to the Irish and Highland famines of the 1840s prove.[35] Relations between the Lowland workers and Highland peasants (i.e. those who had not become proleterianised after migrating to the Lowlands) might be compared to the relations between Northern Italian workers and Southern Italian peasants after the First World War, when Gramsci wrote of the former that 'in order to win the trust and consent of the peasants and of some semi-proletarian urban categories' they needed 'to overcome certain prejudices and conquer certain forms of egoism which can and do subsist within the working class'.[36] Nevertheless, the issue also raises a more general question. Has capitalism, whose world dominance the Scottish Revolution did so much to ensure, been worth the blood it cost to bring it into being?

Documents of Civilisation and Barbarism

The notion that capitalism was unnecessary for development has enjoyed a degree of popularity among radicals, but it is important to understand the implications of this position. The theory of uneven and combined development has certain political implications in the imperialist epoch of capitalist development which began in the last quarter of the nineteenth century. Broadly these are that states in the underdeveloped world can, given certain conditions, overleap the stage of capitalist development to that of socialism. Two of these conditions were that a world capitalist economy already existed and that, through participation in this economy, a working class had been brought into being in the underdeveloped world which could act as the agent of revolutionary change.[37] This is not what the aforementioned radicals are proposing. Far from the dominance of the capitalist mode of production being a necessary precondition for socialism at the international level, the entire capitalist system, from its genesis in Europe during the sixteenth century, is said to have acted as what Immanuel Wallerstein calls a 'virus', infecting other – presumably healthy – societies and preventing them developing in alternatives ways.[38] I regard this view as being profoundly mistaken, but for the purposes of this argument, the point is that it is impossible for Marxists to accept.[39] The expansion of the productive forces brought about by capitalism has been a necessary but insufficient condition for the ultimate goal of human emancipation. Necessary, because without it there will be neither a working class to seize power from the capitalists nor a sufficient level of material resources with which to feed, cloth, house or educate the world's population. Insufficient, because unless the working class is conscious and organised it will not succeed in achieving its revolutionary potential. But the objective situation (the existence of capitalism) precedes the subjective (the conscious mobilisation of the social classes which capitalism has brought into being).

The issue, for socialists at any rate, is therefore whether or not they believe that capitalism is a necessary stage in the development of society, at least for the nations like Scotland which were among the first to break with feudalism, or whether capitalism and its attendant evils might have been avoided altogether. Armstrong has suggested that it might, offering as one of his alternative futures an alliance between the English Levellers and Irish and Scottish 'clan democracy' in order to circumvent 'the Western European pattern of capitalist development'.[40] Young has gone even further, suggesting that even feudalism might have been preferable to capitalism: 'Poverty is inherent in capitalist societies without the caring and sharing of, say, medieval Scotland.'[41] Against such imaginary alternatives or outright fantasies, it is important to restate the Marxist position in its full complexity, as has been done by Jeffrey Vogel:

> Marxist historical theory emphasises the sobering fact about human society hitherto: that all cultural and material progress for the few, all achievements in art, science, industry and culture, have all been the direct result of the misery, degradation, oppression and enslavement of the many. Without ancient slavery, no Aristotle, no Assembly, no Academy. And most importantly, and closest to our own concerns, without the development of modern industry, which crushes children 'beneath the wheels of the juggernaut of capital' we would lack the material basis and the social agent able to achieve a fully human social order under communism.[42]

This is precisely why Marxists regard the development of human society as a tragic process, and not one identifiable with facile notions of 'progress', since we are aware of the price at which progress has been purchased. The point has been best made by Walter Benjamin:

> Whoever has emerged victorious participates to this day in the triumphal procession in which our present rulers step over those who are lying prostrate. According to traditional practice, the spoils are carried along in the procession. They are called cultural treasures, and a historical materialist views them with cautious detachment. For without exception the cultural treasures he surveys have an origin he cannot contemplate without horror. They owe their existence not only to the efforts of the great minds and talents who have created them, but also to the anonymous toil of their contemporaries. There is no document of civilisation which is not at the same time a document of barbarism.[43]

Benjamin speaks here of 'cultural treasures' and this is of special relevance to our subject, since the victory of the Scottish Revolution made possible, in the form of the Scottish Enlightenment, some of the greatest 'treasures' in the history of bourgeois civilisation. In this respect, the Scottish Revolution, far from being exceptional, merely represents, in a more extreme form, the contradictions present in all bourgeois revolutions. One objective of the socialist future – by no means the most important one – will be to make these 'cultural treasures' available to those currently condemned to 'anonymous toil'. For Marxists do not see history as a tragedy without end, but as a period which can be relegated to prehistory if and when human beings succeed in taking democratic control over their world.

This is perhaps the note upon which it is appropriate to end. The Scottish Revolution took a particular form that makes it difficult to celebrate it as part of a revolutionary tradition. It seems to me mistaken to argue that it could have been different – since the alternatives did not exist – and pointless to argue that it should have been different – since this presupposes a normative model of revolutionary development wholly at odds with the actual historical record. The completion of the Scottish Revolution was, at the same time, the completion of the British Revolution. The formation of the Scottish working class was, at the same time, part of the formation of the British working class. These facts make it unlikely, whatever the nature of any subsequent constitutional changes, that there will ever be a second, proletarian Scottish Revolution separate from one in Britain as a whole. Whether or not the Scottish working class will eventually participate in such an event is still an open question. If it does, we can be certain of one thing: the revolution that it helps to make will necessarily be quite unlike the one that brought it into existence, whose history we now draw to a close.

Appendix

Marx and Engels on Scotland

I noted in the Preface that this work would be based on an application of the Marxist method to Scottish history, not an elaboration of any actual analysis Marx and Engels made of that history. This approach is unavoidable, since they made only passing references to Scotland in their work, and these are by no means always accurate. Nevertheless, the various comments that they made on Scotland can be usefully grouped together into one of four contexts.[1]

British Capitalism

The first context was their work on the development of capitalism in their adopted country. Marx and Engels were always careful to include data from Scotland. But whether discussing the nature of the British social formation from the point of view of the working class, or using it as an example of the operation of the capitalist mode of production in general, they considered Scotland as a region, or series of regions, rather than as a nation. Since the national question in Scotland was to remain largely submerged until the formation of the Scottish Home Rule Association in 1886, two years after Marx died, this does not indicate any great insensitivity on their part to the issue.

The exact moment after 1707 at which there ceased to be distinct Scottish and English economies is debatable, but Marx and Engels were clearly right to assume that it had certainly been reached by the mid-nineteenth century. Indeed, a measure of their sensitivity to national differences can be taken from the fact that their writings mark the very moment when the elimination of any residual economic distinctiveness was completed: the 1845 Bank Act that brought the Scottish system into conformity with that of England.[2]

Political Economy and the Scottish Enlightenment

The second context was their critique of the founders of political economy. This was one of the two great intellectual disciplines to emerge from the Scottish Enlightenment (the other being what we now call sociology – although the two were by no means conceptually distinct at the time of their appearance). It is not surprising, therefore, that in what was to prove a lifelong engagement, Marx should return again and again to the works of Sir James Steuart, Adam Smith and their contemporaries.

His interest was by no means confined to these figures from the vanguard of the Enlightenment. Marx thought highly of James Anderson as a theorist, for example, designating him as 'the true discoverer of the modern theory of rent'.[3] He was also aware that the experience of their native country had contributed to the theoretical perspectives of such men. He writes of Steuart, for example, that 'He is particularly interested in the difference between bourgeois and feudal labour, having observed the latter in the stage of its decline in both Scotland and during his extensive journeys on the continent.'[4] This reference is typical, however, in that Scotland features only in so far as it is mentioned by the writers Marx is discussing, that is to say through their writings and not as a subject in its own right. Indeed, where Marx used this aspect of their work as a historical source, rather than as material illustrative of a theoretical position, he was sometimes inclined to treat it too uncritically. One example of this is his repetition of Andrew Fletcher's claim that there were 200,000 beggars in Scotland by 1698, without pausing to consider how Fletcher arrived at a figure which amounted to one fifth of the population. Marx wrote:

> Fletcher of Saltoun declared as late as 1698, in the Scottish Parliament, 'The number of beggars in Scotland is reckoned at not less than 200,000. The only remedy that I, a republican on principle, can suggest, is to restore the old estate of serfdom, to make slaves of all those who are unable to provide for their own subsistence.'[5]

Fletcher was not a commissioner in the Scottish Parliament in 1698, nor did any of his published speeches after election in 1703 refer to this issue. Marx, who was usually scrupulous in such matters, does not give a reference for the quotation, and it may be that he was relying on a summary of the 'Two Discourses Concerning the Affairs of Scotland' and associated this with the speeches subsequently made by Fletcher in Parliament. In any event, I have been unable to trace the quotation, which certainly does not sound like Fletcher. Unfortunately, it is still common to meet Scottish socialists whose sole knowledge of Fletcher derives from this erroneous footnote to *Capital*, and who consequently have the impression that his entire Parliamentary career was taken up with advocating the reintroduction of serfdom, or even slavery.

The Scottish Reformation

The third context is the discussion by Engels of the political and social implications of the Reformation: 'While German Lutheranism became a willing tool in the hands of princes, Calvinism formed a republic in Holland and active Republican parties in England and, above all, Scotland.'[6] Engels' belief that Scotland was one of the principal bases of militant Protestantism is, unlike the neutral references we have quoted so far, a verdict on the political significance of a moment in Scottish history. Unfortunately, his views were expressed in three brief references – one of which remained unpublished during his lifetime – which although suggestive, scarcely amount to a fully developed argument. It would in any event be necessary to disagree with his overestimation of the radical impulses within the Scottish Reformation.

In an unpublished draft which he planned to add to the original text of *The Peasant War in Germany*, Engels described the Reformation as 'the No. 1 bourgeois revolution' which had 'triumphed in Switzerland, Holland, Scotland, England, and to a certain extent, in Sweden (under Gustavus Vasa) and Denmark – here in its orthodox, absolutist form only in 1660'.[7] Even if we accept that the boundaries of the Reformation can be stretched to 1660, this judgement is questionable for both Sweden and Denmark, in addition to Scotland. In fact, the social content of the Reformation in Scotland was remarkably similar to that in Germany, a fact that points to the limited usefulness of the distinction that he draws between Lutheranism and Calvinism. In both cases the nobility saw the new faith as a political weapon with which to break from a temporal power linked to the Catholic Church: in Scotland, that temporal power was the French crown; in the German lands, it was the Holy Roman Empire.

The Constitutional Form of the British State

The fourth and final context is a solitary observation by Engels on the constitutional form of the British state, which does not contain any specific references to Scotland. The supposed significance of this observation has nevertheless been endorsed by James Young in characteristic terms: 'In contrast to auld Freddy Engels who supported the agitation for a Scottish parliament towards the end of his life, most "Marxists" in Scotland simply do not understand the Scottish national question.'[8] This might lead the reader to suppose that Engels had actually made an explicit statement in support of what was then called – from an analogy with current Irish demands – 'Home Rule'. In fact, Engels did no such thing: this is a classic example of what the late Hal Draper variously called 'Marxolalia' or 'Marxophasia' – 'the propensity to garble Marx', or, in this case, Engels.[9]

In *The State and Revolution* Lenin commends a passage by Engels which discusses the most appropriate form of state from the point of view of the working class. Lenin writes: 'He [i.e. Engels] regarded the federal republic either as an exception and a hindrance to development, or as a transition from a monarchy to a centralised republic, as a "step forward" under certain special conditions.' As we shall see, this much is an accurate summary of part of Engels' argument; but then Lenin goes off at a tangent. Starting from the correct assumption that one of these 'special conditions' is the national question, he then moves to the following assertion:

> Even in Britain, where geographical conditions, a common language, and the history of many centuries would seem to have 'put an end' to the national question in the various *small divisions* of that country – even in regard to that country, Engels reckoned with the plain fact that the national question was not yet a thing of the past, and recognised that the establishment of a federal republic would be a 'step forward'.

Following these remarks Lenin returns to the main thrust of his argument: 'Of course, there is not the slightest hint here of Engels abandoning the criticism of the shortcomings of a federal republic or renouncing the most determined advocacy of, and struggle for, a unified and centralised democratic republic.'[10] The digression may have been inspired by a desire to assert the political significance of national self-determination against the position of leading figures on the revolutionary left like Pannekoek and Luxemburg who believed the issue was no longer relevant. Earlier, Lenin had written:

> Engels, like Marx, never betrayed the slightest desire to brush aside the national question – a desire of which the Dutch and Polish Marxists, who proceed from their perfectly justified opposition to the narrow philistine nationalism of 'their' little states, are often guilty.[11]

In any event, this has nothing to do with the passage by Engels that Lenin is discussing. It comes from a letter to Karl Kautsky dated 29 June 1891, unpublished during Engels' lifetime, criticising the draft programme (the 'Erfurt Programme') of the German Social Democratic Party. Here is what the passage says in full, with the section on Britain italicised:

> In my view, the proletariat can only use the form of the one and indivisible republic. In the gigantic territory of the United States, a

federal republic is still, on the whole, a necessity, although in the eastern states it is already becoming a hindrance. *It would be a step forward in Britain where the two islands are peopled by four nations and in spite of a single Parliament three different systems of legislation already exist side by side.*

Engels goes on to point out that federalism has held back development in Switzerland and would be retrogressive in the newly unified Germany. He then goes on to distinguish between a 'union' state [i.e. Britain] and a 'unified' state:

... first, that each member [of a 'union'] state, each canton, has its own civil and criminal legislature and judicial system, and, second, that alongside a popular chamber there is a federal chamber in which each canton, whether large or small, votes as such. The first we [i.e. the Germans] have luckily overcome and we shall not be so childish as to re-introduce it, the second we have in the Bundesrat and we could very well do without it, since our 'federal state' generally constitutes a transition to a unified state. So, then, a unified republic.[12]

The argument stresses the superiority of a 'unified' state over even the federal republic that Engels recommends for Britain. Contrary to what Lenin argues, the central issue for Engels here is not the national question, but the question of which form of the bourgeois state is most useful to the proletariat in its struggle for power. How these remarks can be taken to justify saying that 'auld Freddy' was in favour of Scottish Home Rule, or even an independent Scotland, is a complete mystery, yet the passage is frequently cited to support this very proposition by people who appear not to have read the passage itself, but only Lenin's gloss on it – even though Lenin quotes the passage in full so that his own additions to the argument are quite apparent.[13]

Bibliographical Essay

The purpose of this bibliography is to identify the most useful secondary works for the general reader interested in finding out more about Scottish history for the period discussed in this book. In theoretical terms, the concept of 'bourgeois revolution' around which it is constructed is best explained by Alex Callinicos in 'Bourgeois Revolutions and Historical Materialism', *International Socialism*, Second Series 43, Summer 1989. An essay by Perry Anderson, 'The Notion of a Bourgeois Revolution', *English Questions*, London and New York, 1992, is also useful.

Marxist attempts to trace the overall pattern of Scottish development are few and far between; the most ambitious is the collective effort edited by Tony Dickson and titled *Scottish Capitalism*, London, 1980. This work was produced within the ambit of the Communist Party of Great Britain (as it then was), but essentially reproduces many of the themes of orthodox bourgeois historiography with a left gloss. Chapter 2 is the most relevant, but I radically disagree with its conclusions. A ferocious Trotskyist critique can be found in George Kerevan, 'The Origins of Scottish Nationhood: Arguments Within Scottish Marxism', *The Bulletin of Scottish Politics*, vol. 1, no. 2, Spring 1981. Unfortunately, Kerevan never developed the alternative sketched out in this review and is unlikely to now, given his current role as purveyor of free-market Scottish nationalism. An essay by Tom Nairn, 'Scotland and Europe', first published in *New Left Review* during 1973 and subsequently incorporated into *The Break-Up of Britain*, London, 1977 and 1981, remains a stimulating attempt to place Scotland within the trajectory of European development as a whole, although Nairn accepts the views of the Scottish Enlightenment historians on their own nation too uncritically.

The best narratives of the failed revolution between 1637 and 1651 can be found in two books by David Stevenson, *The Scottish Revolution, 1637–1644*, Newton Abbot, 1973 and *Revolution and Counter-revolution in Scotland, 1644–1651*, London, 1977, both unfortunately out of print.

They should be supplemented with a collection of his essays covering the period as a whole, *Union, Revolution and Religion in Seventeenth Century Scotland*, Aldershot and Brookfield, 1997. For analysis of these decades, however, the key work is Walter Makey, *The Church of the Covenants, 1637–1651*, Edinburgh, 1979, which is simply one of the greatest works of Scottish history to have been written in the twentieth century.

For a general background to Scottish development overall during the period from 1688 to 1746, the two most accessible works are Rosalind Mitchison, *Lordship to Patronage*, London, 1983, Chapters 5–8 and Michael Lynch, *Scotland: A New History*, London, 1991, Part 4, which synthesise much of the best recent research. Ian Whyte performs a similar service more specifically for social and economic history in *Scotland Before the Industrial Revolution*, Harlow, 1995, Chapters 7–17. Despite all the progress in these fields of study during recent years, Christopher Smout, *A History of the Scottish People*, London, 1969, is unlikely ever to be completely superseded, although Christopher Whatley, *Scottish Society 1707–1830*, Manchester, 2000, comes as near as anyone has come yet. In *Scotland's Relations with England*, Edinburgh, 1977 and 1994, William Ferguson conducts a brilliant polemic against most historiography of the subject prior to his own, with particular reference to those interpretations of the Union which see it as inevitable. The Scottish place within the early British state-nation is discussed in Linda Colley, *Britons*, 1992, although the class struggles of the time are not high on her list of priorities. A work which gives proper emphasis to Scotland's role within the early British Empire is Angus Calder, *Revolutionary Empire*, London, 1977 and 1998, a vastly underrated work now available in a paperback edition abridged by the author.

There is no entirely satisfactory discussion of the place of the Highlands in Scottish history, but a helpful discussion for the period before 1688 can be found in the first and last chapters of David Stevenson, *Alasdair MacColla and the Highland Problem in the Seventeenth Century*, Edinburgh, 1980 and 1994, the second edition available under the appalling title of *Highland Warrior*, which MacColla was not. Allan MacInnes, *Clanship, Commerce and the House of Stuart, 1603–1788*, East Linton, 1996, incorporates important material from his earlier essays, many of which I found useful in writing this book. I disagree with both these authors as to the extent to which feudalism was the dominant economic system in the Highlands, but this is as much a disagreement over the nature of feudalism as it is over the Highlands.

Although it too is primarily concerned with the Highlands, the best book on the broader aspects of the Revolution of 1688 is Paul Hopkins, *Glencoe and the End of the Highland War*, Edinburgh, 1986 and 1998. I have dealt with the crucial domestic impact of the Darien expeditions, rather than dwelling on the story of the short-lived colonies that ensued, but for the latter, John Prebble, *The Darien Disaster*, London, 1968 and (as *Darien*) 2000, is both the fullest account and his best book – largely because it does not deal with the Highlands. For all his passionate concern for the fate of the Gaelic-speaking population, few modern writers have done as much as Prebble to perpetuate the myth of that region as one completely distinct from the rest of Scotland. Against this, however, it must also be said that Prebble has also done more to bring the history of the Scots to their attention than any of the academic writers who regularly used to be condescending towards him in the pages of the *Scottish Historical Review*.

The Treaty of Union, to which events at Darien contributed so much impetus, is the single most controversial issue in Scottish history. Chapters 10–14 of Ferguson, *Scotland's Relations with England*, provide a partisan but compelling guide to the sequence of events and a critique of the main pre-1977 interpretations. Another Scottish nationalist inter-pretation can be found in Paul Scott's useful, if sometimes misleading biography of one of the main protagonists, *Andrew Fletcher and the Treaty of Union*, Edinburgh, 1992. The most recent survey of the issues, and itself a valuable contribution to the debate, is Christopher Whatley, '*Bought and Sold for English Gold?*', Glasgow, 1995 and 2001.

The best introduction to Jacobitism is Bruce Lenman, *The Jacobite Risings in Britain 1688–1746*, London, 1980, which despite its title, is actually a history of Scotland for the relevant period refracted through the prism of Jacobitism. The international context and much else besides is discussed in Daniel Szechi, *The Jacobites*, Manchester, 1994. For the '45, two useful works are Jeremy Black, *Culloden and the '45*, London, 1990 – which is particularly good on the military aspects – and A. J. Youngson, *The Prince and the Pretender*, Edinburgh, 1985 and 1996. Youngson attempts a historical experiment by giving two separate accounts from the opposing Hanoverian and Jacobite viewpoints, his point being that an equally convincing case can be made for either. For this reader, however, what his extremely skilful presentation does is to reveal the inadequacies of the Jacobite position. One of the most powerful representations of events during and immediately after Culloden is not a written work at all, but the BBC drama-documentary *Culloden*, 1964, scripted by Prebble from his own book and directed by Peter Watkins. This masterpiece, which is available on video and DVD, manages both to present the complexity of the issues involved and to convey, in human terms, the suffering of the people whose lives were destroyed by the Hanoverian victory. Apart from Watkins' film, the best modern attempt to deal with the significance of the '45 in artistic terms is the two minutes and 29 seconds of Michael Marra's great song, 'Mincing Wi' Chairlhi', which can be found on *Gael's Blue*, ECL CD 9206, 1992.

Thomas Devine, *The Transformation of Rural Scotland*, Edinburgh, 1994 and 1999, proves conclusively that the major advances in Lowland agriculture were accomplished after 1746 – indeed, after 1760. The connections between agricultural Improvement and the Scottish Enlightenment are drawn in a brilliant essay by Eric Hobsbawm, 'Scottish Reformers of the Eighteenth Century and Capitalist Agriculture', first published in French in *Annales: Economies, Societies, Civilizacions*, May/June 1978 and subsequently in English in Hobsbawm, ed., *Peasants in History*, Calcutta, 1980. A reflection on this essay (and others by Christopher Smout and Immanuel Wallerstein) by Tom Nairn, 'Dr Jekyll's Case: Model or Warning?', *The Bulletin of Scottish Politics*, vol. 1, no. 1, Autumn 1980, is one of the first attempts to conceptualise events after 1746 as a 'revolution from above' and remains one of Nairn's sharpest considerations on Scottish history, although it has never been republished.

Study of the Scottish Enlightenment itself has been a postgraduate growth area for the last two decades. For an introduction to the subject, stressing its relationship to the transformation of agriculture, two older Marxist essays are particularly valuable: Roy Pascal, 'Property and Society', *The Modern Quarterly*, March 1938 and Ronald Meek, 'The Scottish Contribution to Marxist Sociology', *Economics and Ideology and Other Essays*, London, 1967. A more recent Marxist analysis of Scottish Enlightenment political economy, with particular reference to the views of Adam Smith, can be found in David McNally, *Political Economy and the Rise of Capitalism*, Berkeley and Los Angeles, 1988, Chapters 4 and 5, and *Against the Market*, London and New York, 1993, Chapter 2. The most useful of the studies which stress the practical implications of the Enlightenment is Richard Sher, *Church and University in the Scottish Enlightenment*, Edinburgh, 1985. Roy Porter, *Enlightenment*, London, 2000, is concerned with Britain as a whole, but contains useful material and analysis of Scottish aspects throughout, particularly in Chapter 10, although Porter fails to differentiate sufficiently between the English and Scottish Enlightenments.

Finally, anyone seeking to approach our period through literature could do worse than to read, in historical sequence rather than order of composition, the novels by Sir Walter Scott that span it; *A Legend of Montrose, Old Mortality, The Black Dwarf, The Bride of Lammermoor, Rob Roy, The Heart of Midlothian, Waverley* and *Redgauntlet*. Christopher Harvie once called Scott, 'the Marxist's favourite novelist', and here at least I am happy to conform to one of Harvie's stereotypes.[1] More than Balzac or any of the other great realists who followed him, Scott made his subject the unfolding of the bourgeois revolution, rather than its outcome. It is perhaps because the existence of the Scottish Revolution itself has been so little recognised that this aspect of his achievement has gone unnoticed for so long.

Notes and References

A Note on the Cover Illustrations

1. J. Uglow, *Hogarth: A Life and a World* (London, 1997), pp. 416–25.
2. R. Paulson, *Hogarth* (second, revised edition, 3 volumes, New Brunswick, 1992), vol. 2, *High Art and Low, 1732–1750*, p. 178; I. Gale, 'A Brush with Bigotry', *Scotland On Sunday*, 16 March 1997.
3. Uglow, *Hogarth*, p. 465; Gale, 'A Brush with Bigotry'. The painting is also known as *O, The Roast Beef of Old England*.

Acknowledgements

1. N. Davidson, 'Scotland's Bourgeois Revolution', in C. Bambery (ed.), *Scotland, Class and Nation* (London, Chicago and Sydney, 1999), Chapter 3.
2. N. Davidson, *The Origins of Scottish Nationhood* (London and Sterling, Virginia, 2000).

Preface

1. See, for example, G. Novack, 'The Civil War – Its Place in History', G. Novack (ed.), *America's Revolutionary Heritage* (New York, 1976) and J. M. McPherson, 'The Second American Revolution', *Abraham Lincoln and the Second American Revolution* (Oxford and New York, 1991).
2. The major exception is B. P. Lenman, *The Jacobite Risings in Britain, 1689–1746* (London, 1980). Scottish historians of the Victorian and Edwardian periods were more inclined to treat the period as a unity. See, for example, A. Lang, *A History of Scotland from the Roman Occupation* (4 volumes, Edinburgh and London, 1900–07), vol. 4. However, both these authors treat the period as beginning with the Glorious Revolution of 1688–89 and its aftermath, which I regard instead as the concluding episode of the process which opened in 1637.

3. D. P. Szechi and D. Hayton, 'John Bull's Other Kingdoms: The English Government of Scotland and Ireland', in C. Jones (ed.), *Britain in the First Age of Party, 1680–1750* (London and Ronceverte, 1987), pp. 239–40.

4. R. Mitchison, *Lordship to Patronage: Scotland, 1603–1746* (London, 1983), p. 3.

5. F. Braudel, *Civilization and Capitalism, 15th–18th Century* (3 volumes, London, 1984), vol. 3, *The Perspective of the World*, p. 370.

6. K. E. Wrightson, 'Kindred Adjoining Kingdoms: An English Perspective on the Social and Economic History of Early Modern Scotland', in R. A Houston and I. D. Whyte (eds), *Scottish Society, 1500–1800* (Cambridge, 1989), p. 255.

7. Nor is the contrary position as original as Mitchison, Braudel and Wrightson evidently believe. As early as 1891 Peter Hume Brown – a writer often accused by nationalist historians of denigrating Scotland – said of the report on Scottish conditions by the Cromwellian officer, Thomas Tucker, that it was 'to this extent misleading, that he evidently measures Scotland by the standard of England, whereas such a country as Denmark would have been a fairer measure to go by'. P. Hume Brown (ed.), *Early Travellers in Scotland* (Edinburgh, 1978, facsimile of the 1891 edition), p. 162.

8. The exceptional nature of English development is a theme usually associated with the work of Robert Brenner, although what distinguishes his work is actually not this position, which was also held by Marx himself, but the reason which he gives for it, and the date at which he argues that it took effect. I disagree with Brenner on both points, but have no wish unnecessarily to burden a book on Scottish history with a detailed discussion about England. The argument of this book is in any event unaffected, since I also accept – albeit for different reasons – that the English state was unique in Europe by 1688, which is the significant issue as far as Scottish development is concerned.

9. G. Lukacs, 'Reification and the Consciousness of the Proletariat', *History and Class Consciousness* (London, 1971), p. 152.

10. A. Gramsci, 'Notes on Italian History', *Selections from the Prison Notebooks of Antonio Gramsci*, edited and translated by Q. Hoare and G. Nowell Smith (London, 1971), p. 119.

11. Peter Burke once rightly criticised the

> false assumption ... that distinguishing events from structures is a simple matter. We tend to use the word 'event' rather loosely to refer not only to happenings which take a few hours, like the battle of Waterloo, but also to occurrences like the French Revolution, a process spread over a number of years.

See 'History of Events and the Revival of Narrative', in P. Burke (ed.), *New Perspectives on Historical Writing* (Pennsylvania, 1992), p. 237.

12. J. M. McPherson, *Battle Cry of Freedom* (Oxford and New York, 1988), p. ix. See also his more general reflections on the difficulties of writing narrative compared with thematic or topic-based history, 'What's the Matter With History?', *Drawn with the Sword* (Oxford and New York, 1996), pp. 248–9.

13. The major exception in a Scottish context is William Ferguson, whose two most recent books, *Scotland's Relations with England* (Edinburgh, 1977 and 1994) and *The Identity of the Scottish Nation* (Edinburgh, 1994) are structured around a series of polemics against historians with interpretations of Scottish history which differ from his own.

14. See, for example, C. Ginzburg, *The Cheese and the Worms* (Harmondsworth, 1992). Ginzburg restricts his comments on other writers to the Preface, see pp. xiv–xxii.

15. See, for example, W. Law Mathieson, *Scotland and the Union* (Glasgow, 1905) and G. Pratt Insh, *The Scottish Jacobite Movement* (Edinburgh, 1952).

16. An anthology published by Canongate Books gives some indication of the treasures available, but republication of the key texts in their entirety would be a genuine service to scholarship. See *The Scottish Enlightenment: An Anthology*, edited and introduced by A. Broadie (Edinburgh, 1997).

17. A. Callinicos, *Theories and Narratives* (Cambridge, 1995), pp. 98–109.

18. Two Scots – John Maclean and James Connolly – certainly belong to the classical tradition, but not primarily as theoreticians of Scottish development. Maclean was an important educator, agitator and organiser, but his occasional excursions into Scottish history, for example on the supposedly communist nature of clan society, have misled successive generations of Scottish socialists. Connolly was a more formidable theoretician, but the very title of his most famous work, *Labour in Irish History*, indicates that his main concern was with the history of his adopted country rather than that of his country of origin.

19. In relation to Marx and Engels themselves, my approach is based on their general method, rather than specific observations on Scotland, where my views are sometimes at variance with theirs. The specific case of the Highlands – the area of Scotland to which they devoted most attention – is the subject of more detailed study in my 'Marx and Engels on the Scottish Highlands', *Science and Society*, vol. 65, no. 3, Fall 2001. The other contexts in which Marx and Engels discussed Scotland are surveyed in the Appendix of the present book, 'Marx and Engels on Scotland'.

Introduction

1. I. Bell, 'The Scottish Parliament, Adjourned on the 25th Day of March 1707, is Hereby Reconvened', A. Taylor (ed.), *What a State!* (London, 2000), pp. 272–6; M. Elder, *Scotland Reclaimed* (Edinburgh, 2000), pp. 160–4.

2. 'Treaty of Union' is technically the correct term for the document which secured the Union of Scotland and England:

> Despite the common mistake, made by some of the most eminent and respected legal historians, of referring to the 'Act of Union' it is plain that the agreement set out in the articles is was *not* an Act of either the Scottish or English Parliament, still less of the Parliament of Great Britain. There was no 'Act of Union'. The agreement was an international treaty between Anne, Queen of Scots and Queen Anne of England, on terms negotiated by commissioners appointed by the two

Queens, signed by them on July 22, 1706, and presented to the two Queens. (D. M. Walker, *A Legal History of Scotland*, 5 volumes, Edinburgh, 1988–, vol. 5, pp. 85–6)

The two Queens were, of course, the same person, although the role of 'Queen of England' weighed rather more heavily on Anne than that of 'Queen of Scots'.

3. Whatever may be said about the second Scottish Parliament, the method by which its Members are elected, or the extent of its powers, it is certainly not a reconvened version of the first. See Chapter 3, 'From Hanoverian Succession to Incorporating Union (1700–1707)'.

4. For the original Scottish proponents of British Unionism, see N. Davidson, *The Origins of Scottish Nationhood* (London and Stirling, Virginia, 2000), pp. 80–2.

5. For a discussion of the confusions in chronology caused by the inability of certain English historians to distinguish between 'England' and 'Britain', see N. Davies, *The Isles* (London, 1999), pp. xxii–xlii.

6. H. R. Trevor-Roper, 'The Anglo-Scottish Union', *From Counter-Reformation to Glorious Revolution* (London, 1992), pp. 295–6.

7. P. H. Scott, 'Why Did the Scots Accept the Union?', *Scottish Affairs* 1, Autumn 1992, p. 126.

8. N. Ascherson, 'Ancient Britons and the Republican Dream', in *Games With Shadows* (London, 1988), p. 148.

9. M. Fry, 'The Whig Interpretation of Scottish History', I. Donnachie and C. A. Whatley (eds), *The Manufacture of Scottish History* (Edinburgh, 1992), p. 87. Fry's own work is by no means immune from this tendency. His massive apologia for Henry Dundas is at one level an attempt retrospectively to defend a Tory regime with minority support in Scotland on the basis of the economic 'opportunities' for which it was supposedly responsible. See *The Dundas Despotism* (Edinburgh, 1992), pp. 382–4. Before the morning of 2 May 1997, Fry used his regular interventions in the Scottish press to defend the Major administration on similar grounds. Readers of his historical work might therefore be justified in thinking that it too 'distort[s] the past by interpreting it in terms of the present'. 'Scratch a Tory, or even a postmodernist, and find a whig,' writes James Holstun. See *Ehud's Dagger* (London and New York, 2000), p. 7.

10. The distinction was first drawn in K. Marx, 'Critical Notes on the Article: "The King of Prussia and Social Reform. By a Prussian"', *Early Writings*, introduced by L. Colletti, translated by R. Livingstone and G. Benton (Harmondsworth, 1975), pp. 419–20. See also L. D. Trotsky, *The Revolution Betrayed* (New York, 1937), p. 288. Much the clearest discussion of the subject is in H. Draper, *Karl Marx's Theory of Revolution* (4 volumes, New York, 1978–90), vol. 2, *The Politics of Social Classes*, pp. 17–21.

11. E. J. Hobsbawm, 'Scottish Reformers of the Eighteenth Century and Capitalist Agriculture', in E. J. Hobsbawm et al. (eds), *Peasants in History* (Calcutta, 1980), p. 7. In other respects this outstanding essay is the most successful attempt to apply Marxist analysis to a specific aspect of Scottish history undertaken to date – a position undiminished by the singular lack of competition.

12. Notes of the Month, 'Scottish Nationalism', *International Socialism*, First Series, 68, April 1974, p. 7. A non-Marxist version of this position is held by Thomas Devine, who writes: 'The claim of the monarchy to rule by divine right was challenged in the civil wars of the middle decades of the seventeenth century and then destroyed at the Revolution of 1688–9.' T. M. Devine, *The Scottish Nation, 1700–2000* (Harmondsworth, 1999), p. 212.

13. J. McGrath, 'Introduction', J. McEwen, *Who Owns Scotland?* (Edinburgh, 1978), pp. 1–2.

14. T. Nairn, 'Scotland and Europe', *The Break-Up of Britain* (second, revised edition, London, 1981), p. 109. Since much of his work has been concerned with the supposed incompleteness of the English revolution, and the backwardness of the state which it produced, this quotation indicates exactly how primitive Nairn considers Scotland to have been to benefit from such an alliance. See N. Davidson, 'In Perspective: Tom Nairn', *International Socialism*, Second Series, 82, Spring 1999, pp. 99–100, 104–5.

15. Virtually the only Marxist to treat the Jacobite rebellions with the seriousness they deserve in relation to the bourgeois revolution in British history was the eccentric figure of Francis Ambrose Ridley. See *The Revolutionary Tradition in England* (London, 1947), Part II, 'The Bourgeois Revolution', Appendix II, 'The Jacobite Counter-Revolution'. This is particularly impressive since he begins this work with a note to the effect that 'for lack of adequate knowledge I do not deal, except incidentally, with the Scotch [sic] revolutionary history' (p. 9, note). A discussion of Ridley's career, in so far as it briefly intersected with the Trotskyist movement in Britain, can be found in S. Bronstein and A. Richardson, *Against the Stream* (London, 1986), Chapter 2.

16. J. Foster, 'Capitalism and the Scottish Nation', in G. Brown (ed.), *The Red Paper on Scotland* (Edinburgh, 1975), pp. 143, 144. Originally published in *Scottish Marxist* 4, June 1973.

17. J. D. Young, *The Rousing of the Scottish Working Class* (London, 1979), p. 29. Young supports this statement with a reference to the article by Foster cited above, even though the latter specifically refuses to take a position on the existence or otherwise of a Scottish bourgeois revolution. See ibid, Chapter 1, note 78.

18. B. Moore, Jr., *The Social Origins of Dictatorship and Democracy* (Harmondsworth, 1969), p. 428.

19. See, in general, R. Brenner, 'Bourgeois Revolutions and the Transition to Capitalism', in A. L. Beier, D. Cannadine and J. M. Rosenheim (eds), *The First Modern Society* (Cambridge, 1989), pp. 285, 294–7; on England, E. M. Wood, *The Pristine Culture of Capitalism* (London and New York, 1991), pp. 6, 125–6, 160; and on France, G. C. Comminel, *Rethinking the French Revolution* (London and New York, 1987), pp. 28–32, Chapter 3, pp. 53–76, 151–2, 180–2.

20. The American War of Independence is the least decisive of the events listed here. From the very beginning of the European settlement in the Americas, the colonists tended to reproduce the social relations prevailing in the metropolitan power. In Portuguese Brazil, the extent of capitalist penetration was therefore minimal, but in some parts of North America, beginning in Massachusetts, where the English Puritans first settled after

1630, it was very far advanced indeed – perhaps in advance of England itself, since the structures of feudal absolutist power were far weaker. On the other hand, the Cavaliers who ran the royal colony of Virginia, particularly after 1642, were intent on recreating precisely the forms of social organisation which were being destroyed across the Atlantic, first with indentured servants, then with African slaves. The War of Independence involved a political revolution against British rule that neither achieved nor consolidated any change in social relations. If anything, it allowed the extension of the very slave relations of production which were to prove the biggest obstacle to further capitalist development. Consequently, the most important episode in United States history, in terms of extending capitalist relations of production and the attendant state apparatus across the entire national territory, was the Civil War, which removed that obstacle. For a discussion of the spectrum of different social relations present in the American colonies before 1776, see J. M. Murrin, 'A Roof without Walls: the Dilemma of American National Identity', in R. Beeman, S. Botein and E. C. Carter II (eds), *Beyond Confederation* (Chapel Hill and London, 1987), pp. 334–6. The growing separation of, and antagonism between, the Northern and Southern social systems after 1784 is briefly but clearly stated in J. M. McPherson, 'Antebellum Southern Exceptionalism', in *Drawn with the Sword* (Oxford and New York, 1996), pp. 12–23.

21. For earlier usages see, in relation to Russia, V. I. Lenin, 'The "Peasant Reform" and the Proletarian–Peasant Revolution', in *Collected Works* (45 volumes, Moscow, 1963), vol. 17, pp. 125–6; and, in relation to France, A. Gramsci, 'The Modern Prince', in *Selections from the Prison Notebooks of Antonio Gramsci*, translated and edited by Q. Hoare and G. Nowell Smith (London, 1971), pp. 179–80. It should be noted, however, that Gramsci overextends the close of this epoch in France by 40 years to 1871, an error repeated independently by Comminel, *Rethinking the French Revolution*, pp. 204–5.

22. G. Therborn, *Science, Class and Society* (London, 1976), p. 117. A similar formulation occurs in an earlier article by Chris Harman, who writes that 'in the transition from feudalism to capitalism there are many cases in which there is not one sudden clash, but a whole series of different intensities and at different levels, as the decisive economic class (the bourgeoisie) forces political concessions in its favour' ('How the Revolution Was Lost', *International Socialism*, First Series, 30, Autumn 1967, p. 14).

23. P. Anderson, 'Marshall Berman: Modernity and Revolution', *A Zone of Engagement* (London and New York, 1992), p. 44. Alex Callinicos, author of the most serious attempt to develop a general theory of bourgeois revolution, quotes this passage on two occasions in support of his contention that such revolutions involve 'episodes of convulsive political transformation'. See 'Bourgeois Revolutions and Historical Materialism', *International Socialism*, Second Series, 43, Summer 1989, pp. 126, 152. Both the context of Anderson's remarks and their subsequent elaboration ('a punctual break with the order of capital'), however, show that he is specifically discussing the socialist revolution, not revolutions in general and certainly not bourgeois revolutions. Indeed, in at least some of

Anderson's writings on the bourgeois revolution he adopts a position near to that taken here; for example, where he writes that

> the historical genesis of the modern bourgeois state has normally taken the pattern of a series of successive ruptures with the existing settlement, concentrated in their rhythm and coercive in their impact, remedying the omissions or reversing the defeats of their predecessors. (See 'The Figures of Descent', in *English Questions*, London and New York, 1992, p. 155)

The weakness of this perspective lies not in the evocation of process, but in the needlessly schematic claims that each process invariably involved a 'second revolution' and that it was not complete until bourgeois democracy was established. Both of these claims are criticised below.

24. Draper, *Karl Marx's Theory of Revolution*, vol. 2, *The Politics of Social Classes*, p. 169.

25. E. P. Thompson, 'The Peculiarities of the English', in *The Poverty of Theory and Other Essays* (London, 1978), p. 51.

26. F. Engels, 'Introduction [to Karl Marx's, *The Class Struggle in France 1848 to 1850*] [1895]', in *Collected Works* (50 volumes, London, 1975–), vol. 29, p. 513.

27. Gramsci, 'Notes on Italian History', in *Selections from the Prison Notebooks of Antonio Gramsci*, p. 115.

28. I have been accused, on the basis of an earlier version of this argument, of believing that 'the bourgeoisie and capitalism are virtually synonymous and that every country dominated by the capitalist mode of production must have undergone its bourgeois revolution' (see J. Conrad, 'Debunking the Myth – Part 1', *Weekly Worker*, 1 June 2000). I do not in fact believe this. The construction of individual capitalist nation-states continued after the 1860s, but in a way that no longer involved revolutions, even revolutions from above such as those which characterised that decade. The triumph of capital after 1871 was so self-evident that the existing ruling classes of Europe and Latin America capitulated to its imperatives, in all but the most backward areas (e.g. the Russian Empire), without the need for a Bismarck or Lincoln to show them the error of their ways. In the colonial or semi-colonial world, however, evolutionary strategies of this sort were rarely an option, and bourgeois revolutions (or their functional equivalents) were still required into the second half of the twentieth century to secure the existence of independent centres of capital accumulation.

29. P. Anderson, 'The Notion of Bourgeois Revolution', *English Questions* (London and New York, 1992), p. 118.

30. Callinicos, 'Bourgeois Revolutions and Historical Materialism', *International Socialism*, Second Series, 43, Summer 1989, p. 124. For an earlier (1949) version of this argument, see M. Shachtman, 'Isaac Deutscher's "Stalin"', *The Bureaucratic Revolution* (New York, 1962), pp. 229–32.

31. G. Lukacs, 'Towards a Methodology of the Problem of Organisation', *History and Class Consciousness* (London, 1971), p. 307.

32. P. Ginsborg, 'Gramsci and the Era of Bourgeois Revolution in Italy', in J. Davis (ed.), *Gramsci and Italy's Passive Revolution* (London, 1979), p. 34. See also the comments by Barrington Moore quoted at note 18, above.

33. G. E. Cockayne, *The Complete Peerage or a History of the House of Lords and All its Members from the Earliest Times* (second edition, revised and much enlarged, 14 volumes, London, 1910–59), vol. 11, *Rickerton to Sisonby*, edited by G. H. White, p. 619. Daer was the second son of the Earl of Selkirk and died of consumption, aged 31, in 1794.

34. Daer to Grey, 17 January 1793, 'The Scottish Reform Movement and Charles Grey, 1792–94: Some Fresh Correspondence', *Scottish Historical Review*, vol. 35, no. 120, October 1956, p. 34.

35. T. Nairn, *The Enchanted Glass* (second edition, London, 1994), p. 375.

36. G. Therborn, 'The Rule of Capital and the Rise of Democracy', *New Left Review* I/103, May–June 1977, pp. 4, 17.

37. Anderson, 'The Figures of Descent', *English Questions* (London and New York, 1992), p. 155.

38. A. Callinicos, 'Trotsky's Theory of Permanent Revolution and Its Relevance to the Third World Today', *International Socialism*, Second Series, 16, Spring 1982, p. 110.

Chapter 1: Scotland After 1688

1. R. E. Tyson, 'Contrasting Regimes: Population Growth in Ireland and Scotland During the Eighteenth Century', in S. J. Connolly, R. A. Houston and R. J. Morris (eds), *Conflict, Identity and Economic Development* (Preston, 1995), pp. 64–7.

2. D. Stevenson, *The Scottish Revolution, 1637–44* (Newton Abbot, 1973), p. 18; G. Donaldson, *Scotland: James V to James VII* (Edinburgh, 1965), p. 277.

3. D. M. Walker, *A Legal History of Scotland* (5 volumes, Edinburgh, 1988–), vol. 4, *The Seventeenth Century*, p. 637.

4. E. Cregeen, 'The Changing Role of the House of Argyll in the Scottish Highlands', in N. T. Phillipson and R. Mitchison (eds), *Scotland in the Age of Improvement* (Edinburgh, 1970), p. 5.

5. [J. Hamilton], 'Dedication to the Young Nobility and Gentry of Scotland', *The Country-Man's Rudiments: Or, an Advice to the Farmers in East Lothian How to Labour and Improve Their Ground* (Edinburgh, 1713), p. [v].

6. The other early theoreticians of Improvement were, in descending order of status: Sir Robert Sibbald, the Geographer Royal; Andrew Fletcher of Saltoun, a laird and, from 1702, a commissioner in the Scottish Parliament; and James Donaldson, a laird. See I. D. Whyte, *Agriculture and Society in Seventeenth Century Scotland* (Edinburgh, 1976), pp. 251–5.

7. W. K. Dickson, 'Heritable Jurisdictions', *Juridical Review* 9, 1897, p. 440.

8. 'The Forbes Baron Court Book', *Miscellany of the Scottish History Society* 3, 1919, pp. 232–3.

9. T. Kirke, 'A Modern Account of Scotland by an English Gentleman', in P. Hume Brown (ed.), *Early Travellers in Scotland* (Edinburgh, 1978, facsimile of the 1891 Edition), p. 261.

10. E. Dunbar Dunbar, *Social Life in Former Days Illustrated by Letters and Family Papers* (Edinburgh, 1866), pp. 141–3.

11. *The Court Book of the Barony of Carnwarth, 1523–1542*, edited with an Introduction by W. C. Dickinson (Edinburgh, 1937), p. xlvii, note 1.

12. *An Ample Disquisition into the Nature of Regalities and Other Heritable Jurisdictions in That Part of Great Britain Called Scotland. By an English Gentleman* (London, 1747), p. 3.

13. [W. Seton], 'An Essay upon the Present State of Scotland', *The Interest of Scotland in Three Essays* (second edition, London, 1702), p. 78.

14. B. P. Lenman, *The Jacobite Clans of the Great Glen 1650–1784* (second edition, Aberdeen, 1995), p. 6.

15. Walker, *A Legal History of Scotland*, vol. 4, *The Seventeenth Century*, p. 463.

16. W. Ferguson, *Scotland: 1689 to the Present* (Edinburgh, 1968), p. 155.

17. Dickson, 'Heritable Jurisdictions', p. 437; I. D. Whyte, *Scotland Before the Industrial Revolution* (Harlow, 1995), p. 211.

18. T. Craig, *The Jus Feudale by Sir Thomas Craig of Riccarton with an Appendix Containing the Books of the Feus*, a translation by J. A. Clyde (2 volumes, Edinburgh and London, 1934), vol. 1, pp. 585–6, 145.

19. J. Dalrymple, *The Institutions of the Laws of Scotland* (Edinburgh and Glasgow, 1981), p. 359. For his deference to Craig, 'our learned countryman', see p. 332.

20. D. Stewart, *Sketches of the Character, Institutions and Customs of the Highlanders of Scotland: With Details of the Military Service of the Highland Regiments* (new edition, Inverness, 1885), p. 58.

21. R. Callander, 'The Pattern of Land Ownership in Aberdeenshire in the Seventeenth and Eighteenth Centuries', in D. Stevenson (ed.), *From Lairds To Louns* (Aberdeen, 1986), pp. 2, 4.

22. T. M. Devine, *The Transformation of Rural Scotland* (Edinburgh, 1994), p. 7.

23. I. D. and K. A. Whyte, 'Debt and Credit, Poverty and Prosperity in a Seventeenth-Century Scottish Rural Community', in R. Mitchison and P. Roebuck (eds), *Economy and Society in Scotland and Ireland, 1500–1939* (Edinburgh, 1988), p. 72.

24. Devine, *The Transformation of Rural Scotland*, p. 7.

25. Ibid.

26. C. Larner, *Enemies of God* (London, 1981), p. 50.

27. [R. Wedderburn], *The Complaynt of Scotland. With an Appendix of Contemporary English Tracts*, re-edited from the originals with an introduction and glossary by J. A. H. Murray (London, 1822), p. 123.

28. Pollock to Douglas, 7 December 1759, quoted in Devine, *The Transformation of Rural Scotland*, p. 14.

29. A. Fletcher, 'Two Discourses Concerning the Affairs of Scotland; Written in 1698', *Political Works*, edited by J. Robertson (Cambridge, 1997), p. 71.

30. [Seton], 'An Essay upon the Present State of Scotland', pp. 77–8.

31. Fletcher, 'Two Discourses Concerning the Affairs of Scotland', p. 72.

32. For a cautious version of this optimistic interpretation, see I. D. Whyte, 'Written Leases and Their Impact on Scottish Agriculture in the Seventeenth Century', *Agricultural History Review*, vol. 27, no. 1, January 1979, pp. 2, 3.

33. I. D. and K. A. Whyte, 'Continuity and Change in a Seventeenth-Century Scottish Farming Community', *Agricultural History Review*, vol. 32, no. 2, April 1984, p. 166.

34. *The Court Book of the Barony of Urie in Kincardinshire, 1604–1747*, edited from the original manuscript with notes and introduction by D. G. Brown (Edinburgh, 1892), entry for 7 May 1669, p. 88.

35. Ibid, sessions for 28 January 1684, p. 99 and 24 May 1698, p. 105.

36. V. G. Keirnan, 'A Banner with a Strange Device: the Later Covenanters', in T. Brotherstone (ed.), *Covenant, Charter and Party* (Aberdeen, 1989), p. 27.

37. T. Johnston, *The History of the Working Classes in Scotland* (Glasgow, 1946), p. 146.

38. [J. Barclay], *The Mirror of Mindes, Or Barlay's Icon Animorum*, Englished by T. M[ay] (London, 1631), pp. 108, 130–1.

39. L. Timperley, 'The Pattern of Landholding in Eighteenth Century Scotland', in M. L. Parry and T. R. Slater (eds), *The Making of the Scottish Countryside* (London and Montreal, 1980), pp. 142–3, 151.

40. W. Makey, *The Church of the Covenant, 1637–1651* (Edinburgh, 1979), pp. 166–8, 170–3, 176–8; A. I. Macinnes, *Charles I and the Making of the Covenanting Movement, 1625–1641* (Edinburgh, 1991), p. 6. Makey emphasises the increase in rents, Macinnes that of entry fines.

41. Makey, *The Church of the Covenant*, p. 166.

42. V. G. Keirnan, 'The Covenanters: A Problem of Creed and Class', in H. G. Kaye (ed.), *Poets, Politics and the People* (London and New York, 1989), p. 46.

43. *The Register of the Privy Council of Scotland*, Third Series, vol. 1, *A.D. 1661–1664*, edited and abridged by P. Hume Brown (Edinburgh, 1908), p. 439.

44. Williamson to Ormonde, 28 September 1678, *Calendar of State Papers, Domestic Series, 1 March 1678 to 31 December 1678, With Addenda, 1674 to 1679*, edited by F. H. Blackbourne Daniell (London, 1913), p. 428

45. Keirnan, 'The Covenanters', p. 46.

46. As Marx writes, in a passage with particular resonance for Scots, or at least those familiar with one of their traditional foods: 'The taste of porridge does not tell us who grew the oats ... does not reveal the conditions under which it took place, whether it is happening under the slave-owner's brutal lash or the anxious eye of the capitalist' (K. Marx, *Capital*, 3 volumes, Harmondsworth, 1976, vol. 1, p. 290).

47. Christopher Whatley argues that 'the process of proletarianisation of the Scottish colliers ... was well under way by the end of the [eighteenth] century'. C. A. Whatley, 'The Dark Side of the Enlightenment? Sorting Out Serfdom', T. M. Devine and J. R. Young (eds), *Eighteenth Century Scotland: New Perspectives* (East Linton, 1999), p. 272.

48. T. Tucker, *Report by Thomas Tucker upon the Settlement of the Revenue of Excise and Customs in Scotland AD 1656* (Edinburgh, 1825), p. 8.

49. *Acts of the Parliament of Scotland*, edited by T. Thomson and C. Innes (12 volumes, Edinburgh, 1814–75), vol. 8, *1670–1686*, pp. 91, 89.

50. G. Marshall, *Presbyteries and Profits* (Cambridge, 1980), pp. 266–7.

51. Whatley, 'The Dark Side of the Enlightenment?', p. 260.

52. For examples of this argument, see H. W. Meikle, *Some Aspects of Later Seventeenth-Century Scotland* (Glasgow, 1947), pp. 8–12; and I. B. Cowan, *The Scottish Covenanters* (London, 1976), pp. 157–8.

53. Dalrymple, *The Institutions of the Law of Scotland*, p. 1013.

54. J. De Vries, *European Urbanization 1500–1800* (London, 1984), p. 39.

55. I. D. Whyte, 'Urbanisation in Early Modern Scotland: a Preliminary Analysis', *Scottish Economic and Social History* 9, 1989, p. 28.

56. G. W. Pryde, 'The Scottish Burgh of Barony in Decline – 1707–1908', *Proceedings of the Royal Philosophical Society of Glasgow*, vol. 73, no. 4, 1949, p. 48.

57. R. A. Houston, *Social Change in the Age of the Enlightenment: Edinburgh 1660–1760* (Oxford, 1994), p. 32.

58. *Extracts from the Records of the Burgh of Edinburgh, 1665 To 1680*, edited by M. Wood (Edinburgh, 1950), p. 50.

59. P. Lindsay, *The Interest of Scotland Considered, with Regard to its Policy in Employing the Poor, its Agriculture, its Trade, its Manufacturies and Fisheries* (Edinburgh, 1733), p. 53.

60. T. M. Devine, 'The Merchant Class in the Larger Scottish Towns in the Later Seventeenth and Early Eighteenth Centuries', in G. Gordon and B. Dicks (eds), *Scottish Urban History* (Aberdeen, 1983), pp. 97–9.

61. D. MacNiven, 'Merchants and Traders in Early Seventeenth Century Aberdeen', in Stevenson (ed.), *From Lairds to Louns*, pp. 64–67.

62. A. Callinicos, 'Bourgeois Revolutions and Historical Materialism', *International Socialism*, Second Series, 43, Summer 1989, p. 134.

63. Marx, *Capital*, vol. 3, pp. 452–4.

64. T. C. Smout, *A History of the Scottish People, 1560–1830* (Glasgow, 1972), p. 157.

65. *Extracts from the Records of the Royal Burgh of Lanark with Charters and Documents Relating to the Burgh AD 1150–1722* (Glasgow, 1893), p. 235.

66. [Seton], 'An Essay upon the Present State of Scotland', p. 75.

67. M. Lynch, 'Introduction', M. Lynch, (ed.), *The Early Modern Town in Scotland* (London, 1987), p. 24.

68. Marshall, *Presbyteries and Profits*, pp. 284–319.

69. Devine, 'The Merchant Class of the Larger Scottish Towns in the Later Seventeenth Century and the Early Eighteenth Century', p. 107. Devine gives his material a more positive gloss than I do here.

70. Marshall, *Presbyters and Profits*, p. 277.

71. R. Brenner, *Merchants and Revolution* (Cambridge, 1993), pp. 83–4 and, more generally, pp. 1–196.

72. *Dictionary of National Biography*, edited by L. Stephen and S. Lee (21 volumes, London, 1908–909), vol. 5, *Craik to Drake*, p. 23.

73. Brenner, *Merchants and Revolution*, p. 115.

74. Ibid, pp. 118, 120, 128–9, 134, 164, 166, 167–8, 500.

75. *Dictionary of National Biography*, vol. 5, *Craik to Drake*, pp. 23–4.

76. Brenner, *Merchants and Revolution*, pp. 435, 549.

77. G. Jackson, 'Glasgow in Transition, c.1660 to c.1740', T. M. Devine and G. Jackson (eds), *Glasgow* (2 volumes, Manchester and New York, 1995), vol. 1, *Beginnings to 1830*, p. 63.

78. T. C. Smout, 'The Glasgow Merchant Community in the Seventeenth Century', *Scottish Historical Review*, vol. 47, no. 143, April 1968, pp. 69–70.

79. Jackson, 'Glasgow in Transition', pp. 72–3.

80. J. Thomas, 'The Craftsmen of Elgin, 1540–1660', in T. Brotherstone and D. Ditchburn (eds), *Freedom and Authority* (East Linton, 2000), pp. 143, 150–1, 152–4.

81. The classic statement of this position is in P. Hume Brown, *Scotland in the Time of Queen Mary* (London, 1904), pp. 144–61, where the craft and merchant guilds are respectively held to represent 'the democratic spirit' and 'exclusive privilege'. (p. 157).

82. M. Lynch, 'Whatever Happened to the Medieval Burgh?', *Scottish Social and Economic History*, 4, 1984, p. 12.

83. Thomas, 'The Craftsmen of Elgin', pp. 145, 150, 153.

84. M. Lynch, 'Urban Society, 1500–1700', in R. A. Houston and I. D. Whyte (eds), *Scottish Society 1500–1800* (Cambridge, 1989), p. 111.

85. W. Hamish Fraser, *Conflict and Class* (Edinburgh, 1988), p. 5.

86. J. Banaji, 'Modes of Production in a Materialist Conception of History', *Capital and Class* 3, Autumn 1977, p. 30 (Banaji's emphasis). See also K. Marx, *Grundrisse* (Harmondsworth, 1973), pp. 106–7, for the much misunderstood passage from which Banaji draws this interpretation.

87. I. D. Whyte, 'The Occupational Structure of the Scottish Towns in the Late Seventeenth Century', Lynch (ed.), *The Early Modern Town in Scotland*, pp. 224–5.

88. Houston, *Social Change in the Age of the Enlightenment*, p. 290.

89. H. M. Dingwall, *Late 17th Century Edinburgh* (Aldershot and Brookfield, 1994), pp. 196–201.

90. N. Davidson, *The Origins of Scottish Nationhood* (London and Sterling, Virginia, 2000), pp. 113–14; N. Canny, 'The Origins of Empire: An Introduction', *The Oxford History of the British Empire* (5 volumes, Oxford and New York, 1998–99), vol. 1, N. Canny (ed.), *The Origins of Empire*, p. 12.

91. K. M. Brown, 'From Scottish Lords to British Officers: State Building, Elite Integration and the Army in the Seventeenth Century', in N. Macdougall (ed.), *Scotland and War AD 79–1918* (Edinburgh, 1991), p. 143.

92. T. Barnard, 'Scotland and Ireland in the Later Stewart Monarchy', in S. G. Ellis and S. Barber (eds), *Conquest and Union* (London and New York, 1995), p. 271.

93. G. Donaldson, 'The Legal Profession in Scottish Society in the Sixteenth and Seventeenth Centuries', *Juridical Review*, New Series, 21, 1976, pp. 3–9; R. Mitchison, 'The Social Impact of the Clergy of the Reformed Kirk of Scotland', *Scotia* 6, 1982, pp. 5–6.

94. M. Lynch, *Scotland: A New History* (revised edition, London, 1992), p. 254.

95. N. Phillipson, 'Lawyers, Landowners and the Civic Leadership of Post-Union Scotland', *Juridical Review*, New Series, 21, 1976, p. 100.

96. S. J. Davies, 'The Courts and the Scottish Legal System, 1600–1747: The Case of Stirlingshire', in B. P. Lenman, G. Parker and V. A. C. Gatrell (eds), *Crime and the Law: The Social History of Crime in Western Europe since 1500* (London, 1980), pp. 132–4, 144–5.

97. R. Mitchison, *Lordship to Patronage: Scotland, 1603–1746* (London, 1983), p. 165.

98. S. R. Gardiner, *The History of the Great Civil War, 1642–1649* (4 volumes, London, 1987), vol. 1, *1642–1644*, p. 226.

99. W. Thompson et al., 'From Reformation to Union', in T. Dickson (ed.), *Scottish Capitalism* (London, 1980), p. 65.

100. M. Lynch, 'Calvinism in Scotland, 1559–1637', in M. Prestwich (ed.), *International Calvinism, 1541–1715* (Oxford, 1985), p. 252.

101. Mitchison, 'The Social Impact of the Clergy of the Reformed Kirk of Scotland', p. 5.

102. I. B. Cowan, 'Church and Society in Post-Reformation Scotland', *Records of the Scottish Church History Society* 17, 1969–71, pp. 197–9.

103. Makey, *The Church of the Covenant*, pp. 86–7.

104. Ibid, pp. 98, 102.

105. Ibid, p. 99.

106. Davies, 'The Courts and the Scottish Legal System', pp. 122–48. Stirlingshire was also the location for a sheriff court, a Royal Burgh court and several Justices of the Peace.

107. C. Hill, 'Puritans and "the Dark Corners of the Land"', *Change and Continuity in Seventeenth-Century England* (London, 1974); H. M. Jewell, 'North and South: The Antiquity of the Great Divide', *Northern History* 27, 1991.

108. D. Forbes, 'Memoir of a Plan for Preserving the Peace of the Highlands', *Culloden Papers. From the Year 1625 to 1748* (London, 1815), p. 14.

109. A. Cunningham, *The Loyal Clans* (Cambridge, 1932), pp. 14–15.

110. E. J. Hobsbawm, *Industry and Empire* (Harmondsworth, 1969), p. 300.

111. Smout, *A History of the Scottish People*, p. 43. See also R. Nicholson, *Scotland: The Later Middle Ages* (Edinburgh, 1974), pp. 206–7. In the hands of authors influenced by Smout it is nevertheless the contrast between the Highlands and the Lowlands, rather than their comparability that tends to be highlighted. See, for example, the comments of Peter Linebaugh: 'In Scotland during the 1690s Moloch [i.e. the English state] dealt with two profoundly different societies. In the Lowlands, there was an urban society whose rulers, through the Kirk, were able to make this area one of the most dynamic and enterprising of capitalist zones. In the Highlands, however, material and social life was not only pre-capitalist, it was pre-feudal; Gaelic culture and clan organisation were militarist and without notions of private property' (*The London Hanged*, Harmondsworth, 1993, p. 46). None of this is actually true. Of course, these are merely passing comments in an otherwise excellent historical study, and Linebaugh makes no claim to be an expert in Scottish matters. Nevertheless, it is through such casual repetitions that misleading notions become part of 'common sense'. Linebaugh gives Smout, *A History of the Scottish People*, Chapters 9 and 14, as his main secondary source. Perry Anderson makes essentially the same error, on the basis of the same secondary source, in *Lineages of the Absolutist State* (London, 1974), pp. 135–6.

112. J. Harrington, 'The Art of Lawgiving in Three Books', *The Political Works of James Harrington*, edited with an introduction by J. G. A. Pocock (Cambridge, 1977), p. 624.

113. R. A. Dodgson, *Land and Society in Early Scotland* (Oxford, 1981), pp. 153–4.

114. M. Weber, *General Economic History* (New York and London, 1961), p. 29.

115. R. A. Dodgson, '"Pretence of Blude" and "Place of Their Duelling": The Nature of the Scottish Clans, 1500–1744', in Houston and Whyte (eds), *Scottish Society*, p. 187.

116. Scott to Lord Dalkeith, 23 November 1806, *The Letters of Sir Walter Scott*, edited by H. J. C. Grierson, 12 volumes (London, 1932–37), vol. 1, *1787–1807*, p. 331.

117. The Duke of Argyll, *Scotland as it Was and as it Is* (Edinburgh, 1888), pp. 25, 31.

118. D. Stevenson, *Alasdair MacColla and the Highland Problem in the Seventeenth Century* (Edinburgh, 1980), p. 296; B. P. Lenman, *The Jacobite Risings in Britain, 1689–1746* (London, 1980), p. 139.

119. In Poland, the nobility was also organised in clan structures only during the feudal period. 'These clans were not direct descendants of tribal units of organisation,' writes Perry Anderson, 'but more recent formations modeled on them' (*Lineages of the Absolutist State*, p. 283, n. 10). Norman Davies, who is aware of the similarities between the Scottish Highlands and Poland, treats the clannic aspects of the Polish nobility as a relatively superficial phenomenon – correctly, in my view, since they were as feudal in essence as their Scottish analogues: 'Members of the same clan usually fought side by side in battle, forming the basic unit of the feudal host' (*God's Playground*, 2 Volumes, Oxford, 1981, vol. 1, p. 209).

120. J. Walker, *An Economical History of the Hebrides and Highlands of Scotland* (2 volumes, Edinburgh, 1808), vol. 1, p. 51.

121. *An Ample Disquisition into the Nature of Regalities and Other Heritable Jurisdictions in that Part of Great Britain Called Scotland. By an English Gentleman*, p. 13.

122. A. I. Macinnes, *Clanship, Commerce and the House of Stuart, 1603–1788* (East Linton, 1996), p. 143.

123. Ibid, pp. 143–6.

124. Lenman, *The Jacobite Risings in Britain*, p. 245.

125. P. H. Hopkins, *Glencoe and the End of the Highland War* (Edinburgh, 1986), p. 25–6.

126. Macinnes, *Clanship, Commerce and the House of Stuart*, p. 143.

127. G. Donaldson, 'Scotland's Conservative North in the Sixteenth and Seventeenth Centuries', *Transactions of the Royal Historical Society*, Fifth Series, 16, 1965, p. 74.

128. Donaldson himself suggests that the origins of this division may lie at least partly in the extent of English penetration into Scotland, particularly during the occupation of 1547–49, which extended no further than the mouth of the Tay at Dundee. See ibid, pp. 76–9.

129. E. Burt, *Burt's Letters from the North of Scotland*, with an introduction by R. Johnson (2 volumes, Edinburgh, 1974), vol. 2, pp. 24–5.

130. These are features which would today be taken to indicate the existence of different 'ethnic' communities, although I believe that the concept is as misleading, if not quite so actively dangerous, as that of 'race', which is why I also enclose it in quotation marks. For a critique of the concept, see N. Davidson, 'The Trouble With "Ethnicity"', *International Socialism*, Second Series, 84, Autumn 1999.

131. S. Johnson, 'A Journey to the Western Isles of Scotland', *Johnson's Journey to the Western Isles of Scotland and Boswell's Journal of a Tour to the Hebrides with Samuel Johnson, LLD*, edited by R. W. Chapman (Oxford, 1970), p. 40.

132. Fletcher, 'Two Discourses Concerning the Affairs of Scotland; Written in the Month of July, 1698', p. 70.

133. *Extracts from the Records of the Royal Burgh of Lanark with Charters and Documents Relating to the Burgh* AD *1150–1722*, p. 144.

134. A. I. Macinnes, 'Repression and Conciliation: The Highland Dimension, 1660–1688', *Scottish Historical Review*, vol. 65, no. 180, October 1986, pp. 169, 171.

135. *The History of the Affairs of Scotland from the Restoration of King Charles II in the Year 1660. And of the Late Great Revolution in that Kingdom* (Edinburgh, 1690), pp. 128–9.

136. J. Jordun, *John of Fordun's Chronicle of the Scottish Nation*, edited by W. F. Skene (2 volumes, Edinburgh, 1872), vol. 2, p. 38.

137. J. Mair, *A History of Greater Britain As Well England As Scotland, Compiled from the Ancient Authorities by John Mair, by Name Indeed a Scot but by Profession a Theologian*, translated and edited by A. Constable (Edinburgh, 1892), p. 48.

138. C. Kidd, *British Identities before Nationalism* (Cambridge, 1999), p. 125.

139. *Extracts from the Records of the Synod of Moray*, edited by W. M. Cramond (Elgin, 1906), entry for 13 and 14 April 1624, p. 7.

140. Tucker, *Report by Thomas Tucker upon the Settlement of the Revenue of Excise and Customs in Scotland AD 1656*, p. 36.

141. W. J. Withers, 'The Scottish Highlands Outlined: Cartographic Evidence for the Position of the Highland–Lowland Boundary', *Scottish Geographical Magazine*, vol. 98, no. 3, July 1982, p. 154.

142. Walker, *An Economical History of the Hebrides and Highlands of Scotland*, vol. 1, p. 19.

143. Contrary to what is claimed in L. Colley, *Britons* (New Haven and London, 1992), pp. 14–15 and, following her rather too closely on this occasion, Davidson, *The Origins of Scottish Nationhood*, p. 72.

144. J. Macinnes, 'The Gaelic Perception of the Lowlands', in W. Gillies (ed.), *Gaelic and Scotland Alba Agus A' Ghaidhlig* (Edinburgh, 1989), pp. 92–100.

145. Stevenson, *Alasdair MacColla and the Highland Problem in the Seventeenth Century*, p. 19.

146. I. L. MacDonald, 'Resurrection of the Old Scottish Tongue: The Author's Praise of the Old Gaelic Language', translated by and partially reproduced in M. Chapman, *The Gaelic Vision in Scottish Culture* (London and Montreal, 1978), pp. 60–1.

147. D. Forbes, 'Some Thoughts Concerning the State of the Highlands [In the Lord President's Handwriting. Perhaps 1746]', *Culloden Papers*, p. 297.

148. Jordun, *John of Fordun's Chronicle of the Scottish Nation*, p. 38.

149. *The History of the Affairs of Scotland*, p. 240.

150. Which is why it is implausible to speak, as Simon Schama does, of the 1640s as being characterised by 'relentless war between the Calvinist Lowlands and the largely Catholic northwestern Highlands'. See *A History of Britain* (3 volumes, London, 2001–02), vol. 2, *The British Wars, 1603–1776*, p. 149.

151. A. Bellesheim, *History of the Catholic Church in Scotland from the Introduction of Christianity to the Present Day* (4 volumes, Edinburgh, 1890), vol. 4, p. 128.

152. A. Webster, 'An Account of the Number of People in Scotland in the Year One Thousand Seven Hundred and Fifty Five', in *Scottish Population Statistics Including Websters's Analysis Of Population 1755*, edited by J. G. Kyd (Edinburgh, 1952), pp. 68–77. The figures concerning the number of Catholics in Scotland are among the most reliable in Webster's account. See R. Mitchison, 'Webster Revisited: A Re-examination of the 1755

"Census" of Scotland', in T. Devine (ed.), *Improvement and Enlightenment* (Edinburgh, 1989), p. 68.

153. J. Dawson, 'Calvinism and the Gaidhealtachd in Scotland', in A. Pettegree, A. Duke and G. Lewis (eds), *Calvinism in Europe, 1540–1620* (Cambridge, 1994), p. 247.

154. M. Martin, *A Description of the Western Isles of Scotland Circa 1695, etc.*, edited with an introduction by D. J. Macleod (Edinburgh, 1994), p. 372. For his comments on the second sight, see pp. 321–48.

155. H. Mackay, *Memoirs of the War Carried Out in Scotland and Ireland 1689–1691*, edited by J. M. Hog, P. F. Tytler and A. Urquahart (Edinburgh, 1833), p. 16.

156. *Extracts from the Records of the Synod of Moray*, entry for 13 and 14 April, 1624, p. 7.

157. Dawson, 'Calvinism and the Gaidhealtachd In Scotland', p. 251.

158. Larner, *Enemies of God*, p. 80.

159. G. Gordon, 'The Continuation of the History and Genealogy of the Earls of Sutherland Collected Together by Gilbert Gordon of SallaghfFrom the Year 1630', *A Genealogical History of the Earldom of Sutherland from its Origin to the Year 1630; Written by Sir Robert Gordon of Gordonstoun, Baronet, with a Continuation to the Year 1651* (Edinburgh, 1813), p. 521.

160. Stevenson, *Alasdair MacColla and the Highland Problem in the Seventeenth Century*, p. 136.

161. J. Rawson Elder, *The Highland Host of 1678* (Aberdeen, 1914), pp. 45–6.

162. A. Shiel[d]s, *A Hind Let Loose; Or, A Historical Representation of the Testimonies of the Church of Scotland, for the Interest of Christ. With the True State Thereof in All its Periods* (Edinburgh, 1797), pp. 133–4.

163. J. Kirkton, *The Secret and True History of the Church of Scotland from the Restoration to the Year 1678*, edited by C. K. Sharpe (Edinburgh, 1817), pp. 387, 390.

164. 'A Short Account of the Extraordinary Sufferings of the Burgh of Lanark', *Extracts from the Records of the Royal Burgh of Lanark with Charters and Documents Relating to the Burgh AD 1150–1722*, p. 229.

165. 'A Copie of a Letter From the Host About Glasgow', *Blackwood's Edinburgh Magazine*, vol. 1, no. 1, April 1817, pp. 68–9.

166. Kirkton, *The Secret and True History of the Church of Scotland from the Restoration to the Year 1678*, p. 391.

167. *The Register of the Privy Council of Scotland*, Third Series, vol. 5, AD 1676–1678, edited and abridged by P. Hume Brown (Edinburgh, 1912), pp. 578, 579–80.

168. A. Brodie, *The Diary of Alexander Brodie of Brodie, 1652–1680, and of His Son, James Brodie of Brodie, 1680–1685, Consisting of Extracts from the Existing Manuscripts and a Republication of the Volume Printed at Edinburgh in the Year 1740* (Aberdeen, 1863), entry for 2 February 1678, p. 397.

169. 'A Copie of a Letter From the Host About Glasgow', p. 68.

170. J. Prebble, *Glencoe* (Harmondsworth, 1968), p. 59. This comparison was first made by Sir Walter Scott, who noted that 'when we took up the account of Kabul ... we were forcibly struck with the various points of parallelism between the manners of the Afghan tribes and those of the ancient Highland clans. They resembled these oriental mountaineers in their feuds, in their adoption of auxiliary tribes, in their laws, in their modes of conducting war, in their arms, and, in some respects, even in

their dress' ('Review of the *Culloden Papers*', *Quarterly Review* 18, January 1816, p. 288). For further parallels, see ibid, p. 289.

171. H. Henderson, 'Glencoe On Our Minds', *Alias MacAlias* (Edinburgh, 1992), pp. 259–60.

172. G. Wade, 'Report, etc., Relating to the Highlands, 1724', *Highland Papers Relating to the Jacobite Period 1699–1750*, edited by J. Allardyce (2 volumes, Aberdeen, 1895), vol. 1, pp. 132–3.

173. I. L. MacDonald, 'The Battle of Inverlochy', in D. Thomson (ed.), *An Introduction to Gaelic Poetry* (London, 1974), p. 122.

174. A. I. MacInnes, 'Scottish Gaeldom, 1638–1651: the Vernacular Response to the Covenanting Dynamic', in J. Dwyer, R. A. Mason and A. Murdoch (eds), *New Perspectives on the Politics and Culture of Early Modern Scotland* (Edinburgh, n.d. [1985]), p. 77.

175. Stevenson, *Alasdair MacColla and the Highland Problem in the Seventeenth Century*, p. 23.

Chapter 2: Three Dimensions of Socio-economic Crisis (the 1690s)

1. I. Wallerstein, *Historical Capitalism* (London, 1984), p. 42.

2. Marx to Annenkov, 28 December 1846, *Collected Works* (50 volumes, London, 1975-), vol. 36, p. 97 and K. Marx, *Capital* (3 volumes, Harmondsworth, 1976), vol. 1, p. 884. For the views of a contemporary Marxist historian, see J. Saville, *The Consolidation of the Capitalist State, 1800–1850* (London and Boulder, Colorado, 1994), p. 6.

3. E. J. Hobsbawm, 'Revolution', in R. Porter and M. Teich (eds), *Revolution in History* (Cambridge, 1986), pp. 23–4.

4. R. Porter, *Enlightenment* (London, 2000), p. 27.

5. F. Halliday, *Revolution and World Politics* (Houndmills, 1999), p. 185.

6. J. Rosenberg, *The Empire of Civil Society* (London and New York, 1994), p. 42.

7. De Cominges to Louis, 4 February 1664, J. J. Jusserand, *A French Ambassador at the Court of Charles the Second. Le Comte de Cominges from His Unpublished Correspondence* (London, 1892), p. 100 and Chapter 6, 'The Liberties of England', more generally.

8. *Memorials and Correspondence of Charles James Fox*, edited by Lord J. Russell (4 volumes, London, 1853), vol. 2, p. 38.

9. A. Smith, *Lectures on Jurisprudence*, edited by R. L. Meek, D. D. Raphael and P. G. Stern (Oxford, 1978), p. 265.

10. C. Mooers, *The Making of Bourgeois Europe* (London and New York, 1991), pp. 161–2.

11. F. J. McLynn, *The Jacobites* (London, 1985), p. 29.

12. P. Anderson, *Arguments Within English Marxism* (London, 1980), pp. 55–6. See also 'Geoffrey de Ste. Croix and the Ancient World', *A Zone of Engagement* (London and New York, 1992), p. 17.

13. T. C. Smout, *Scottish Trade on the Eve of Union* (Edinburgh and London, 1963), pp. 244–56; B. P. Lenman, *An Economic History of Modern Scotland* (London, 1977), pp. 45–52. Lenman follows Smout in referring to four economic crises affecting Scotland during this period but, for reasons explained below, I have treated acts of war and the imposition of tariff barriers as different aspects of the same process of inter-state competition.

14. *Acts of the Parliament of Scotland*, edited by T. Thomson and C. Innes (12 volumes, Edinburgh, 1814–75), vol. 9, *1689–1695*, pp. 314–15.
15. Ibid, pp. 377–80.
16. Ibid.
17. Ibid, p. 421.
18. Ibid, p. 462.
19. Ibid, pp. 316–19.
20. Ibid, pp. 494–7.
21. G. Marshall, *Presbyteries and Profits* (Cambridge, 1980), p. 209.
22. R. Saville, *Bank of Scotland* (Edinburgh, 1996), pp. 3, 4.
23. Ibid, p. 3.
24. S. G. Checkland, *Scottish Banking: A History, 1695–1973* (Glasgow and London, 1973), pp. 16–18, 26, 33–7.
25. P. Lindsay, *The Interest of Scotland, with Regard to its Policy in Employing the Poor, its Agriculture, its Trade, its Manufactuories and Fisheries* (Edinburgh, 1733), p. 92.
26. A. M. Carstairs, 'Some Economic Aspects of the Union of Parliaments', *Scottish Journal of Political Economy*, vol. 2, no. 1, February 1955, p. 65–6.
27. G. Pratt Insh, *The Company of Scotland Trading to Africa and the Indies* (London, 1932), p. 35.
28. J. Prebble, *The Darien Disaster* (Harmondsworth, 1970), p. 33.
29. Marshall, *Presbyteries and Profits*, pp. 202–3.
30. L. Kerr, '"A Matter of the Highest Consequence": Anglo-Scottish Parliamentary Rivalry over Trade in the Age of the Glorious Revolution', *Scottish Tradition* 18, 1992, p. 71.
31. B. P. Lenman, 'The Highland Aristocracy and North America', Inverness Field Club (ed.), *The 17th Century in the Highlands* (Inverness, 1986), p. 179.
32. T. Crawford, 'Political and Protest Songs in Eighteenth-Century Scotland 1: Jacobite and Anti-Jacobite', *Scottish Studies*, vol. 14, no. 1, 1970, pp. 5–6.
33. Rycaut to Turnbull, 17 November 1697, *Papers Relating to the Ships and Voyages of the Company of Scotland Trading to Africa and the Indies, 1696–1707*, edited by G. Pratt Insh (Edinburgh, 1924), p. 13.
34. M. Martin, *A Description of the Western Islands of Scotland Circa 1695, etc.*, edited with an introduction by D. J. Macleod (Edinburgh, 1994), p. 14.
35. P. H. Hopkins, *Glencoe and the End of the Highland War* (Edinburgh, 1986), p. 439.
36. R. E. Tyson, 'Famine in Aberdeenshire, 1695–1699: Anatomy of a Crisis', D. Stevenson (ed.), *From Lairds to Louns* (Aberdeen, 1986), pp. 32, 34–8, 50.
37. P. Walker, 'Some Remarkable Passages in the Life and Death of Mr Daniel Cargill', *Biographia Presbyteriana* (2 volumes, Edinburgh, 1727), vol. 1, p. 26.
38. R. S. Doctor of Medicine [R. Sibbald], *Provision for the Poor in Time of Dearth and Scarcity* (second edition, Edinburgh, 1709), p. 3.
39. Walker, 'Some Remarkable Passages in the Life and Death of Mr Daniel Cargill', p. 28.
40. [Sibbald], *Provision for the Poor in Time of Dearth and Scarcity*, p. 3.
41. In 1698, for example, a Solemn Humiliation and Fast was ordered for Scotland as a whole on 5 May, and specifically for Lothian and Tweedale

on 17 May. See R. Chambers, *Domestic Annals of Scotland from the Revolution to the Rebellion Of 1745* (3 volumes, Edinburgh and London, 1874), vol. 3, pp. 195–6.

42. A. Fletcher, 'Two Discourses Concerning the Affairs of Scotland; Written in 1698', *Political Works*, edited by J. Robertson (Cambridge, 1997), pp. 66–7.

43. K. E. Wrightson, 'Kindred Adjoining Kingdoms: An English Perspective on the Social and Economic History of Early Modern Scotland', in R. A. Houston and I. D. Whyte (eds), *Scottish Society, 1500–1800* (Cambridge, 1989), p. 255.

44. In his great work on the relationship between the El Nino cycle and Third World famine, Mike Davis points out that one of the most extreme of all El Nino events, that of 1743–44, devastated crops in the Shandong region of China, but did not lead to mass mortality, unlike the lesser El Nino droughts of 1877 or 1899, which did. Davis identifies the crucial difference as being the ability of the eighteenth century Qing state to provide famine relief, in contrast to its successor of the following century, enfeebled by internal division and Western imperialist intervention. See *Late Victorian Holocausts* (London and New York, 2001), pp. 280–5.

45. W. P. L. Thompson, *History of Orkney* (Edinburgh, 1987), pp. 185, 186.

46. As Robert Brenner writes:

> What ... marks off the English economy from those of all its European neighbours in the seventeenth century was not only its capacity to maintain demographic increase beyond the old Malthusian limits, but also its ability to sustain continuing industrial and overall growth in the face of the crisis and stagnation of the traditionally predominant cloth export industry. ('The Agrarian Roots of European Capitalism', in T. H. Aston and C. H. E. Phillip (eds), *The Brenner Debate*, Cambridge, 1985, p. 325)

Brenner correctly points out that even the United Netherlands, England's closest rival in capitalist terms, failed to make this breakthrough to industrialisation. The problem with his analysis is that it assumes capitalism had failed to develop anywhere else in Europe outside of these two states, but even in Scotland there had been some capitalist development. The questions raised by Brenner are important but too complex to discussed adequately here, although as a general observation Perry Anderson is surely right to say that: 'The idea of capitalism in one country, taken literally, is only a bit more plausible than that of socialism [in one country]' ('Maurice Thompson's War', *London Review of Books*, 4 November 1993, p. 17).

47. E. Richards, 'Scotland and the Uses of the Atlantic Empire', in B. Bailyn and P. D. Morgan (eds), *Strangers in the Realm* (Chapel Hill and London, 1991), p. 78.

48. J. Donaldson, *Postscript to 'Husbandry Anatomized' or an Addition to the Enquiry into the Present Manner of Ordering, Drilling and Manuring the Ground in Scotland for Most Part; Whereby it is Further Explained and Applied, and Several Good Effects that May Follow Hinted At* (Edinburgh, 1698), pp. 5, 7.

49. Fletcher, 'Two Discourses Concerning the Affairs of Scotland', p. 68.

50. Ibid, p. 69.

51. Both suggestions are implausible, but the first in particular is not strengthened by Scott bringing on young Ramsay MacDonald as a character witness on behalf of Fletcher's 'humane and enlightened' proposals. See P. H. Scott, *Andrew Fletcher and the Treaty of Union* (Edinburgh, 1992), pp. 66–7.

52. W. F. Gray, 'The Woeful Tale of Scottish Slavery', *Juridical Review* 45, 1933, pp. 135–6.

53. Fletcher, 'Two Discourses Concerning the Affairs of Scotland', pp. 76–9.

54. J. G. A. Pocock, *The Machiavellian Moment* (Princeton and London, 1975), pp. 431–2.

55. Another proposal which aimed to deal with the long-term implications of the crisis came from John Law, the only other Scottish figure comparable to Paterson and Fletcher in respect of the boldness of his thought, but one whose innovations were applied almost exclusively outside his native land, notably in the Mississippi Scheme which he oversaw from the court of Regency France between 1715 and 1720. (His peripheral role in the affairs of his own country is indicated by his relegation to the footnotes of this history.) His sole contribution to the debate over the Scottish economy was in a book called *Money and Trade Considered, with a Proposal for Supplying the Nation with Money*, published in Edinburgh in 1705 during the debate over the Union. His book starts from the same problem that exercised Fletcher – the presence of large numbers of unemployed people – but proposes that they could be put to work, not through forcible enserfment, but by ensuring that there was enough money in circulation to stimulate the economy. The proposal, which involved issuing a paper currency (of which Law was the first proponent) is based on classic Physiocratic assumptions about land being the source of all value. According to Adam Smith, who is politely scathing about 'Mr Law', the proposal was considered and rejected by the Scottish Parliament. See *An Inquiry into the Nature and Causes of the Wealth of Nations*, with an introduction by A. S. Skinner (Harmondsworth, 1970), pp. 416–17. For an appropriately kaleidoscopic account of Law's career and reputation, see J. Buchan, 'Mississippi Dreaming: On the Fame of John Law', *New Left Review* I/210, March–April 1996. Buchan discusses the 'land bank' scheme on pp. 54–5.

56. Thomson, *History of Orkney*, pp. 186–7.

57. I. D. Whyte and K. A. Whyte, 'Continuity and Change in a Seventeenth-Century Scottish Farming Community', *Agricultural History Review*, vol. 32, no. 2, 1984, pp. 166–7.

58. T. M. Devine, *The Transformation of Rural Scotland* (Edinburgh, 1994), p. 8.

59. Smout, *Scottish Trade on the Eve of Union*, p. 255.

60. W. Paterson, 'A Proposal to Plant a Colony in Darien', *The Writings of William Paterson*, edited by S. Bannister (3 volumes, New York, 1968, facsimile of the 1859 Edition), vol. 1, p. 159.

61. For the place of Darien in the construction of this empire during the period 1688–1707, see A. Calder, *Revolutionary Empire* (New York, 1981), pp. 336–429. Calder discusses the expeditions themselves on pp. 378–82. The fullest account is given in Prebble, *The Darien Disaster*.

62. W. L. Mathieson, *Scotland and the Union* (Glasgow, 1905), p. 38.

63. C. Storrs, 'Disaster at Darien (1698–1700)? The Persistence of Spanish Imperial Power on the Eve of the Demise of the Spanish Habsburgs', *European History Quarterly*, vol. 29, no. 1, January 1999, pp. 8–10.

64. Mathieson, *Scotland and the Union*, p. 38–9.
65. 'Letter by the Council of Caledonia to the Governor of Carthegena', 11 March 1699, *The Darien Papers: Being a Selection of Original Letters and Official Documents Relating to the Establishment of a Colony at Darien by the Company of Scotland Trading to Africa and the Indies 1695–1700*, (Edinburgh, 1859), p. 91.
66. Wodrow to Thomson, 30 August 1699, *Early Letters of Robert Wodrow, 1698–1709*, edited by L. W. Sharp (Edinburgh, 1937), pp. 16–17.
67. 'Phil-Caledon', *A Defence of the Scots Settlement at Darien, with an Answer to the Spanish Memorial Against It* (Edinburgh, 1699), p. 17; see also pp. 42–43.
68. Melville to Carstares, 4 June 1700, *State Papers and Letters Addressed to William Carstares*, edited by J. McCormick (Edinburgh, 1774), pp. 516–17.
69. Wodrow to Wallace, 16 July 1700, *Early Letters of Robert Wodrow*, p. 92.
70. Fletcher, 'Two Discourses Concerning the Affairs of Scotland', pp. 36, 37.
71. Letter dated 25 December 1699, quoted in H. MacPherson, *The Cameronian Philosopher: Alexander Shields* (Edinburgh and London, 1932), p. 144.
72. T. Gallagher, *Glasgow: The Uneasy Peace* (Manchester, 1987), p. 2.
73. M. P. Maxwell, 'The Ulster Plantation: Scotland's First Colonial Venture', *Scottish Colloquium Proceedings* 2, 1969, p. 2.
74. It may also have been the case that the very success of the Ulster colony added to the difficulties which the Scots experienced at Darien and all previous attempts at colonisation. It had already drawn off and provided a profitable home for many of those who might otherwise have been prepared to emigrate further afield. The planters themselves were often heavily indebted from the cost of transporting, housing and equipping tenants, as were the tenants themselves. The debts drew heavily from the available supply of credit. The success of this first British colony therefore acted to prevent a specifically Scottish one from coming into being. See N. Canny, 'The Origins of Empire: An Introduction', *The Oxford History of the British Empire* (5 volumes, Oxford and New York, 1998–99), vol. 1, *The Origins of Empire*, N. Canny (ed.), p. 15–16.
75. Storrs, 'Disaster at Darien (1698–1700)?', p. 27. See also Lenman, *An Economic History of Modern Scotland*, p. 51.
76. 'Letter by the Council of Caledonia to the Governor of Carthegena', p. 92.
77. Lenman, *An Economic History of Modern Scotland*, p. 51.
78. Fletcher, 'Two Discourses Concerning the Affairs of Scotland', p. 37.
79. M. Lynch, *Scotland: A New History* (revised edition, London, 1992), p. 309.
80. W. Thompson, 'Scotland', in A. L. Morton, *1688: How Glorious Was the Revolution?, Our History* 79, July 1988, p. 30.
81. M. Hunter, '"Aitkenhead the Atheist": The Context and Consequences of Articulate Irreligion in the Late Seventeenth Century', in M. Hunter and D. Wooton (eds), *Atheism from the Reformation to the Enlightenment* (Oxford, 1992), pp. 224–6, 240–1, 253. The Act under which Aitkenhead was sentenced states: 'And for the third fault he shall be punished by death as an obstinate blasphemer' (*Acts of the Parliament of Scotland*, vol. 9, *1689–1695*, p. 387).
82. Hunter, '"Aitkenhead the Atheist"', p. 237; C. Larner, *Enemies of God* (Oxford, 1983), p. 77. The last official executions were in Inverness in

1706, although the last person to be executed – apparently by an illegal local initiative – was Janet Cornfoot in Dornoch during 1727. See ibid, p. 78.

83. Marchmont to Pringle, 22 June 1700, *A Selection from the Papers of the Earls of Marchmont. Illustrative of Events from 1685 to 1750* (3 Volumes, London, 1831), vol. 1, p. 210.

84. Marchmont to Seafield, 7 October 1699, ibid, vol. 3, p. 178.

85. Marchmont to Pringle, 23 December 1699, ibid, vol. 3, p. 199.

86. Lenman, *An Economic History of Modern Scotland*, p. 52.

Chapter 3: From Hanoverian Succession to Incorporating Union (1700–1707)

1. Shaftesbury to Le Clerc, 6 March 1705, *The Life, Unpublished Letters and Philosophical Regimen of Anthony, Earl of Shaftesbury*, edited by B. Rand (London, 1992, facsimile of the 1900 Edition), p. 353. Shaftesbury commends his correspondent for defending the works of the Scottish writer George Buchanan, which he claims 'will oblige all British men, and can offend no English, but such as are slaves, or in slavish principles' – an interesting use of the notion of Britishness, before the Union was an accomplished fact.

2. J. Robertson, 'Union, State and Empire: The Britain of 1707 in its European Setting', in L. Stone (ed.), *An Imperial State at War* (London and New York, 1994), p. 236.

3. *The Correspondence 1700–1711 of John Churchill, First Duke of Marlborough and Anthony Heinsius, General Pensionary of Holland*, edited by B. Van 'T Hoff (The Hague, 1951), p. 5.

4. Pringle to Marchmont, 26 February 1702, Historical Manuscripts Commission, 'Marchmont MSS', *The Manuscripts of the Duke of Roxburghe; Sir H. H. Campbell, Bart.; The Earl of Strathmore; and the Countess Dowager of Seafield* (London, 1894), Fourteenth Report, Appendix, Part 3, p. 154.

5. Godolphin to Seafield, 24 July 1703, ibid., p. 199.

6. Marchmont to Devonshire, 12 December 1704, *A Selection from the Papers of the Earls of Marchmont. Illustrative of Events from 1685 to 1750* [hereafter *The Marchmont Papers*] (3 volumes, London, 1831), vol. 1, pp. 278–9.

7. C. S. Terry, *The Scottish Parliament: Its Constitution and Procedures, 1603–1707* (Glasgow, 1905), p. 164.

8. P. H. Scott, 'The Truth About the Union', *Scottish Affairs* 11, Spring 1995, p. 57.

9. B. Coward, *The Stuart Age* (Harlow, 1980), p. 306.

10. R. A. Houston, 'Popular Politics in the Reign of George II: The Edinburgh Cordiners', *Scottish Historical Review*, vol. 72:2, no. 194, October 1993, p. 167.

11. E. B. Thomson, *The Parliament of Scotland 1690–1702* (Saint Andrews, n.d. [1929]), p. 14.

12. Entry for 14 January 1701, *A Diary of the Proceedings in the Parliament and Privy Council of Scotland 21 May, 1700 to 7 March 1707 by Sir David Hume of Crossrigg, One of the Senators of the College Of Justice* (Edinburgh, 1828), pp. 51–2.

13. Thompson, *The Parliament of Scotland*, p. 21.

14. J. Dalrymple, *An Essay Towards a General History of Feudal Property in Great Britain* (London, 1757), pp. 342, 338–9.

15. J. H. Burton, *The History of Scotland from Agricola's Invasion to the Extinction of the Last Jacobite Insurrection* (8 volumes, Edinburgh, 1898), vol. 8, p. 85.

16. See, for example, W. Speck, *Stability and Strife*, (London, 1977), pp. 152–3.

17. P. K. Monod, *Jacobitism and the English People* (Cambridge, 1989), p. 349.

18. A. Smith, *An Inquiry into the Nature and Causes of the Wealth of Nations*, edited by A. S. Skinner (Harmondsworth, 1970), p. 358.

19. J. Brewer, *The Sinews of Power* (London, 1989), p. 171.

20. A. I. Macinnes, 'Influencing the Vote: The Scottish Estates and the Treaty of Union, 1706–07', *History Microcomputer Review*, vol. 6, no. 2, Fall 1990, p. 15.

21. A. Fletcher, 'Speeches by a Member of the Parliament Which Began at Edinburgh the 6th of May, 1703', Speech 3, 22 June 1703, *Political Works*, edited by J. Robertson (Cambridge, 1998), pp. 138–9.

22. Fletcher to Russell, 8 January 1689, Scottish Record Office, Andrew Russell Papers, RH15/106/690, no. 7. This letter was first cited in T. C. Smout, 'The Road to Union', in G. Holmes (ed.), *Britain After the Glorious Revolution* (London and Basingstoke, 1969), pp. 183–4, although Smout offers no suggestions as to why Fletcher subsequently changed his mind. Ferguson's discussion can be found in *Scotland's Relations with England* (Edinburgh, 1977), p. 171 and Scott's in *Andrew Fletcher and the Treaty of Union* (Edinburgh, 1992), pp. 44–6.

23. J. Clerk, *Memoirs of the Life of Sir John Clerk of Penicuik, Baronet, Baron of the Exchequer, Extracted by Himself from His Own Journals 1676–1755*, edited from the manuscript in Penicuik House with an introduction and notes by J. M. Gray (Edinburgh, 1892), p. 49.

24. [?G. Ridpath], *An Historical Account of the Ancient Rights and Power of the Parliament of Scotland* (Edinburgh, 1703), p. xiii.

25. Fletcher, 'Speeches by a Member of the Parliament Which Began at Edinburgh the 6th of May, 1703', Speech 13, 9 September 1703, *Political Works*, pp. 160–1.

26. Seafield to Godolphin, 18 August 1705, *Letters Relating to Scotland in the Reign of Queen Anne by James Ogilvy, First Earl of Seafield, and Others*, edited by P. H. Brown (Edinburgh, 1915), pp. 73, 75–6. Seafield is commenting on a speech by Fletcher during 1705, but the point is equally relevant to his interventions in 1703.

27. Ferguson, *Scotland's Relations with England*, p. 192.

28. Bruce Lenman therefore exaggerates when he says that 'there was no Scottish army after 1688'. The official record of the Establishment of land forces in Britain for 1692, which he cites, provides a separate return for Irish and indeed for Danish and Dutch forces, but none for Scotland, although there were still distinct Scottish regiments like the Coldstream Regiment of Foot Guards. B. P. Lenman, *The Jacobite Clans of the Great Glen, 1650–1784* (second edition, Aberdeen, 1995), p. 46.

29. S. H. F. Johnston, 'The Scots Army in the Reign of Anne', *Transactions of the Royal Historical Society*, Fifth Series, 3, 1952, pp. 14–15; 'Establishment for the Pay of Her Majesty's Standing Forces in the Kingdom of Scotland, 15 May 1702', *Miscellany of the Maitland Club* 3, Edinburgh, 1843, pp. 87–98.

30. Scott, *Andrew Fletcher and the Treaty of Union*, p. 121.

31. J. Morrill, 'The English, the Scots and the British', in P. S. Hodge (ed.), *Scotland and the Union* (Edinburgh, 1994), p. 82.

32. P. W. J. Riley, *The Union of England and Scotland* (Manchester, 1978), p. xvi.

33. R. Mitchison, *Lordship to Patronage: Scotland, 1603–1746* (London, 1983), p. 132.

34. J. Swift, 'The Publick Spirit of the Whigs', *The Prose Writings of Jonathan Swift* (14 volumes, Oxford, 1953), vol. 8, *Political Tracts 1713–1719*, edited by H. Davis and I. Ehrenpreis, pp. 49–50.

35. G. Burnet, *The History of My Own Time* (6 volumes, London, 1725–34), vol. 5, pp. 920–1.

36. Between 1660 and 1707, 41 Scottish peers or their heirs married English wives, at a time when there were 135 peers. As Keith Brown has noted, these marriages were often not undertaken for the purpose of producing heirs, since many of the males were entering their second or third marriage and already had successors; see 'The Origins of a British Aristocracy: Integration and Its Limitations Before the Treaty of Union', in S. G. Ellis and S. Barber (eds), *Conquest and Union* (Harlow, 1995), pp. 227, 231.

37. Baillie to Roxburgh, 11 April 1705, *Correspondence of George Baillie of Jerviswood 1702–1708* (Edinburgh, 1842), p. 75.

38. For a later example of Edinburgh crowd activity which can be more plausibly described as a 'kind of wild justice', see H. T. Dickinson and K. Logue, 'The Porteous Riot: A Study in the Breakdown of Law and Order in Edinburgh, 1736–1737', *Journal of the Scottish Labour History Society*, 10 June 1976.

39. [W. Forbes], *A Pill for Pork Eaters: Or, a Scots Lancet for an English Swelling* (Edinburgh, 1705), pp. 3, 4.

40. J. Taylor, *A Journey to Edenborough in Scotland by Joseph Taylor, Late of the Inner Temple, Esq.*, with Notes by W. Cowan (Edinburgh, 1903), pp. 95, 126.

41. Hamilton to Orkney, 16 November 1706, Historical Manuscripts Commission, *Report on the Manuscripts of His Grace the Duke of Portland, K. G., Preserved at Wellbeck Abbey* [hereafter *Portland Manuscripts*] (9 volumes, London, 1891–1923), vol. 8, p. 266.

42. Scott, *Andrew Fletcher and the Treaty of Union*, pp. 119–20, 141–4.

43. J. S. Gibson, *Playing the Scottish Card* (Edinburgh, 1988), p. 59.

44. [Forbes], *A Pill for Pork Eaters*, p. 5.

45. Mar to Carstares, 9 March 1706, *State Papers and Letters Addressed to William Carstares*, edited by J. McCormick (Edinburgh, 1774), pp. 743–4.

46. For the military and fiscal transformation of the English state after 1688, and the British state after 1707, see Brewer, *The Sinews of War*.

47. J. Robertson, 'An Elusive Sovereignty: The Course of the Union Debate in Scotland 1698–1707', J. Robertson (ed.), *A Union for Empire* (Cambridge, 1995), p. 209.

48. Nairne to Mar, 21 November 1706, Historical Manuscripts Commission, *Report on the Manuscripts of the Earl of Mar and Kellie* [hereafter *Mar and Kellie Manuscripts*] (London, 1904), p. 329.

49. Riley, *The Union of England and Scotland*, p. 189.

50. Marchmont to Soames, 27 February 1707, *The Marchmont Papers*, vol. 1, p. 322.

51. Mar to Carstares, 9 March 1706, *State Papers and Letters Addressed to William Carstares*, p. 744.

52. G. Lockhart, *'Scotland's Ruine': Lockhart of Carnwarth's Memoirs of the Union*, edited by D. Szechi (Aberdeen, 1995), p. 147.

53. See his request for instructions from Robert Harley and the (unfortunately incomplete) reply by the latter: Defoe to Harley, 13 September 1706, *Portland Manuscripts*, vol. 4, pp. 326–8 and Harley to Defoe, ? September 1706, ibid, p. 334.

54. Riley, *The Union of England and Scotland*, p. 245.

55. R. A. Houston, *Scottish Literacy and the Scottish Identity* (Cambridge, 1985), pp. 34–5, 46–7.

56. Lockhart, *'Scotland's Ruine'*, p. 150.

57. Atholl to the Atholl Lairds, 24 October 1706, *Chronicles of the Atholl and Tullibardine Families Collected and Arranged by John, Seventh Duke of Atholl, KT* (5 volumes, Edinburgh, 1908), vol. 2, p. 68.

58. Ibid.

59. Lockhart, *'Scotland's Ruine'*, p. 148.

60. 'Stirling Address', 18 November 1706, Perth Burgh Records B59/34/17/3, quoted in C. A. Whatley, *'Bought and Sold for English Gold?'* (Dundee, 1994), p. 41.

61. 'Instructions by the Magistrates and Town Council of the Burgh of Lauder, to their Commissioner in Parliament, in Relation to the Union Proposed Betwixt the Kingdoms of Scotland and England', National Library of Scotland, Ry. III.a. 24 (74).

62. Lockhart, *'Scotland's Ruine'*, p. 158.

63. 'The Burgh of Montrose and the Union of 1707: a Document', edited by T. C. Smout, *Scottish Historical Review*, vol. 66, no. 182, October 1987, p. 184.

64. Riley, *The Union of England and Scotland*, pp. 278–9.

65. W. Thompson et al., 'From Reformation to Union', in T. Dickson (ed.), *Scottish Capitalism* (London, 1980), p. 87.

66. [J. Hodges], *The Rights and Interests of the Two British Monarchies Inquir'd Into, and Clear'd; With a Special Respect to an United or Separate State* (London, 1703), pp. 56–7.

67. John Law opposed the Union, but we will never know what his objective assessment of the implications for Scottish society were, since his opposition was based on the fact that in 1694 he had been found guilty and convicted of murder at the Old Bailey, but had subsequently escaped from prison and returned to Scotland: 'Law opposed the union of the Scots and English parliaments, not out of some precocious nationalism, but to save his life: for with the union would come the warrant' (J. Buchan, 'Mississippi Dreaming: On the Fame of John Law', *New Left Review* I/210, March–April 1995, p. 54).

68. W. Paterson, Fourth Letter, 8 October 1706, *The Writings of William Paterson*, edited by S. Bannister (3 volumes, New York, 1968, facsimile of the 1859 edition), vol. 3, p. 18.

69. W. Patterson, Fifth Letter, 15 October 1706, ibid., p. 24.

70. An anticipation of what was to follow can, however, be found in the paper requesting resources and permission to invade French Canada presented by Colonel Samuel Vetch to the Board of Trade on 27 July 1708. Vetch, a classic early representative of the Scot On The Make, refers throughout to

the 'British Interest', the 'British Monarchy' and the 'British Empire'. The latter was not the only resonant term which he seems to have been the first to use: Canada is described as potentially being 'a noble Colony, exactly calculate for the constitutions and genius of the most Northern of North Britons'; S. Vetch, 'Canada Survey'd. Or the French Dominions Upon the Continent of America Briefly Considered in Their Situation, Strength, Trade and Number, More Particularly How Vastly Prejudiciall They Are to the British Interest, and a Method Proposed for Easily Removing Them', *Calendar of State Papers, Colonial Series, America and West Indies, June, 1708–1709*, edited by C. Headlam (London, 1922), pp. 41–51. For the central role Scots subsequently played in the British Empire, with particular reference to the contribution this made to the formation of both Scottish and British national consciousness, see N. Davidson, *The Origins of Scottish Nationhood* (London and Sterling, Virginia, 2000), Chapter 6, 'British Imperialism and National Consciousness in Scotland'.

71. Logan to Mar, 27 August 1706, *Mar and Kellie Manuscripts*, p. 274.
72. [J. Logan], *A Sermon Preached Before His Grace James Duke of Queensberry, Her Majesty's High Commissioner. Upon the 27 October 1706. By Mr John Logan, Minister of the Gospel at Alloa* (Edinburgh, 1706).
73. Mar to Nairne, 26 October 1706, *Mar and Kellie Manuscripts*, p. 298.
74. Lockhart, *'Scotland's Ruine'*, pp. 143–4.
75. Mar to Nairne, 26 October 1706, *Mar and Kellie Manuscripts*, p. 299.
76. Same to same, 3 November 1706, ibid, p. 309.
77. W. Seton, *A Speech in Parliament the Second Day of November 1706 on the First Article of the Treaty of Union* (Edinburgh, 1706), pp. 4, 7, 11–12. Only one anonymous pamphleteer seems to have seriously argued for a Union with the United Provinces. See *A Letter Concerning the Consequence of an Incorporating Union in Relation to Trade* (Edinburgh, 1706).
78. J. Hamilton, *The Lord Beilhaven's Speech in Parliament the Second Day of November 1706 on the Subject Matter of an Union Between the Two Kingdoms of Scotland and England* (Edinburgh, 1706), pp. 2, 7–8.
79. D. Defoe, *The History of the Union Between England and Scotland, with a Collection of Original Papers Thereto* (London, 1786), p. 328. According to Paterson, Marchmont actually said:

> Methinks I see, I see, hath a vision, and what then? He talked of things 1700 years past, and I'm assured, were that member once awake, he'll find all is a dream, and all he hath spoken containeth more of imagination and fantasy than anything real or solid. (Paterson to Lewis, 5 November 1706, *Portland Manuscripts*, vol. 8, p. 262).

80. Mitchison, *Lordship to Patronage*, p. 135. For the details, see R. Mitchison, *The Old Poor Law in Scotland* (Edinburgh, 2000), p. 41.
81. *Acts of the Parliament of Scotland*, edited by T. Thomson and C. Innes (12 volumes, Edinburgh, 1814–75), vol. 11, *1702–1707*, pp. 313–15.
82. Mar to Nairne, 5 November 1706, *Mar and Kellie Manuscripts*, p. 312.
83. Defoe, *The History of the Union Between England and Scotland*, p. 269.
84. Defoe to Harley, 7 December 1706, *Portland Manuscripts*, vol. 4, p. 364.
85. Gibson, *Playing the Scottish Card*, p. 82.

86. Defoe to Harley, 7 December 1706, *Portland Manuscripts*, vol. 4, pp. 365–6.

87. Same to same, 9 December 1706, ibid, p. 366.

88. W. McDowall, *History of the Burgh of Dumfries with Notices of Nithsdale, Annandale and the Western Borders* (fourth revised edition, Dumfries, 1986), p. 509.

89. 'An Account of the Burning of the Articles of Union at Dumfries', National Library of Scotland, Ry. III.a. 24 (9).

90. Mar to Nairne, 12 November 1706, *Mar and Kellie Manuscripts*, p. 318.

91. Lockhart, *'Scotland's Ruine'*, p. 155.

92. Seafield to Carstares, 27 March 1707, *State Papers and Letters Addressed to William Carstares*, p. 764.

93. Lockhart, *'Scotland's Ruine'*, p. 179.

94. *The Smoaking Flax Unquenchable; Where the Union Between the Two Kingdoms is Dissecated, Anatomised; Confuted and Annuled. Also, that Good Form and Fabrick of Civil Government, Intended and Espoused by the True Subjects of the Land, is Illustrated and Held Out* (n.p., 1706), pp. 13, 14, 16, 22.

95. W. Houston, 'A Succinct Deduction of the Series of Affairs Relating to Church and State of Scotland from the Year 1679 to and with This Present State', *Portland Manuscripts*, vol. 8, pp. 373, 374.

96. Lockhart, *'Scotland's Ruine'*, p. 180.

97. Mar to Harley, 21 September 1706, *Mar and Kellie Manuscripts*, p. 281.

98. J. Ker, *The Memoirs of John Ker of Kersland in North Britain, Relating to Politics, Trade and History* (3 volumes, London, 1727), vol. 1, p. 37–8.

99. W. Alexander, *An Essay Showing that There's No Probability of There Being So Much French Interest, as it's Certain There's English Influence in Our Present Parliament of Scotland* (Edinburgh, 1704), pp. 7, 8. The same author does note, however, that 'the English are much better masters than the French, neither do the English Enslave their Subjects as the French do' (ibid, p. 7).

100. Lockhart, *'Scotland's Ruine'*, pp. 183–4.

101. N. Hooke, *The Secret History of Colonel Hooke's Negotiations in Scotland in Favour of the Pretender In 1707. Written by Himself* (London, 1760), p. 8.

102. Lockhart, *'Scotland's Ruine'*, pp. 183–4.

103. Nairne to Mar, 29 November 1706, *Mar and Kellie Manuscripts*, pp. 305–6.

104. Defoe to Harley, 13 November 1706, *Portland Manuscripts*, vol. 4, p. 350.

105. K. Brown, 'From Scottish Lords to British Officers: Elite Integration and the Army in the Seventeenth Century', in N. McDougall (ed.), *Scotland and War AD 79 To 1918* (Edinburgh, 1991), p. 149.

106. Johnston, 'The Scots Army in the Reign of Anne', p. 7.

107. Defoe, *The History of the Union Between England and Scotland*, pp. 265, 266.

108. *A Short Letter to the Glasgow Men* (n.p., n.d. [1706]), p. 2.

109. Defoe to Harley, 27 December 1706, *Portland Manuscripts*, vol. 4, p. 374.

110. See the evidence assembled in A. Lang, *A History of Scotland from the Roman Occupation* (4 volumes, Edinburgh and London, 1900–07), vol. 4, pp. 130–1.

111. Ker, *Memoirs*, vol. 1, p. 61.

112. [J. Hodges], *War Between the Two British Kingdoms Considered. For the Mutual Interest of Both* (London, 1705), p. 40.

113. All their denials stem from the period after the Union had come into effect, beginning with a Protestation posted in Sanquhar during October 1707, so this may be retrospective. See the evidence assembled in D. H. Fleming, 'Mr Lang's Cameronian and Jacobite Alliance', *Critical Reviews Relating Chiefly to Scotland* (London, 1910), pp. 406–10 and Appendix B, 'Did the Cameronians Coquet with the Jacobites in 1707?', pp. 502–4.

114. As late as 1725 Lockhart was writing to a fellow Jacobite, whom he evidently expected to be sceptical ('you'd be surprised and scarce credit me'), that there was 'a fair probability of a conjunction of measures betwixt the Highlanders and the Cameronians', although predictably this also came to nothing. Lockhart to Cameron, 5 October 1725, *Letters of George Lockhart of Carnwarth, 1698–1732*, edited by D. Szechi (Edinburgh, 1989), p. 245.

115. Scott, *Andrew Fletcher and the Treaty of Union*, p. 200.

116. Paterson to ?Harley, 21 December 1706, *Portland Manuscripts*, vol. 8, p. 274.

117. Riley, *The Union of England and Scotland*, p. 12.

118. C. A. Whatley, 'Coal, Salt and the Treaty of Union of 1707: A Revision Article', *Scottish Historical Review*, vol. 66, no. 181, April 1987, pp. 31–9.

119. Defoe to Harley, 16 December 1706, *Portland Manuscripts*, vol. 4, p. 373.

120. For this distinction, see Davidson, *The Origins of Scottish Nationhood*, pp. 13–15.

121. J. Goodare, *State and Society in Early Modern Scotland* (Oxford, 1999), p. 338.

122. Defoe to Harley, 4 January 1707, *Portland Manuscripts*, vol. 4, p. 374.

123. Defoe to Harley, 6 January 1707, ibid, p. 379.

124. Lockhart, *'Scotland's Ruine'*, p. 195.

125. Patterson to ?Lewis, 29 October 1706, *Portland Manuscripts*, vol. 9, p. 254.

126. *Acts of the Parliament of Scotland*, vol. 11, *1702–1707*, pp. 404–6.

127. Roxburgh to Baillie, 28 November 1705, *Correspondence of George Baillie of Jerviswood*, p. 138. For an example of the uses to which this quotation had been put, see C. Harvie, *Scotland and Nationalism: Scottish Society and Politics, 1707–1994* (second edition, London and New York, 1994), p. 38.

128. For Weymss, see Whatley, 'Coal, Salt and the Union of 1707', p. 35; for Galloway, see D. Woodward, 'A Comparative Study of the Irish and Scottish Livestock Trades in the Seventeenth Century', in L. M. Cullen and T. C. Smout (eds), *Comparative Aspects of Scottish and Irish Social and Economic History, 1600–1900* (Edinburgh, 1977), p. 157.

129. William Ferguson is frequently mentioned in the same context as Riley and Scott as a writer with a sceptical view of the motivations behind the Union. Indeed, Ferguson may be said to have begun this historiographical trend with an essay of 1964 in which he described the Treaty as 'probably the greatest political "job" of the eighteenth century' (see 'The Making of the Treaty of Union of 1707', *Scottish Historical Review*, vol. 43, no. 136, October 1964, p. 110). But while Ferguson has been insistent on the role of patronage in the ratification of the Treaty, he has never reduced his explanation to the type of monocausality favoured by the other two writers. His views are given their fullest expression in *Scotland's Relations with England*, pp. 180–277.

130. R. Burns, 'Such a Parcel of Rogues in a Nation', *The Cannongate Burns*, edited by A. Noble and P. Scott Hogg (Edinburgh, 2001), p. 394.

131. J. G. Simms, 'The Establishment of Protestant Ascendancy, 1691–1714', in T. W. Moody and W. E. Vaughn (eds), *A New History of Ireland* (10 volumes, Oxford, 1976–), vol. 4, *Eighteenth Century Ireland 1691–1800*, p. 7.

132. W. R. Scott, 'Scottish Industry Before the Union', in P. Hume Brown (ed.), *The Union of 1707* (Glasgow, 1907), p. 101. This judgement has been quoted favorably by several later writers. See, for example, T. C. Smout, *Scottish Trade on the Eve of Union* (Edinburgh and London, 1963), p. 275.

133. Riley, *The Union of England and Scotland*, p. 215.

134. Macinnes, 'Influencing the Vote', p. 19.

135. Brown, 'The Origins of a British Aristocracy', pp. 244–5.

136. Johnston, 'The Scots Army in the Reign of Anne', p. 19.

137. Brown, 'From Scottish Lords to British Officers', p. 149.

138. Ibid, p. 152.

139. Parke to Hedges, 19 January 1707, *Calendar of State Papers, Colonial Series. America and West Indies. 1706–1708, June*, p. 358.

140. Quoted in J. T. Finlay, *Wolfe and The '45 and from 1749 to 1753* (London, 1928), p. 226. It should be noted that Wolfe later changed his mind; see ibid., p. 229.

141. Sunderland to Parke, 28 March 1707, *Calendar of State Papers, Colonial Series. America and West Indies. 1706–1708, June*, p. 411.

142. Council of Trade and Plantations to Handasyd, 11 March 1707, ibid, p. 393.

143. Brown, 'From Scottish Lords to British Officers', p. 149.

144. B. P. Lenman, '"Garrison Government"?: Governor Alexander Spotswood and Empire', in G. G. Simpson (ed.), *The Scottish Soldier Abroad, 1247–1967* (Edinburgh and Maryland, 1992), pp. 67–8, 73.

145. L. D. Trotsky, *The History of the Russian Revolution* (London, 1977), p. 268.

146. Baillie to Roxburgh, 29 December 1705, *Correspondence of George Baillie of Jerviswood*, pp. 143–4.

147. Goodare, *State and Society in Early Modern Scotland*, p. 321.

148. A. L. Murray, 'Administration and Law', in T. I. Rae (ed.), *The Union of 1707: Its Impact on Scotland* (Glasgow and London, 1974), p. 34.

149. B. P. Lenman, *An Economic History of Scotland* (London, 1977), p. 60.

150. Robertson, 'An Elusive Sovereignty', p. 227.

151. Stair to Harley, 26 November 1706, *Portland Manuscripts*, vol. 4, p. 360. For Lockhart, Stair was the 'Judas of his country' (See Lockhart, '*Scotland's Ruine*', p. 58). Stair died after a four-hour long contribution to the debate over Article 22, it is assumed from a heart attack brought on by his exertions. See, for example, L'Hermitage to Heinsius, 14 January 1707, *The Correspondence 1700–1711 of John Churchill, First Duke of Marlborough and Anthony Heinsius, General Pensionary of Holland*, pp. 88–9.

152. 'News Letter', 29 October 1706, *Portland Manuscripts*, vol. 8, p. 258.

153. *Public General Statutes Affecting Scotland from the Beginning of the First Parliament of Great Britain, 6 Anne, AD 1707, to the End of the Fourteenth Parliament of the United Kingdom, 10 and 11 Victoria, AD 1847* (3 volumes, Edinburgh, 1876), vol. 1, p. 5.

154. Defoe, *The History of the Union Between England and Scotland*, p. 456.

155. I. D. Whyte, *Agriculture and Society in Seventeenth-Century Scotland* (Edinburgh, 1976), p. 12.

156. [Hodges], *The Rights and Interests of the Two British Monarchies*, p. 29.

157. [J. Arbothnot], *A Sermon Preached to the People at the Mercat-Cross of Edinburgh on the Subject of the Union* (London, 1707), p. 3. The text for this thoroughly political sermon is Ecclessiastes 10:7: 'Far better is he that Laboureth and aboundeth in all Things, than he that boasteth himself and wasteth Bread.'

158. Defoe, *The History of the Union Between England and Scotland*, pp. 458–9.

159. Davenant to Godolphin, 31 January 1704, 'An English Economist's View of the Union, 1705', edited by D. A. G. Waddell, *Scottish Historical Review*, vol. 35, no. 120, October 1956, p. 147.

160. H. R. Trevor-Roper, 'The Anglo-Scottish Union', *From Counter-Reformation to Glorious Revolution* (London, 1992), p. 296.

161. M. Davis, 'The Political Economy of Late Imperial America', *Prisoners of the American Dream* (London and New York, 1986), p. 185, note 3. The strategy of the British had become general for all of the capitalist and semi-capitalist powers by the eve of the First World War. The only criterion for support that any local pre-capitalist regime required was that they genuinely represented some effective form of social power, thus excluding, for example, the Emperor of China, but including various Arab Emirates. As Trotsky wrote in 1906: 'We thus see that the world bourgeoisie has made the stability of its State system profoundly dependent on the unstable pre-bourgeois bulwarks of reaction' (L. D. Trotsky, 'Results and Prospects', *The Permanent Revolution* and *Results and Prospects*, London, 1962, p. 240).

162. R. Burns, 'To a Mouse, on Turning Up Her Nest with the Plough, November 1785', *The Cannongate Burns*, p. 96.

163. 12 November 1706, 'To His Grace, Her Majesties High Commissioner, and Honourable Estates of the Parliament, the Humble Address of a Considerable Body of People in the South and Western Shires', [G. Mitchell], *Humble Pleadings for the Good Old Way* (n. p. [Edinburgh], 1713), p. 253.

164. Lockhart, *'Scotland's Ruine'*, p. 204. Needless to say, Lockhart puts the worst possible complexion on this rueful comment, describing it as a 'despising and contemning' remark.

Chapter 4: Scotland and the British State: From Crisis to Consolidation (1708–1716)

1. See for example, T. Nairn, 'Scotland and Europe', *The Break-Up of Britain* (second, expanded edition, London, 1981), pp. 108–10 and 'Old and New Scottish Nationalism', ibid, pp. 135–9. The actual concept of 'structural assimilation' was developed in the Trotskyist movement to describe the transformation of the Eastern European states on the Russian Stalinist model during and after 1947. See T. Wohlforth, 'The Theory of Structural Assimilation', *'Communists' Against Revolution* (London, 1978).

2. C. A. Whatley, *Scottish Society, 1707–1830* (Manchester, 2000), for example, devotes precisely 5 out of 337 pages to discussing the movement, despite carrying the subtitle, 'Beyond Jacobitism, Towards Industrialisation'.

3. C. von Clausewitz, *On War*, edited by A. Rapoport (Harmondsworth, 1968), p. 119.

4. Ibid, p. 376. For a study of the intellectual relationship between Clausewitz and Marxism, for which the philosophy of Hegel provides the common reference point, see A. Gat, 'Clausewitz and the Marxists: Yet Another Look', *Journal of Contemporary History*, vol. 27, no. 2, April 1992.

5. H. T. Buckle, *The History of Civilization in England* (3 volumes, London, 1904), vol. 3, p. 155.

6. G. Pratt Insh, *The Scottish Jacobite Movement* (Edinburgh and London, 1952), pp. x, ix.

7. E. J. Hobsbawm, 'Scottish Reformers of the Eighteenth Century and Capitalist Agriculture', in E. J. Hobsbawm et al. (eds), *Peasants in History* (Calcutta, 1980), pp. 6–7.

8. N. Davidson and D. Gluckstein, 'Nationalism and the Class Struggle in Scotland', *International Socialism*, Second Series, 48, Autumn 1990, p. 115.

9. See, however, C. Tilly, *European Revolutions, 1492–1992* (Oxford and Cambridge, Massachusetts, 1993), p. 114, for a work whose author can still describe the civil war of 1745–46 as a 'Scottish rising'.

10. J. G. A. Pocock, 'The Fourth English Civil War: Dissolution, Desertion and Alternative Histories in the Glorious Revolution', *Government And Opposition*, vol. 23, no. 2, Spring 1988, pp. 154, 166; 'The Significance of 1688: Some Reflections on Whig History', in R. Beddard (ed.), *The Revolutions Of 1688* (Oxford, 1991), pp. 279–80. This is a particularly curious position for Pocock to take, since he has elsewhere been one of the leading advocates of a new British history. On the other hand, as Michael Fry suggests, perhaps this has simply turned out to be an old English history with a new name. See 'Past Imperfect', *Scotland on Sunday*, 9 January 1995.

11. D. Cannadine, *Class in Britain* (New Haven and London, 1998), p. 51. Earlier in the same chapter Cannadine had informed us that Gaelic, Catholicism and clanship were cultural, and not simply geographic identities. Despite his error over the supposed Catholicism of the Highland population, this is obviously nearer the truth, since it is difficult to conceive of an identity that could simply be 'geographic' without also being social and cultural; see ibid, p. 43.

12. A. Cunningham, *The Loyal Clans* (Cambridge, 1932), p. 435.

13. Pratt Insh, *The Scottish Jacobite Movement*, p. 105.

14. Cunningham, *The Loyal Clans*, p. 311.

15. J. C. D. Clark, 'On Moving the Middle Ground: The Significance of Jacobitism in Historical Studies', in E. Cruikshanks and J. Black (eds), *The Jacobite Challenge* (Edinburgh, 1983), pp. 177–8.

16. W. Ferguson, *Scotland's Relations with England* (Edinburgh, 1977), p. 168.

17. M. G. H. Pittock, *The Myth of the Jacobite Clans* (Edinburgh, 1995), pp. 118, 6–9.

18. E. P. Thompson, 'Patricians and Plebs', *Customs in Common* (London, 1991), pp. 68, 75–6; N. Rogers, 'Riot and Popular Jacobitism in Early Hanoverian England', in E. Cruikshanks (ed.), *Ideology and Conspiracy* (Edinburgh, 1982), pp. 70–2, 82–3; N. Rogers, 'The Urban Opposition to the Whig Oligarchy, 1720–69', in M. C. and J. R. Jacob (eds), *The Origins of Anglo-American Radicalism* (revised edition, New Jersey and London, 1991), p. 155.

19. F. J. McLynn, *The Jacobites* (London, 1985), p. 123.

20. [W. Forbes], *A Pill for Pork-Eaters: Or, a Scots Lancet for an English Swelling* (Edinburgh, 1705), pp. 6, 8.

21. 'Come Let Us Drink a Health, Boys', *The Jacobite Relics of Scotland: Being the Songs, Airs and Legends of the Adherents of the House Of Stuart*, collected and illustrated by James Hogg (2 volumes, Edinburgh, 1819–21), vol. 1, p. 100.

22. R. D. MacKay, 'A Song to Prince Charles', *Highland Songs of the Forty-Five*, edited by J. L. Campbell (Edinburgh, 1984), p. 231.

23. J. Spalding, *The History of the Troubles and Memorable Occurrences in Scotland and England, from 1624 To 1645* (2 volumes, Edinburgh, 1828), vol. 2, p. 266.

24. Gordon to Stoneywood, 26 November 1745, 'Letters from Lord Lewis Gordon, and Others, to the Laird of Stoneywood, 1745–46', *Miscellany of the Spalding Club* 1, 1841, p. 408.

25. To describe Jacobitism as the expression of a 'reactionary nationalism', as Chris Harman as done, is therefore doubly wrong. On the one hand, because it assumes the position that I just criticised, namely that the movement was entirely based on 'Highland society'. On the other, because Highlanders were in any case incapable of regarding themselves in national terms. Harman groups Jacobitism together with other counter-revolutionary movements such as those of the Breton *chouans* and the Basque and Navarese Carlists, but to describe any of these as national movements seems misplaced, since they were ultimately attempts to protect an anti-national feudal particularism; see 'The Return of the National Question', *International Socialism*, Second Series, 56, Autumn 1992, pp. 13–14.

26. *The Miserable State of Scotland Since the Union Briefly Represented; And the Only Way to Render it Happy Plainly Pointed Out in a Letter to a Friend* (Perth, 1716), p. 1.

27. D. Szechi, *The Jacobites* (Manchester and New York, 1994), pp. 87–90.

28. N. Hooke, 'A Memorial Concerning the Affairs of Scotland', *The Secret History of Colonel Hooke's Negotiations in Scotland in Favour of the Pretender in 1707. Written by Himself* (London, 1760), p. 166.

29. F. J. McLynn, *France and the Jacobite Rising of 1745* (Edinburgh, 1981), p. 11.

30. Quoted in J. Black, *Culloden and the '45* (London, 1990), p. 29.

31. G. Lukacs, 'Critical Observations on Rosa Luxemburg's "Critique of the Russian Revolution"', *History and Class Consciousness* (London, 1971), p. 282.

32. E. Cregeen, 'The Changing Role of the House of Argyll in the Scottish Highlands', in N. T. Phillipson and R. Mitchison (eds), *Scotland in the Age of Improvement* (Edinburgh, 1970), p. 10.

33. [E. Bruce], *The Highlands of Scotland in 1750*, with an introduction by A. Lang (Edinburgh, 1898), p. 40.

34. [J. Hodges], *War Between the Two British Kingdoms Considered. For the Mutual Interest of Both* (London, 1705), p. 152.

35. D. Szechi, 'Introduction', *Letters of George Lockhart of Carnwarth, 1698–1732*, edited by D. Szechi (Edinburgh, 1989), p. xiii.

36. Although, unlike them, Szechi is in the position of offering a revisionist account in the absence of an orthodoxy to revise. The only examples which Szechi gives of the supposed conventional wisdom, to which he

claims Carnwarth stands as a reproach, are Insh's *The Scottish Jacobite Movement* and Plumb's *The Growth of Political Stability in England, 1675–1725*, dating from the 1950s and 1960s respectively. Leaving aside the age of these works – which scarcely suggests an interpretation sweeping all before it – the former is notable among Jacobite studies precisely for the exceptional nature of its Hegelian–Marxist framework and the latter, as the title suggests, is principally concerned with England.

37. G. S. Pryde, *Scotland from 1603 to the Present Day* (London, 1962), p. 81.

38. E. Cruikshanks, *Political Untouchables* (London, 1979), p. 70.

39. J. Home, *The History of the Rebellion in the Year 1745. The Works of John Home, Esq. to which is Prefixed an Account of his Life and Writings by Henry MacKenzie* (3 volumes, Edinburgh, 1822), vol. 3, p. 7.

40. Home appears to have been following the method outlined by Thucydides in *The History of the Peloponnesian War*, which was 'while keeping as closely as possible to the general sense of the words that were actually said, to have speakers say what, in my view, was called for in each situation'. See the critique by Moses Finley, who quotes this passage, in *Ancient History* (Harmondsworth, 1987), pp. 13–15.

41. Quoted in R. Mitchison, 'The Government and the Highlands 1707–1745', Phillipson and Mitchison (eds), *Scotland in the Age of Improvement*, p. 31.

42. A. Smith, *An Inquiry into the Nature and Causes of the Wealth of Nations*, edited by A. S. Skinner (Harmondsworth, 1970), p. 511.

43. *The Prisoners of the '45*, edited from the State Papers by B. G. Seton and J. G. Arnot (3 volumes, Edinburgh, 1928), vol. 1, pp. 270–1.

44. Huntly to the Lairds of Achloyne and Knockespack, 28 September 1715, *Correspondence of Sir George Warrender, Baronet, Lord Provost of Edinburgh and Member of Parliament for the City, with Relative Papers*, edited with an introduction and notes by W. K. Dickson (Edinburgh, 1935), pp. 99–100.

45. Mar to Forbes, 9 September 1715, quoted in A. and H. Tayler, *1715* (London, 1936), pp. 43–4.

46. V. I. Lenin, 'The Tasks of the Proletariat in Our Revolution', *Collected Works* (45 volumes, Moscow, 1963), vol. 24, p. 59.

47. L. D. Trotsky, *The History of the Russian Revolution* (London, 1977), p. 223.

48. *An Ample Disquisition into the Nature of Regalities and Other Heritable Jurisdictions in That Part of Great Britain Called Scotland. By an English Gentleman* (London, 1747), pp. 3, 13.

49. *A Letter to an English Member of Parliament from a Gentleman in Scotland Concerning the Slavish Dependence which a Great Part of that Nation is Still Kept Under, by Superiorities, Wards, Reliefs and Other Remnants of the Feudal Law, and by Clanship and Tithes* (Edinburgh, 1721), pp. 13, 16, 29–30, 34. Significantly, this pamphlet was republished in 1746 during the propaganda onslaught preceding the abolition of feudalism in Scotland.

50. C. Innes, *Sketches of Early Scotch History and Social Progress* (Edinburgh, 1861), pp. 455–6.

51. Argyll to Townshend, 24 September 1715, quoted in Tayler and Tayler, *1715*, p. 60.

52. E. K. Carmichael, 'Jacobitism in the Scottish Commission of the Peace, 1707–1760', *Scottish Historical Review*, vol. 48, no. 165, April 1979, pp. 58, 61.

53. Lockhart to Oxford, 23 December 1712, *Letters of George Lockhart of Carnwarth, 1698–1732*, p. 63; same to same, ibid, p. 66.

54. Marchmont to Seafield, 7 November 1699, *A Selection from the Papers of the Earls of Marchmont. Illustrative of Events from 1685 to 1750* (3 volumes, London, 1831), vol. 3, pp. 188–9.

55. C. A. Whatley, 'How Tame Were the Scottish Lowlands During the Eighteenth Century?', in T. M. Devine (ed.), *Conflict and Stability in Scottish Society 1780–1850* (Edinburgh, 1990), p. 7.

56. Smith to Strachan, 4 April 1760, A. Smith, *The Correspondence of Adam Smith*, edited by E. C. Mossener and I. S. Ross (Oxford, 1977), p. 68.

57. Wodrow to Black, 8 November 1715, *The Correspondence of the Rev. Robert Wodrow*, edited by the Rev. T. McCrie (3 volumes, Edinburgh, 1842), vol. 2, p. 90.

58. B. P. Lenman, *The Jacobite Risings in Britain, 1689–1746* (London, 1980), p. 98.

59. Balmerino to Maule, 2 June 1713, quoted in W. Ferguson, *Scotland: 1689 to the Present* (Edinburgh, 1978), p. 61.

60. Lord Bolingbroke, 'A Letter to Sir William Windham', *The Works of Lord Bolingbroke. With a Life, Prepared Expressly for this Edition Containing Additional Information Relative to His Personal and Public Character, Selected from the Best Authorities* (4 volumes, Philadelphia, 1841), vol. 1, p. 129.

61. P. K. Monod, *Jacobitism and the English People* (Cambridge, 1989), p. 323.

62. Lenman, *The Jacobite Risings in Britain*, pp. 116–18.

63. L. Gooch, *The Desperate Faction?* (Hull, 1995), p. 178.

64. Lenman, *The Jacobite Risings in Britain*, p. 118.

65. F. J. McLynn, 'Newcastle and the Jacobite Rising of 1745', *The Journal of Local Studies*, vol. 2, no. 1, Spring 1982, p. 58. McLynn argues that Jacobitism in the north-east of England had two other social bases apart from the Catholic gentry, 'Tory country gentlemen' and 'the Newcastle proletariat' or, more specifically, the colliers and keelmen who were also affected by the economic crisis. The question here is whether the latter two were capable of rising in the absence of the former. As McLynn notes, the failure of the '15 effectively led to the destruction of the Catholic gentry and, in their absence, there was no rising in the north-east during the '45. As I argued earlier in this chapter, the ascription of 'Jacobite' motives to the early proletariat is in any case extremely questionable: 'The authorities could never make up their minds whether the colliers were activated more by Levelling or Jacobite principles' (ibid, pp. 58–9).

66. Gooch, *The Desperate Faction?*, pp. 60–61. Correctly noting that 'feudalism was long dead' in the region, Monod goes on to claim that servants also fought as Catholics, not because they were forced by their masters: 'No legal bond required servants to fight for their masters, and had they been forced, they would have run away at the first shot.' To say the least, this expresses a certain degree of naivety concerning the powers which members of even a post-feudal ruling class can exercise over their subordinates, particularly if the former are armed, as these were. See Monod, *Jacobitism and the English People*, p. 323.

67. Mar to Erskine, 17 January 1712, Historical Manuscripts Commission, *Report on the Manuscripts of the Earl of Mar and Kellie* (London, 1904), p. 494.

68. 'Memorial as to the State of the Prisoners on Account of the Late Rebellion, 1715', *The Spottiswoode Miscellany: A Collection of Original Papers and Tracts Illustrative of the Civil and Ecclesiastical History of Scotland* (2 volumes, Edinburgh, 1845), vol. 2, pp. 476–7. Haldane was subsequently accused of having Jacobite sympathies because he recommended leniency in the treatment of prisoners; this may be so, but it is obvious that his account is scarcely flattering to the Jacobite cause.

69. M. G. H. Pittock, *Jacobitism* (Houndmills, 1998), pp. 60–1.

70. A. Keith, *A Thousand Years of Aberdeen* (Aberdeen, 1972), pp. 273–4.

71. A. Smith, 'Dundee and the '45', in L. Scott-Moncrieff (ed.), *The '45: To Gather an Image Whole* (Edinburgh, 1988), p. 100.

72. Glasgow Magistrates to George II, 26 August 1715, *Extracts from the Records of the Burgh of Glasgow* (12 volumes, Glasgow, 1876–1917), vol. 4, *1691–1717*, pp. 539–40.

73. Townshend and Argyll to the Glasgow Magistrates, 12 October 1715, ibid, pp. 545–6.

74. W. L. Mathieson, *Scotland and the Union* (Glasgow, 1905), p. 301.

75. Wodrow to Flint, 23 December 1714, *The Correspondence of the Rev. Robert Wodrow*, vol. 1, p. 633.

76. Wodrow to Erskine, 2 February 1715, ibid, vol. 2, p. 21.

77. Wodrow to Black, 8 November 1715, ibid, p. 92.

78. Mathieson, *Scotland and the Union*, p. 312.

79. D. Szechi, 'The Hanoverians and Scotland', in M. Greengrass (ed.), *Conquest and Coalescence* (London, 1991), p. 124.

80. [Forbes] to Walpole, August 1716, *Culloden Papers. From the Year 1625 to 1748* (London, 1815), p. 61.

81. Lockhart to the Earl Marischal, April 1719, *Letters of George Lockhart of Carnwarth*, p. 141.

82. D. Hume, 'Of the Parties of Great Britain', *Political Essays*, edited by K. Haakonsen (Cambridge, 1994), p. 282. The concluding section of this essay, from which the passage quoted is taken, was omitted in editions published after 1770 and replaced by a shorter concluding paragraph. It is restored in this edition as an endnote; see ibid, p. 279, note 10.

Chapter 5: Social Transformation and Agricultural Improvement (1716–1744)

1. D. Defoe, 'An Explanatory Preface to *The True-Born Englishman*', *The Shortest Way with Dissenters and Other Pamphlets* (Oxford, 1927), p. 24.

2. K. Marx, 'Preface to the First Edition', *Capital* (3 volumes, Harmondsworth, 1976), vol. 1, p. 91. This very condensed formula was not, of course, his last word on the subject. In 1877 Marx wrote a letter to the Russian journal *Otechesivenniye Zapiski* criticising the interpretation of *Capital* made in its pages by the populist N. K. Mikhailovsky. Marx proposes two hypotheses. First, that the Russian peasant commune might provide the launching pad for the advance to communism in Russia, but the possibility of that happening was already being undermined by the development of capitalism. Second, that even if the commune failed to play this role, capitalist development would in any event not proceed in the same manner as in England or France, contrary to what was asserted

by Mikhailovsky in his desire to turn a 'historical sketch of the genesis of capitalism in Western Europe into a historic–philosophical theory of general development, imposed by fate on all peoples, whatever the historical circumstances in which they are placed'. See '[Letter to *Otechesivenniye Zapiski*]', *Collected Works* (50 volumes, London, 1975–), vol. 24, pp. 199, 200. See my discussion in 'Marx and Engels on the Scottish Highlands', *Science and Society*, vol. 65, no. 3, Fall 2001, pp. 307–18.

3. See, for example, T. Nairn, 'The Modern Janus', *The Break-Up of Britain* (second, revised edition, London and New York, 1981), pp. 334–5.

4. L. D. Trotsky, *The History of the Russian Revolution* (London, 1977), p. 27.

5. Ibid.

6. C. Trebilcock, *The Industrialization of the Continental Powers* (Harlow, 1981), p. 208 and pp. 221–7 more generally.

7. H. R. Trevor-Roper, 'The Scottish Enlightenment', *Studies on Voltaire and the Eighteenth Century* 58, 1967, p. 1650.

8. B. F. Duckham, 'English Influences in the Scottish Coal Industry 1700–1815', in J. Butt and J. T. Ward (eds), *Scottish Themes* (Edinburgh, 1976), pp. 28–34.

9. B. F. Duckham, *A History of the Scottish Coal Industry* (2 volumes, Newton Abbot, 1970), vol. 1, *1700–1815*, p. 169.

10. C. A. Whatley, 'The Dark Side of the Enlightenment? Sorting Out Serfdom', T. M. Devine and J. R. Young (eds), *Eighteenth Century Scotland: New Perspectives* (East Linton, 1999), pp. 268–72 and '"The Fettering Bonds of Brotherhood": Combination and Labour Relations in the Scottish Coal-Mining Industry c. 1690–1775', *Social History*, vol. 12, no. 2, May 1987, pp. 139–46.

11. Contrary to what is argued in J. Saville, *The Consolidation of the Capitalist State, 1800–1850* (London and Boulder, 1994), p. 17. See Whatley, '"The Fettering Bonds of Brotherhood"', pp. 146–53. A study by Rab Houston of labour relations in the mines at Lasswade during the first half of the eighteenth century gives detailed support to Whatley. See R. A. Houston, 'Coal, Class and Community: Labour Relations in a Scottish Mining Community, 1650–1750', *Social History*, vol. 8, no. 1, January 1983.

12. C. A. Whatley, 'New Light on Nef's Numbers: Coal Mining and the First Phase of Scottish Industrialisation, c.1700–1830', in A. J. G. Cummings and T. M. Devine (eds), *Industry, Business and Society in Scotland Since 1700* (Edinburgh, 1994), pp. 7, 15.

13. Ironically, Ireland, a country that had failed to adapt even to this extent was rewarded by conquest from England. As a result Ireland overtook Scotland in most indices of economic growth by the end of the seventeenth century, precisely because the conquest involved the smashing of existing feudal relations and the substitution of capitalist ones in the context of the colonial-settler regime – although this is not to say that subjugation by England would have been any more desirable a route to development for the Scottish people than it actually was for the majority of the Irish. See R. Mitchison, 'Ireland and Scotland: The Seventeenth-Century Legacies Compared', in T. M. Devine and D. Dickson (eds), *Ireland and Scotland, 1600–1850* (Edinburgh, 1983), pp. 4, 6.

14. T. M. Devine, 'The Anglo-Scottish Union of 1707 and Scottish Development: The Case Re-Opened', *Scotia* 8, 1984, p. 7.

15. J. Clerk, 'Sir John Clerk's Observations on the Present Circumstances of Scotland, 1730', edited by T. C. Smout, *Miscellany of the Scottish History Society* 10, 1965, pp. 96–212. The quote appears on p. 212.

16. D. Defoe, *A Tour Through the Whole Island of Great Britain*, abridged and edited with an introduction and notes by P. Rodgers (Harmondsworth, 1974), pp. 596–7, 614–15.

17. Cockburn to Bell, 3 June 1735, *Letters of John Cockburn of Ormistoun to his Gardener, 1727–1744*, edited with introduction and notes by J. Colville (Edinburgh, 1904), p. 25.

18. P. Lindsay, *The Interest of Scotland Considered, with Regard to its Policy in Employing the Poor, its Agriculture, its Trade, its Manufacturies and Fisheries* (Edinburgh, 1733), pp. 38–9.

19. [W. Mackintosh], *An Essay on Ways and Means of Inclosing, Fallowing, Planting, etc., in Scotland; and that in Sixteen Years at Farthest* (Edinburgh, 1729), p. 257.

20. A. Smith, *An Inquiry into the Nature and Causes of the Wealth of Nations*, edited by A. S. Skinner (Harmondsworth, 1970), p. 520. Note the lack of reference to industry. In fact, Smith devotes far more space to discussing agriculture than to any other sector of the economy in this work. There is now an extensive literature devoted to questioning the extent to which Smith was aware even of the developments in industry taking place while he wrote, let alone of their importance. For the case that where his comments extend beyond agriculture they relate to 'proto-industrialisation' rather than industrialisation proper, see C. P. Kindleberger, 'The Historical Background: Adam Smith and the Industrial Revolution', in T. Wilson and A. S. Skinner (eds), *The Market and the State* (Oxford, 1976), and the dissenting comments by A. Briggs and R. M. Hartwell which follow. One interpretation of Smith, which I find persuasive, argues that his work constitutes a defence of 'agrarian-based capitalist development in a landed commonwealth ruled by prosperous and public-spirited country gentlemen' against the emergent 'industrial and commercial capitalists' whose amorality Smith distrusted; see D. McNally, *Political Economy and the Rise of Capitalism* (London and New York, 1993), pp. 256–7 and pp. 228–57 more generally. For an earlier version of this argument, see R. Koeber, 'Adam Smith and the Industrial Revolution', *Economic History Review*, Second Series, vol. 11, no. 3, July 1959, pp. 389–91.

21. C. Harman, 'From Feudalism to Capitalism', *International Socialism*, Second Series, 45, Winter 1989, p. 82.

22. K. Marx, *Theories of Surplus Value* (3 volumes, Moscow, 1963), vol. 1, p. 43. See also Appendix, 'Marx and Engels on Scotland', in the present volume.

23. Marx, *Capital*, vol. 1, p. 895.

24. 'The accumulation of gold and silver, of money, is the first historic appearance of the gathering-together of capital and the first great means thereto; but, as such, it is not yet the accumulation of capital. For that, the re-entry of what has been accumulated into circulation would have to be posited as the moment and the means of accumulation' (K. Marx, *Grundrisse*, Harmondsworth, 1973, p. 233).

25. I. D. Whyte, 'Proto-Industrialisation in Scotland', in P. Hudson (ed.), *Regions and Industries* (Cambridge, 1989), pp. 244–5.

26. J. M. Dickie, 'The Economic Position of Scotland in 1760', *Scottish Historical Review*, vol. 18, no. 69, October 1920, p. 19.

27. Ibid, p. 17; T. M. Devine, *The Transformation of Rural Scotland* (Edinburgh, 1994), pp. 15–16.

28. Smith, *The Wealth of Nations*, pp. 327–8; T. C. Smout, 'Where Had the Scottish Economy Got To by the Third Quarter of the Eighteenth Century?', in I. Hont and M. Ignatieff (eds), *Wealth and Virtue* (Cambridge, 1983), pp. 55–7;

29. Atholl to Murray, 23 May 1717, L. Leneman, *Living in Atholl, 1685–1785* (Edinburgh, 1986), p. 47.

30. J. Clerk, *Memoirs of the Life of Sir John Clerk of Penicuik, Baronet, Baron of the Exchequer, Extracted by Himself from His Own Journals 1676–1755*, edited from the manuscript in Penicuik House with an introduction and notes by J. M. Gray (Edinburgh, 1892), p. 137.

31. H. Hamilton, 'Introduction', *Life and Labour on an Aberdeenshire Estate 1735–1750 (Being Selections from the Monymusk Papers)*, transcribed and edited by H. Hamilton (Aberdeen, 1946), p. xxvii.

32. V. G. Keirnan, 'The Covenanters: A Problem of Creed and Class', *Poets, Politics and the People*, edited by H. G. Kaye (London and New York, 1989), p. 56.

33. Wilson to Grant, 6 June 1735, *Selections from the Monymusk Papers (1713–1755)*, transcribed and edited by H. Hamilton (Edinburgh, 1945), p. 128. 'Porteous Rolled' is not a reference to the fate of Captain John Porteous, who was not lynched by the Edinburgh crowd until the following year. Rather, it refers to the process by which the High Court began the process of indicting suspected law-breakers. The Court would issue a letter to all the sheriffs asking if anyone within their jurisdiction had committed any crimes from an enclosed list. The sheriff would then put the same question to a number of local worthies, whose responses were collected and returned to Edinburgh. The list of responses was known as a 'Porteous Roll'. See S. J. Davies, 'The Courts and the Scottish Legal System, 1600–1747: The Case of Stirlingshire', in B. P. Lenman, G. Parker and V. A. C. Gatrell (eds), *Crime and the Law: The Social History of Crime in Western Europe Since 1500* (London, 1980), pp. 147–8.

34. H. Hamilton, *An Economic History of Scotland in the Eighteenth Century* (Oxford, 1963), p. 86; 'Economic Growth in Scotland, 1720–1770', *Scottish Journal of Political Economy*, vol. 6, no. 2, June 1959, pp. 91–2.

35. E. Kerridge, *The Agricultural Revolution* (London, 1967), p. 24. As David McNally has pointed out, the onslaught against the remaining English common lands after 1760 (when the great period of English parliamentary enclosure began) was therefore the culmination of a centuries-long attempt to dispossess the peasantry, 'seal[ing] the fate of the small tenants or cottagers by making them irreversibly reliant on wage-labour for their subsistence' (*Against the Market*, p. 127).

36. P. Linebaugh and M. Rediker, *The Many-Headed Hydra* (London and New York, 2000), p. 19; J. Holstun, *Ehud's Dagger* (London and New York, 2000), p. 372.

37. *Letter to the Right Hon. Augustus Du Cary, Commander of His Majesty's Troops at Kirkcudbright, from the Poor Distressed Tenants of Galloway*, National Library of Scotland, Wodrow MSS, XL94.

38. J. Leopold, 'The Leveller's Revolt in Galloway in 1724', *Journal of the Scottish Labour History Society* 14, 1980, p. 15.

39. A. Webster, 'An Account of the Number of People in Scotland in the Year One Thousand Seven Hundred and Fifty Five', *Scottish Population Statistics Including Websters's Analysis of Population 1755*, edited by J. G. Kyd (Edinburgh, 1952), pp. 24–5.

40. Clerk to Clerk, 6 May 1724, 'Letters Reporting the Rising of the Levellers in 1724', edited by W. A. J. Prevost, *Transactions of the Dumfries and Galloway Natural History and Antiquarian Society*, Third Series, 44, 1967, p. 199.

41. Quoted in A. S. Morton, 'The Levellers of Galloway', *Transactions of the Dumfries and Galloway Natural History and Antiquarian Society*, Third Series, 16, 1936, p. 239.

42. Leopold, 'The Levellers Revolt in Galloway in 1724', p. 16.

43. *An Account of the Reasons of Some People in Galloway, Their Meetings Anent Public Grievances Through Enclosures*, New College Library, Bc4.8.

44. *Letter to the Right Hon. Augustus Du Cary, Commander of His Majesty's Troops at Kirkcudbright, from the Poor Distressed Tenants of Galloway*, National Library of Scotland, Woodrow MSS, XL94.

45. T. C. Smout, *A History of the Scottish People, 1560–1830* (Glasgow, 1972), p. 304.

46. C. W. J. Withers, 'Education and Anglicisation: The Policy of the SSPCK Towards the Education of the Highlander, 1709–1825', *Scottish Studies* 26, 1982, p. 40.

47. Quoted in ibid.

48. *The Highlander's Complaint, Transmitted by a Gentleman of That Country to His Friends at Edinburgh* (Edinburgh, 1737), p. 24.

49. Lindsay, *The Interest of Scotland*, pp. 31–2.

50. Lockhart to the Old Pretender, 2 September 1725, *Letters of George Lockhart of Carnwarth, 1698–1732*, edited by D. Szechi (Edinburgh, 1989), p. 239.

51. G. Wade, 'Report Relating to the Highlands, 1727', *Historical Papers Relating to the Jacobite Period 1699–1750*, edited by J. Allardyce (2 volumes, Aberdeen, 1895), vol. 1, p. 161.

52. E. Burt, *Burt's Letter's from the North of Scotland*, with an introduction by R. Johnson (2 volumes, Edinburgh, 1974), vol. 2, pp. 246–7.

53. 'Memorial Anent the True State of the Highlands as to Their Chieftainries, Followings and Dependencies Before the Late Rebellion', *Historical Papers Relating to the Jacobite Period*, vol. 1, pp. 172, 174, 176.

54. Erskine to Farquharson, 15 September 1726, *The Records of Invercauld*, edited by J. G. Michie (Aberdeen, 1901), pp. 315–16.

55. Campbell to Mar, 29 July 1718, Historical Manuscripts Commission, *Calendar of the Stuart Papers Belonging to His Majesty the King, Preserved at Windsor Castle* (7 volumes, London, 1923), vol. 7, pp. 94, 95, 97.

56. E. R. Cregeen, 'The Tacksmen and Their Successors: A Study of Tenurial Reorganisation in Mull, Morven and Tiree in the Early Eighteenth Century', *Scottish Studies* 13, 1969, p. 99.

57. Ibid, p. 107.

58. Ibid, p. 118.

Chapter 6: The End of the British Revolution (1745–1746)

1. As indeed do many modern historians, for example, Keith Brown: 'As a meaningful political force jacobitism was finished at Sheriffmuir.' See *Kingdom or Province?* (Houndmills, 1992), p. 196.

2. G. Lockhart, *The Lockhart Papers; Containing Memoirs and Commentaries upon the Affairs of Scotland from 1702 to 1715, by George Lockhart Esq. of Carnwarth* (2 volumes, London, 1817), vol. 2, p. 405. These passages are not included in 'Scotland's Ruine'.

3. Quoted in J. Black, *Culloden and the '45* (London, 1990), p. 46.

4. H. Fielding, *The History of Tom Jones. A Foundling*, in *The Writings of Henry Fielding Comprising His Celebrated Works of Fiction* (London and Edinburgh, 1875), p. 300.

5. Lord Kames, *Essays upon Several Subjects Concerning British Antiquities* (Edinburgh, 1747), p. 208.

6. R. Blackburn, *The Making of New World Slavery* (London and New York, 1997), pp. 569–70.

7. Wodrow to Black, 8 November 1715, *The Correspondence of the Rev. Robert Wodrow*, edited by T. McCrie (3 volumes, Edinburgh, 1842), vol. 2, p. 91.

8. From this point onwards I will refer respectively to the Hanoverian and Jacobite armies. Stuart Reid has argued against this usage on the grounds that the term 'Hanoverian' should be reserved for the army of that particular German statelet, the appropriate term for the forces of George II being the 'British' army. This seems excessively formalistic. I use the terms to denote the possibility of a change of regime and the Jacobite army consequently becoming the basis of a new 'British' army in its turn. See 'Introduction', *1745: A Military History of the Last Jacobite Rebellion* (Staplehurst, 1996), no pagination [p. i].

9. F. J. McLynn, *The Jacobite Army in England 1745* (Edinburgh, 1983), p. 28.

10. D. Stevenson, *Alasdair MacColla and the Highland Problem in the Seventeenth Century* (Edinburgh, 1980), p. 298.

11. J. Dalrymple, *Considerations upon the Policy of Entails in Great Britain; Occasioned by a Scheme to Apply for a Statute to Let the Entails of Scotland Die Out, on the Death of the Possessors and Heirs Now Existing* (Edinburgh, 1764), pp. 66–7.

12. A. Ferguson, *A Sermon Preached in The Ersh Language to His Majesty's First Highland Regiment of Foot, Commanded by Lord John Murray, at Their Cantonment at Camberwell on the 18th Day of December, 1745* (London, 1746), pp. 15, 17. Tom Nairn has described this sermon as 'dire stuff', consisting of little more than 'eulogies of the Protestant–Hanoverian way, conventionally counterpointed against stern denunciations of the Pretender, Popery and wooden shoes'; see 'From Civil Society to Civic Nationalism: Evolution of a Myth', *Faces of Nationalism* (London and New York, 1997), p. 76. In fact, it contains in embryo many of the ideas which Ferguson was to elaborate 20 years later:

    > If Society is a thing so indispensably necessary to the human Nature, and if every individual Member reaps such inestimable Advantages from their joint Confederacy; can we no longer hesitate in drawing our Conclusion, that each member is bound, both on account of his own and the public Welfare, to maintain that League from which he derives

so many blessings. (Ferguson, *A Sermon Preached in the Ersh Language to His Majesty's First Highland Regiment of Foot*, p. 9)

Compare A. Ferguson, *An Essay on the History of Civil Society*, edited with an introduction by D. Forbes (Edinburgh, 1966), Part 1, Section 3, 'Of the Principle of Union Among Mankind'.

13. Forbes to Tweedale, 8 August 1745, *Culloden Papers. From the Year 1625 to 1748* (London, 1815), p. 204.
14. J. S. Gibson, *Locheil of the '45* (Edinburgh, 1994), p. 35.
15. 'Donald Cameron of Clune's Evidence at the Trial of John Cameron of Fassifern', 15 February 1754, J. Stewart, *The Camerons* (Stirling, 1974), pp. 307–8.
16. E. Richards and M. Clough, *Cromartie* (Aberdeen, 1989), pp. 55–6.
17. 'Memoirs of the Rebellion in 1745 and 1746, So Far as It Concerned the Counties of Aberdeen and Banff', *Origins of the 'Forty-Five*, edited by W. B. Blaikie (Edinburgh, 1916), pp. 130–1, 116, 121.
18. Richards and Clough, *Cromartie*, p. 56.
19. J. Foster, *An Account of the Behavior of the Late Earl of Kilmarnock After His Sentence, and on the Day of His Execution* (London, 1746), p. 10–11.
20. Quoted in C. Petrie, *The Jacobite Movement: The Last Phase 1716–1807* (London, 1950), p. 126.
21. *The Prisoners of the '45*, edited from the State Papers by B. G. Seton and J. G. Arnot (3 volumes, Edinburgh, 1928), vol. 3, pp. 300–26.
22. E. R. Cregeen, 'The Tacksmen and Their Successors: A Study of Tenurial Reorganisation in Mull, Morven and Tiree in the Early Eighteenth Century', *Scottish Studies* 13, 1969, p. 127.
23. Quoted in G. Menary, *The Life and Letters of Duncan Forbes of Culloden* (London, 1936), p. 311.
24. Quoted in W. Wilson, *The House of Airlie* (2 volumes, London, 1924), vol. 1, p. 171.
25. Gordon to Stoneywood, 26 November 1745, 'Letters from Lord Lewis Gordon, and Others, to the Laird of Stoneywood, 1745–46', *Miscellany of the Spalding Club* 1, 1841, p. 408.
26. Bisset to Harrison, 28 September 1745, L. Leneman, *Living in Atholl, 1685–1785* (Edinburgh, 1986), p. 220.
27. Bisset to Atholl, 15 October 1745, ibid, p. 221.
28. R. Chambers, *History of the Rebellion in 1745–6* (Edinburgh, 1869), pp. 68–9.
29. McLynn, *The Jacobite Army in England 1745*, pp. 25–6.
30. M. G. H. Pittock, *The Myth of the Jacobite Clans* (Edinburgh, 1995), pp. 57–61.
31. J. M. McPherson, *Battle Cry of Freedom* (Oxford and New York, 1988), pp. 317–21, 614.
32. In a later work, *For Cause and Comrades* (Oxford and New York, 1997), McPherson uses the letters and memoirs of rank-and-file troops on both sides of the American Civil War to reconstruct the reasons why they fought. Those given by Confederates ranged from the open defence of slavery on the one hand to more idealistic positions based on states rights (and 'liberty' more generally) on the other. For examples of the former, see ibid, pp. 19–20, 107–10; for examples of the latter, see ibid, pp. 20–1, 170–1.
33. Reid, *1745*, p. 200.

34. B. P. Lenman, *The Jacobite Risings in Britain, 1689–1746* (London, 1980), p. 253.

35. Pittock, *The Myth of the Jacobite Clans*, p. 60; see also Chapter 3, 'Nationalists or Jacobites?'.

36. 'Proclamations of Prince Charles: F – 10 October 1745', *Historical Papers Relating to the Jacobite Period*, edited by J. Allardyce (2 volumes, Aberdeen, 1895), vol. 1, p. 189.

37. Lenman, *The Jacobite Risings in Britain*, p. 253; Pittock, *The Myth of the Jacobite Clans*, p. 93.

38. E. Cruikshanks, *Political Untouchables* (London, 1979), p. 100.

39. S. Reynolds, *Kingdoms and Communities in Western Europe, 900–1300* (second edition, Oxford, 1997), pp. 251–4. An example of 'proto-nationalism' identified by Eric Hobsbawm is where 'the political bonds and vocabularies of select groups are more directly linked to states and institutions, and which are capable of eventual generalization, extension and popularisation'. See *Nations and Nationalism Since 1780* (Cambridge, 1990), p. 47. This might include the identification of a territory and its population with a specific dynastic succession, but only where the Crown becomes the figurehead for the 'people' in a way incompatible with the powers of the feudal monarchy. These powers – or their equivalent at the local jurisdictional level – were precisely what the Jacobite lords wished to maintain. For a discussion of the issues involved see N. Davidson, *The Origins of Scottish Nationhood* (London and Sterling, Virginia, 2000), pp. 24–6, 32–3 (for Europe in general) and 47–51, 59–61 (for Scotland in particular).

40. Lenman, *The Jacobite Risings in Britain*, p. 250.

41. *The Woodhouslee Manuscript: A Narrative of Events in Edinburgh and District During the Jacobite Occupation, September to November 1745*, edited by A. F. Stewart (London and Edinburgh, 1907), p. 89.

42. Kames, *Essays upon Several Subjects Concerning British Antiquities*, pp. 205, 208; see also p. 217. For an anonymous contemporary pamphlet devoted entirely to this theme see *A Comparison of the Spirit of the Whigs and Jacobites; Being the Substance of a Discourse Delivered to an Audience of Gentlemen in Edinburgh, December 24, 1745* (Edinburgh, 1746). Compare both to Alexander Shields in 1685: 'When a ruler, in direct opposition to the ends of government, seeks the ruin not only of religion, but also of the people's safety, he must certainly forfeit his right to reign.' *A Hind Let Loose* (Edinburgh, 1797), p. 411.

43. Ferguson, *A Sermon Preached in the Ersh Language to His Majesty's First Highland Regiment of Foot*, pp. 18–19.

44. Gordon to Stoneywood, 29 October 1745, 'Letters from Lord Lewis Gordon, and Others, to the Laird of Stoneywood', p. 403.

45. Bisset to Athol, 15 October 1745, Leneman, *Living in Atholl*, p. 222.

46. Cochrane to Argyll, 4 October 1745, *The Cochrane Correspondence Regarding the Affairs of Glasgow 1745–46* (Glasgow, 1836), p. 23.

47. Aberdeen Town Council to Falconer, 9 April 1745, 'Extracts from Aberdeen Burgh Records, 1745–46: D – Town Council Letters, 1746', *Historical Papers Relating to the Jacobite Period*, vol. 1, p. 240. The same letter gives some indication of the extent of British-wide trading networks by that date: 'Our Provisions and Necessaries, which we used to get from

London, Newcastle and the Firth of Forth, are quite exhausted by the long Stagnation of Trade, and the army's being for sometime here.'

48. L. Colley, *Britons* (New Haven and London, 1992), pp. 83, 377–8.
49. Cochrane to Maule, 4 January 1746, *The Cochrane Correspondence*, p. 66.
50. 'Extracts from the Diary of the Reverend John Bisset, Minister at Aberdeen, 1745–46', entry for 1st November 1745, *Miscellany of the Spalding Club* 1, p. 352.
51. Ibid, p. 253.
52. Gordon to Stoneywood, 26 November 1745, 'Letters from Lord Lewis Gordon, and Others, to the Laird of Stoneywood', p. 407.
53. T. L. Kington Oliphant, *The Jacobite Lairds of Gask* (London, 1870), p. 128.
54. A. Smith, 'Dundee and the '45', L. Scott-Moncrieff (ed.), *The '45: To Gather an Image Whole* (Edinburgh, 1988), pp. 102–5. Compare that account with the enthusiastic, if not entirely accurate version found in the correspondence of William Mure of Glasgow:

> Last Wednesday, being his Majesty's birth-day, the inhabitants of Perth inclined to give some public evidence of their loyalty, in which they were interrupted by a party of Highlanders, then in the town, upon which the mob rose, disarmed the whole party, killed a French officer who happened to be among them, injured several, and drove the rest out of town. Poor wretches! It would pity you to hear how their parties which are come from the army are hunted down in their passage through the west country homewards. (Miller to Mure, 4 November 1745, *Selections from the Family Papers Preserved at Caldwell*, 2 volumes, Glasgow, 1854, part 2, vol. 1, *1733–1764*, p. 68)

55. The Perth Hanoverians fled to Stirling after the failure of their uprising, only to be enrolled by General Blackeney into a 'volunteer' regiment called the Company of Perthmen. Most of their subsequent efforts were directed towards digging fortifications around Stirling Castle. See B. Harris and C. A. Whatley, '"To Solemnize His Majesty's Birthday": New Perspectives on Loyalism in George II's Britain', *History*, vol. 83, no. 271, July 1998, pp. 418–19.
56. *Jacobite Memoirs of the Rebellion of 1745*, edited by R. Chambers (Edinburgh, 1834), pp. 96–7.
57. Harris and Whatley, '"To Solemnize His Majesty's Birthday"', p. 419.
58. David, Lord Elcho, *A Short Account of the Affairs of Scotland, in the Years 1744, 1745, 1746*, with a memoir and annotations by E. Charteris (Edinburgh, 1973), pp. 423–4; K. Tomasson and F. Buist, *Battles of the '45* (London, 1962), p. 202.
59. A. Carlyle, *Autobiography of the Reverend Dr Alexander Carlyle, Minister of Inveresk Containing Memorials of the Men and Events of the Time* (Edinburgh, 1840), p. 147.
60. Forbes to Tweedale, 8 August 1745, *Culloden Papers*, p. 205.
61. G. D. H. Cole and R. Postgate, *The Common People, 1746–1946* (second, revised edition, London, 1961), p. 2.
62. A. Smith, *Lectures on Jurisprudence*, edited by R. L. Meek, D. D. Raphael and P. G. Stern (Oxford, 1978), p. 541.
63. H. Fielding, *A History of the Present Rebellion in Scotland* (London, 1745), pp. 9–10.

64. This absence of military power in Scotland casts doubt on the claims which are often made about the supposed colonial relationship which existed between England and Scotland at the time. As Linda Colley remarks: 'We know that English politicians neglected Scotland from the Act of Union to the '45 (which would scarcely have reached such terrifying proportions had English imperialism been assiduous)' (L. Colley, 'The Multiple Elites of Eighteenth-Century Britain', *Comparative Studies in History and Society*, vol. 29, no. 2, April 1987, p. 409).

65. J. Johnstone, *A Memoir of the 'Forty-Five*, edited with an introduction by B. Rawson (second edition, London, 1970), p. 41.

66. J. Youngson, *The Prince and the Pretender* (Edinburgh, 1996), p. 237. It should be noted that Youngson is deliberately trying to argue – none too convincingly – from a pro-Jacobite position at this point in his extremely interesting book.

67. Lockhart to the Old Pretender, 25 July 1725, *Letters of George Lockhart of Carnwarth, 1698–1732*, edited by D. Szechi (Edinburgh, 1989), p. 232.

68. F. J. McLynn, *France and the Jacobite Rising of 1745* (Edinburgh, 1981), p. 17.

69. J. Maclean, 'A Journall of the Travells and Marches of John Maclean in His Highness's Army 1745', I. G. Brown and H. Cheape (eds), *Witness to Rebellion* (East Linton, 1996), p. 27.

70. H. Cheape, 'The Journal of Captain John Maclean', ibid., p. 15.

71. Cole and Postgate, *The Common People*, p. 2.

72. I. Gilmour, *Riots, Risings and Revolutions* (London, 1990), p. 114. For Gilmour's inverted Marxism, see E. P. Thompson, 'Tory with a Marxist Touch', *Guardian Weekly* (London), 19 April 1992.

73. I. R. Christie, 'The Tory Party, Jacobitism and the 'Forty-Five: A Note', *Historical Journal*, vol. 30, no. 4, October 1987, p. 931.

74. Gilmour, *Riots, Risings and Revolutions*, p. 116.

75. Pittock, *Jacobitism*, p. 67.

76. Ibid, pp. 67–8.

77. Gilmour, *Riots, Risings and Revolutions*, pp. 116.

78. Colley, *Britons*, p. 81.

79. *An Ample Disquisition into the Nature of Regalities and Other Heritable Jurisdictions In That Part Of Great Britain Called Scotland. By an English Gentleman* (London, 1747), p. 32.

80. Quoted in B. Harris, '"A Great Palladium of Our Liberties": The British Press and the 'Forty-Five', *Historical Research*, vol. 68, no. 165, February 1995, p. 73.

81. Lord Elcho, *A Short Account of the Affairs of Scotland in the Years 1744, 1745, 1746*, p. 337.

82. Johnstone, *A Memoir of the 'Forty-Five*, pp. 59–60. Elcho gives a shorter, but similar account in *The Affairs of Scotland*, pp. 337–8.

83. J. Black, 'Could the Jacobites Have Won?', *History Today*, vol. 45, no. 7, July 1995, p. 28.

84. *The Contrast: Or Scotland as it Was in the Year 1745, and Scotland in the Year 1819* (London, 1825), Letter 6, 16 March 1746, p. 90.

85. G. Murray, 'Lord George Murray's Account of the Defeat of the Prince's Army at Culloden, 16th April 1746', *The Spottiswoode Miscellany: A Collection of Original Papers And Tracts Illustrative of the Civil and*

Ecclesiastical History of Scotland (2 volumes, Edinburgh, 1845), vol. 2, pp. 507–8.

86. Ibid, p. 494.
87. J. Black, *A Military Revolution?* (Houndmills, 1991), pp. 20–34. For the application of this theory to the '45, see *Culloden and the '45*, pp. 172–4.
88. J. Sinclair, *Memoirs of the Insurrection in Scotland in 1715* (Edinburgh, 1858), p. 130.
89. *The History of the Rebellion in 1745 And 1746 Extracted from 'The Scots Magazine' with an Appendix Containing an Account of the Trials of the Rebels; the Pretender and His Son's Declarations etc.* (Aberdeen, 1755), p. 198.
90. Cole and Postgate, *The Common People*, p. 4.
91. Maclean, 'A Journall of the Travells and Marches of John Maclean in His Highness's Army 1745', p. 37. From the internal evidence of his journal John Maclean was killed in the days directly after Culloden; his journal was continued by one of his kinsmen, Donald, who entered these lines some time after 19 April.
92. R. Forbes, *The Lyon in Mourning, or a Collection of Speeches, Letters, Journals, Etc. Relative to the Affairs of Prince Charles Edward Stuart 1745–1775*, edited with a Preface by H. Paton (3 volumes, Edinburgh, 1895), vol. 1, p. 251.
93. Ibid.
94. 'O'Sullivan's Narrative', *1745 and After*, edited by A. and H. Tayler (London, 1938), p. 167, note 1. Macdonald was one of the 'seven men of Moidart' who accompanied Charles Stuart from France. Extracts from his unpublished memoirs were used by the editors of this work as a commentary on the account by another of the seven, John William O'Sullivan.
95. A. J. Guy, 'King George's Army 1714–1750', in R. C. Woosnam (ed.), *1745: Charles Edward Stuart and the Jacobites* (Edinburgh, 1995), pp. 51–2.
96. *The Prisoners of the '45*, vol. 1, pp. 152–3.
97. Forbes, *The Lyon in Mourning*, vol. 1, pp. 217, 218.
98. Bisset to Atholl, 22 June 1746, Leneman, *Living in Atholl*, p. 230.
99. *The Contrast*, Letter 7, 30 April 1746, p. 123.
100. Ibid, Letter 8, 3 September 1746, p. 156.
101. J. Prebble, *Culloden* (Harmondsworth, 1965), p.182.
102. Forbes, *The Lyon in Mourning*, vol. 1, p. 218.
103. See, for example, Reid, *1745*, p. 177.
104. *The Woodhouslee Manuscript*, p. 17.
105. See, for example, the following comments: 'The immediate aftermath of the 'Forty-Five was marked by systematic state terrorism, characterised by a genocidal intent that verged on ethnic cleansing' (A. I. Macinnes, *Clanship, Commerce and the House of Stuart, 1603–1788*, East Linton, 1996, p. 213). For similar comments see ibid, pp. 32, 215.
106. E. Burt, *Burt's Letters from the North of Scotland*, with an introduction by R. Johnson (2 volumes, Edinburgh, 1974), vol. 2, p. 24; vol. 1, pp. 4–5.
107. W. Speck, *The Butcher* (Caernarfon, 1995), pp. 96, 147.
108. Johnstone, *A Memoir of the 'Forty-Five*, p. 75.
109. 'Extract of a Letter from a Gentleman at Derby', *The Gentleman's Magazine and Historical Chronicle*, vol. 16, no. 1, January 1746, p. 16.
110. Robb Donn MacKay, 'A Song to Prince Charles', *Highland Songs of the Forty-Five*, edited by J. L. Campbell (Edinburgh, 1984), p. 119.

111. J. Fergusson, *John Fergusson, 1727–1750* (London, 1948), p. 99.
112. *The Woodhouslee Manuscript*, p. 69.
113. 'A Short Account of the Behaviour of the Rebel Army at Hamilton, in a Letter from a Friend, 6th January 1746', *The Spottiswoode Miscellany*, vol. 2, pp. 493, 494.
114. 'Extracts from the Diary of the Reverend John Bisset', entry for 24 October 1745, p. 352.
115. Mitchell to Dundas, 12 September, *The Arniston Memoirs: Three Centuries of a Scottish House 1571–1838*, edited from the family papers by G. W. T. Omond (Edinburgh, 1888), p. 129.
116. Albemarle to Newcastle, 2 February 1746, *The Albemarle Papers Being the Correspondence of William Anne, Second Earl of Albemarle, Commander in Chief of Scotland, 1746–1747*, edited with introduction and notes by C. S. Terry (2 volumes, Aberdeen, 1902), vol. 1, p. 357.
117. *The Gentleman's Magazine and Historical Chronicle*, vol. 16, no. 12, December 1746, pp. 633–4.
118. Johnstone, *A Memoir of the 'Forty-Five*, p. 128.
119. Kilkerran to Halifax, 2 December 1745, Fergusson, *John Fergusson*, pp. 118–19.
120. 'Diary of Hugh Earl of Marchmont, from September 26th, 1745 to May 1st, 1746', *A Selection from the Papers of the Earls of Marchmont. Illustrative of Events from 1685 to 1750* (3 volumes, London, 1831), vol. 1, p. 163.
121. [E. Bruce], *The Highlands of Scotland in 1750* with an introduction by A. Lang (Edinburgh, 1898), pp. 144–5.
122. *The Gentleman's Magazine and Historical Chronicle*, vol. 16, no. 5, May 1746, pp. 261, 262.
123. Pringle to Marchmont, 20 March 1746, 'Marchmont Correspondence Relating to the '45', edited by C. F. C. Hepbourne Scott, *Miscellany of the Scottish History Society* 5, 1933, p. 344.
124. J. MacDonald, *Memoirs of an Eighteenth Century Footman, Travels (1745–1779)* with an introduction by J. Beresford (London, 1927), p. 12.
125. [William Murray], *The Thistle: A Dispassionate Examination of the Prejudices of Englishmen in General to the Scottish Nation. In a Letter to the Author of 'Old England', of December 27 1746* (London, 1747), p. 9.
126. C. Kidd, 'Gaelic Antiquity and National Identity in Enlightenment Ireland and Scotland', *English Historical Review*, vol. 109, no. 434, November 1994, pp. 1206–7.
127. K. Marx, 'Another English Revelation', *Collected Works* (50 volumes, London, 1975-), vol. 14, p. 516.
128. 'Copy of a Letter from a Gentleman in London to his Friend in Bath', 17 September 1750, *Jacobite Memoirs of the Rebellion of 1745*, p. 333.
129. Newcastle to Cumberland, 23 May 1746 and Cumberland to Newcastle, 5 June 1746, *The Prisoners of the '45*, vol. 1, pp. 4–5.
130. Quoted in Black, *Culloden and the '45*, pp. 191–2.
131. Fletcher, 'Proposals for Civilising the Highlands', *The Albemarle Papers*, vol. 2, pp. 483–4.
132. Ibid, pp. 482–3.
133. Kames, 'Introduction', *Essays upon Several Subjects Concerning British Antiquities*, no pagination [p. ii].
134. J. Craig, 'An Account of the Life and Writings of the Author', J. Millar, *The Origin of the Distinction of Ranks: Or, an Inquiry into the Circumstances Which*

Give Rise to Influence and Authority in the Different Members of Society (fourth
edition, Edinburgh, 1806), pp. xxxvii–xxxviii.

135. W. Ferguson, *Scotland: From 1689 to the Present* (Edinburgh, 1978),
p. 156.

136. *An Enquiry into the Causes of the Late Rebellion and the Proper Methods for
Preventing the Like Misfortune for the Future* (London, 1746), pp. 63, 64, 56.

137. *Public General Statutes Affecting Scotland from the Beginning of the First
Parliament of Great Britain, 6 Anne, AD 1707, to the End of the Fourteenth
Parliament of the United Kingdom, 10 and 11 Victoria, AD 1847* (3 volumes,
Edinburgh, 1876), vol. 1, p. 107.

138. G. Pratt Insh, *The Scottish Jacobite Movement* (Edinburgh, 1952), p. 150.

139. Lenman, *The Jacobite Risings in Britain*, p. 278.

140. A. Mackillop, '"Plough-shares into Broadswords": The Scottish Highlands
and War, 1750–1810', a paper read at the Association of Scottish
Historical Studies Annual Conference, 'Scotland and War', Perth, 1995,
p. 53.

141. 'Extract of a Letter from Dr Birch to the Hon. Phillip Yorke, London, 9
August 1746', *The Parliamentary History of England from the Earliest Period
to the Year 1803* (London, 1812), vol. 13, p. 1418.

142. *Public General Statutes Affecting Scotland*, vol. 1, p. 108.

143. Quoted in C. Nordmann, 'Choiseul and the Last Jacobite Attempt of 1759',
in E. Cruickshanks (ed.), *Ideology and Conspiracy: Aspects of Jacobitism,
1689–1759* (Edinburgh, 1982), p. 208.

144. The question of what would have happened had Charles Stuart
successfully landed in Scotland after 1746 is of course the theme of
Redgauntlet, one of Sir Walter Scott's last fully realised novels. Scott's
answer, delivered in the novel by Darsie Latimer, was that no one would
'at this time of day, think of subjecting their necks again to the feudal
yoke'. The conversation in which Darsie makes this point to his sister Lilias
in Chapter 18 is laboured as a dialogue, but as historical analysis it
demonstrates one of the reasons why Scott was so avidly read by two
young Germans, K. Marx and F. Engels.

Epilogue: The Scottish Path to Capitalist Development (1747–1815)

1. A. Gramsci, 'Notes on Italian History', in *Selections from the Prison
Notebooks of Antonio Gramsci*, edited and translated by Q. Hoare and G.
Nowell Smith (London, 1971), p. 105.

2. E. J. Hobsbawm, *The Age of Capital, 1848–1875* (London, 1975),
pp. 150–1.

3. James McPherson goes so far as to say that 'the northern states, along
with Britain and a few countries in northwestern Europe, were cutting a
new channel in world history that would doubtless have become the
mainstream even if the American Civil War had not happened' (J. M.
McPherson, *Battle Cry of Freedom*, Oxford and New York, 1988, p. 861).

4. E. P. Thompson, 'The Peculiarities of the English', in *The Poverty of Theory
and other Essays* (London, 1978), pp. 40–5; 'Patricians and Plebs', in
Customs in Common (London, 1991), p. 84, note 1.

5. T. C. Smout, 'Scottish Landowners and Economic Growth, 1650–1850', *Scottish Journal of Political Economy*, vol. 11, no. 4, November 1964, p. 229.

6. J. D. Young, *The Rousing of the Scottish Working Class* (London, 1979), p. 29.

7. E. M. and N. Wood, *A Trumpet of Sedition* (London and Boulder, 1997), p. 96.

8. J. G. A. Pocock, *The Machiavellian Moment* (Princeton and London, 1975), p. 477. Elsewhere, Pocock argues that 'Enlightenment in Protestant culture' like that of England 'had a conservative face, because it was directed against sect, as well as Pope in the movement away from the wars of religion'. See 'Conservative Enlightenment and Democratic Revolutions: The American and French Cases In British Perspective', *Government and Opposition*, vol. 24, no. 1, Winter 1989, p. 91 and pp. 83–94 more generally.

9. R. Porter, *Enlightenment* (Harmondsworth, 2000), pp. 30–1.

10. Ellen Meiksins Wood has written of the 'bourgeois actors' of the French Enlightenment and Revolution that: 'Their quarrel with the aristocracy has little to do with liberating capitalism from the fetters of feudalism.' This, apparently, is because the Enlightenment itself was 'rooted in non-capitalist social property relations' which represented 'an alternative route out of feudalism'. Meiksins Wood is referring, of course, to absolutism – or rather, her own special conception of absolutism as a mode of production, rather than the form taken by the late feudal state. The relationship of the Scottish Enlightenment to capitalist development must cast doubt on this thesis, not least because, whatever else might be said about the work of Kames et al it could not have been directed against a nonexistent Scottish absolutism. See E. Meiksins Wood, 'Modernity and Postmodernity', *The Origins of Capitalism: A Longer View* (London and New York, 2002), pp. 183, 184.

11. A. Smith, *Lectures on Jurisprudence*, edited by R. L. Meek, D. D. Raphael and P. G. Stern (Oxford, 1978), p. 264.

12. The situation in Scotland after 1746 was in fact more typical of the aftermath of a proletarian than a bourgeois revolution, in the sense that the economy had to be consciously reconstructed after the conquest of political power. Eight months after the October Revolution, Lenin noted that the Russian economy still contained five intermingled 'socio-economic structures': patriarchal or 'natural' peasant farming, small commodity production, private capitalism, state capitalism and socialism. His point – sadly lost on subsequent generations of would-be Leninists – was that the nature of the workers' state was not defined by state ownership of the economy but by whether the working class were in political control of the state ('the Soviet state is a state in which the power of the workers and the poor is assured'). In May 1918, this was still true, if only just. See V. I. Lenin, '"Left-Wing" Childishness and the Petty-Bourgeois Mentality', *Collected Works* (45 volumes, Moscow, 1963), vol. 27, pp. 335–6, 339.

13. T. Nairn, 'Dr Jekyll's Case: Model or Warning?', *The Bulletin of Scottish Politics*, vol. 1, no. 1, Autumn 1980, p. 140.

14. E. J. Hobsbawm, 'Scottish Reformers of the Eighteenth Century and Capitalist Agriculture', in E. J. Hobsbawm et al. (eds), *Peasants in History* (Calcutta, 1980), p. 5.

15. See, in relation to England, R. Brenner, 'Bourgeois Revolution and the Transition to Capitalism', in A. L. Beier, D. Cannadine and J. A. Rosenheim (eds), *The First Modern Society* (Cambridge, 1989), pp. 285, 294–7, and 302; and, as a general proposition, I. Wallerstein, *Historical Capitalism* (London, 1984), pp. 105–6. Brenner mistakes the extent to which capitalist relations had become dominant by the Civil War; Wallerstein mistakes the nature of capitalism for the existence of world markets. It should be noted, however, that in every respect other than their dating of its origin, these writers have diametrically opposite views on the mechanisms by which capitalism came to be the dominant mode of production within the world economy.

16. V. I. Lenin, 'The Agrarian Programme of Social Democracy in the First Russian Revolution 1905–1907', *Collected Works* (45 volumes, Moscow, 1963), vol. 13, p. 239; Preface to the second edition, *The Development of Capitalism in Russia*, ibid, vol. 3, pp. 32–3.

17. T. J. Byers, *Capitalism from Above and Capitalism from Below* (Houndmills, 1996), pp. 27–8.

18. Ibid, pp. 106–7, 113–14.

19. T. M. Devine, *The Transformation of Rural Scotland* (Edinburgh, 1994), p. 63.

20. Lenin, *The Development of Capitalism in Russia*, pp. 194, 197.

21. R. Mitchison, 'Patriotism and National Identity in Eighteenth-Century Scotland', in T. W. Moody (ed.), *Nationality and the Pursuit of National Independence* (Belfast, 1978), p. 88.

22. *The Statistical Account of Scotland, 1791–1800* edited by Sir John Sinclair (20 volumes, Wakefield, 1975–85), vol. 16, *Banffshire, Moray and Nairnshire*, with a new introduction by D. J. Withrington, p. 142.

23. Lord Kames, *Sketches of the History of Man* (Glasgow, 1802), p. 219.

24. A. Calder, *Revolutionary Empire* (New York, 1981), pp. 536–7, 538.

25. Lord Kames, Preface, *The Gentleman Farmer: Being an Attempt to Improve Agriculture by Subjecting it to the Test of Rational Principles* (sixth edition, Edinburgh, 1815), p. xii.

26. 'A Supplement, Containing an Account of the Present State of Agriculture, and the Improvements Recently Introduced', ibid, p. 537.

27. *The Statistical Account of Scotland*, vol. 14, *Kincardineshire and South and West Aberdeenshire*, with a new introduction by D. J. Withrington, p. 155.

28. L. Timperley, 'The Pattern of Landholding in Eighteenth-Century Scotland', in M. L. Parry and T. R. Slater (eds), *The Making of the Scottish Countryside* (London and Montreal, 1980), p. 141.

29. Smout, 'Scottish Landowners and Economic Growth', pp. 219–28.

30. J. Strawhorn, 'Ayrshire in the Enlightenment', in G. D. R. Cruikshank (ed.), *A Sense of Place* (Edinburgh, 1988), p. 189.

31. R. Blackburn, *The Making of New World Slavery* (London and New York, 1997), pp. 527–8.

32. J. G. Lockhart, *The Life of Sir Walter Scott, Bart.* (London, 1893), p. 255.

33. W. Scott, *Waverley; Or, 'Tis Sixty Years Since*, edited by A. Hook (Harmondsworth, 1972), p. 492.

34. Scott to Montagu, 2 January 1820, *The Letters of Sir Walter Scott*, edited by H. J. C. Grierson (12 volumes, London, 1932–37), vol. 6, *1819–1821*, p. 103.
35. Scott to Morritt, 19 May 1820, ibid, p. 190.

Conclusion

1. W. Benjamin, 'Theses on the Philosophy of History', *Illuminations*, edited with an introduction by H. Arendt (London, 1973), p. 259.
2. E. J. Hobsbawm, 'The Sense of the Past', *On History* (London, 1997), pp. 20–1.
3. Benjamin, 'Theses on the Philosophy of History', p. 262.
4. L. Grassic Gibbon, *Grey Granite*, in *A Scots Quair*, edited and introduced by T. Crawford (Edinburgh, 1995), p. 73.
5. N. Davidson, *The Origins of Scottish Nationhood* (London and Sterling, Virginia, 2000), pp. 190–3.
6. W. Aiton, *A History of the Rencounter at Drumclog and the Battle of Bothwell Bridge in the Month of June, 1679, with an Account of What is Correct, and What is Fictitious in* The Tales of My Landlord *Respecting These Engagements, and Reflections on Political Subjects* (Hamilton, 1821), pp. 98–9; see also pp. 7–8.
7. A. Armstrong, 'Back to the Future Part 1: 1688 and 1989 – Revolution, "Progress" and Reaction', *Cencrastus* 50, Autumn 1994, p. 3.
8. J. Vogel, 'The Tragedy of History', *New Left Review* I/220, November–December 1996, pp. 56, 57.
9. C. Hill, *God's Englishman* (Harmondsworth, 1972), p. 266.
10. F. Engels, 'Introduction to the English Edition (1892) of *Socialism: Utopian and Scientific*', *Collected Works* (50 volumes, London, 1975–), vol. 27, pp. 291–2.
11. G. Stedman Jones, 'Society and Politics at the Beginning of the World Economy', *Cambridge Journal of Economics* 1, 1977, p. 87.
12. A. Armstrong, 'Jacobite or Covenanters: Which Tradition?', *Jacobites or Covenanters: A Scottish Republican Debate* (Glasgow, 1994), p. 29.
13. Grassic Gibbon, *Grey Granite*, p. 154. These were not necessarily Grassic Gibbon's own views, although they reflect accurately enough a strand of thinking within the Scottish socialist movement which absorbed an earlier Presbyterian hagiography.
14. L. Spence, 'Edinburgh – Scotland – 1936', *The Nineteenth Century and After*, vol. 120, no. 717, November 1936, pp. 635–6.
15. Spence also maintains another venerable Covenanting tradition in his contemptuous dismissal of the Highlanders as 'a people so utterly comatose' that they would never rebel against their landlords (ibid, p. 640).
16. Armstrong, 'Back to the Future Part 1: 1688 and 1989 – Revolution, "Progress" and Reaction', p. 3.
17. J. T. Callender, *The Political Progress of Britain; Or an Impartial Account of the Principal Abuses in the Government of This Country from the Revolution in 1688* (Edinburgh, 1792), Part 1, p. 34. The bourgeoisie themselves were quite prepared to make such parallels:

There came to be built into the Protestant and Enlightened historical consciousness the memory of the two cycles of war against Catholic universal monarchy: one against Spain which had ended at Westphalia, the other against France which had ended at Utrecht – though wherever France was seen to be sponsoring Jacobite enterprises this memory was likely to become active; this is why Handel's oratorio casts Butcher Cumberland in the unlikely role of Judas Maccabeus. (J. G. A. Pocock, 'Conservative Enlightenment and Democratic Revolutions: The American and French Cases in British Perspective', *Government And Opposition*, vol. 24, no. 1, Winter 1989, p. 92)

Judas Maccabeus led the Jewish revolt against the Seleucid Empire during the second century BC, entering Jerusalem in triumph in 165 (an event commemorated by Handel in 'Hail! The Conquering Hero Comes') and rededicating the Temple to Jahveh after it had been dedicated to the Greek god Zeus by the Seleucid king Antiochus IV. The psalms associated with the Maccabean revolt were of course highly regarded by religious radicals in seventeenth-century England.

18. T. Cliff, 'On the Class Nature of the People's Democracies', *Neither Washington nor Moscow* (London, 1982), p. 66 and *Trotskyism After Trotsky* (London, Chicago and Sydney, 1999), p. 27.

19. W. Makey, *The Church of the Covenant, 1637–1651* (Edinburgh, 1979), p. 185.

20. J. D. Young, 'Marxism, Liberalism and the Process of Industrialization', *Survey* 70–71, 1969, p. 215.

21. R. Burnett, 'Past Imperfect but Better than Nothing', *Scotland on Sunday*, 23 July 1995.

22. K. Marx, *Capital* (3 volumes, Harmondsworth, 1976), vol. 1, p. 926.

23. D. Craig, *On the Crofter's Trail* (London, 1992), p. 273.

24. Indeed, Craig himself suggests a parallel between Nazi atrocities and those committed by the Highland landowners elsewhere in the same book; see ibid, p. 310.

25. These remarks are also applicable to the repression after Culloden. Allan MacInnes refers to the 'genocidal intent' of the British state and of Cumberland having 'instigated and encouraged genocide'. Whatever Cumberland or his officers may have wished to carry out in the Highlands, the fact is that they did not do so. See A. I. MacInnes, *Clanship, Commerce and the House of Stuart* (East Linton, 1996), p. 211, 213.

26. C. Harvie, *Scotland and Nationalism* (London, 1977), p. 26. Harvie sensibly omits this comment from the second edition (London and New York, 1994). See p. 10.

27. The late Raphael Samuel refers to 'Scotland's most celebrated heiress, Elizabeth, Countess of Sutherland, whom readers of *Capital* will know as an architect of the Highland Clearances.' Many people – not least those who live in the region of Sutherland – are quite aware of the life and crimes of Elizabeth Gordon without ever having read *Capital*. See 'Four Nations History', *Island Stories: Unraveling Britain*, edited by A. Light with S. Alexander and G. Stedman Jones (London and New York, 1998), p. 28.

28. Marx, *Capital*, vol. 1, pp. 889–95. This is the volume to which Harvie presumably refers (see note 26 above). For the references to the Duchess of Sutherland (not the Duke), see ibid, pp. 891–2.

29. J. Hulston, *Ehud's Dagger* (London and New York, 2000), p. 115.

30. Ibid, pp. 431–2. For a similar argument about the ongoing nature of 'primitive accumulation, see M. Perelman, *The Invention of Capitalism* (Durham and London, 2000), pp. 31–2.

31. Hulston, *Ehud's Dagger*, p. 429.

32. K. Marx, *Grundrisse* (Harmondsworth, 1973), p. 133. Marx is allowing his understandable outrage to overcome his own historical understanding: events in England were infinitely more violent and ruthless than in the Highlands of Scotland. See, for example, P. Linebaugh and M. Rediker, *The Many-Headed Hydra* (London and New York, 2000), pp. 17, 18, 51.

33. T. M. Devine, 'The Highland Clearances', *Exploring the Scottish Past* (East Linton, 1995), p. 140.

34. R. H. Campbell, 'Too Much on the Highlands? A Plea for Change', *Scottish Economic and Social History* 14, 1994, pp. 58–64.

35. Davidson, *The Origins of Scottish Nationhood*, pp. 116–51.

36. A. Gramsci, 'Some Aspects of the Southern Question', *Selections from the Political Writings (1921–1926)*, translated and edited by Q. Hoare (London, 1978), p. 448.

37. The clearest and most detailed exposition of this aspect of the theory is to be found in M. Lowy, *The Politics of Combined and Uneven Development* (London, 1981), Part 1. The second part, which seeks to apply the theory to explain revolutions in the underdeveloped world after the Second World War, fails because Lowy insists on treating the nature of resulting states at their own estimation as 'post-capitalist'. For an infinitely more realistic assessment, which treats the Third World revolutions after the Second World War as the modern equivalents of the bourgeois revolution, see T. Cliff, 'Permanent Revolution', *International Socialism*, First Series, 12, Spring 1963, reprinted in *International Socialism*, First Series, 61, August, 1973. For a more detailed application of the theory, with specific reference to China, see N. Harris, *The Mandate of Heaven* (London, 1978), pp. 267–81.

38. I. Wallerstein, 'Eurocentrism and its Avatars: the Dilemmas of Social Science', *New Left Review* I/226, November–December 1997, pp. 104–5.

39. Although not for the reasons given by James Young, who writes: 'There has long been a tendency amongst some "marxist" historians to portray any expansion of the productive forces as being the key to human emancipation from either nature or feudal oppression' (J. D. Young, *The Rousing of the Scottish Working Class*, London, 1979, p. 46). That there have been such tendencies is a historical fact, most importantly in the Second International before the First World War – an institution much admired by Young, incidentally – and by Stalinism after 1929, but the answer to such determinism is not the voluntarism he advocates. See, for examples of Young's uncritical attitude towards the Second International, J. D. Young, *John MacLean: Clydeside Socialist* (n.p. [Glasgow], 1992), pp. 95, 102, 218, 223, etc.

40. Armstrong, 'Jacobite or Covenanter', p. 21; 'Back to the Future Part 2: 1492 and 1992 – Redemption, Improvement and Progress', *Cencrastus* 51, Spring 1995, p. 36.

41. J. D. Young, 'What Kind of Socialist Scotland?', paper presented to a meeting of the Movement for a Socialist Scotland, Edinburgh, 14 January 1989, p. 4. To be charitable, this may be a reference to the fictitious 'clan

democracy' which Armstrong also sets so much store by, rather than to medieval feudalism as such.

42. Vogel, 'The Tragedy of History', p. 41. The quote is from Marx, *Capital*, vol. 1, p. 799.
43. Benjamin, 'Theses on the Philosophy of History', p. 258.

Appendix: Marx and Engels on Scotland

1. Their observations on the Highlands were both more numerous and more closely integrated into the central theoretical concerns of historical materialism than those discussed below. I have therefore discussed them separately in 'Marx and Engels on the Scottish Highlands', *Science and Society*, vol. 65, no. 3, Fall 2001.
2. K. Marx, *Capital* (3 volumes, Harmondsworth, 1976), vol. 3, pp. 658, 696–7; K. Marx, *Grundrisse* (Harmondsworth, 1973), p. 133.
3. Marx, *Capital*, vol. 3, p. 757. The theory itself is discussed in K. Marx, *Theories of Surplus Value* (3 volumes, Moscow, 1969), vol. 2, pp. 114–17, 121–5, 144–9.
4. K. Marx, *A Contribution to the Critique of Political Economy*, *Collected Works* (50 volumes, London, 1975–), vol. 29, p. 298.
5. Marx, *Capital*, vol. 1, p. 882–3, note 9.
6. F. Engels, 'Introduction to *Socialism: Utopian and Scientific*', *Collected Works*, vol. 27, p. 291. See also F. Engels, *Ludwig Feuerbach and the End of Classical German Philosophy*, *Collected Works*, vol. 26, pp. 395–6.
7. F. Engels, 'On the Peasant War', *Collected Works*, vol. 26, p. 554 (translation modified).
8. J. D. Young, 'What Kind of Socialist Scotland?', a paper read at a meeting of the Movement for a Socialist Scotland, Edinburgh, 14 January 1989, p. 1.
9. H. Draper, *Karl Marx's Theory of Revolution* (4 volumes, New York, 1978–), vol. 2, *The Politics of Social Classes*, p. 1.
10. V. I. Lenin, 'The State and Revolution', *Collected Works* (45 volumes, Moscow, 1963), vol. 25, p. 447.
11. Ibid, pp. 446–7. These remarks were also true of some members of the Bolshevik Party itself, such as Bukharin.
12. F. Engels, 'A Critique of the Draft Social Democratic Programme of 1891', *Collected Works*, vol. 27, p. 228.
13. See, for example, S. Freeman, 'For a Scottish Workers' Republic', *Socialist Review* (London) 1, April 1978, pp. 30–1.

Bibliographical Essay

1. C. Harvie, 'Grasping the Thistle' in K. Cargill (ed.), *Scotland 2000* (Glasgow, 1987), p. 11.

Index

Compiled by Sue Carlton

Argyll, Archibald Campbell, 5th Earl
of 63
Argyll, Archibald Campbell, 7th Earl
of 18
Argyll, Archibald Campbell, 9th Earl
of 48
Argyll, Archibald Campbell, 10th
Earl and 1st Duke of 18, 293
Argyll, George Campbell, 8th Duke of
55
Argyll, John Campbell, 2nd Duke of
200, 224, 225–6, 241
  and dissolution of Privy Council
  192
  and Treaty of Union 126–7, 128,
  131, 135, 158, 161
Argyll Militia 248
Argyllshire 56, 61, 66
Aristotle 289
Armstrong, Alan 289, 291–2,
  299–300
Ascherson, Neal 3
Atholl Highlanders 151
Atholl, James, 2nd Duke of 238, 244,
  259
Atholl, John Murray, 2nd Marquis of
  128, 135, 139, 150, 160, 214
Atwood, William 133
Auerstadt, battle of (1806) 279
Austria 76
Austrian Succession, War of
  (1740–48) 230, 231
Ayr 44, 137
Ayrshire 28, 30, 44

bagpipes, banning of 269
Baillie, George, of Jerviswood 124–5,
  159, 165–6
Balfour, James 84
Banaji, Jairus 44
Bank Act 1845 302
Bank of England 82
Bank of Scotland 81–2, 101, 210
Bannockburn 179
Barclay, Colonel David 27
Barclay, John 27–8
baron courts 19, 20–1, 49, 51, 168,
  207, 280
Belhaven, John Hamilton, 2nd Baron
  19, 90, 143, 193, 195, 211
Benjamin, Walter xix, 286
Bisset, Reverend John 245, 264

Bisset, Thomas (Commissary) 238,
  244, 259–60
Black, Jeremy 254, 256
Blackburn, Robin 230
Blackwood, Robert 84
Blair Castle 255
Blair, Robert 29
blasphemy law (1661) 102–3
Blenheim, battle of (1704) 121, 152
Bohemia 73
Bolingbroke, Henry Saint John,
  Viscount 196–7
Bonaparte, Napoleon 284, 287
bonnet lairds 22–3, 24, 28, 29, 71,
  197, 275
Bothwell Bridge, battle of (1679) 60
bourgeois revolution 5–8, 170, 175,
  182, 276–7, 300
  and capitalism 12, 16, 182, 272,
  274
  Company of Scotland and 86
  conditions for 9, 16, 275
  and Highland Clearances 295–9
  irreversibility of 273
  and national populism 288
  as passive revolution 275–80
  patterns of 9–15
  in Scottish history 7, 15–16
  and socialist tradition of struggle
  290–4
bourgeoisie 10–11, 45, 49, 211
  and bourgeois revolution 11,
  12–13
  and Union 137–8
Braes of Mar 198
Brand, Sir Alexander 90
Braudel, Fernand xiv
Breadalbane, John Campbell, 1st Earl
  of 21
Brenner, R. 40
Brewer, John 112
Bristol 197
Britain
  constitutional form of 04–6
  expansionism 181, 230
  imperialism 294–5
  relations with France 181, 229–32
British Army 46–7, 120, 231
  atrocities 257–61
  Highland Regiments 269
  role of Scots 152, 162–5, 269